MW00396228

LATE ROMANCE

ALSO BY DAVID YEZZI

Poetry

More Things in Heaven: New and Selected Poems
Black Sea
Birds of the Air
Azores
The Hidden Model

Anthologies

The Swallow Anthology of New American Poets

LATE ROMANCE

Anthony Hecht—
A Poet's Life

DAVID YEZZI

St. Martin's Press

New York

First published in the United States by St. Martin's Press, an imprint of St. Martin's Publishing Group

www.stmartins.com

Design by Susan Walsh

Library of Congress Cataloging-in-Publication Data

Names: Yezzi, David, author.
Title: Late romance : Anthony Hecht, a poet's life / David Yezzi.
Description: First edition. | New York : St. Martin's Press, 2023. | Includes bibliographical references and index.
Identifiers: LCCN 2023027937 | ISBN 9781250016584 (hardcover) | ISBN 9781250016591 (ebook)
Subjects: LCSH: Hecht, Anthony, 1923–2004. | Poets, American—20th century—Biography.
Classification: LCC PS3558.E28 Z95 2023 | DDC 811/.54 [B]—dc23/eng/20230713
LC record available at https://lccn.loc.gov/2023027937

Our books may be purchased in bulk for promotional, educational, or business use. Please contact your local bookseller or the Macmillan Corporate and Premium Sales Department at 1-800-221-7945, extension 5442, or by email at MacmillanSpecialMarkets@macmillan.com.

First Edition: 2023

10 9 8 7 6 5 4 3 2 1

For
Sarah Harrison Smith
Michael Anderson
and in memory of
J. D. McClatchy

CONTENTS

INTRODUCTION
Recognition and Reversal

per·i·pe·'tei·a: *noun, formal,* a sudden reversal
of fortune or change in circumstances . . .

A nthony Hecht came to a turning point in his life in 1967, when
he was in his mid-forties. He had not published a book of poems
in thirteen years. His first marriage had ended. His memories of
World War II still nagged at him, its traumas close to the surface. His life
in New York City, where he had been raised, was coming to a close. Never
completely at home as a child, now he was without a home, a physical
and spiritual exile; it was a period he looked back on as "the hard hours."

Things had been bleak for a long time. Several years earlier, his wife,
Pat, had divorced him and taken their two young sons to live with her
new husband in Belgium. Hecht broke down. Losing his sons was more
than he could bear. In 1961, he checked himself into Gracie Square Hospital, near the East River, where three months of Thorazine treatments
made him dull and groggy. His family's medical history would have given
his doctors pause. During the Depression, his father fell into despair and
attempted suicide. (He would make several attempts over the years.) And
there were other childhood anxieties, chiefly caused by the chronic illness
of his brother, Roger, whose epileptic seizures prompted mysterious, upsetting treatments.

As a Private First Class in Germany, he had served as a translator at
the liberation of Flossenbürg Concentration Camp, near the Czech border, an hour's drive from his Jewish great-grandfather's hometown of
Buttenheim. His company had passed right through it, a horrible homecoming. What he saw in that camp and in combat ruined his sleep. He
would "wake up shrieking," and these nightmares persisted for the rest
of his life.[1] He "experienced a very profound and fully conscious sense
of guilt at surviving when others, including friends, had not."[2] This guilt

was compounded by a secret that Hecht harbored, which he spoke of only once: a confession about the war that he kept to himself for nearly thirty years.

All of this weighed on him, so much so that he feared he would go mad.[3] Forty-three, bearded, and both playful and brooding, he was finishing his final semester of teaching at his alma mater, Bard College, before taking up a new post at the University of Rochester. The move caused many ripples: geographic, professional, cultural, and—importantly— meteorological. (Hecht took puckish delight in lambasting Rochester for its punishing winters, even skewering the city in a satiric sestina.[4]) Personally, he was at loose ends: an itinerant professor-poet, single, and, though widely acknowledged by his peers, relatively unsung. But *everything* in his life was about to change—and, blessedly, for the better.

He had just completed a new book of poems called *The Hard Hours*. The new poems were blistering, more forthright than his previous collection and roiled by misgivings. For the first time in his life, under intense emotional strain, Hecht wrote poems of "absolute raw simplicity and directness."[5] The fluent, at times fulsome, ornamentation of his first collection, *A Summoning of Stones*, was simplified, as if worn down, by grief. *The Hard Hours* won the Pulitzer Prize for 1968.

Hecht's ultimate reversal—his peripeteia, as he termed it, after Aristotle—remained just over the horizon. True, the prize had bolstered his reputation and his career. He was much in demand for readings, and further honors followed. But Hecht described the most profound change, when it came, as a rebirth. He acknowledged that, like Ferdinand, saved from drowning in Shakespeare's late romance *The Tempest*, he had "received a second life."[6] In March 1971, Hecht met Helen D'Alessandro, a young editor at the publishing house of Walker and Company. Or, rather, they met again after many years; Helen had been his student at Smith College. They married three months later.

Both felt as if something supernatural had intervened. Helen had been in love with Hecht since college. After their marriage, the two were seldom apart: they traveled together to readings and lectures, and, after Hecht's retirement in 1990, to Venice each summer. At their wedding, lines from *The Tempest* were read out in the courtyard garden of Helen's apartment on East 94th Street:

Look down, you gods,
And on this couple drop a blessèd crown;
For it is you, that have chalk'd forth the way
Which brought us hither!

Visitors to Hecht's grave at Bard College can see a selection of these words carved there, backgrounded by a field of green.

In public, Hecht came across like one of his own poems—formal on first acquaintance, at times even dandyish, but with a fraught inner life. His eyes gleamed with wit, and he could be raucously funny, but he was slow to reveal this side of himself and then only to trusted friends. His personal style was essentially professorial, but with an aristocratic bearing and flare: a pocket square; a bow tie; a neat, Renaissance-style beard, and swept-back hair.[7] To those who did not know him well, he could appear intimidating. An interview from 1982, when he was US Poet Laureate, attests to his keen self-awareness: "I think I am a moody, generally good-natured person with an impish sense of humor, subject to occasional fits of melancholy and self-doubt, troubled by the standard vanities and fears that go with being a poet."[8]

Then there was his accent, a mid-Atlantic lilt that struck some American ears as mandarin or even British.[9] One acquaintance, Nancy Lewis, wife of the critic R. W. B. Lewis, described it as resembling an English public school boy's accent; she wondered if it weren't a protective measure.[10] It also may have been a way of fitting in:

I've heard my voice recorded and by now I feel it sounds like me. Doubt-less it's a mask of some sort; a fear or shame of something, very likely of being Jewish, a matter I am no longer in the least ashamed of, though once it was a painful embarrassment.[11]

Part of it was the stage actor in him, a voice he developed as a young man performing in plays; his manner was a choice he made, a product of self-creation. His younger brother, Roger, by contrast, sounded exactly like a born-and-bred New Yorker.

Hecht's surfaces could be deceiving. As he puts it in *The Hidden Law*, his book on W. H. Auden, "everything that counts is well veiled."[12] He would never write "confessional" poems like his friends or colleagues W. D. Snodgrass, Robert Lowell, Sylvia Plath, and Anne Sexton. "I work at disguising the autobiographical," he told one reporter.[13] "What I hope to do," he told another, "is to conceal my identity by putting it into a whole cast of characters in which the reader can't tell who the real Anthony Hecht is." He saw how Robert Frost and Wallace Stevens "contrived to deal with very personal, sometimes emotionally devastating matters in their poetry. In Frost's case this is well recognized, even when he took certain precautions."[14] Hecht was "urged by the same sort of tact and discretion" to avoid raw disclosure. A slight scuffing of the surface, however, reveals the searingly personal.[15] "There are, after all, poets, like Frost, whose poems are remarkably intimate, once you crack their codes," he acknowledged.[16]

Like Frost, Hecht became a poet with a key. In his poems, "a bleak and forlorn landscape" could "assemble and convey a deep sense of despair."[17] Into seemingly offhand images, Hecht could encode the carnage of war. "Death the Whore," for example, unfolds beneath a sky of "German silver,"[18] a column of smoke rising.[19] "Still Life" ends abruptly with an act of re-experiencing typical of post-traumatic stress; the speaker is transported in an instant from a peaceful natural setting to standing "somewhere in Germany, / A cold, wet, Garand rifle in my hands."[20] Several autobiographical undercurrents animate "The Venetian Vespers," including a father's mysterious disappearance.[21]

Hecht understood the complex connections between a poet's life and work. His lengthy appreciation of Auden, which came pouring out of him after his retirement from teaching, led him to the conclusion that "it may ultimately be impossible to pluck out the core of the mystery of any man after his death."[22] But Hecht, like Frost before him, left clues. They are there, often beneath a layer of leaves and twigs, in the dank landscapes of his poems. His life holds essential keys; turning them opens realms at once "impersonal" (in the sense that T. S. Eliot praised) and deeply felt. Hecht never broadcast his pain, nor did he succumb to it. Writing poetry brought him joy. After long suffering came a reversal, almost as an act of grace. And the poems tell this story, too. No poet of the twentieth century has better expressed the trauma to the American psyche caused by the Second World War, a horror deepened by his experience of his own German

Jewish heritage as well as the bitter legacy of antisemitism he encountered in his youth. No American poet has expressed such traumas so exquisitely, steeped in the language of Shakespeare and the Bible, and fluent in the fine arts of painting, music, and drama. His poems are an indelible record of suffering and joy, darkness and light.

PART ONE

ONE

HECHT & SONS
(1923–1934)

Hinx, minx, the old witch winks,
The fat begins to fry;
Nobody home but Jumping Joan,
Father, mother, and I.[1]

1. "Death Sauntering About"[2]

Adead body lay on the sidewalk. The boy didn't know what it was at first. He saw the commotion and wondered at the crowd of grown-ups milling around. His stout governess—excited, curious—pushed him forward. Then he saw the draped form, "covered for decency's sake with blankets."[3] In that moment, the Great Depression—what it meant to him (and to his parents and grandparents)—came into sharp relief. All the recent agitation of his household, his father's erratic moods, his mother's scolding, found an immediate expression in that dark object. He had been lying low, keeping to himself as much as possible. His family was reeling in a city- and countrywide frenzy of decimated fortunes, as well as in dramas of their own making, of mental and physical illnesses, punctuated by long silences and sudden eruptions. The grown-ups were keeping secrets. Was he being shielded or merely ignored? And shielded from what, exactly? Now he saw something with his own eyes that confirmed his fears without explaining them. The boy's name was Tony Hecht; he was six years old.

Actually, Tony saw bodies, plural.[4] It was the winter of 1929, in New York City. That first, anonymous suicide, face masked from view, took him off guard. He would never forget this first encounter with death, and the many subsequent deaths he witnessed, as a soldier in wartime, would not displace it. Tony was standing on the sidewalk beside his brother, Roger, three years his junior, still in a stroller, when they happened on the sight. Some distraught person had thrown himself out of a window. The boys' governess, who took them for daily walks around the neighborhood, would have been particularly interested. She relished lurid tabloid scenes, poring over her sensationalist newspapers on a bench in Central Park, while Tony played at Cowboys and Indians. The grisly scene would have drawn her.

Roger may have slept on, oblivious. His frailty, the product of childhood illness, afforded him a kind of protected status in the family. Whatever Roger wanted, Roger got, from the earliest age. What he most often wanted, as he grew older, was to be like his big brother, whom he admired but also slyly competed with. In the struggle for their parents' deference and attention, however, there was no competition; Roger always won. Fräulein, as the family called their governess, might have even relished exposing Tony to the horrific sight. She had a sadistic streak, routinely meting out mental and physical shocks to the older boy, while pampering the younger.

For Tony, the disturbance on the street was further proof that something in the grown-up world was horribly wrong. Whisperings at home and even outright arguments created a baleful atmosphere, the causes of which he could only wonder at. His father, Melvyn, seemed at times utterly distraught, and Tony's mother, Dorothea, countered Melvyn's outbursts with stony stoicism and tacit reproof. The newspapers were full of direful predictions, and—somehow related, Tony sensed—things at home had grown worse as well. The Hechts no longer bought their clothes at the fancier department stores on the East Side. Dorothea, an independent and intelligent woman, known to friends as Dottie or Dot, was livid about her husband Melvyn's ineptitude with money. As the disaster wore on— both public and private—the family began to scrimp in ways they never had before.

In the years following Black Friday, as Manhattan adjusted to the shock of the Crash, with its soup lines and carts of nickel apples, the Hechts were never in "serious want."[5] There was no shortage of food, and they even had someone to cook it for them. Though his parents were well enough off, Tony was terrified. The family's "downward mobility," conceived in the mind of a child, seemed at times to threaten their very existence. *What was going on?* he repeatedly wondered. No one would tell him. That was grown-up talk, nothing for little boys to bother about. But the taciturn and sensitive child, frequently left to his own anxious thoughts, wondered where it would end. Melvyn, mortified and guilty about his fruitless business dealings, certainly shed no light. Would they wind up like the homeless people he saw depicted in his father's copy of *The New York Times?*

A year after the Crash, nearly fifty thousand men crowded into the Municipal Lodging House near the East River on 25th Street; by the winter of 1931 that number had more than doubled, including nearly two thousand white-collar workers—bankers, doctors, lawyers, and businessmen. Meals were served by the Salvation Army, provided one stood through a Christian sermon first. (The Hechts were Jewish, though non-observing. They attended services at Temple Emanuel only at the High Holidays, at the invitation of older relatives.) Hoovervilles of makeshift shanties sprang up in Central Park, a few blocks from the Hechts' apartment. The old reservoir in their neighborhood became known as Hoover Valley or Forgotten Men's Gulch, and the presence of a tightrope walker and other out-of-work hawkers and performers made it a kind of tourist destination, which the rubbernecking Fräulein no doubt observed with the boys in tow.

The Hechts were insulated by family money from the worst of the crisis, but they were not immune. In distress over his own botched business dealings, Melvyn tried to commit suicide, the first of several attempts.[6] This became a family secret, which Hecht glimpsed only at a distance—his father's sudden absence, his wrists wrapped in gauze on his return. He was a striking example of unfulfilled promise—handsome, well-dressed, even stylish; from a prosperous family; Harvard educated; a Navy veteran of the First World War. During Hecht's childhood and adolescence, Melvyn "lost every cent he had, not once but three times; and not only his own money but that of friendly investors, who came to regard him as either a crook or stupid."[7] Each time, they relied on Dorothea's family for a "bailout," and each time Melvyn was deeply ashamed, wanting forgiveness or, failing that, a quick end to his suffering. Dorothea's anger at her husband's incompetence "almost unhinged her."[8]

They lived in a handsomely appointed apartment building at 1327 Lexington Ave., which ran the length of an entire block, with entrances on 88th and 89th Streets.[9] The layout was sprawling, full of corners where Tony could escape notice, watching out the windows onto the streets below for long hours by himself. It was a shifting, "unhappy" time. He took things hard, fear being one of his childhood's "chief ingredients, and as for love, it is too strongly fused with dependence and anxiety to be anything like the mature feelings we commonly think of." Forty years later, Hecht recounted this painful time in his longish autobiographical poem "Apprehensions":

> We were living at this time in New York City
> On the sixth floor of an apartment house
> On Lexington, which still had streetcar tracks.[10]

The poem is filled with apprehensions in both senses of the word—both gleanings and fears. Unable to decipher the tangle of ominous clues about the state of his household, his imagination filled in the blanks with his worst suspicions. His parents left him wondering. Was it their idea to shield the boys? Or was there simply no thought of them; they were, after all, merely children, occasionally seen and never heard.

With Roger there was no question. He was young for his age, much too young for adult confidences. He was ill and had been from birth. He required regular house calls from physicians. Tony wondered about that, too. Who were these doctors, with their strange treatments and mysterious pills? Roger's illness—he was eventually diagnosed with epilepsy—was a further occasion for silence and secrets in the house. Seeing his brother's seizures, Tony must have thought he was dying.

Children, Hecht later reflected,

> know from a remarkably early age that things are being kept from them,
> that grown-ups participate in a world of mysteries (death being a major
> one, but also liquor and procreation, not sex, about which children have
> a scant notion when very young) from which children are debarred, to

their continuing frustration and ineradicable curiosity. These mysteries, like the Masonic rites, are ones parents and elders are sworn not to reveal to the uninitiated, which include all children. And so we sought for signs.[11]

Hecht believes that all children exhibit a natural curiosity about the adult world, but not all of them experience it under such a dark cloud, as a looming threat. This was true of *his* childhood, *his* parents. When he looked back on his boyhood and adolescence—in poems like "A Hill," "Apprehensions," and "A Certain Slant of Light"—his search for clues is infused with sadness, a bleakness in which the soul of childhood becomes alienated and beleaguered. His parents' erratic behavior compounded these dark mysteries. Made hyperaware by this, Tony noticed everything. At one point a bottle of Roger's phenobarbital and a razor blade went missing, after which Melvyn returned home with bandaged wrists.

To make matters even more worrying, much of what Hecht learned about his surroundings came from Fräulein, whom he remembered as:

> . . . *a Teutonic governess*
> *Replete with the curious thumb-print of her race,*
> *That special relish for inflicted pain.*[12]

With Dorothea often secluded in her room (she, too, was a melancholic) and Melvyn away at the office, it was Fräulein who ran the house, a stolid, brutish presence. Hecht's memory of her, filtered through hindsight in the years after the war, mingles her native cruelty with images of the Holocaust. Though it would only become clear later, the mental and physical abuses he suffered at her hands foreshadowed the horrors he witnessed in Germany at the liberation of Flossenbürg Concentration Camp. What does Hecht mean when he speaks of the "thumb-print of her race"? Some innately "German" quality, long dormant perhaps, which revealed itself in the Final Solution? The Hechts were themselves German, from Bavaria. As a young boy, Hecht's Jewishness, downplayed by his family, had been a cause for ridicule from teachers, and now his Germanness, too, would raise eyebrows. Unlike her employers, who had made their home in New York for generations, Fräulein was likely a more recent arrival, and Christian, not Jewish. That Fräulein secretly looked down on her employers is easy to imagine, possibly gossiping about them with the other governesses at the Cosmopolitan Club on 65th Street, founded by German nannies, a few blocks from the Hechts' apartment.

If she managed to hide her prejudices from the elder Hechts, it was clear to Tony that she did not intend him much good, cowing him daily into "acts of shameless, mute docility."[13] Her primary concern was for Roger, who required constant attention. Dorothea had made it clear: Roger needed looking after, while Tony could be expected to tag along unobtrusively. On their strolls around the Upper East Side, Fräulein always stopped with the boys at a sidewalk fruit stand. Each day the same routine: she asked Roger what he wanted ("he always chose a banana"), and then she would buy Tony the same as Roger was having. He was not asked his preference or even spoken to much. Roger's health was a constant worry to his parents, and Fräulein understood that it was in her interest to favor the younger boy.[14]

To Tony, Fräulein was terrifying. She relished violence, spending each morning poring over photographs in her favorite tabloid, the *Journal-American*. Her paper of choice traded in the grisliest stories they could dig up to titillate the reader, and she was hooked. The black-and-white images became seared into Hecht's memory in grainy chiaroscuro:

> *A child chained tightly to a radiator*
> *In an abandoned house; the instruments*
> *With which some man tortured his fiancée,*
> *A headless body recently unearthed*
> *On the links of an exclusive country club. . . .*[15]

The corpse they had witnessed on that fateful day would have caused Fräulein great excitement. She had stumbled on an exclusive, as the crowd stood shading their eyes and pointing up to a high window. But Tony was not looking up; he was looking at the fallen form. Unlike his mother, who is almost entirely absent from the memories in "Apprehensions," Fräulein did not hide the worst from her charge. Was this another form of the pain she liked to inflict? If so, it paled compared to the thrill of inflicting physical pain. In her fits of irritation and brutishness, she resorted to whatever was to hand. She kept the six-year-old in psychological darkness, a "cloudy world of inference / Where the most solid object was a toy / Rake that my governess had used to beat me." She became for him the stuff of nightmares, eventually morphing in his dreams into a harbinger of the global conflict quickly coming over the horizon. She comes back at the conclusion of the poem as a specter, a haunting:

> Just when it was that Fräulein disappeared
> I don't recall. We continued to meet each other
> By secret assignations in my dreams
> In which, by stages, our relationship
> Grew into international proportions
> As the ghettos of Europe emptied, the box cars
> Rolled toward enclosures terminal and obscene,
> The ovens blazed away like Pittsburgh steel mills,
> Chain-smoking through the night, and no one spoke.
> We two would meet in a darkened living room
> Between the lines of advancing allied troops
> In the Wagnerian twilight of the Reich.
> She would be seated by a table, reading
> Under a lamp-shade of the finest parchment.
> She would look up and say, "I always knew
> That you would come to me, that you'd come home."
> I would read over her shoulder, "In der Heimat,
> Im Heimatland, da gibts ein Wiedershenen."
> An old song of comparative innocence,
> Until one learns to read between the lines.[16]

She returns to him, not surprisingly, during wartime. As a soldier on the Western Front, Hecht marched through his great-grandfather's hometown of Buttenheim, near Bamberg. Hecht and his company often slept out, on bivouac, but toward the end of the war, as the Allies advanced, he was garrisoned in private homes, which had been abandoned by the Nazis as they fled. At night, silent, in the eerie and unaccustomed comfort of a German living room, this specter from childhood returned, the song of homecoming pitched as a deathly threat.

The storms of childhood were not without their moments of brilliant sun. Hecht always knew that he was in many ways fortunate. The family's financial troubles after the Crash and their social decline proceeded only so far. They continued to enjoy a good deal of freedom and comfort. There were regular trips abroad (though somewhat less frequent), and summers in leafy Westchester County or in Connecticut, on the Long Island Sound, a short train ride from the city. That Tony was the favorite of his paternal great-grandmother, Amalie, was another bright spot. He always looked forward to her attentions and the secret language of the bond they shared. Granny Amalie, then in her nineties, doted on him, giving him the kind of special affection that he missed. Left out when his mother and grandmother gossiped, Granny sat apart with Tony playing card games. Hecht later felt that it was Amalie alone that first taught him how to love.[17]

His parents were not esthetes, but they were cultured, well-traveled New Yorkers, and even a little snobbish about their social standing. Hecht was exposed to music and art at an early age, and his parents were "good about giving him books," a number of which made a lasting impression on him.[18] Dorothea had a crackling intelligence, the brains of the operation, and Melvyn, while he had a poor head for business, studied Classics at Harvard and had an appreciation for literature. Among the books in their apartment were a number of old volumes and sets of a certain value. Rare books that the newlyweds had requested as wedding gifts lined the shelves in shades of brown calfskin. The book that Hecht first lit on was a collection of nursery rhymes, illustrated by the Dutch watercolorist Henriette Willebeek le Mair. One verse in particular—a common mishearing of the old Scottish folksong "My Bonnie lies over the ocean"—fascinated him:

> My body lies over the ocean,
>   My body lies over the sea,
> My body lies over the ocean.
>   O bring back my body to me.

Hecht memorized these lines, singing them over and over, almost obsessively, to himself, when no one was paying attention, which was much of the time. He later remembered "brooding upon these lines, like darkness upon the face of the waters,"[19] circling around questions of meaning and implication that interested him more than his schoolwork. They performed a kind of magic trick in his imagination. Its mysteries

> bespoke a remarkable spiritual condition, possibly a ghoulish one. What was my body doing out there, anyway? Was it getting wet? And where was I in the meantime? These questions absorbed me at an age when I was supposed to be getting down the rudimentary facts of American history, which I carelessly neglected. I had a vision of my body in mid-Atlantic, hanging unsupported just about three feet above the white caps, looking as if you could pass steel hoops along it from end to end by way of demonstrating that there were no wires or hidden brackets to keep it aloft. It was very cold, and getting dark.
>
> Scary as this vision was, it encouraged my appetite for poetry, which instinctively I knew to be about the unspoken and unspeakable. And in this I was absolutely right. Poetry operates by hints and dark suggestions. It is full of secrets and hidden formulae, like a witch's brew. A lot of the fun lies in trying to penetrate the mystery; and this is best done by saying over the lines to yourself again and again, till they pass through the stage of sounding like nonsense, and finally return to a full sense that had at first escaped notice.[20]

The strategies of indirection that Hecht later practiced in his poems, the hints and dark suggestions, which both occluded and slyly hinted at a personal source, took root at an early age, at a time when he dearly needed them. Like Joyce's Stephen Dedalus, he felt like an outsider:

> *My own devices came to silence and cunning*
> *In my unwilling exile, while attempting*
> *To put two and two together, at which I failed.*
> *The world seemed made of violent oppositions:*
> *The Bull and Bear of Wall Street, Mother and Father,*
> *Criminals and their victims, Venus and Mars,*
> *The cold, portending graphics of the stars.*[21]

These morbid tunes he memorized from books simmered in his imagination, circulating in the cloud of childhood unknowing. He could still hear them some sixty years later as he composed a suite of nursery rhymes for "The Presumptions of Death," a series of personations of the grim reaper in different guises:

> *Weep, baby, weep!*
> *No solaces in sleep.*
> *Nightmare will ruin your repose*
> *And daylight resurrect your woes.*
> *Weep, baby, weep![22]*

"'It Out-Herods Herod. Pray You, Avoid It.'"—one of Hecht's poems about the war—begins with fairy tales in which the "warty giant and witch / Get sealed in doorless jails." Referring to his own children, it proceeds toward its bitter conclusion in the music of the nursery, at Christmastime:

> *A hero comes to save*
> *The poorman, beggarman, thief,*
> *And make the world behave*
> *And put an end to grief.*
>
> *And that their sleep be sound*
> *I say this childermas*
> *Who could not, at one time,*
> *Have saved them from the gas.[23]*

The family photos from before the Crash depict a life of comfort and adventure. In a photo from around 1927, Tony, age four, sits on a small white bench of slatted woodwork. Pulled snugly over his tiny brow, a tan felt hat with a broad silk ribbon frames his cherubic face. Beneath a camel hair topcoat peeks a cravat and white collar, with a carnation draped blowzily from his buttonhole. In his hands, gloved in pale calfskin, is a tiny ebony walking stick, held across his lap, one leg cocked under the opposite knee, with the free leg dangling down a few inches from the ground. He is wearing shiny leather boots that extend over his thighs and disappear under his coattails. His eyes shine out from beneath the brim of his hat, bright but also a little bemused and sad. If he is smiling, it is a tentative smile, lips parted as if poised to speak.

In another suite of pictures, from a large family album, the Hechts are traveling with friends aboard the SS *Milwaukee*. With them are the Geisels, Ted and Helen. Ted was a Dartmouth man and now made a handsome living as an illustrator, under the sobriquet Dr. Seuss (Seuss being his mother's maiden name). Also of German extraction, Ted was thirteen at the outbreak of the First World War. His family became roundly ostracized, and discrimination against German-Americans was widespread in his hometown of Springfield, Massachusetts. The Geisels were longtime family friends of the Hechts, and when Tony later expressed an interest in poetry, Ted was called in to sound him on the matter. Life on the Atlantic was gay: lounge chairs and cocktails, an outdoor pool, fancy dinners. Everyone dressed to the nines, including Tony and Roger, who sported new sandals and gleaming white beach-wear. The Geisels posed for a photo with a ship's lifesaver wreathed around their necks. On their trip, they visited Paris and Switzerland, took in ancient monuments and picturesque lakes. It was a last hurrah before the Crash.

2. Out of the Swamp

Hecht's great-grandfather, Joseph, came to New York from Butten-heim, Germany, in the mid-1800s, at age seventeen. He made his name in the hide business. The New York City leather district was known as the Swamp and its dealers as Swampers. Joseph was already estab-lished in the business after only six months as a New Yorker. His scrappy entrepreneurship quickly paid off, and his business grew. He took a wife, named Amalie ("Malie") Fleishmann, also arrived recently from Bavaria, and subsequently moved with her to 133 Henry Street.

Hecht & Sons, as it became known, took over a sizable stretch of Cliff Street, with stores at number 92, 94, 96, and 98. The family produced shoe leather—uppers, vamps, and quarters—developing a strong reputa-tion in the trade and an international reach.[24] The rise in family fortunes found its expression in real estate. As the Lower East Side became increasingly identified with Eastern European Jewry, the prosperous German Jews began to move uptown. They thought of themselves as "our crowd," an affiliation of well-to-do recent immigrants who had made good in a single generation.[25] Not to be deterred by the resistance, born of antisemitism, that excluded them from New York's social clubs, they founded their own, most notably the Harmonie Club, of which Hecht's grandfather was a member, and erected their own cultural institutions such as the Young Men's Hebrew Association on East 92nd Street. (Hecht would have a lifelong association with this institution's renowned Poetry Center, where many of his poetic heroes had read their work, including T. S. Eliot and W. H. Auden.)

When Tony's grandfather, Aaron, entered the business, the company logo featured an eight-point elk's head inside a double diamond, bordered along the bottom by the name. The Hechts were "said to be the largest dealer[s] in deer and elk skins, and probably handle[d] more horse hides than any other dealer in the United States," declared *Hide and Leather: An International Weekly*.[26] The trade journal followed the Hechts' doings as movers and shakers. Hecht & Sons was one of the leading concerns in the Swamp by March 1893, when Melvyn, Tony's father, was born.

Melvyn tried to escape the family business, but fate intervened to block his plans. He had gotten as far as Harvard. By the twenties, Harvard, along with Yale and Princeton, imposed quotas on the number of Jewish students who were granted admission, but in Melvyn's day, admission was based solely on passing the entrance exam, and he had passed. But the triumph was short lived. He left without a degree. When Aaron's eyesight failed, Melvyn was called home to run things for his father. Perhaps it was because his interests lay elsewhere, but Melvyn showed no particular aptitude for business. It was certainly a comedown for the bookish young man. In 1920, the Merchants Association Yearbook lists the office of the New England Enameling Co. at 200 Fifth Avenue, on the southwest corner of Madison Square Park, and a census from around this time blandly lists Melvyn as "a salesman."

Still, it was good for him to have work, particularly when he was looking to start a family, and, that same year, Melvyn married Dorothea Grace Holzman. Dorothea was born a year after her husband, in 1894. Her parents, Elkan and Jennie Goldman Holzman, were Midwesterners by birth. The Goldmans and the Holzmans came from Hessen-Darmstadt, south of Frankfurt in what was then Prussia. They had arrived, like Joseph Hecht, with the waves of German Jewish immigrants in the 1850s, settling in Ohio and Illinois. In 1880, the Holzmans moved to New York, with the Goldmans following in 1910. Both landed on or near Park Avenue, and Tony's maternal grandparents were married at Temple Israel of Harlem in 1894. Both families were in the garment business and owned successful retail stores, and Cohen Goldman & Co. Clothing thrived for many years at 45 West 18th Street. Melvyn and Dorothea married at the Ritz Carlton, the luxury hotel, now gone, at 46th Street and Madison Avenue, on January 19, 1920. Prohibition had gone into effect two days before, and the dozen cases of champagne ordered for the occasion went unopened. The waiters stowed one case in the bride and groom's limousine, which they took home to 1327 Lexington Avenue at 89th Street.

Joseph did not live to see his grandson married; he had died the year before. The wedding was packed with extended family. As a boy, Tony observed this same parade of distant relatives during the holidays, constituting "the regulation hive of more remote aunts and uncles— grandparental siblings and their issue—who are now lost to time. There was a tennis freak, whose name was Goldman . . . There was a family named Raphael, but whether they were family-related or merely friends is clouded in mist."[27] According to Hecht, Dorothea's mother, Jennie, had an older brother, William Goldman, born 1868, "who was rich and successful, and a collector of paintings."[28] The jewel of his collection was a painting by the sixteenth-century Flemish master Adriaen Isenbrandt, famous for his Christian religious subjects. So prominent were the works in William's collection, which "Tony admired greatly,"[29] that they were exhibited at the World's Fair in New York in 1939, before being broken up for sale.[30] Tony would have thought of William's collection when he began acquiring his own pictures, numbered prints mainly, which became the prized showpieces of his living room, where guests were entertained. (In Paris, after the war, for example, Tony acquired a number of excellent prints—by Rouault and Braque, and a lithograph by Matisse—at reasonable prices.)

Melvyn had made a handsome match. Dorothea's family came from

the same part of Germany and prospered among the same German Jewish community on the Upper East Side of Manhattan. (It would not have
done for him to marry into a family of Eastern European Jews from
the Lower East Side, who, in contrast to "our crowd," were thought of
as "the rest of us.")[31] The tightknit Goldmans and Holzmans enjoyed
even greater prosperity than the Hechts. Elkan belonged to the exclusive
and dues-heavy Harmonie Club and managed a number of lavish trips
en famille to Europe (at around $5,000 per passenger in today's money),
with one travel visa even signed by William Jennings Bryan (The Great
Commoner) himself.

The suave and mercurial Melvyn appreciated art and literature, but
Dorothea (with her family's financial backing) oversaw the most important decisions. Like most women of her circle, Dorothea did not attend
college. After finishing school in Switzerland, where she polished her
French conversation, she embarked on a self-directed course of study
in the "social graces." When Melvyn moved from sales to investments,
it's likely that his father-in-law, Elkan, helped him with connections and
capital. Jewish banking families approached a kind of aristocracy that the
well-to-do Jewish merchant class aspired to. Melvyn was no exception.
He must have felt that finance was more elegant than trade. A shrewd
investor, Elkan continued to prosper through his mercantile business. He
made periodic gifts to his children of several thousand dollars for "everyday" expenses, which took the pressure off of Melvyn as he stumbled
forward in a business that he loathed. In fact, he loathed business generally.[32] Melvyn was encouraged to take positions of less and less responsibility, until Dorothea believed he could no longer cause financial harm
to others. In abdicating from the family business, Melvyn may have set a
precedent for Tony to go another way. (The neurasthenic Roger was not
a candidate.) The chain of Hecht & Sons broke with Melvyn. Tony was
"urged by many family members, on many occasions" to join the family
firm, but he had no interest, due no doubt to seeing how wretched it
made his father.

Melvyn was a shy, but amiable clubman, and cut a striking figure in
an English suit, his pipe habitually to hand. (His grandson Adam remembered him as always smelling of tobacco.) Many Upper East Side Jews did
not believe in making a point of being Jewish. Tony's parents were very

much of this ilk. The newlyweds were "not very observing Jews."[33] Her family attended services on Rosh Hashana, though more for social reasons than religious, or headed "to the home of some aunt or uncle, never seen on any other occasion, to celebrate the Passover. . . . My father, an uncommonly superstitious man, declared himself a complete atheist."[34] Jewishness was something about which they were both ashamed and secretly proud. "The shame was the kind engendered by the conventional antisemitism, and the social ostracism experienced by virtually all Jews in a gentile society" and the "pride was based on a fantasy that the Jews were somehow all 'brilliant' as a race (a conviction they must have realized they were both exceptions to), and that many of the greatest men and women, if the truth were but known, were actually Jews."[35] His parents played a game in which they asserted that numerous great men and women, all geniuses, were secretly Jews, such as Charlie Chaplin and Copernicus. As an adult, looking back, Hecht puzzled over his parents' sense of exceptionalism. They could be a little snobbish. Surely, they knew that they were no Einsteins, but in many senses they were to be envied, part of the cultured Western European Jewish diaspora that had made a place for themselves in Manhattan.

3. "A grave and secret malady . . ."[36]

Anthony Evan Hecht was born on January 16, 1923, at the Sloane Hospital for Women, located on the campus of the Columbia University College of Physicians and Surgeons, at Amsterdam Avenue and 59th Street. The hospital was a short cab ride, across Central Park and down, from his parents' Upper East Side apartment. It's possible Dorothea's family helped the young couple with the medical costs, as they had with much else, as Melvyn worked to secure his prospects at New England Enamel.

An early photo of Tony—possibly the earliest of the newborn—taken at only a few weeks old, shows four generations. At bottom right is the babe in a white gown, the crown of his head illuminated by light from an elegantly draped window above a velvet window seat. Three women, in a descending line from standing to sitting, loom over him like a row of nesting dolls, each in an elegant black gown, their hair in stylish updos. Standing on the left, at a remove of several feet from the main event, is the baby's mother, an attractive young woman with raven hair and small hands. She's holding a rattle on which the infant's gaze is fixed, aiming outward toward the photographer. In the middle, perched on the arm of a high-backed upholstered chair, sits his grandmother, Jennie, wearing a single strand of pearls and a thin smile. She peers over the shoulder of the third woman, Tony's great-grandmother, Amalie, age eighty-seven, with a long double row of pearls and snow-white hair. Amalie smiles down warmly at the baby in her arms. She took a particular shine to Tony, showering him with attention, which was not forthcoming from the other women.

The Hecht boys were often isolated from the adults, with a nanny to look after them during the day. Also, they spent a great deal of time with doctors, Roger especially. Roger's numerous ailments meant a rotating cast of physicians visiting the home, but Tony, too, had a serious early health scare. At age one, he developed a dangerous ear infection. A doctor was sent for, and when he arrived at the Hechts' Lexington Avenue apartment, he determined that "the situation was urgent."[37] He operated on the infant on the kitchen table. Hecht remembered two images from the convalescence: the spindles of his crib and, catching the sunlight on a nearby windowsill, a goldfish in a bowl—as in a painting by Matisse—that someone (perhaps one of his "many aunts") bought for him as a get-well gift. The fish must have glowed in the sun. Hecht's memories are frequently of light and shadow, the way the sun streams into a basilica in Venice, or the first, ominous hints of dawn on a battlefield, or the transcendent, gleaming taxi that would transfix him in early childhood. The yellow cab becomes a key image in "Apprehensions," an image of Dame Kind and a reprieve from the shadowy world of 140 East 89th Street. This fascination stayed with him his whole life, his wife, Helen, remembers: "He was enchanted by the various effects of sunlight—slanting across the lawn during late-summer afternoons, gilding the sides of buildings, illuminating the leaves of trees. He often commented on the beauty of such effects."[38]

The apartment on 89th Street was vast, still, and deathly quiet. His memories of it were leached of color and life:

In the parlor, which was never used,
Under a glass bell, the dried hydrangeas
Had bleached to the hue of ancient newspaper,
Though once, someone affirmed, they had been pink.[39]

Seasonally, through the gloom, light would break into the parlor in shafts:

Green velvet drapes kept the room dark and airless
Until on sunny days toward midsummer
The brass andirons caught a shaft of light
For twenty minutes in the late afternoon
In a radiance dimly akin to happiness—
The dusty gleam of temporary wealth.

Hecht constructs a still life of the transient—light, happiness, wealth—though the memory itself is indelible, the vision of a solitary child, who in fact was never alone. There was always Roger. A number of traumatic memories grew out of Hecht's "uninformed and ungoverned fantasies about the consequences of the Depression,"[40] but there was another major event that greatly shaped his young life and compounded his childhood insecurities: the birth of his brother.

Roger Deer Hecht was born on October 22, 1926. He was smaller than Tony and fairer. Where Tony's face was oval, with deep-set eyes, Roger's was round and sunny. But Roger was unwell, and his illness introduced into the already fraught apartment an added anxiety. In fact, Roger suffered from no single illness but rather a host of ailments:

[he] was not only epileptic; he limped, he had a semi-paralyzed right hand, and eyesight so poor that as a child he was made to exercise his eyes every day for long periods with a stereopticon, the focusing of which was meant to limber the muscles of his eyes and correct his tendency to be cross-eyed.[41]

At a loss for what to do, Dorothea employed a psychotherapist to treat his seizures. Talk therapy, a newly fashionable import from Europe popularized in New York society by the salons of Mabel Dodge, did nothing to allay Roger's episodes in childhood. Roger was also prescribed medications early on, though none did the trick. "Only when he was fully grown," his older brother remembered, "did they find the right medications that could control" the seizures.[42]

Roger often followed onto ground cleared by Tony—an uneasy shadowing at times. Tony went to Bard, Roger went to Bard. Tony went to Kenyon (on the GI Bill), Roger followed after. Roger would himself become a poet of some accomplishment. The two even shared a number of subjects and themes, such as Judaism, war, and the Bible. "It is uncommon enough for two siblings to be so allied in their professional ambitions," Hecht felt in retrospect. "Roger himself once remarked that the two of us had more in common than William and Henry James. . . . These parallels were not coincidental; indeed they represented a bond so close as to trouble both of us from time to time."[43] As a boy, Roger was devoted to Tony, acting as his literary secretary when Tony was living abroad. Increasingly, he became a kind of doppelganger, always wanting to do what his brother did, attend the same schools, achieve the same things. Both boys inherited their father's raucous sense of humor, though Roger's "sense of comedy leaned heavily towards absurdity and ridiculousness." His brother remembered, "There were times when he was so joyfully transported by some lunacy of which he had read, or by some absurdity of his own invention, that his exhilaration knew no bounds, and he was mercifully, powerfully, utterly freed from all the afflictions he was born with."

Hecht knew in his gut that his family life was deeply unhealthy for him at that formative age: "Some instinct," which he trusted completely, told him "that the interrelationships and interdependencies of my immediate family were draining and dangerous to me":

> I was not free to be myself—though of course I hadn't the faintest notion of what I would be if I were free. I wanted to be an adult, not for the pleasures of adulthood (whatever they were—the only one that appealed to me in those days was the right to stay up late) but to be at least exempted from the routine and humiliating scrutiny of my elders (including my teachers), by whom I was inevitably weighed and found wanting. And a

child who is told he is not good at anything is likely sooner or later to give into a mood of defeat. And this was pretty much the situation in which I found myself; parental dissatisfaction was a kind of tyranny, developed to encourage the symbiotic relationship, though I scarcely could have known this at the time.[44]

His father, Melvyn, behaved like "a shackled and enfeebled man," and Roger was physically weak and vulnerable. Their weakness left Hecht without a family structure he could either embrace or rebel from. Melvyn and Roger were "the two people who, in my childhood, would have been my natural rivals; and since each was handicapped, I felt I had to pull my punches. I remember feeling from very early on that any success of mine was *ipso facto* painful to both of them. My father was ashamed of his failures and resented my successes, and I was completely aware of this. No doubt I chose poetry in the first place because in at least one sense it may be regarded as uncompetitive." The full impact of this unhealthy dynamic would reveal itself in time on one of several psychiatrists' couches that Hecht later resorted to for help with these traumas. He found it hard to take pride in his accomplishments, even when completing a new book of poems, receiving an acceptance from Howard Moss at *The New Yorker,* or garnering a prestigious award. His awareness of the issue hardly made it better: "I have never been able to free myself of this self-imposed constraint and feeling of guilt about such accomplishments as have been mine," nor was there any positive acknowledgment coming from his parents.

For long hours he was left to his own devices, with no relief for his restlessness beyond what distractions he could invent for himself around the apartment. There were rows of books in expensive sets, but it would be years before he could master their contents and lose himself in them. The formal living room had little else that would draw his interest except for the piano—a Steinway grand in dark-brown figured wood, like the books a wedding gift to his parents. His mother played, and he would sit by and listen. She did not instruct Tony or encourage him to play, but, likely on his own, barely tall enough to pull himself up on the bench, he would open the cover and sit at the keys when no one was around. He found that he could recall melodies he had heard and pick them out by ear. He developed a "fierce interest in music," and it wasn't long before he was playing whole tunes. "The first kind of art that I really instantly recognized and reacted to . . . was classical music, which I heard on WQXR in New York City."[45] A Hungarian uncle named Leonard Wolf gave him classical records for Christmas every year, and one of his prized possessions was a volume of brief lives of the great composers.

Tony hoped his playing would draw the approval of his mother, but it did not; in fact, quite the opposite. After he had mastered a few tunes, his "mother then lost all interest in music, and quit playing." Similarly, when Tony and Roger "started to write poetry, she stopped reading poetry abruptly, and firmly declared she 'couldn't understand' anything written by either" of them.[46] His parents were not completely discouraging of his playing. When he was seven or eight, he attended music school, though the lessons were short-lived. Tony enjoyed playing by ear, which came to him naturally and easily, but "he refused to learn to read music."[47] He had "not perfect but relative pitch" and was "afflicted with [a] particular kind of auditory memory" that enabled him to "recall a good deal of intricate classical music after a single hearing, and to pick out fugues and canons by ear."[48] Long passages from Whittier's "Snow-Bound" and Bryant's "Thanatopsis," memorized in school, lodged themselves where they were hard to get rid of. He later wished that it was passages from Milton or Shakespeare, and not "To him who in the love of nature holds . . . ," that had provided his early models for the iambic pentameter line. He would "measure out [his] lines against that one, not because [he] liked it, but because it was a certified Bureau of Weights and Measures Standard Iambic Pentameter Line." His magpie ear also collected whole songs—tunes and lyrics—by Cole Porter and Noël Coward. He found that "he could also recall words if they appeared in a patterned order," and his "interest in poetry began there."[49] Part of his love of poetry from the beginning lay in its formal properties, as he explained to Langdon Hammer in an interview from mid-career:

> I share with John Hollander and a great number of others the delight in formality. It is useful and valuable in any number of ways. It has its musical component, a metrical and rhythmical component; but it is also a valuable form of artistic discourse. In *Homo Ludens* Johan Huizinga

speaks of play as something confined within a certain limit. It has rules. If it's an athletic thing like tennis, it has a court. These limitations Huizinga finds analogous to religious ceremonies and rituals, the marking out of sacred space and the confining of activity within prescribed limits. Huizinga finds this absolutely characteristic of all aesthetic undertakings, and I can't help but believe that that's true. This is part of the way the imagination takes pleasure in its own life. Without the limitations there would be less pleasure.[50]

The delineation of ritualized or sacred space elevates some of Hecht's most ambitious and serious poems (such as "Rites and Ceremonies"), while the ludic charge of form lends spark and wit to poems in a lighter vein ("The Ghost in the Martini," as only one example).

His parents resisted his wish to be a poet, at least initially. In all things he was "encouraged to be mediocre." And as far as his mother was concerned, he succeeded brilliantly in this. She told him

in a tone of mild regret and resignation that the aptitude tests indicated that I had no aptitudes whatever. As the evidence continued to pile up on all sides it became increasingly difficult to attain any confidence in myself; and I wanted alternately to be dead or to be "old," which meant to me, in either case, no longer under the scrutiny of authorities I was powerless to combat.[51]

The "sadness" that came to infuse his poems was "the matured and mellowed residue of what in childhood had been a poisonous brew of fear, hatred, self-loathing, impotence and deep discouragement."[52]

Through all of this, Tony's great-grandmother always had time for him, providing the love and attention that he sorely missed from his mother. During their regular visits all together, Dorothea and Jennie would "pursue their interests and gossip together."[53] His "Granny" was left out of his mother's koffee klatches, as was Tony himself, of course. The two "found comfort in one another's company."[54] They played Parcheesi and kept out of the way.

Her death, when it came, was concealed from him by the adults, like so much else. He would later remember visiting his grandmother's apartment and running to his Granny's room, but his mother held him back. When he strained in protest, he was told simply that he could not see her. Nothing further was explained. He realized later, from her continued absence, that his great-grandmother must have died, though no one in the family ever said as much. Perhaps they were protecting him, or, as he came to suspect, this was another example of how little they paid attention to or understood his feelings at that age. His great-grandmother had been precious to him, and now she was gone. Tony thought of her often, believing in his innocence that he could call her back to life by doing so. In his quiet moments at the window, she was still with him, he was sure.[55]

A scene from "The Venetian Vespers" resonates with the event, though in the poem it is the speaker's mother who has died: "When I was six years old it rained and rained / And never seemed to stop."[56] Something secret ripples through the family, and the child is the last to find it out:

> Next day they told me that my mother was dead.
> I didn't go to school. I watched the rain
> From my bedroom window or from my burlap nest
> Behind the counter. My whole life changed
> Without my having done a single thing.
> Perhaps because of those days of constant rain
> I am always touched by it now, touched and assuaged.
> Perhaps the early vigilance at windows
> Explains why I have now come to regard
> Life as a spectator sport.[57]

To the outside world, Hecht's parents seemed all one might wish—handsome, affluent, worldly. From a financial standpoint, there was enough of a cushion, particularly from the older generation, that life after the Crash appeared to carry on as before. Tony, a "child of privilege"[58] to onlookers, had already seen more of the world than most boys his age, having traveled to Europe by ocean liner a few years before. In 1934, the Hechts allowed themselves another extended tour through France and Switzerland. Roger documented the entire trip in a small leather-bound diary, with the year printed in gold on the cover. In September, they sailed on the SS *Lafayette* for Le Havre. The boys played pirates aboard ship, lying in ambush with toy guns and posting lookouts. While Hecht's parents dressed up for afternoon activities, followed by dinner in the grand dining room, the boys scrambled around on deck under the supervision of Mademoiselle, who had succeeded Fräulein to Tony's great relief.

In Paris, the boys played in the park with Mademoiselle or visited sights with their parents. Among the photos from the trip is a postcard of a hotel on the side of a mountain, Hôtel Pensione Caldaro-Herrnhofer in the Mendel Pass near Bolzano in the Tyrolean Alps. The chalet-style building is gleaming in the sun as the valley below fills up with shadows. The Hechts had a balcony overlooking the pass and slopes of the mountains on the opposite side, much like the setting of the poem "The Grapes." By evening, the less-fashionable hotel is cloaked in shade, while the places across the way get the light:

> . . . it is strange and sad, at cocktail time,
> To look across the valley from our shade,
> As if from premature death, at all that brilliance
> Across which silently on certain days
> Shadows of clouds slide past in smooth parade,
> While even our daisies and white irises
> Are filled with blues and darkened premonitions.[59]

Like Hecht's childhood, "The Grapes" reverberates with premonitions and diminished fortunes. His stay in the Tyrol, age eleven, was his first trip to Italy, the country that would become his psychic home. Like his parents, he prized connections to the Old World. In Zurich, the family posed for photos in the Hecht Platz—no known relation, though the name itself derived from that part of the world. As an adult, Hecht would return to Europe as often as he could, occasionally for months at a time, and after his retirement from teaching he returned every summer to the Veneto. Italian painting and architecture, French poetry, English and Greek drama: these would become touchstones of his sensibility. When he arrived in Paris in wartime, he was already familiar with how a walk down the Champs-Élysées would take one to the Opera, and the

Luxembourg Gardens were only a short walk from Notre Dame. With the sun on his face as he wandered St. Germain, he could remember the day that he and Roger wore their new berets and posed with their father, with Tony holding one of his father's cigarettes in the European style. That was a good day, though the good days came fleetingly to the boy, like light on a bead of water, briefly reflecting his surroundings and elevating his spirits, then gone.

TWO

"AN EDUCATION FOR WHICH I RECEIVED NO GRADES . . ."[1]
(1935–1941)

1. "A corn roast and bonfire in summer camp . . ."[2]

Life on East 89th Street in the mid-thirties continued much as it had—relentless and bleak. "For many complicated reasons, my childhood was a rather bitter and lonely one," Hecht disclosed years later.[3] Nothing the twelve-year-old Hecht did seemed to win his parents' approval. He was solitary, adrift, and could not hope to garner the kind of concern and support from his parents that his brother received. When, years later, Roger became a poet, very much in his brother's footsteps, it was clear to outsiders that Dorothea prized Roger's poems—as she did everything produced by her dear, infirm son—while paying scant attention to Tony's. Whenever Tony got his name in the papers for a prize or a publication, she was pleased, but showed little interest in his poetry otherwise. Everything Roger wrote, by contrast, was deemed "wonderful."[4]

Hecht's early schooling—first at Mrs. Oast's Nursery School in Manhattan, and then at the elite day schools Dalton (for K-3) and Collegiate (for middle school)—entailed not so much an escape from isolation and insecurity as a continuation and a deepening of them. The progressive Dalton would have valued his musical talents, if he had dared to reveal them. Dalton's innovative, wholistic approach—derived in part from its founder Helen Parkhurst's experience teaching with child-centered education innovator Maria Montessori—appealed to Dorothea as a follower of intellectual fashion, but it may have overwhelmed Hecht, who tended to retreat into a defensive shell.

His artistic abilities—for singing, acting, piano—seem not to have found an outlet at the school, where children's creativity was valued. It would be years before he came into his own creatively, developing greater confidence and autonomy a little at a time. Things got worse, before they got better. His propensity for seeing himself as an outsider was abetted by the other children and even some teachers, who made him feel that he did not belong. In photographs from these years, Hecht looks haunted—shorn hair, sunken eyes, and a sad smile. Instead of despairing, however, he kept quiet, hoping for a change. From an early age, he worked to check his pride, which he held to be the worst sin of the Seven Deadlies. This much was Granny Amalie's influence, no doubt; it was she alone who made him feel loved.

For middle school, the stricter, all-boys Collegiate was chosen. Where Dalton had been modern and experimental, Collegiate was hidebound and traditional. Chartered by the Dutch West India Company as part of the Reformed Dutch Protestant Church of New Amsterdam in 1638, Collegiate claimed to be the oldest independent school in the country. Dalton was nearby, on East 72nd Street; Collegiate necessitated a crosstown bus to West 77th, though in good weather it was an easy walk across the park. If Dalton was home to nurturers, free-thinkers, philosophers, and child-psychologists, then Collegiate retained a strong whiff of sacral incense and WASP parochialism. Hecht made no close friends there. It was a sporty school, and he was not especially sporty at that age (though he later picked up baseball, swimming, and shooting). Nor was he particularly engaged with academics. Even subjects like literature and languages, which drew him later on, left him cold. The fault was in the place and not the pupil.

Occasionally, his mother or Mademoiselle would arrange for a play-date with boys of Hecht's acquaintance, either from school or summer camp. Hecht later remembered one boy in particular named Maurice, whom all of the kids called "Two Potato," possibly from the rhyming, elimination game played by rapping fists one atop another. Whenever Two Potato came to the Hechts', he behaved beautifully—always "kind and well-meaning." But Two Potato was a shattering bore; at least Hecht thought so. He resented being saddled with the boy for hours at a time in his parents' very grown-up apartment, with lots of dark and dusty corners and no ready amusements. So, he "invented a story that there was hidden treasure in the apartment," and Two Potato was sent in search of it. This relieved Hecht of his unwanted hosting. The boy's lumpish nickname amused Hecht. He remembered calling his friend's house one day and asking, "Is Two Potato home?" The boy's mother replied tartly, with "great hauteur," "Do you mean *Maureeece*?"[5] Maurice makes a striking cameo in "The Short End," Hecht's longer poem about the disintegration of a marriage, which ends in a fatal fire. The newlyweds Norman and Shirley Carson arrive at a sales convention in Atlantic City, where Shirley stands out as the only spouse in sight. At a party in the Plantagenet Bar and Tap Room, the couple are introduced around to the drunken salesmen, including "Maurice, / Whose nickname it appeared, was Two Potato." The salesmen take to taunting the pair:

> *Two Potato particularly seemed*
> *aggressive both in his solicitude*
> *And in the smirking lewdness of his jokes*
> *As he unblushingly eyed the bride for blushes.*[6]

It becomes clear to Shirley that they have become "mere hostages / Whom nobody would ransom." Like his namesake, the fictional Maurice is a bore from whom the Carsons cannot escape. They wind up feeling "Timid and prepubescent and repressed."

The occasional playdate, followed by afternoons in Central Park: each day followed the same progress. In the park he was allowed to venture off by himself, or perhaps Mademoiselle, who would be fussing with Roger, just lost track of him. The park could be a wild place, even in broad daylight, with countless shadowed paths winding unseen through the Ramble and the Ravine's steep slopes cut off from any adult supervision. Even structured activities could take a sinister turn. One afternoon, Hecht returned home from a summer playgroup with his face bloodied and bruised. His nose was broken. He had been badly beaten by older boys. Where were the grown-ups when this was going on? How had they allowed it to happen? Dorothea called up the other mothers to register her concern, and Hecht was met the next day with what he took to be sincere apologies. But "he never forgot the hurt of that incident,"[7] and he would always wonder what he would have looked like had his nose not been broken.

The previous summer the Hechts had gone abroad, staying in posh hotels and traveling by train through the Alps. No such trip was planned for this year. Despite their straitened circumstances, the Hechts continued to do as their friends did, making day trips to nearby beaches with occasional outings to Coney Island or even Atlantic City. Through the height of the season, the two boys were thrown together as usual and rarely met any local children their age to play with.

The boys were older now and harder to keep occupied. If Dorothea was to get any peace, she would have to take matters in hand. A suitable sleepaway camp was found in North Belgrade, Maine. Camp Kennebec, with its bone-chilling lake and sprawling woods, and its bluff and boyish camaraderie, would change Hecht's young life dramatically for the better, though it would take more than one summer to do it. Like many camps of that era, Kennebec's names and traditions were all drawn from their version of Native American culture. Though there were weekly Bible readings, the camp had no explicit religious affiliation. Still, it was widely known as a "camp for Jewish boys."[8] Founded by two lawyers from Philadelphia, Louis M. Fleisher and Samuel G. Friedman, Kennebec drew boys from the major urban centers of the Northeast, as well as attracting a "national patronage." It included a junior camp for boys aged ten to twelve, which is where Hecht began that first summer.

Hecht needed a couple of weeks to settle in. At first, the camp's precise rituals, rustic dining hall, cabin living, and elaborate daily schedules were strange for someone who had never been away from home. The counselors, known to the kids as Uncles or "Unks," were strapping, well educated, athletic, and handsome. The dress code among the Unks, not surprisingly in Maine, was early Preppy Handbook: tennis whites, plaid flannel in the evenings, horn-rimmed glasses, tousled hair. The camp prided itself on employing a staff of "university trained men," who had specialties in woodworking, horsemanship, engine repair, hiking, and general fitness. In July, there were swim meets with other camps, tennis, and fishing, and in August the kids would go on overnights in the woods and take long trips on horseback.

Hecht was starved for male role models at home, and here were a host of smart, capable young men, who took an interest in what he was doing and could show him the right way to do it. Hecht returned for the next several summers. The motto appended to the camp history—"the man in every boy and the boy in every man"[9]—rang true for Hecht. In the wilds of the Maine woods, over successive summers through 1938, he blossomed from a taciturn loner to a hearty adolescent, who enjoyed sports and rough play—a regular gangly kid, with lively friends and outdoorsy interests.

To her credit, Dorothea had found the perfect place for her son. From her perspective, the $400 fee (more than $7,000 in today's value for July and August) was worth every penny. Perhaps Melvyn and Dorothea drove him on his first trip north, but mostly he took the overnight train. On these long trips, which rolled through the green New England landscape, Hecht might catch a couple hours of sleep, but his excitement was such that he arrived most years entirely sleepless. He rejoiced in his freedom— from his parents, his governess, and, most significantly, his brother.

Hecht embraced the traditions of the place with enthusiasm. Buoyant letters about his escapades and accomplishments came winging home, his prolific correspondence owing partly to a camp policy, whereby letters home were their "tickets" to dinner on Wednesdays and Sundays. His penciled notes were full of the usual boilerplate—"having a swell time," etc.—but they featured wondrous details, which Hecht was keen to share. "The other night we had grand council. We were dressed with blankets and walked slowly down to the council ring. Mr. Fleisher dressed as an Indian Chief was beating a drum. Uncle Mac who was medicine man blew the pipe of peace and the chieftains of each tribe were chosen."[10] Hecht participated eagerly in camp activities, which stretched from before sunrise to the nightly bonfire. Playing Indians and going on raids was hilarious fun and a long-standing tradition at Kennebec, from its beginning in 1912:

> The youngest boys were divided into two tribes, each under the chieftainship of a master, and camp grounds were established across the lake for them. . . . With it arose the custom of midnight raids on enemy campsites (participated in then even by the directors) and ingenious reprisals for the raids that have survived over the years as a lively facet of the Kennebec Way.[11]

In the pitch dark, through overgrown woods, under brilliant star-filled skies, the boys huddled together in silence, barely breathing, hoping not

to be detected. For such stealth operations, Hecht made a war club out
of wood.

When Hecht first arrived at Kennebec, he walked through the quad
of tents, which ran in two long rows down toward the lake. There was a
camp flag, which was lowered at sunset to the report of "the unpredict-
able cannon." Other elements included a tree house, an old Shinto gate,
a bocce court, and trampolines. An array of tennis courts sat behind the
tents, and down a dirt path a baseball diamond opened out against a backdrop of woods. Reveille was at 6 A.M. As a camp freshman, he hadn't yet
learned to swim. He was more interested in indoor activities: he earned
the nickname The Maestro, "the quiet but witty boy of the cabin. His
interests leaned more to the cultural side of camp than to athletics."[12]
When his parents sent him an instrument to play around the campfire,
he quickly became known as "a fine ukulele player and a good entertainer
on and off the stage."[13] By his second summer, he had mastered swimming more or less: in the interval between the wake-up bugle and the
flag raising, it was "normal to see Tony Hecht, sleepy-eyed, but cheerfully
calm and composed, thinking over his activities on the water front as an
energetic 'sinker.'"[14] In his cabin was one Maurice Rashbaum, Jr., from
West 73rd Street in New York—Two Potato himself.

The photo from his second summer is more bright-eyed. Hecht's expression shows his increasing comfort and contentment in the woods and
with these boys. Writing home, he referred to several of them by name.
More than at school, he found boys he liked to play and fish with; they
put on plays, hatched plots, and sang. Even his athletics improved; he
learned baseball, boxing, rowing, and riflery. The camp's crowded schedule of activities had a positive effect on his physique and his confidence.

The first swim of the day came at 7 A.M.—the lake was frigid at that
hour—followed by "setting up exercises" and then breakfast. Counselors
mentored the boys in academics and the arts. After breakfast, there were
lessons in literature, algebra, history, French, and natural science, before
more swimming at eleven. In the afternoon, Hecht played baseball and
tennis, ran track, swam, wrestled, boxed. The boys learned canoeing,
piling into the camp's two monstrous war canoes. Hecht also learned
shooting, lying on his stomach at the rustic gun range, the butt of a gun
snugged between his shoulder and cheek. He proved an accomplished

marksman, a fact he boasted about in letters home. He even sent his parents the paper targets, endorsed by the National Rifle Association, with his scores recorded at the bottom. One bullseye, featuring a lattice of tightly grouped bullet holes, records a forty-seven out of a possible fifty for prone shooting at fifty feet. Hecht, of course, had no inkling that he would eventually be called upon to carry a rifle in the service of his country. A number of the boys on the range that summer would likely be doing the same.

When the time came, even the Unks would join up and ship out, but for now life in North Belgrade was still idyllic:

> In the evenings there were sometimes tramping parties to Great Pond to see the sunset, or quiet times with music at the lake front. Assembly programs often featured story reading, or boxing exhibitions, or "moving pictures" lit by arc lights. When the pictures were clear, special mention was made of it. There were magic lantern shows, accompanied by appropriate readings.[15]

In addition to Two Potato, Hecht's cabin included a pair of boys he knew from home—Buddy and Dicky—likely the sons of family friends. The other three—Alan Shwarbacher, Donald Iceman, and Robert Bernbaum—quickly made friends with this cohort, and Hecht and Shwarbacher in particular fished and played together. Their counselor was Uncle Stan, who led the boys in Indian chants. One camp tradition that Hecht never wrote home about and showed no signs of participating in was a blackface minstrel show led by the Unks, not unusual for 1930s white America, which had absorbed minstrelsy in films and radio shows.

Hecht at first received hazing from the older boys, who liked to pounce on the junior campers without warning. He fended off two bullies— Cohen and Klingenstein—by fighting them: "I didn't win but I was far from lost. I can beat up Cohen and both of them are beginning to respect [me]." Of course, when it was his turn to dish it out, he enjoyed razzing the younger boys, carrying out good-natured stunts such as forcing the freshmen to wear their pants inside-out and backwards for a week. In his second summer, Hecht moved up from Junior to Senior camp. He took great pleasure in belonging: "I am getting along this year so much better than last it isn't funny. . . . The older boys are swell to me and Cohen and Klingenstein never bother me. I can't exaggerate what a good time I am having."[16]

Roger, too, came north to Maine in the summer of 1935, though he attended Camp Androscoggin, where presumably allowances could be made for Roger's lack of physical strength and where he might receive extra care if needed. Wherever Tony went, Roger usually followed, as if Tony were an advance guard for his less-hardy brother. It's easy to imagine Hecht resenting his brother's shadowing, especially since Roger had always been the one who got more credit for his accomplishments. But Hecht supported his brother. If he was jealous at times, he never overtly took it out on Roger. He truly wished his brother well. At Kennebec, at any rate, he was glad to be on his own, making his own way, on his own terms, without comparison or association. When Melvyn sent letters to the boys, Tony reminded him that they needed to go under separate cover, since he would not be seeing Roger. As Dorothea may have feared, camp was not as good a fit for Roger. In subsequent summers, he stayed behind in New York because of his health. Tony's letters asked after him.

Hecht's parents wrote to him often. Even Melvyn liked to dash off notes from his office, and Hecht was glad when mail call produced new letters from home. Camp life required lots of special gear and clothing, and Hecht, still concerned about his family's finances, hated to ask his mother for extra money unless unavoidable: "I wanted to tell you that it has been raining here for two days and it is necessary to wear boots. I am very sorry I have to ask for these things and I don't care if you don't want to send them." Melvyn liked to kid with Tony, preferring to trade bawdy jokes than to lay down the law. That was Dorothea's job. Jokes were the private language between father and son, and the disapproving Dorothea was not included in them. After several summers of receiving his father's humorous squibs, Hecht was emboldened to enclose a note to Melvyn for his eyes only:

Story—
Two men were going to a masquerade ball as a cow, one to be the front, the other back. They were walking across a field when suddenly a real bull started chasing them. The back man said "Can you run?"

Front man: "I'll be fucked if I can"
Back man: "Well, [I'll] be fucked if you can't"
End—Tony[17]

Where Hecht heard this joke he doesn't say. He felt a growing camaraderie with the other boys and described their joint escapades in his letters. The tonic note was wild hilarity, and the Unks fostered their earthy esprit de corps. If one boy's fishing line broke, a friend would lend him one. Together, they performed a series of practical jokes, had egg fights, short-sheeted (or "pied") beds, and even sent one boy's cot out into the middle of the lake on a raft. Hecht liked jokes that told stories, and he excelled in performing them, able to put on a variety of voices. To the Unks, he may have seemed quietly witty, but, like Melvyn, his low-key exterior masked a wicked sense of humor, a quality he retained throughout his life and brought to bear in his more satiric poems.

Overnight trips were a regular feature of the camp. Boys made campfires to cook their own food and clambered to the top of Mount Katahdin. They took long walking trips with full packs to the Rangeley Lakes and canoe trips to Moosehead Lake. According to the camp history, "Some of these were successful, some left to chance, with campsites often requested in fields and barns, and supplies purchased at random farmhouses. The party of the first trip to Moosehead was put off the train at Dead Water, beyond Bingham, because of lack of fare, and hiked five days back into camp."[18]

A long trek that Hecht took in the summer of 1938 "was handicapped slightly by a few minor accidents," including a mild case of impetigo and a broken ukulele. The biggest mishap resulted from a run of bad weather along a portion of the Appalachian Trail formerly used by Benedict Arnold in his attempt to capture Quebec:

The first night we camped at Carry Pond. On the following day we hiked twelve miles to West Carry Pond and camped at Dead River. The campsite was lousy since there were cowflop and flies all over the place. We had to lay over the third day because of bad weather. The next day we climbed Mt. Bigelow (4150 ft.), a tough climb but we had good weather. . . . On the sixth day, we climbed Mt. Saddleback, which is not

quite as high as Bigelow but a lot harder. We were caught in a storm
on top and were almost blown away. The fog was so thick we couldn't
follow the trail.[19]

With the trail lost, the trip took a nasty turn, as the boys wished for the
safety of home and a dry bed. Hecht put on a good face: "But we came
out all right and it was swell." Perhaps because Roger gave his parents
such regular concern, Hecht resisted the temptation to elicit sympathy for his hardships. In his letters, at least, he was uncomplaining and
sturdy, which his parents must have valued, even if they rarely praised
him for it.

Hecht's upbeat tone in his letters masked a number of challenges, but
the overall memory of camp was fond. His accomplishments at Kennebec were among the few positive experiences from childhood to make it
into his poems, though always in a darkened context. In "The Book of
Yolek," Hecht recalls a children's summer camp much like his own, with
its ritual bonfires and feasts. The word *camp* becomes a focal point in the
poem, a sestina, as one of the form's repeating end-words. At first, *camp*
infuses the poem with a piquant nostalgia, as a place of bucolic if long-
lost recreation:

> *You remember, peacefully, an earlier day*
> *In childhood, remember a quite specific meal:*
> *A corn roast and bonfire in summer camp.*
> *That summer you got lost on a Nature Walk:*
> *More than you dared admit, you thought of home . . .*

The youthful memory of a leafy summer camp takes on shades of
another camp. The thought of home becomes an orphanage raided by
the Nazis. At the very center of the poem, summer camp becomes concentration camp:

> *They came at dawn with rifles to The Home*
> *For Jewish Children, cutting short the meal*
> *Of bread and soup, lining them up to walk*
> *In close formation off to a special camp.*

How often you have thought about that camp,
As though in some strange way you were driven to,
And about the children. . . .

Peaceful seclusion gives way to a site of mass extermination; the safety of his parental home becomes the vulnerable home for orphans, these two strains interweaving in his recollection. Hecht's memories of Camp Kennebec become even more poignant when one realizes that the Jewish children with whom he swam and played baseball could have, in a not-too-distant time and place, been the very children rounded up and sent to that special camp from which Yolek does not return. Hecht makes this connection between the Jewish children of the camps and his own young sons at the end of "'It Out-Herods Herod. Pray You, Avoid It.'"

The woods of Maine were as far away from Hecht's wartime experiences as it was possible to get. The place was pure innocence. Hecht did a lot of singing at that age. All the kids at Kennebec were full of songs. Hecht, the "Maestro," earned his nickname in the camp orchestra. He deepened his love of classical music, including Wagnerian opera (which he never much cared for later on): "We have a swell Victrola up in the lodge with both popular and classical recordings, and they have a set of about 12 records with songs from *The Mikado* besides having the *Nutcracker Suite, Scheherazade, Lohengrin, Tannhauser,* and a million others."[20] At Kennebec, Hecht finally received praise for his artistic abilities, and his knowledge and love of the arts became part of his identity as a gifted and versatile performer.

On the outdoor stage, Hecht developed his boyhood passion for acting. What verse he wrote at this point was in the form of comic songs for performance by the camp Theatre Guild and the annual Songfest. It must have surprised the Unks that such a quiet kid could launch abruptly into boisterous singing. Hecht's ability to cut up in front of a crowd won him early admiration from his cabinmates. Drawing on a quickly growing repertoire, he aped a crotchety old man from the *Mike and Meyer* film shorts, with his friend Alan taking Mike and Hecht playing Meyer. The films, in circulation since the mid-teens, depicted two old men whose jealousy of each other sours their friendship. In *The Delicatessen* (1915), Mike and Meyer operate a prosperous deli, until their squabbling lands them in jail. The boys relished mocking these stereotypes from their parents' generation—and in a sense, they were making fun of their own parents. The sketch "went over with a bang,"[21] and the boys were called on to reprise their roles on numerous occasions.

On the strength of his turn as Meyer, Hecht was cast in three plays at once. His star turn came as the sweet and guileless maid Buttercup in Gilbert and Sullivan's *H. M. S. Pinafore*. Hecht was one of the only boys who could still sing the highest notes, so the warbling soprano role fell to him. Appearing in a dress would have certainly cracked up the other campers, and he was game to play for big laughs. On the strength of *Pinafore*, he was elevated, along with a few of his castmates, to the camp's drama club.

The official camp history identifies Hecht as a snappy writer of camp songs. "Sing of a Summer's Day," composed by a camper "who was to win a Pulitzer Prize for poetry," was no doubt Hecht's work. Hecht's earliest attempts at verse were "doggerel" and light verse, and he was exceedingly good at it, far surpassing his fellows. He "had committed to memory not only a lot of classical music but the tunes and words of songs by Cole Porter and Noël Coward." He loved the "highly formal patterns of those lyrics, as well, of course, as their wit and charm."[22] When it was his cabin's turn to enter a song in the yearly camp-wide competition, all eyes turned to Hecht, who produced a delightful parody of Rodgers and Hart's standard "The Lady Is a Tramp," first heard on Broadway the previous year. Sung to the tune of the intro ("I've wined and dined on Mulligan Stew," etc.), Hecht penned:

> *Our first year here, we will admit*
> *We were a bunch of mockies.*
> *We took one look at Cowflop Hill*
> *And said, "We're in the Rockies."*

The song took home top prize at Songfest, and the lyrics were printed in the *Kennebecamper*. This parody was one of the first things of his devising that he ever saw in print. It pleased him greatly. Soon he would become a regular contributor to his school's literary magazine.

In his fourth summer, Hecht was appointed "dramatic commissioner."[23] He became an associate editor on the *Kennebecamper*, which touted him as "the aggregation's council member, wit, and songwriter."[24] He also gained confidence on the baseball diamond, tennis court, and shooting range, which were essential parts of the "Kennebec Way." The paths matted with pine needles and the icy lake water, the mischievous plots hatched and executed, the long fishing trips and overnights on horseback contributed greatly to his physical and mental health. The more time away from his New York school and his high-strung family, the better he felt and the more he grew into himself. This sort of self-actualization was at the heart of the camp's mission. A camp motto by the naturalist John Burroughs reads: "I am a saner, healthier man, with truer standards, for all my loitering in the fields and woods." In one of the Unks' campfire talks there is reference to "the boy as nature's priest," and the camp founders were not shy about touting the spiritual benefits of woodsmanship in thoroughly Thoreauvian manner. At the end of each summer, the campers gathered at the last campfire and heard this heartfelt plea:

> *Oh boys! Will glare of noisy streets and theatres blur*
> *The vision of the meadows green where cattle low and songbirds stir?*
> *Will pleasures that are bought with gold be thought by you the greater*
>   *part,*
> *Remembering not the simple joys that lie so near to nature's heart?*
> *Or will you be true to all the tests that Kennebec imposed,*
> *Where naked as at morning dip your faults and virtues stood disclosed.*[25]

Each fall, he would miss the soft air and star-filled skies of Maine. New York felt to Hecht increasingly claustrophobic. His family moved to a smaller apartment in 1936, closer to the Park, at 40 East 83rd Street, when Hecht was thirteen. (They would move one final time when he went away to college, landing at 163 East 81st Street, the apartment where Roger lived with his parents and where he stayed on after their death.) Escaping the city for two months a summer for the past several years had meant the world to him. In the woods, he found a degree of peace. The natural landscape became a psychic touchstone for him and a valuable resource for his poems. He came to feel that "The eloquence of the physical universe, the demonstration on the part of the natural world,

amounts to a revelation to all who are not blind and deaf."[26] As in "A Hill,"
landscape becomes an "infinitely lavish hall of mirrors, the Versailles of
facets and reflections, in which whenever we look we see, as we must,
unfailingly, some unexpected aspect of ourselves."[27]

His earliest published poems, though still a decade away, recalled the
contours of Maine's lakes and crystal skies, finding in them a framework
through which to reveal his inner life. Observing clouds in the surface
of a lake, the two become indistinguishable; they are composed of the
same element:

> We may consider every cloud a lake
> Transmogrified, its character unselfed,
> At once a whale and a white wedding cake
> Bellowed into conspicuous ectoplasm.[28]

Hecht learned from Shakespeare and Frost—and from others later on
like Bishop and Merrill—how landscape might be used for powerful, often bitter, effects. Thomas Hardy became a key figure for him in this
regard. Hecht defended Ruskin's notion of the "pathetic fallacy," embracing the possibility of the *paysage moralisé* in early poems such as "La
Condition Botanique," "Spring for Thomas Hardy," and "The Gardens of
the Villa d'Este." His first published poem, never collected and written
after returning home from the war, finds in the landscape a dark corollary
for the trauma he felt at the time:

> And seeing this broken landscape toed by the wind together,
> I wanted to drop down on my paper knees,
> And become some wind-bitten plant, and bend in the weather,
> And I wanted to scream.[29]

The city spoke a different language, one of art and culture, of grit
and rapid change. It was the language that his parents and his teachers
at the Collegiate School spoke. It was a social language, bumptious and
intrusive. In Maine, he learned an alternate language of high-spirited
games and quiet contemplation, which greatly transformed his inner life,
though back in the city it was difficult to sustain.

2. "Lingering flavors of the clergy"

Hecht dreaded returning to school each fall. In North Belgrade, he had felt at home among the other campers—city kids like him, who acknowledged their families' Judaism but wore it lightly. In the woods, an unspoken bond of kinship and recognition existed between boys just beginning to discover their resilience and independence, much as the camp founders envisioned.

The Collegiate School, by contrast, was never a good fit for him. Despite growing up nearby and acting and dressing indistinguishably from his schoolmates, Hecht never fit in there. Collegiate had a reputation for the highest academic rigor, and Melvyn, being a Harvard man, wanted his son to follow in his footsteps. It was an era when certain private schools maintained quotas for Jewish students, with a few exceptions made for token "our crowd" families.[30] Christian religious observance played a regular part in each school day, beginning with a morning chapel service. Hecht had no objections; he was content to follow the school's traditions without feeling at all invested in them. Hecht's family was almost entirely, even pointedly, secular. Reflecting back, Hecht saw that Christian belief and practice played a large part in his upbringing:

> I live in what is, nominally at least, a Christian society, and I have been a student at what were actually sectarian schools—the Collegiate School, which is a Dutch Presbyterian school, and Bard College, which was founded as an Episcopal institution, though it was completely secular by the time I got there.
>
> Even so, it had lingering flavors of the clergy, and I sang in the choir on Sundays. I liked to sing, and they gave me a dollar a shot. So you grow up in a kind of culture which is Christian, and it's impossible not to notice this. . . . It's nothing you can ignore unless you are yourself someone of an orthodox faith of a different sort, and I'm not.[31]

Since he paid no particular mind to organized religion, Christian culture became the default. The issue rarely came up. Certain teachers, however, liked to make a point of Hecht's difference, barely masking their distaste for Jews and singling him out for ridicule.

It is a bitter irony of Hecht's childhood that his most beloved writer, Shakespeare, was used against him. Hecht came to admire Shakespeare above all other writers, but his first exposure to him, at Collegiate, was devastating. The experience left a shockingly sour taste in his mouth and registered as one of the low points in an already fraught childhood. Hecht remembered how one afternoon, while reading *The Merchant of Venice* in class, the teacher began quoting Antonio's screed against Shylock:

> *Mark you this, Bassanio,*
> *The devil can cite Scripture for his purpose.*
> *An evil soul, producing holy witness,*
> *Is like a villain with a smiling cheek,*
> *A goodly apple rotten at the heart.*[32]

The boys took turns reading out the parts, working slowly through the text. Early in the play, Antonio admits to spitting on Shylock in the Rialto, to kicking him and calling him a dog. Hecht's teacher thrilled at these insults, relishing Launcelot Gobbo's appraisal: "Certainly the Jew is the very devil incarnation." The experience was

> mortifying, and in complicated ways. I was being asked to admire the work of the greatest master of the English language, and one universally revered, who was slandering all those of my race and religion. I was not even allowed to do this in private, but under the scrutiny and supervision of public instruction. And it took many class periods to get through the whole text. I can also remember the unseemly pleasure of my teacher in relishing all the slanders against the Jews in general and Shylock in particular. It was a wounding experience and the beginning of a kind of education for which I received no grades. And it has continued for the rest of my life.[33]

He never forgave that teacher with the disdainful look on his face, and many years later he revisited his quarrel with *Merchant* in a long essay. Shakespeare, though subject to the prejudices of his age, was, among countless things, a great poet of the outsider. Racial bias and the notion of the stranger, the shadow, the other, figure importantly in a number of Shakespeare's greatest dramas.[34] Hecht's first classroom exposure to Shakespeare ushered in this unsettling awareness, and all three of the essays he came to write on the plays consider in varying degrees how prejudices held by the characters (as well as by Shakespeare and his audience) inform the portrayals of Shylock, Othello, and Caliban.

In the fall of 1936, he moved on to the Horace Mann School for Boys in Riverdale, at 246th Street in the North Bronx—a welcome change. Sitting on the dock of Salmon Lake that summer watching his bobber hover on the surface, he imagined what his new school might bring. For one thing, he would have to leave the house early, waking up before his family, with only their dog, Peppy, seeing him off as he left the apartment. After school he reversed the long commute by bus and subway between boroughs, often arriving home after dark in the winter months. The reward for this trek was more open space than schools in Manhattan enjoyed, with playing fields and walks spread out over acres of green. The student body was made up of boys much like Hecht himself—young men from well-to-do Jewish families in Manhattan. One estimate put the Jewish enrollment in the late 1930s at 80 percent.

Apart from the student body, much about the school resembled Collegiate. Equally remote from the progressive attitudes at Dalton, Horace Mann followed the British system of forms, with ninth grade as the third form and twelfth as the sixth. As one prominent alumnus remembered, there was chapel every Wednesday, and

> Students wore jackets and neckties to class; faculty members were addressed as "sir." . . . Competition was considered a fact of life; class standings with detailed numerical grades were openly discussed, and the names and subjects of students receiving "honors" (86 and above) and "high honors" (95 and above) were printed each quarter in the Horace Mann Record. . . .
>
> That atmosphere reflected what was considered best practice at the time, but it also suited the parents of a student body which, in the teens, 1920's and even 1930's had been essentially patrician but, by the 1940's, had increasingly become composed of the children of upwardly mobile business and professional parents who wanted their offspring worked

hard, trained well, and sent off for polishing to first-rate colleges, Ivy League if possible. . . . Horace Mann prided itself on having brighter students, a heavier workload and what were generally believed (by us, at least) to be higher academic standards.[35]

This kind of social and intellectual training was exactly what Hecht's parents wished for him. He was too quiet, too often by himself. The rigors and proud elitism of a classic preparatory academy would be just what he needed. The affable but demanding headmaster Charles Carpenter Tillinghast would remind students that "a Horace Mann boy is a young gentleman."[36] But Hecht was not interested in rising to the academic challenges at Horace Mann. He coasted on his native intelligence while pursuing other interests, and his grades reflected his lack of engagement: "He was too troubled and unhappy, living in an atmosphere of family crisis and intermittent hysteria to devote himself to study."[37] His poor performance did not go unnoticed. One particularly sadistic history teacher jeered that he "would never amount to anything," with the whole class looking on. This mortifying episode soured him on the school. According to his youngest son, Evan, he "had some really disturbing experiences at Horace Mann. He had a lot of really difficult teachers," including one "who said that he would do everything in his power to see to it that my father never went to college."[38] Harry Wheeler Martin, a history teacher, rattled on about a Catholic conspiracy in politics, and "he didn't think much of Zionism either, or—according to one of his students—Jews. This same student said that Martin believed Jews to be dishonest and blacks stupid."[39] Hecht continued to receive the brunt of this sinister extracurricular education: "There was a history teacher named Martin who hated Roosevelt, and, only slightly less, me. He avowed in class before all my classmates, that I did not deserve to go to college."[40]

Eventually, Hecht found ways to pursue interests close to his heart, almost all of them elective. In a school of fewer than 400 students, there were extensive opportunities beyond the classroom, including

an excellent weekly newspaper (The Record); a yearbook comparable in quality to those of major colleges (The Mannikin); a glossy, illustrated literary magazine (The Quarterly); a yearly school guide book (The Manual); an impressive First Form language magazine (The Linguist); a Dramatic Club and Stage Crew that mounted and elaborately staged two short presentations and one full-length production each year; a Glee Club of some 50 members and a 20-member school orchestra; and active and relatively well-supported clubs for Music, Chess, Debating, Speaking, Political Science, Public Events, Science, Photography, Skiing and Scouting.[41]

Hecht worked a bit on the yearbook, but he preferred performing on stage to editing and the literary arts. Building off of his newly won confidence for acting at camp, he made a splash in the Dramatic Club.

One teacher who left a huge impression was Al Baruth. Baruth was a Horace Mann tradition in himself. He taught English to generations of boys. In addition to literature, he insisted on teaching speech and rhetoric, and his classes in elocution were an important aspect of their "training." The boys were taught how to speak clearly and forcefully. When the poet Nicholas Christopher first met Hecht at Harvard in 1977, he had only recently graduated from Horace Mann. The two soon realized they had Baruth in common. He was a burly figure, more like something out of a Jack London novel than the typically bookish educator. He had

> been a lumberjack, a boxer, he was a self-taught guy. In the days when they had guys like that. And he'd gone to school, probably at night. His tie was always pulled down, very blustery.[42]

Baruth had been a crime reporter and a PhD student at Columbia University. He was also a savvy entrepreneur, running a car service for students from wealthy Manhattan families. Each morning he drove down from Riverdale to pick boys up on Park Avenue, at one point in the late 1930s shuttling the young Si Newhouse and Roy Cohn in the same car. He also founded a summer camp, much like Kennebec, whose largely Jewish clientele typically ran afoul of locals' anti-Jewish biases: "Baruth briefed his charges that the townspeople had never seen a New Yorker or a Jew and that combination might be overwhelming." (He was himself Jewish, but "pretended he wasn't.") He advised campers with particularly

Jewish-sounding names to change them, to avoid the sort of thing that sometimes happened: when the local undertaker's wife noticed one boy's nametag, for example, she saw it "was a Jewish name . . . and said, 'Oh, you're Jewish. You can't work for me.'"[43]

To the boys at Horace Mann, Baruth was larger than life. With broad shoulders, a square jaw, and a cresting wave of chestnut, pomaded hair, he embodied the school's ideal of "manliness." His nose looked like it had been broken in the ring, but his gray flannel suit suggested refinement. To his students' delight, Baruth "made literary texts come vibrantly alive," so that boys "came away with an appreciation of the musical quality of great po-etry, an ear attuned to the well-turned phrase."[44] He "boomed out poetry or dramatic dialogue with such obvious relish and conviction that the most apathetic student was moved. 'And men in England now abed will hold their manhood cheap, that they were not with us on St. Crispin's Day!'—and the class could see the sunlight sparkle on Harry's blade."[45] Baruth was the fa-vorite of Hecht's year, and, when the time came to name a class advisor, he was chosen to oversee their activities.

Public speaking was reinforced by the school's Speakers Club and De-bating Club, and it played a key role in the classroom and at school assem-blies. Baruth would have the boys recite Shakespeare or Marlowe as part of their speech training. Hecht, who had caught the acting bug at Ken-nebec, added to his natural stage presence a facility for elevated speech. Poetry recitation was also a requirement of Baruth's class, and students memorized lyric poems as well as speeches from *Tamburlaine* and *Julius Caesar*. Gifted with a nearly photographic recall, Hecht committed long passages of Shakespearean blank verse to memory, and he quickly became known for his sonorous and elegant recitations.

As Christopher recalls, Baruth "taught us how to speak to the person in the back of the room, how to speak very slowly. And Tony was the best reader I ever heard—incredible. He was the best." Hecht worked closely with Baruth. On his college applications, he put Baruth down as a "teacher best acquainted with applicant's abilities." Not only did his high-school speech classes improve his diction and timing, but they also altered the sound of his voice. Precise and refined, Hecht's speech recalled the classical actors of his day. Among the literati, it was a means of acceptance and distinction. It was most pronounced around strangers, and it relaxed into a more plain-spoken jocularity with his intimates. Hecht became "convinced that it served as a mask." He recalled that "when I used to drink a lot, everyone remarked that my speech became more precise and fastidious the more I drank. I used to be pleased by this observation. I suppose I felt it meant I was giving nothing away."[46]

In interviewing Hecht for *The Paris Review* in 1988, the poet J. D. McClatchy observed that "most striking of all" about him was his voice: "a plummy, resonant baritone that, to my ear, sounds like no one else so much as the actor Claude Rains."[47] To some, it seemed distancing, formal, asserting a high degree of cultivation and learning. To his longtime friends like Annie Wright, the widow of the poet James Wright, he just sounded like himself, that is to say mild, amusing, and intelligent. From the school's perspective, it was part of the desired effect—that of the English public-school boy—which its students adopted to move seamlessly within the Ivy League colleges for which they were being groomed. This was also to a good extent Dorothea's accent. Hecht's son Evan noticed that it could be more pronounced at certain times and less at others: "I would notice it would come out in degrees. If he was a bit nervous in, say, addressing a large group of perhaps cynical college students it would come on a little bit thicker. But if he was hanging out with me and complaining about somebody he'd refer to as a 'sonofabitch,' he'd really embellish it in an American folksy-sounding drawl by comparison. He would adjust it according to the audience."[48]

Taciturn and a little morose, Hecht found a way to win the attention of his peers. Much as he had at camp, he became known as a performer. In his junior year, Horace Mann's fifth form, Hecht performed in concerts by the Glee Club. He was the club's librarian and contributed his "rich baritone" in a featured quartet, called the small chorus. The quartet, dressed in black tie with wide silk lapels, provided comic relief with their selection of novelty songs. So striking was Hecht's "never-to-be-forgotten" solo rendition of Victor Herbert and Henry Blossom's "Every Day Is Ladies' Day with Me" that the yearbook hailed him as "Every Day Is Ladies' Day" Hecht. His performances in the Dramatic Club's productions of "The Tavern" and "The Bishop Misbehaves" were also highly touted.

As with his rendition of Little Buttercup at Kennebec, Hecht excelled in comic and romantic roles. With a glint in his eye he could intone the Herbert-Blossom lines: "It's a frightful thing to think of all the hearts that I have broken, / Altho' each one fell in love with me without the slightest token, / That my fatal gift of beauty had inflamed her little heart, / But I found that some small favor always seemed to ease the smart." The laughter and applause he received were dizzying and addictive.

In the spring of 1940, the last term of his senior year, Hecht's fellows voted him best actor. Earlier in the school year, he'd donned the embroidered frock coat and hose of a saber-wielding seventeenth-century French nobleman in Rostand's comedy of manners *The Romancers*. His crowning achievement in Dramatic Club (while also serving as president of the music club) came that May, as the eponymous suitor in Oscar Wilde's *The Importance of Being Earnest*.[49] All of the women were played by men, and Julian Beck carried off the show-stealing drag portrayal of Lady Bracknell. (Beck later famously co-founded the experimental Living Theater, with his wife the director and actress Judith Malina.)

The production meant a good deal to Hecht. Acting became his identity. On his senior yearbook page, the aspiring thespian appears as himself and in character (possibly as the dandified John Worthing, in natty attire with a monocle affixed in the nook of his left eye). He brought this "foppish" élan to his portrayal of Wilde's sandwich-savoring aristocrat. As the chronicler of the Dramatic Club noted: Hecht "handled both the love scenes and the glib, sarcastic lines of the author with a sure touch." Hecht developed instinctively as an actor, feeling his way by natural ability, he later explained: "Whatever drawing or acting I had done [in high school] was entirely extracurricular and with that kind of supervision which taught me no more [than] I had already sensed intuitively." In acting, as in the other arts, particularly piano, Hecht proved to be an autodidact.[50]

With his dewy eyes and pendulous forelock, Hecht was a type of the young romantic lead. He had always felt things deeply. One boy, Armand Schwab, a year younger than Hecht, remembered a grand passion that the two of them shared in the spring of 1940:

We were both infatuated with one Pat Mayer. She was not terribly pretty, but she was terribly intellectual and interesting to be with. . . .

The height or depth of that situation came one evening—one of those scenes that remain almost tacitly in the memory—when he and I sat on a bench under an arbor (wood, with stringy bark hanging off the wood) at the 72nd Street entrance to Central Park. . . . we had actually walked there from our homes across the Park to perform this act of homage. We even, in effect, serenaded her; we recited to each other bits of Browning's "Last Ride Together."[51]

Hecht remembered that time as full of "giddy innocence and blameless fatuity," and yet he was "anything but cheerful," for reasons he himself "utterly failed to understand" at the time.[52] Even more alluring than Pat Mayer was a sexually flirtatious beauty, a widely popular (and now nameless) girl who seemed to Hecht "a would-be Salome or Delilah."[53] The two girls provided a great distraction from schoolwork, which Hecht found it difficult to engage with—all except for Geometry, which he loved and excelled at, receiving honors from the kindly math teacher, a hoary-headed man named Callahan.

"What does it all mean, poet?" the Browning poem asks. Hecht had no answers as of yet. He showed no ambitions for serious verse writing—least of all love poetry—though he did develop an exceptional prosodic facility and a fine ear. Four times a year, the boys' best writing was chosen to appear in *The Quarterly,* and Hecht was among a select few who routinely appeared there. Another star of *The Quarterly* was his friend Jack Kerouac, of Lowell, Massachusetts, who had arrived in the sixth form as a post-graduate recruit for the football team. (Kerouac played baseball, too, as "an outfielder on the Varsity nine.") His senior page in the *Mannikin* captures him mid-play in full uniform and pads, with the number two blazoned across his striped jersey. He was equally admired for his writing: "Brain and brawn found a happy combination in Jack. . . . A brilliant back in football, he also won his spurs as a Record reporter and a leading Quarterly contributor."[54]

Baruth advised on the school's publications and likely assisted in the selection of Kerouac's and Hecht's work for the magazine. Hecht liked Jack for his easygoing kindness. Both were conspicuously talented though not very studious. According to one of his biographers, Ellis Amburn, when Kerouac did attend classes, "he found himself surrounded by rich boys who were eager to share their turkey sandwiches, napoleons, and chocolate milk with him."[55] Like Hecht, he felt estranged from the children of the very rich who arrived at school each morning in chauffeur-driven limousines (or Al Baruth's car). But Kerouac thrived at Horace Mann, very much enjoying his role as a star athlete. He performed legendary feats on the football field and contributed two stories to *The Quarterly*— "Brothers," a plain-spoken detective story, and "Une Veille de Noel," about the hard-drinking denizens of a Greenwich Village bar. He also wrote a jazz column and interviewed Glenn Miller for the *Horace Mann Record*. Meanwhile, Hecht contributed pieces on classical music, based on concerts he attended and his growing record collection.

Hecht's longest swatch of verse in *The Quarterly* was a parody of Oliver Wendell Holmes's "The Deacon's Masterpiece, or The Wonderful 'One-Hoss Shay': A Logical Story." The poem appeared in his fourth-form English textbook, *The Book of American Literature*, edited by Franklyn and Edward Snyder. Hecht's answer to Holmes's bit of Victoriana was "A True and Authentique History of the Cardinal's False Teethe," in which the "logic" behind Holmes's jeu d'esprit gets applied to a set of dentures. In Holmes, the shay, a small carriage, endures for a hundred years (amazingly to the precise moment of the 100th anniversary of the Lisbon Earthquake) and then goes to pieces "All at once . . . , and nothing first,— / Just as . . . as bubbles do when they burst." Hecht's poem collapses in absurdist humor and a consideration of the cleric's dentures:

> One Tuesday after eating lunch
> When there was nothing left to munch
> He took the teeth out of their socket
> And he put them in his left hip pocket.
> Unfortunately he forgot
> He'd put his teeth in such a spot
> For, that same afternoon in town,
> He bit himself when he sat down.[56]

It ends:

> The moral, dear reader, is easily written—
> "Who strives for perfection is usually bitten."

The first strains of a more serious lyric ambition emerged in junior year, with his entry "The Sea," which begins much like Arnold's "Dover Beach." Hecht's poem begins, "We stood in humble silence there / Before the vast and glorious sea," and proceeds in tight, rhymed stanzas:

> Again we looked, and now beheld
>   A miracle, a fantasy;
> An army not to be repelled
>   By humans such as you or me.
>
> An infantry of froth or foam
>   Paraded in majestic might.
> A cavalry's white armour shone
>   Reflecting morning's radiant light.

As in Arnold's poem (which the boys read for class), the sea conjures armies, and armies were very much on everyone's mind in September 1939, the beginning of Hecht's senior year.

On September 1, *The New York Times'* three-tiered banner headline traversed the page: GERMAN ARMY ATTACKS POLAND; / CITIES BOMBED, PORT BLOCKADED; / DANZIG IS ACCEPTED INTO REICH. In downtown Manhattan, the English poet W. H. Auden, recently arrived in New York, penned one of his most famous poems, "September 1, 1939," set "in one of the dives / on Fifty-second Street." By the time Hecht became friends with Auden in Italy, years later, Auden repented the poem as sentimental, but it has never wanted for admirers. Auden captured the crushing anxiety of that moment. For Hecht and the boys at Horace Mann, news of the rising unrest in Europe was not just something they read about in the paper. Several boys new to the sixth form had experienced it firsthand and fled to the United States in the nick of time. One of them was Rudolf Ernst Henning, who had just arrived from Hamburg. Henning spoke very little English at first but worked hard to earn good grades, joining the Radio Club and becoming an "ardent German Clubber." Alfred Bloch came via Paris from "war-torn Poland," and his gift for languages gave him a boost in the French and German clubs.

A touching photo of him for his yearbook page has him smiling and pointing to Poland on a large wall map. Then there was Kerouac's "really best friend," Seymour Wyse, whose parents sent him to New York from London "to avoid the blitz." It was Wyse who turned Kerouac onto jazz: "At Kelly's Stable in Harlem, Jack lit up his first joint and listened to Roy Eldridge blow the wildest trumpet since Louis Armstrong and Dizzy Gillespie." Kerouac was decidedly cooler than Hecht. He once passed Hecht a joint at a New Year's Eve party, but Hecht demurred, saying he'd rather have more booze. In fact, he had "never taken anything at all of that sort" and, he joked, "thought of anyone who did as a 'dope fiend' out of Victorian melodrama."[57]

The two boys liked each other, but had little in common. Kerouac knew that he would be heading to Columbia in the fall to play football, but as of early spring Hecht was still unsure where he would land. The admissions officers at Swarthmore told him that they were not able to welcome him into their freshman class, because of the large number of applications from Jewish students. On his senior page, Hecht listed Oberlin as the place he hoped to attend. This, too, was not to be. Increasingly worried about his prospects, he traveled with his family north of the city to the Hudson Valley, made famous by the Hudson River School painters for its beautiful vistas. As the name Annandale-on-Hudson suggests, it was a stone's throw from the river that ran from the Adirondack mountains, through the state capital in Albany, and south into New York Harbor. Overlooking the water was a series of grand estates that housed Bard College. "At the time I went to Bard it was not a difficult place to get into," Hecht later admitted. "My father had dreams that I would follow him to Harvard, but that was out of the question, and my interview there, carried out at his initiative, was humiliating."[58] Things worked out for the best, however. Attending Bard College was one of the greatest bits of good fortune in Hecht's life.

3. Dr. Seuss Makes a House Call

Hecht was preparing to decamp to his new home at Bard in the fall of 1940. Two hours north of New York, it was easily accessed by train from Grand Central Terminal. The campus was nestled in the rural hamlet of Annandale, part of the town of Red Hook. Founded as St. Stephen's College, in association with the Episcopal Church of New York City, it originally offered young men a classical education in preparation for the seminary. During the Depression, St. Stephen's became an undergraduate school of Columbia University, furthering the classical and progressive traditions of the place and one of the first institutions of higher learning to fully credit the study of the creative and performing arts. As the school grew more secular, the name was changed in 1934 to honor John Bard, who founded the school with a land gift from his Annandale estate. In time, the campus would sprawl over some of the most beautiful countryside in the Hudson Valley, combining several estates including Bartlett, Blithewood, Ward Manor, and Sands.

"It seems that the nervous tension of the trip up to college was too much for my Victrola, which is not in working order," Hecht wrote to his parents.[59] That first week was "quite an overwhelming experience. I was extremely happy and very depressed within the same hour." He felt deeply self-conscious at first: "I thought everyone was laughing at me behind my back." He found his teachers encouraging and was greatly heartened by their enthusiasm for his abilities. Mr. Grassi, a professor of art, was so impressed by a set of drawings Hecht showed him that the new student was encouraged to begin his college career as an art major. With an open-ended curriculum and no course requirements, Bard allowed Hecht to enroll in the classes that excited him most: art, music, English, writing, and drama. In addition to his regular music class, he signed up for piano, voice, and glee club. During their initial class meeting, the professor asked Hecht to play the piano, and he regaled the small class of eight with an excerpt from the final fugue movement of Bach's Concerto for Two Keyboards and Orchestra in C Major, which impressed them all greatly.

The students, too, put Hecht at ease: "People simply flock to your room and introduce themselves and sit around and bull for hours on end. None of the conversations is particularly lofty, but it's lots of fun." Before the month was out, he bought a one-fifth share in a car, which he could use for errands. For the first time since camp, he was having fun. Being away from home freed him from a world of anxiety, and there was so much to do at school that it was easy to find excuses to stay at college rather than return

to New York on the weekends. He was still reeling from the bombshell his
father dropped at the end of the summer. Maybe Melvyn was thinking
of the last Christian school his son attended. Wanting to spare him future
awkwardness, he floated a nervous suggestion. Perhaps Hecht should take
the opportunity, before he was known at school, to change his name to
something less Jewish sounding, to avoid discrimination. Hecht was "ap-
palled."[60] This was typical of his father's sentimental cowardice. He had
seen his son's upset over his treatment at Collegiate, and, perhaps, he had
experienced this sort of prejudice himself in the business world.

In any case, Hecht had already begun to invest in his name as a
writer, publishing articles and poems, though it would be a few years
before "Tony" was replaced by the more formal "Anthony" on the page.
Melvyn's fears were not unfounded. Bard, for all its free-spiritedness, was
a product of its age. Richard F. Koch, who was a senior the year Hecht
arrived, recalled, "There were very, very few Jews at Bard—and we were
not welcome in the fraternities, of which there were three."[61] Despite
this, Koch fell in love with the place, and Hecht did as well. On a campus
with fewer than 150 students in those years, everybody knew everybody.
Such exclusivity wasn't cheap: tuition, room, and board were among the
costliest in the country.

Often characterized as "an experimental adjunct of Columbia University," it was far enough away from home for Hecht to escape his parents'
gravity. At first, he managed a balance between family life, schoolwork, and
his artistic pursuits. As Mr. Grassi wrote at the end of Hecht's first term in
the fall of 1940, "The boy is not a genius, for which we can be thankful,"
pronouncing him "a well-rounded college man with a sufficient devilry to
keep him human." Hecht excelled on stage: "His work in the theater, particularly in his very realistic characterization of the late Neville Chamberlain,
has established his reputation as an actor without in the least disturbing
his sense of balance and perspective."[62] In his second semester, after a stint
as soundman and walk-on in *Thunder Rock,* he played the lead in Edna St.
Vincent Millay's "Aria da Capo." His advisor, Dr. Gray, acknowledged that
Hecht's talents were considerable; his teachers, he said, "recognize potential abilities and assume that sufficient education is taking place. I believe
it is taking place, though it *need* not be so imperceptibly documented. . . .
It must be added," Dr. Gray hastened to extenuate, "that he has played

large roles in two plays during the term. . . . He profits a great deal from his acting."[63] (Hecht's acting partner in "several plays at Bard"[64] was a girl named Lois Montgomery, who went on to pursue a career in Hollywood.)

He filled his schedule of classes with the courses he liked, in the hopes of making a strong first impression: Theory and Practice of Play Production, Acting, and Stage Direction, as well as summer classes in Acting and the Development of French Drama. His advisor Paul Morrison, a theater veteran who directed Hecht in his classmate Al Sapinsley's play *Not in Our Stars,* thought Hecht was the real deal. In his recap of the show in the *Bardian,* he singled Hecht out for particular praise:

> First honors go to Tony Hecht. His performance throughout was sincere, valid and theatrically effective; the transition from the miserable youth of the first scene reaping the just fruits of a nasty manner, to the episodes of his childhood, were affected gracefully and without self-consciousness; a creditable feat which we appreciate all the more when we imagine what a less sensitive actor might have done, especially with some of the later scenes necessitating a jump from the age of ten to twenty within a few seconds. Tony has authority, interest and imagination. We recall particularly the underlying poignancy of the first scene and are grateful. Actual communication between an actor and his audience is a rare thing. Tony can do it.

Then suddenly Hecht changed direction, dropping theater as a course of study, and choosing instead to concentrate on literature—poetry in particular. Morrison applauded the move, commending again Hecht's dramatic flair (he was a particularly fine mimic), but acknowledging his new choice as the more viable course.

From here on out, he would be a poet. He flatly rejected his parents' wishes for him to go into business, and even his interests in music and drama would take a back seat. He knew what he wanted to do with his life and how this change had come about: "It was Larry Leighton who aroused my delight in poetry." Leighton was "a strange man, gentle but in some ways forbidding. For one thing he was a complete alcoholic, more addicted than anyone I've ever known."[65] Hecht was one of five or six students in a class held in Leighton's rooms. The class met in the morning, and it was often the case that, when they arrived, Leighton was still in bed asleep. It was the students' job to rouse him. Even after he was conscious, he could only regain his capacity for speech after drinking off a quantity of gin, which one of the students had dutifully set out for him in his toothbrush glass. Only then would he rise, clad in nothing but a bathrobe, and haltingly begin the lesson. That Leighton, "a quite unembarrassed homosexual," seemed to enjoy the company of the all-male undergraduates was not lost on them. He would summon his students with Gaveston's lines from *Edward II*: "I must have wanton poets, pleasant wits . . ."[66] He would poets tease the boys by winkingly pointing out any homoerotic undertones in the poems under consideration. He had read all of the modern poets as well, and introduced his students to them:

> Leighton was often talking to us about poets so new, and so little mauled over by critical comment, that his reactions were almost as fresh as our own. In 1940 or '41 I bought Eliot's *Collected Poems: 1909–1935*, the copy I still own. I bought Dylan Thomas's *Twenty-Five Poems*, large quantities of Auden, the second edition of Hopkins, Stevens's *Harmonium*, and much else. About all these poets he was lively, conjectural, imaginative, and open to dissenting opinion.[67]

At one point in the semester, Leighton founded the all-male Blithe Spirit Society "to which one was bidden because 'bird thou never wert.' It was an invitation issued to students he found attractive to come to his rooms and drink as heavily as they wished in the evenings."[68] Made uneasy by this dynamic, Hecht steered clear of these after-hours gatherings.

Through Leighton's mentorship, Hecht awoke "to the life of the mind," immersing himself in the work of poets who would have a lasting influence, often acquiring their work as it appeared.[69] He also read the literary criticism of Eliot, I. A. Richards, William Empson (whom he later met at Kenyon College), Edmund Wilson, R. P. Blackmur, and Yvor Winters. He bought copies of Cyril Connolly's *Horizon* (one shilling) and *Partisan Review* (twenty-five cents), talismans of his new trade, which he kept for the rest of his life, inscribed "Tony Hecht."

In fulfillment of Bard's winter term, Hecht worked as a cub reporter at *The New Yorker.* Years after the war, *The New Yorker* would play an important role in his career as a poet—its renowned poetry critic Louise Bogan would write admiringly about his first book of poems, and its longtime poetry editor Howard Moss would include him in the magazine's regular stable of poets. Though Hecht never landed an article in the magazine as a wide-eyed student intern, he worked hard at his reporting and caught the notice of the editor William Shawn, who wrote favorably of his work to the faculty at Bard.

Back in Annandale, Hecht began writing for the *Bardian.* The issue for April 1941 announced Hecht as a clever satirist, with a lengthy, illustrated romp entitled "A Pox on Your Vobiscum, or Three Sheets to the Wind." In it, a man creates a ghost to haunt the ghost that is haunting him:

> *With litmus papers, beakers, and some lead,*
> *He manufactured spirits from the dead.*
> *He held within an arsenic solution*
> *The shadow of his clever retribution.*

That spring, he was also working on a volume of light verse called *Pigs Have Wings,* which included a poem about the king of Tibet and his pet yak, John. By December of his sophomore year, his tone and intention changed, newly reflecting the modernist and post-symbolist poetry he had been reading. "Poem" reads as a youthful homage to Eliot and Yeats:

> *This is the song*
> *Of a bright passion,*
> *Metal truth in a white sun.*
>
> *Loud from the wind's rocky throat,*
> *Wild and pure,*
> *It spins to the chasm depth,*
> *and hurls hard to the cliff . . .*

By May, he had arrived at an idiom much closer to the music of his mature poetry. Writing of the transformative effects of musical performance in "The Concert," he concludes:

groping for a new environment, [it]
Extends itself within our consciousness
Beyond the single place or single man,
To an unmargined realm—
Into, perhaps, an infinite orchard or vineyard,
Where it may roll down the crossed vistas in a vast plaid of power,
Or cause the grape to burst its skin of its own accord.

When Hecht returned to New York on winter break, he could barely contain his enthusiasm. He gushed to his parents about his plans to become a poet. The senior Hechts were decidedly taken aback:

> I don't seem to recall that my parents took much interest in what happened to me at college, with one exception. They were understandably too preoccupied with more urgent matters—my poor brother's illness, domestic hostility, financial travails. The exception occurred when, having fallen head over heels with poetry for the first time in my life, I came home for some holiday, and cheerfully, naively announced to my parents that I planned to become a poet.[70]

This news was met with distress by Hecht's parents:

> Not only did they wish that I go into business, but they specifically rejected and reprehended the calling of a poet. Their whole concern was for my material success, not because they wanted me to get rich, but simply to be able to survive—which poetry was not likely to achieve for me.[71]

Dorothea acted quickly and decisively. She scanned the list of their friends for someone to advise Hecht on his poetry. She enlisted the help of Dr. Seuss, the pen name of Theodor Seuss Geisel, who had known the boy since early childhood. Geisel was a political cartoonist at this time, contributing to *PM*, the liberal paper that began publication in June 1940. He was also known for drawing the popular ads for Flit bug repellent, which featured his characteristic array of fanciful creatures. *PM* featured contributions by prominent writers and artists of the day, such as I. F. Stone, Ernest Hemingway, Dorothy Parker, Jack Coggins, and

James Thurber. Geisel contributed hundreds of cartoons for the paper's editorial page over its eight-year run. He was also a celebrated versifier. His first children's book, *And to Think That I Saw It on Mulberry Street,* appeared a couple years before, in 1938, with its charming and memorable doggerel: "All the long way to school / And all the way back, / I've looked and I've looked / And I've kept careful track, / But all that I've noticed, / Except my own feet, / Was a horse and a wagon / On Mulberry Street."

Dorothea, with Melvyn's passive assent, invited Ted and his wife to dinner. At some point in the evening, Ted was meant to lead their son back from the brink of self-destruction. Hecht remembered:

> I had no reason to suspect that he was there for any sinister purpose until, at the end of dinner, we rose to leave the dining room and Ted put his arm around my shoulder and said, "Tony, what do you want to be when you grow up?" And I knew right away that something was up. So I said, I'm going to be a poet. And he said, "Fine, and I have some advice for you. I think the first thing you should do is to read the life of Joseph Pulitzer." Well, I didn't know anything about Pulitzer except that he was a news-paper publisher. But I knew instantly that Ted was trying to discourage me from becoming a poet, so I assumed there must be something in Pulitzer's life that was as threatening as it could possibly be. Whereupon I resolved never to read the life of Joseph Pulitzer. . . .[72]

To this simple act of omission, Hecht later joked, he owed his career as a poet. Despite the evidence of Geisel's collusion, Hecht's affection for him was untarnished by the awkward exchange. The two would remain friends and see quite a bit of each other when they were stationed separately on the West Coast during their Army service. Undeterred by the encounter, Hecht composed poems that became a regular feature of the *Bardian* literary journal.

After only one year at college, he had come into his own as a writer and performer. (He also composed a musical piece about Bard and was pleased with several portraits he had drawn of fellow students.) In the meantime, a need had arisen at Camp Kennebec, and Hecht was particularly well suited to meet it. Rex Beach, a twenty-year veteran Uncle in charge of the camp's theatrical productions, was slowing down: the after-dinner dramatic events had become too exhausting, and more and more he retreated at twilight to the calm and comfort of his house across the lake. He assumed a largely supervisory role, conferring on younger strengths the duties of rehearsal and production. The baton was passed to Roland Ball, known to the boys as "Buck." He and Hecht got on wonderfully. Buck roused audiences with his virtuosity at the piano, a talent Hecht shared. He relied on Hecht for help with everything from writing songs and sketches to filling the largest roles. In the summer of 1940, Hecht worked side by side with Buck, as a writer, composer, and performer. The yearbook lauded him as "'Star' Hecht."

When Ball was called up for military service, he arranged to have Hecht return, not as a camper—he was now too old for that—but as a counselor, a junior Uncle. Confident of Hecht's talents and his rapport with the boys (for whom he was now something of a legend), Buck put him in charge of directing. "With its old director in the rigors of national defense and its advisor officially out of camp, the reins of the stage fell to Freshman Uncle Tony Hecht, who one year out of the First Section, turned in an amazing performance. His directing ability, pointless jokes, and under-cover songwriting made him famous throughout the camp."[73] A photo from the summer of 1941 shows Hecht looking like a young lumberjack. Plaids and flannels were de rigueur for the Maine woods, where nights and even days could be chilly. Hecht tucked his dark broad-checked shirt into rolled up dungarees and sported a pair of well-worn moccasins. Sitting beside him on the ground was another freshman counselor, Paul Herb, who served as "manager of the stage crew, make-up man, and jack-of-all-trades."

The main stage itself was open to the stars. Hecht's first effort was Chekhov's *The Marriage Proposal,* with three experienced hands in the cast including Hecht himself, who played a "neurotic and very excitable young Russian." As in Shakespeare's theater, the women's roles were taken by boys, with Bob Smith playing the bride-to-be. Hecht then directed a mystery called *Banquo's Chair* and a drama titled *The Rising of the Moon* by Lady Gregory, co-founder with W. B. Yeats of the Irish National Theatre. These highly literary choices went over well with the campers, or at least no objections were raised. Hecht directed eight shows altogether, including George S. Kaufman's comedy *The Still Alarm* and the season finale, a musical (perhaps based on *Measure for Measure*?) performed by the First Section called *The Duke Is on the Job*, for which Hecht also wrote the book and songs.

With such a packed schedule Hecht would have needed a break from his summer break, but the school year started right away with no time for him to catch his breath. Then, out of nowhere, he had the wind completely knocked out of him. "In my second year of college, I was suddenly sent home because my brother's shrink believed that my father, who had disappeared (a matter of which I knew nothing) was planning to kidnap me . . ."[74] Hecht's father went missing in the fall of 1942—only temporarily, as it turned out—but, for a time, no one knew where he had gone. This intrigue proved extremely unsettling for Hecht. The gangly, soulful-eyed sophomore was sent home from college, for his own protection, lest his father show up unannounced and with ominous intent. The reasons for his father's behavior were never made clear; it's likely they were again financial and that this was the second of Melvyn's three attempts to end his own life. Hecht knew all about his father's emotional instability, including the earlier suicide attempt. He had lived for over a decade under its pall. High-spirited and erratic, Melvyn at times behaved like "a near hysteric" and, if triggered by some obscure anxiety, could "have done anything," Hecht feared.[75]

Overwhelmed with anxiety, Hecht lost his grip on his schoolwork, and his professors noted his lack of focus. The head of the drama department, Paul Morrison, sounded the alarm in his Adviser's Semester Summary, wondering in evenly ruled, official cursive if Hecht hadn't undergone "what might be called a mild nervous breakdown,"[76] for which the well-intentioned Morrison recommended a vigorous regimen of physical exercise. Here was a bitter inheritance: Melvyn's breakdown led to his son experiencing the same, or something close to it. It was something that Melvyn battled his whole life. The same would be true for his son.

In many ways, college up to this point had been Hecht's first prolonged experience of "something like happiness,"[77] but, with this latest upheaval, feelings of "insufficiency and inferiority" overtook him. Professor Morrison saw how insecurities repeatedly drove the young student "into corners of acute depression."[78] He "even developed physical symptoms—nervousness and lassitude." The uncertainty of his father's desperate behavior pushed him beyond his limits until, finally, he "lost control and needed help."

He managed to finish the semester, barely. Professor Morrison praised his maturity in dealing with

> the recent upheaval in his family circle. Stunned as he was at first by the complexity of the situation, he managed to think very clearly with re-spect to his position in relation to it and behaved with genuine maturity in a situation which might easily have floored another boy of his age.[79]

He had just turned nineteen. When he went back to Bard for the spring semester, it was deep winter in the Hudson Valley—cold, bleak, and bar-ren, as in his poem "A Hill." His teachers were patient and encouraging, even as his performance continued to suffer. Incompletes mounted up during these periods. Hecht suffered from lassitude and severe depres-sion, though generally he kept his head above water in those subjects and pursuits that most attracted his interest. His grades "grew better with time." By the end of his career at Bard, he won two annual awards for his writing. He continued to make "real friends" for the first time, and with effort, put his father's strife behind him. He discovered new enthusiasms, such as the Brahms piano quartet, which he first heard

> when I was roughly nineteen years old, during what was one of the happiest intervals of my young life. That happiness was to be cut short by the war, and for some time thereafter. And so it was both natural and easy for me to identify this music with a period in my life almost approaching bliss. . . . There is a shimmer to the piano part of the first movement that is like the sunlit surface of a fast-flowing stream in early morning.[80]

Just then, the war broke through the music. The United States, neu-tral up to that point, had been attacked, and it was joining the fight. Hecht remembered vividly the instant

> when, on a mild December Sunday afternoon, the broadcast of the New York Philharmonic was interrupted for the announcement that Japan had

bombed Pearl Harbor. I, as it happened, had chosen to go for a walk instead of staying in my room to listen to the symphonic concert, as most
of my college classmates had done, so it was only when I returned, feeling virtuously healthy, that I found out what had happened. Of course,
the full significance of the event would not be felt for quite some time.[81]

He was safe for the time being, but that would soon change. Having
only recently regained something of the happiness he discovered when
he began college, he "was now required to give it up, and perhaps [his]
life as well."[82]

THREE

"GHOSTS FROM THE OVENS"[1]

(1942–1946)

1. You'll Be Sorry

H echt was at ease in his own skin at Bard. His sense of belonging—to a community of students, scholars, and writers—had been almost entirely unfamiliar up to that point. College became a high point of his early life, and the memories of that time would draw him back to Bard more than once, as a professor of English, in subsequent years. And yet the speed with which Hecht's brightening outlook at Bard came and went took his breath away: "things picked up" but "not for long."[2]

In the fall of 1942, Hecht made his way north from Manhattan to Annandale for the start of his junior year. In many ways, the term began as it usually did. The campus was filled with students tanned from summer break, the lawns were lush, and the nearby countryside sprawled with an overgrowth of greenery. Things appeared placid, but the mood among the students and faculty was anxious. Foremost in everyone's mind was the war. Two years earlier, in 1940, Congress had passed the Burke-Wadsworth Act, instituting the first peacetime draft, with the US entering the war the following year, on the day after Pearl Harbor was attacked. The younger faculty on campus were now being called up; their absence was notable and disrupted certain classes. Headlines and newsreels enumerated the casualties of war, vivid images of the brutal fate that awaited the boys who shipped off to fight. Hecht's thoughts were full of direful prediction. To his great relief, students under twenty-one were exempt from the draft, and he had every reason to expect that his life at college would continue uninterrupted. Delighted with his newfound independence, he kept to Annandale as much as possible, while back in Manhattan his parents and Roger moved to a new apartment at 163 East 81st Street.

Hecht had a room there, naturally—one he shared with Roger—but he now realized the more physical and psychic distance he put between himself and his family, the better off he felt.

Hecht continued to follow the news, and in November, heavy casualties in Europe created a need for replacements. As he prepared to head home for the Thanksgiving holiday, word came from Washington that Congress had amended the Selective Training and Service Act, lowering the draft age to eighteen. Hecht would turn twenty in January, placing him squarely within the new pool of potential conscripts. Everything changed in a moment. The rare joy he had come to associate with Bard was replaced by a febrile uncertainty. Would he be called up? Would he be forced to quit Bard? Could he bring himself to fight and even kill for his country? Would he himself be killed or maimed?

The Hechts were not a military family, though Melvyn's grandfather, Joseph, had served in the Union Army during the Civil War. As unlikely as it must have seemed to Hecht, Melvyn himself had been a Navy man, serving during the First World War. Hecht rarely recalled this fact when characterizing his father (to himself or others), but an old family scrapbook contains a testament to his service: a photograph of Melvyn in his Navy uniform, smiling, fresh-faced, and young—several years before his emotional and financial troubles began and only a year or two before his marriage to Dorothea.[3] In 1917, Dorothea, too, refused to remain on the sidelines, working for the Postal Censorship Committee, and using her knowledge of German to detect possible enemy communications. (Hecht later came to suspect that she worked for the War Department as a spy.) Like so many recent Americans of German stock, Melvyn and Dorothea would have been at pains to demonstrate that they were no fans of the Kaiser and that their loyalties lay firmly with their adopted home.

After the United States entered the Second World War in 1941, Dorothea resumed her duties as a censor. Her appointment, through the War Department, as a clerk and translator for the French paid more than $2,000 per annum, by the end of the war. Through her involvement in the Military Intelligence Division, Dorothea gained some experience of how military bureaucracies worked. She knew more than her neighbors about what was going on with the war effort at home. As savvy as ever, she conferred with her son on how best to navigate his future military service, which was likely imminent. Mother and son concluded that the draft wouldn't do. It left too much to chance. Enlistment, by contrast, might improve his situation in a number of ways. If drafted, he would have no say in his assignment, likely lumping him in with the infantry, where casualties were highest. As an enlistee, he might have more input as to his preferences. He could pursue roles other than combat, such as the ones offered by the Army Specialized Training Program, or ASTP.

Less than two weeks after the lowering of the draft age, Hecht returned home to New York City. It was Thanksgiving week. Rockefeller Center, which had been adorned each year since 1931 with an enormous spruce tree for Christmas, sported three smaller trees this year, each decorated in a color of the American flag. Hecht might have stopped off to see them on Saturday the 21st, as he made his way to the recruiting office at 480 Lexington Avenue. In the shadow of the Chrysler Building in Midtown Manhattan, Hecht presented himself to enlist in the Army Reserves. With him was Melvyn, who added his signature to the paperwork. (Since Hecht was a minor, the Army required that a parent fill out a notarized statement of consent.) After Hecht completed his forms, including an initial aptitude screening called the Army General Classification Test, there came a lull. As a reservist, his active duty would not begin immediately.

Following the holiday, he returned to Bard and began the Army Enlisted Reserve Corps program, along with a suite of courses that might serve him in the ASTP. Meanwhile, the Army-Navy fitness regimen that he had been following since fall continued to improve his physical health and mood. More and more, Hecht and his parents set their sights on the ASTP. The program had been developed by the army to steer students with college credits or special skills toward further training in areas useful to the war effort—engineering, say, or in Hecht's case, translation. Ultimately, the ASTP promised to confer a higher rank commensurate with candidates' backgrounds and education, which Hecht believed might keep him safe from the worst of the fighting. His parents, constantly concerned with Roger's health, now extended their protective instincts to their elder son, looking out for him however they could.

Hecht's trajectory toward the ASTP succeeded, at least at first. His courses in calculus, physics, and trigonometry went well, and he was surprised at how much he excelled in math. (At one point, due to the thinning of the faculty at Bard, he even taught math to undergrads, his first experience of teaching.) In the ASTP, he could look forward to "specialized, i.e., *non-infantry, duty*," but it would be months before the qualifying exam was offered. With a plan in place, he anxiously awaited the next steps. In the meantime, his projected path did not excuse him from the mind-numbing routines of army training. Before the ASTP might return him to the classroom for six months, "infantry basic was required first."[4]

On June 12, 1943, with his junior year at Bard behind him, Hecht reported to Fort Dix in New Jersey for "sorting."[5] As the term suggests, it was a mindless and mechanical process: "The most unpleasant thing I've encountered so far is standing endlessly at 'Formations'—three or four each day—and not being able to take a crap whenever I want to; especially since there's no time for it till about 4:30 PM."[6] Days were filled with seemingly pointless activity. No sooner had he arrived at Fort Dix than the company sergeant sent everyone out under cover of night on a "commando raid" that "involved stealing cement from a nearby civilian construction company to use for sidewalks at the base."[7] Hecht wrote sardonically about this to his parents, whom he kept abreast of his movements, as much as was allowed. In fact, he wrote often, and their correspondence would remain frequent throughout the war. The sheer number of letters bespeaks a fundamental connection and affection, despite the rocky dynamic he had navigated during his years at home.

After Fort Dix, he was sent in July to Fort McClellan, Alabama, for basic training. The goal was to transform "the wide variety of individuals who entered the service into teams of fighters who could work seamlessly with one another to achieve their objectives."[8] The process of converting hordes of teenagers into well-oiled teams meant overlooking the needs of the one for the needs of the many. Decisions about when to eat, sleep, and even move one's bowels, were no longer in Hecht's control. Using the latrine out in the open, where everyone could see, was one of the things he resented most.

He was warned by soldiers who had preceded him there by only a few days, "You'll be sorry." They jeered this at all new arrivals, but, in fact, he was already sorry. Nothing about this training appealed to him, though he was later proud of his improved physical condition. (For years after the war he remained whippet-slim, with lean musculature.) His mind was filled with horrible scenes from the newsreels in the local cinemas. He recalled one film about building the Burma Road, through seven hundred miles of mountains and jungle: "the road builders were frail Burmese women, some of them with their babies slung over their backs, as they sat cross-legged, fitting small pieces of stone. . . ."[9] The newsreels suggested a long global conflict. Hecht admitted that he began to rue his situation "even before receiving his uniform."[10] He encountered all the storied discomforts and humiliations of basic: KP duty and scrubbing latrines, "mind-numbing calisthenics, thirty-mile marches, close-order drills"; one learned to "crawl, with lowered head and on your belly toward an active machine-gun firing live ammunition."[11] He remembered receiving a glimmer of hope before he enlisted from a *Reader's Digest* article, which suggested that men with flat feet were being rejected. Any such loophole would have been welcome. He was briefly exultant, until the story turned out to be false. Now he was stuck in Alabama with no hope of reprieve.

Basic training, or "boot camp," was designed to break young soldiers down, curbing their wills. Hecht turned in his civilian clothes, had his head shaved, and received an identifying serial number. He was never alone: All new trainees ate, slept, and performed endless hours of physical fitness training together; they "practiced the same basic skills over and over—marching, loading, unloading, and cleaning their weapons."[12] Drill instructors browbeat the men until they snapped to at the least command. Even slight lapses could result in grueling physical punishments— "sometimes for the entire group."[13] Non-Coms—non-commissioned officers—excelled at instilling fear, and the only defense against retribution was to always obey orders without question. Hecht wrote to his parents on Army stationery, at the height of the Alabama summer, on July 26, 1943, addressing them playfully (as he often did) with "Dear Kids":

> First of all it's hot as hell. . . . The indoctrination process is very thorough. We received our rifles the second day we arrived, and also our bayonets . . . and there are an infinite number of little things that conspire to make us forget we were ever civilians. The most important one is when you wake up in the morning it's too early to think, during the day you're too busy to think, and at night you're too tired to think.[14]

Woken up for rifle drills at 3:30 A.M., Hecht and the other bleary-eyed soldiers would leave the company area for the range, where they remained until 5:30 or 6. In the first light of dawn, he learned how to "operate, aim and fire the M1 rifle."[15] The marksmanship he'd practiced at Kennebec came in handy: "I'm doing well so far," he updated the Kids. "I'm in the sharpshooter class and just one point below the expert class."[16] Then came instruction in hand-to-hand combat, called "dirty fighting," which culminated in a final free-for-all.

Sheer exhaustion, brought on by incessant drilling and round-the-clock hazing, crushed Hecht's spirit. The spark that had taken so long to kindle in him—a passion for literature and music and learning—dimmed and went out. He kept a few books with him, mostly unread. His old boss at *The New Yorker,* William Shawn, invited Hecht to keep in touch while in the army. Shawn encouraged him "to write as much as possible and send it in to them." Hecht was prepared to make "a determined effort," but "the training program . . . interfere[d]."[17] The only writing he managed were his frequent letters home.

Staying positive challenged Hecht's resources, as the dark clouds that marked his early teenage years gathered again, leaving him stunned and listless: "The only way I was able to keep up my spirits during basic was the hope, based on ASTP, that once basic was over (thirteen weeks of the summer in Alabama) I would be sent to some college or university for training in 'intelligence' work."[18] In August, he received his score for the ASTP screening test. He passed, a great relief. He hoped they might place him back at Bard, where an arm of the program was in session, but he was shipped off instead to Carleton College in Northfield, Minnesota, for language training in German. He described the change in humorous, theatrical terms, moving "from the red clay and sun of Alabama to a colorful campus in Minnesota. Beautiful setting. Cast of about 900 and dialogue will be in German." The lack of privacy and free time persisted at Carleton, where instruction and physical training ran from early morning to late at night. Hecht took classes in economics and sociology. He became proficient in German, the study of which came easily to him, his mediocre grades at Carleton notwithstanding. He hadn't spoken it as a child, but he'd heard it in his grandparents' apartment. Dorothea knew enough German, as well as French, to facilitate her translation work for the Office of Censorship. On the strength of these courses, Bard awarded Hecht his B.A. in the spring of 1944. He also garnered in absentia the college's John Mills Gilbert Poetry Prize two years running and received a copy of T. S. Eliot's *Four Quartets* as a token, along with an invitation from President Gray for Hecht to visit campus on his first furlough.

Back in the welcome surroundings of a college classroom, he studied German language and history, political science, and European geography. To capitalize on this slight return to normalcy, he brought, as mementoes of his student days, books by his favorite poets:

> I did this for reasons that are probably extra-literary; that is, I was very happy in college, I really was, I studied hard and learned a great deal and enjoyed myself enormously. It was like carrying a token of a life that I very much prized with me into a life that I knew I was going to hate, as I did hate the entire time I spent in the army. I know of someone else who arrived at basic training camp carrying his violin, for the same reason, not because he played, because it was a talisman of some sort representing a life to which he was dedicated. I wasn't that dedicated to literature, but I was dedicated to my undergraduate days when I was happy and constantly learning and constantly excited. I brought with me the things that represented that to me.[19]

Tucked in his bag, with his shaving kit and gear and the few odds and ends that he was instructed to bring with him to Fort McClellan, was:

> a little set of paperbacks: Shakespeare plays and an anthology of English and American poetry. . . . [T]hey symbolized sanity and joy; they were the lovely inventions of admirable minds, and they were moreover meant to remind me of the happy place where I first encountered them.[20]

The books' power to preserve something of the recent past may have had an initial effect, but it couldn't withstand the depredations of military life:

> They were *not* meant to serve as pseudo-Victorian "consolations" for anticipated hours of distress. The distress was certainly expected, but

literature, in my experience, does not console, and isn't meant to; and I seemed to have believed that even then. Those texts were instead goals of a sort; realms of coherence and happiness. At the critical moment it turned out that they failed me completely.[21]

The beauty and order found in the plays and poems drained away, until the words became utterly inert on the page. During his three years of service, his time was never his own, and when he did manage to steal a free moment, the last thing he felt like doing was rereading Shakespeare:

> Anyone who's been through infantry basic in wartime will understand that there is little in the way of leisure or energy for the reading of literature. . . . About the third week, when I found myself unexpectedly gifted with an off-duty afternoon, [I] dug my books out of my footlocker and started to read some texts I all but knew by heart; they had that day all the vitality and impact of a random page of the Oswego telephone directory.[22]

Hecht became despondent, disoriented, but, of course, there was no one to complain to. In his letters home, full of Shakespearean quotations from memory, he betrayed no sign of the hopelessness of his situation, though he did admit to bouts of depression returning in waves. His books became a marker of how much he had lost:

> I read and reread, with mounting terror, those lyrics and speeches that had enthralled me only a month before—and it was as if I had been lobotomized. My mind was gone, or completely numbed. I tried twice during the following weeks, with the same heartbreaking results. I put the books away, and never looked at them again during the entire time I spent in the army.[23]

As he explained to Lawrence Rhu in *The Harvard Advocate,* he could still recall how in those months of stateside training "the English language, let alone poetry, meant nothing to me anymore, and I was afraid I'd never recover it."[24]

Then he was blindsided. It was announced that the ASTP was being

discontinued. Hecht felt as if a promise had been broken. This betrayal—
he saw it as one—landed him in the exact position he was hoping to
avoid. The Army scattered the members of the ASTP (which initially
numbered as many as 150,000 men) into other outfits, just as Hecht was
completing his requirements:

> In the twenty-fourth week the entire nationwide program was cancelled
> by an act of Congress. The ostensible reason was that the program was
> "undemocratic," favoring either those who had college educations where
> they learned foreign languages, or the children of immigrants who learned
> it at home. The real reason (which, of course, could not be uttered in pub-
> lic) was that military debacles made the need for more "cannon fodder"
> imperative. They needed more infantry men, and "intelligence" was a su-
> perfluous luxury at that point.[25]

The cadets from the ASTP were farmed out to the divisions as infantry
replacements. They went from believing they would be kept from the
fighting to being thrown into some of the worst of it. According to the
military historian Roger Spiller: "Of the millions of Americans sent
overseas by the Army during World War II, only 14 percent were infantrymen. Those 14 percent took more than 70 percent of all the battle
casualties among overseas troops."[26]

Life at Carleton College had been bad enough. Everything there followed a set routine, down to making the bed and hanging up clothing. Any
lapses were totted up through the "Gig System." Four gigs, or infractions,
meant a loss of one's good conduct pass. Eight gigs, and the cadet was
confined to his barracks for the weekend. A dirty ashtray could receive one
gig. But as uncomfortable as Carleton was, life at Fort Leonard Wood in
Missouri, where he was sent in April 1944, was infinitely worse:

> Being sent back to the infantry was crushing to the morale, and seemed
> to increase, if possible, the emotional and mental torpor (a protective
> reaction, of course) that had made it impossible for me to read. I stayed
> in that numbed state until long after I was discharged, having seen over
> half my company killed or wounded in action.[27]

He again attempted to read in his copy of Shakespeare: "I have been reading 'King Lear' a fine play by William Shakespeare—I'm sure you've heard of him. He used to write sonnets for high-school anthologies," he joked with his parents, who were now extremely worried for him.[28] The attempt to find pleasure in poetry failed again, and eventually he returned most of his books to his parents for safekeeping. It would be a long time before he would take any joy in them:

> I fear that I shall once again fall into that mental slump, which is so necessary to being a good soldier. After one week here, my thoughts have already become less coherent. This is liable to be the most depressing feature of army life for me. Even on your own free time you cannot manage to think the thoughts you want to, and escape from the army for a while. Everywhere you look you see barracks, jeeps, rifles, soldier insignias and everything that pertains to the army. You can't get away from it. It's like a horrible obsession.[29]

His depression returned. It was a familiar feeling—he'd "had it all along through high school" and even into college. He assured himself and his parents that it would pass, though to be mired in it again even temporarily was excruciating.

In Missouri, Hecht joined the 97th Division, commonly known as the Trident Division, whose symbol, worn as a patch by its members, was a white trident on a blue ground. There he waded into the sea of replacements. One former ASTP trainee put it this way: "As soon as we arrived, we were sucked into the innards of the division, whose officers and non-commissioned officers could hardly believe their eyes when they saw us. New Meat, in their hungry words, fresh beef, and young (virginal, too, in most cases), a windfall of malleable human flesh when it was really needed."[30] This GI, Private First Class Robert Kotowitz, could have been Hecht's doppelganger: of Jewish descent, "highly intelligent with a valuable gift for subtle irony, an unlikely infantry man—so civilized as to be close to an anomaly."[31] Perhaps it was their intelligence and education that made the transfers from the ASTP widely mistrusted and disliked by the officers in the division. The critic Paul Fussell describes it this way: seventy-one thousand troops "had their program cancelled and from nirvana were plunged into hell: they became infantry replacements and were sent to the hardest-hit divisions. . . . In their infantry companies they were buddyless and shunned as almost dangerous strangers. These embittered replacements were a most pitiable group, lonely, despised, and untrained, deeply shocked by the unexpected brutalities of the frontline and often virtually useless."[32] Hecht felt that Fussell's account came extremely close to his own experience.

Hecht spent the summer months on maneuvers, with two weeks out of doors followed by a fortnight back at camp. Conditions, as Geoffrey Lindsay writes, were miserable: "The physical demands of infantry training were much more challenging than those of basic training and included running obstacle courses, twenty-five-mile forced marches up and down the Ozark Mountains, and hand-to-hand combat. Then there were copperhead snakes, lizards, wild hogs, and rats that trainees would encounter on bivouac."[33]

When his parents learned of the situation with the ASTP, they tried to intervene on Hecht's behalf. Melvyn's misguided attempt fell flat, and may have even made matters worse. Hecht was mortified by his father once again:

> My father made a foolish and pitiful attempt to get me discharged while I was training in Missouri. . . . He somehow managed to inform officers of the division of his own mental breakdowns, and to imply that I was subject to the same frailties. I was called away from a bivouac to be interviewed by a military shrink. When I figured out what was going on, I realized I had only to put on an act in order to get discharged on what the army called a Section Eight, or "mental" grounds. I really felt that my life that morning was in my own hands. At the same time, I felt unwilling to fake, and, ashamed of what my father had done, I confined myself to acknowledging that I hated the army—like *Catch-22,* this was regarded as a sign of mental soundness—and refusing to address the interrogating officer as "Sir," an act of mild but, to me, meaningful insubordination.[34]

By his own admission Hecht was not an exemplary soldier, but neither was he a coward. He was not feeling so low as to capitalize on his father's ruse.

In the fall of 1944, the 97th headed west to California, with Japan likely their ultimate destination. At Camp Callan, near San Diego, Hecht received amphibious assault training, which would be needed if they deployed in the Pacific Theater. The landings exposed Hecht to prolonged wet and cold, and he wound up in the hospital, with pneumonia and a 104°F fever. He was not sick enough for furlough, as his parents had hoped; that required a condition near to death, he told them. After spending several days in an oxygen tent ("which has many advantages over the little tent I used to live in" at Callan),[35] routine testing revealed no further issues, though each minute phase of his care was documented ad nauseam by the army.[36] Hecht welcomed the escape from camp drudgery, even if it meant confinement to a hospital bed, "leading a much happier life . . . with my own private illness, than I did when I was with the company, sharing the great public woe."[37] He remained weak, but discouraged a cross-country trip by his father, since he would likely be released soon. Mentally he felt refreshed, and he took advantage of his free time to read and daydream. He remembered his grandfather Aaron's old saying, which Melvyn liked to repeat: "Wenn Man krank ist, / fàugt's im kopf an" ("When you are sick, it starts in the head"). Though Hecht does not suggest it, this could have been Melvyn's personal motto. His parents did fly to California for a whirlwind weekend visit the following month, and Hecht let them know how grateful he was for the effort and expense.

His parents reminded him that Ted Geisel worked for the Armed Forces Motion Picture Unit in Hollywood, producing instructional films under the eye of Frank Capra. The films were designed to build morale and warn the troops against everything from malaria and syphilis to booby traps. Lindsay speculates that "Hecht may have asked if Geisel could help with a transfer to the motion picture unit," but the reply came back in the negative, along with an explanation from Helen Geisel to Hecht's parents. Such transfers were out of Geisel's control, which was no great difficulty to accept. Harder to countenance was the advice Geisel sent along through his wife: Hecht should look on his service as an opportunity for important life experience and not merely long years of marking time. If he was to, in fact, become a writer, then here was his material. He had a point, though Geisel, from his comfy creative perch, was in no danger of seeing actual combat. On a furlough to Los Angeles in August, Hecht visited Geisel, who told him that he would again look into the possibility of a transfer but "not to stake any hopes on it."[38]

The remainder of the fall, into January of 1945, was spent at Camp Cooke, nearer to San Luis Obispo. Further training included "clearing minefields, attacking entrenched positions with tanks and armored vehicles, and running live ammunition simulations," which, due to accidents, occasionally proved fatal. In something of a reversal with regard to his reading, he requested more books from home—*Finnegans Wake* and a subscription to the *Partisan Review*. He worked his way through volumes of fiction (Bowen, Huxley, Sterne) and poetry (Marianne Moore and a long-poem anthology). He acquired volumes by Spinoza and Euclid. "I'm accumulating quite a library," he wrote to his parents.[39] This is an ambitious reading list for someone who no longer took pleasure in books. Perhaps he read them but not in the old way, as the burgeoning poet. Hecht wrote no poetry during his years of service, except for doggerel scribbled in letters to make his parents smile. That part of himself was gone, in danger of never returning. The dark waters of his depressions continued to gather; when at times they receded, he felt partly restored, though still disoriented.

He commiserated, in a highly literary way, with his friend from the ASTP Albert F. Millet, who was already stationed abroad. He rattled through a tongue-in-cheek litany of highbrow references for his parents' amusement, though it would scarcely have left them laughing:

> Got a letter from Al, who attended the Shakespeare Festival Stratford-on-Avon just previous to his writing. Said he "immersed himself in the sacred writing." I also wrote to him—sort of a frenzy of Joyce + Eliot and Thomas Aquinas, all tending to the opinion that existence per se, is a rather screwed up affair. Both his letters and mine are suffused with a minor form of Weltschmerz, the gist of which has been most successfully captured in the peerless lines—
>
> "Happy the foetus that miscarries, and the frozen idiot that cannot cry 'Mama.' Happy those run over in the street today, or drowned at sea, or sure of death tomorrow from incurable diseases[;] they cannot be made a party to the grand fiasco."[40]

Hecht had been reading *Lear* so intently at Camp Cooke that he committed much of it to memory and would have had the king's admonition on the tip of his tongue: "Better thou hadst not been born . . . !" His worsening mood was compounded by a month of maneuvers in February, during which he wrote no letters. The exercises were cut short, however, when Hecht's company was deployed.

Casualties in Europe, particularly at the Battle of the Bulge that winter—some seventy-five thousand souls lost in the counter-surge against the German army—meant that Hecht's division would be needed most urgently in Europe, and not in the Pacific as they had believed. On December 16, 1944, the German army launched a massive attack in Belgium's Ardennes Forest, and the large ulceration in the front line gave the campaign its name. By mid-January, the US Army had battled back. The army began mobilizing replacements. In early February, Hecht crossed the country by train, arriving at Camp Kilmer in New Jersey. On the nineteenth, he and about fourteen thousand men sailed from New York in a convoy of ships. They were conveyed by destroyers to Le Havre. They then headed north to nearby Camp Lucky Strike, with some hundred thousand men sleeping in tents.

Hecht had been to Le Havre before, as a ten-year-old. He remembered the shape of the harbor as they approached and the smell of diesel mixed with seawater. Unlike most of his fellow infantrymen, Hecht felt an attachment to Europe. He had walked the boulevards of Paris and hiked in the Austrian mountains, been to zoos and parks, seen monuments and museums. Now this magical land was submerged in war. He would travel for the first time to Germany, the land of his ancestors. He would pass through the very town in which his great-grandfather Joseph was born and lived until, as a teen, he boarded a steamer and crossed the Atlantic the other way, to America.

2. In the Ruhr Pocket

Somewhere in France": that was the date line of his long letter home in early March 1945. Arriving in the dark, Hecht watched as the city slowly revealed itself in the rising light. It was familiar and horribly strange at once. The crossing had been rough at times, but he managed to keep his sea legs and not succumb to seasickness. He joked with his parents that, "All in all, this voyage falls quite short" compared with his previous two visits to Europe. The charming seaboard accommodations of the SS *Lafayette*, which he had sailed on as a boy, had been replaced by a vessel "obviously constructed to carry miscreants from the Venetian Doge's Palace to the prison, in the event that the Bridge of Sighs broke down."[41] Once ashore, he noted in a letter on his father's birthday, March 3, that France "has altered considerably since we were last here together."[42]

After a brief stay in Le Havre, visiting bookstores (where he acquired Rimbaud's *Illuminations* and reproductions of Toulouse-Lautrec), drinking in bars, and flirting with girls in French, he began his journey with the division east, toward the war. In a long letter to his family—which included jaunty asides to Roger; Paula, his parents' cook (to whom he always sent regards); and a family friend named Kathryn Swift—he assured everyone that he'd felt in "remarkably high spirits" since he arrived. "Perhaps it is because France is practically a second home to me now."[43] He signed the letter Pascal, in a final Gallic flourish. As an expression of his enthusiasm for the Old World, Hecht liked to end his letters at this point with a playful European persona, such as W. F. Hegel, Antoine, J. S. Bach, Paul Claudel, Françoise Villon, Erasmus, etc.

In troop sleepers marked "40 hommes—8 Chevaux," Hecht and his company rattled through Belgium and Holland on their way to "somewhere in Germany." "I have arrived in the Vaterland," he reported to the Kids. On his way to the front lines in the Ruhr Pocket, Hecht was billeted in private homes, at one point "having quite a time" on a piano, despite his fingers being "very stiff from lack of practice."[44] A sense of almost eerie calm enveloped Hecht as his company made its way across the Rhineland:

> For as long as I've been in this country, I've only slept on the ground one night (so far). In every other case I've slept on the floor, sofa, or bed in a German house. The inhabitants are told (by me, of course) either to move to the cellar for the night, or to move out altogether. They generally prefer to stay in the cellar—an old habit of theirs for which our Air Force and Artillery are responsible. . . . I am naturally required to do all

translating, to secure mattresses, hot water, and whatever accessories are necessary. On the whole the Germans we have "stayed with" have done their best to impress us with the idea that they were never Nazis, they hated the party, they're glad the war's almost over, they're delighted that we've come and assorted fairy tales of this kind. Every single family— and many prisoners that we took—told us the same story.

Though Hecht may have had his suspicions, there was no way for him to know that in a month, the war in Europe would be over. It did not come in time to save him from the worst days of his life. A week of relatively cushy travel deposited him in the middle of the fighting.

From Dusseldorf, the 386th Infantry moved south, through Bonn. One of Hecht's first missions was to establish positions on the southern bank of the Sieg River, which runs at a right angle to the Rhine. On April 7, his company was ordered to cross the river, establishing positions on the northern bank. An official history of the division notes that "Most units met only light resistance crossing the river. A few companies received heavy enemy machine guns, mortar, and artillery. Some of the machine gun fire came from a castle on the northern bank." It's possible that Hecht witnessed this heavy fire from a nearby house, or perhaps it was reported to him in detail by someone who had. Months later he typed up this account, in the form of a news article. Perhaps he had in mind Siegfried Sassoon's public statement against the conduct of the Great War, published in *The Times*. Though he took great care with the details, Hecht's account was never published:

This column will be devoted to the most monstrous accusation any man can make against one of his superior officers.

Its contention is that an officer wittingly sent men out to their al-most inevitable death, on a mission that could never be accomplished, and did this for the sole purpose of appeasing and placating his superior officers.

It concerns a unit which was stationed on the bank of a river. The unit's mission was to hold its position, and to be on constant guard against enemy patrols, which were coming across the river at night. The author of this column was stationed in an isolated house on the very bank of the river, an observation post from which the opposite river bank was clearly visible. In daylight, it was possible to look out of the window of this house and see all that one could see of enemy territory—a fifteen-foot height cement wall.

The unit had not been stationed at this place very long, when orders were received from higher headquarters that patrols should be sent out into enemy territory to get information concerning the strength and position of the hostile forces. So that night a patrol was sent.

It was a small patrol of about eight or ten men, and they started out on a particularly windy, cold, and dark night admirably suited for such a patrol. The darkness was obviously in their favor. The sound of wind would nullify, to an extent, the noises they might make in crossing the river. And the cold would keep the enemy guards distracted with their own discomforts.

Nevertheless, they had not paddled half way across the river in their rubber boat, when an enemy machine gun opened up. A moment later another machine gun opened fire. The patrol was almost helpless, stranded there in the middle of the river, with nothing but rifles to fire back at the machine guns which were located behind the cement wall.

After a short period of considerable confusion, the patrol returned to the "friendly" shore; several men were severely wounded. The following night another patrol started out on the same mission. They got all the way across, but still could not get past the wall. Patrols were sent out every night from then on, some large and some small, but in every case, at least one man was hit. One night a thirty-man patrol returned with all but four men either wounded or dead. And the sum of all the information which these patrols were able to report was that the wall was cement, it was fifteen feet high, and the enemy was behind it.

Yet nothing was done about it. One officer was in a position to do something; he didn't have the authority to stop the patrols but he could have informed his superiors that the patrols were purposeless. Why he chose not to mention this cannot be said with any certainty, but the character of the man would suggest that he [wanted to impress his superiors with his ability to carry out orders to the word and without question].

That this officer is, in the opinion of the men who worked with him, morally guilty for the deaths of these American soldiers, there can be no doubt. But the burden of guilt falls on the American Army for permitting a man of this caliber to hold a position of such vast responsibility.[45]

Hecht's own sense of morality had been strained almost beyond endurance by what he was being asked to do. So much seemed pointless. Now here was a case where responsible leadership would have prevented senseless deaths, and yet no steps were taken, when he felt they could have been. His life and the lives of his platoon lay in the hands of an incompetent, he felt. It is difficult to imagine that this "column" was ever submitted for publication, but the reasons why Hecht wrote it may be found in the closing lines. He blamed the Army for subjecting him and his fellows to almost certain death. The mission was what the GIs called FUBAR ("Fucked up beyond all recognition").

Hecht's company worked to clear towns and take German prisoners as they made their way through the Ruhr Valley. As Lindsay has it, "they took their first casualties on 9 April and were pinned down for ninety minutes outside Niederalben until they could retreat. They met stiff resistance on 10 April as well, when several troops were injured."[46] An action report, or diary, of C Company, written by one of its members, notes the death on April 9 of "one of 'C' Company's best drivers, T/5 Donald Holstein," and several others were "shocked" by mortar fire. One soldier was wounded in the temple and behind the ear.[47] For Hecht, "These first casualties and deaths came to us as a rude shock; our friends and comrades, with whom we had trained, undergone real privations and endured grave dangers, were now legless, armless, or dead."[48] A fragment describing the Ruhr Pocket that never found its way into a poem has a documentary feel:

> Near a small German town
> On the day of which I sing
> The Krauts had the advantage
> Of superior position,
> Superior fire-power,
> Superior everything.
> (God knows what's the advantage
> In this abused profession.

We had crouched all night in the rain,
Our breath and socks were sour
With a glandular fear of death
Mixed with a fear of pain.)
And there we were pinned down,
Having lost twenty men,
Not counting the captain
Who was heaving behind a tree.
He gagged and sucked for breath
And watered at the eyes—
Not out of cowardice,
For on the following day
We all came down with it.[49]

Perhaps the fiercest action involving the 386th was the assault on the small town of Drabenderhöhe. "The town was located on a high hill defended by 88s, 20mm guns, 40mm dual purpose flak guns, small arms, and automatic weapons. Company C, commanded by Captain Llwellyn R. Johnson, was given the job of taking the town."[50] On April 12, artillery fire was laid down on the town of Drabenderhöhe. Company C attacked, and after a short, fierce battle, was thrown back with massive casualties. US artillery and mortar fire then effectively neutralized most of the enemy's firepower. The official account has the company's Captain Johnson leading his troops under heavy fire over 1,500 yards of terrain. He was awarded the silver star for his action in taking the town.

Hecht's perspective was decidedly different:

Our company commander was a fool, wholly incapable of any initiative, who slavishly obeyed commands, however uninformed or ill-considered, from battalion or regimental HQ, and without regard to the safety or capacity of his own troops. . . . Anyway, on this day when we were hopelessly kept flat on the ground by superior fire-power, some idiot at an upper echelon, far behind the lines and blissfully unaware of our situation regarding the enemy (though probably eager to keep all forward movements abreast of one another to protect all flanks), ordered my company to move forward, and the captain ordered us to ready ourselves, though there would have been nothing but total annihilation in prospect. At the last second, higher command called for artillery, which turned the trick. And as we slowly rose from prone positions, I confessed to my platoon commander, a second lieutenant just about my age, that if the order to advance had not been countermanded I was very unsure whether I would have obeyed.[51]

Once inside the town, Hecht was likely called on to translate what the townspeople were saying as they readily surrendered to the American troops. One historian describes the scene:

Within minutes, the first files of American infantry troops were cautiously probing the bullet-riddled streets, now bedecked with white sheets, and they began searching the homes and buildings. The Muth family remained huddled in their cellar until the Americans entered the home. A GI immediately discovered the frightened residents and drove them into the street, where they were questioned by an American soldier speaking broken but intelligible German. The interrogator seemed to be well informed about the village and its inhabitants, including the Nazi Party members and the administrative officials.[52]

"Could this unnamed German-speaking American have been PFC Hecht?" wonders Lindsay. "It is very likely: Hecht's ASTP training had included lessons on the Nazi Party structure and administration,"[53] making him a prime candidate for leading such an exchange.

In writing about the war in subsequent years, Hecht makes use of that ambiguous moment of calm and threat that comes over the battlefield at dawn. Will it dispel the fears that breed in the darkness or bring a renewed attack? Hecht's most traumatic memory of combat took place shortly after daybreak:

The mood of the company was shaken when, one morning, we found ourselves hugging the ground at the crest of a hill, in the shadow of trees, looking out across a green field that dipped shallowly in the middle before rising to a small height not far away, and behind which German troops were lobbing mortar shells at us. We fired back, and the exchange went on for a while, until at last the enemy simply stopped firing. This could, of course, have been preliminary to something else, a trick, anything. We remained exactly where we were. And then, to my astonishment, a small group of German women, perhaps five or six, leading small children by the hand, and with white flags of surrender fixed to staves and broom-handles, came up over the far crest and started walking slowly toward us, waving their white flags back and forth. . . . When they were about half way, and about to climb the slope leading to our position, two of our machine guns opened up and slaughtered the whole group.[54]

Afterward, Hecht held no further illusions about the valor of battle or the humanity and integrity of his fellow GIs. He had seen them at their worst, as craven, frightened animals. After this, Hecht could never hope to partake of the usual bonding and loyalty to one's fellows that combat fostered: "That morning left me without the least vestige of patriotism or national pride. . . . The men in my company, under ordinary circumstances, were not vicious or criminal, but I no longer felt close to any of them. Battle, which is supposed to bring soldiers together, failed to do that."[55]

3. "How often you have thought about that camp . . ."[56]

At the end of April, Hecht was "whisked out of 'front-line' Infantry Co., and sent back to Battalion, then to Regiment, and finally to Division." He wrote to his parents on April 26 to announce these "tidings of great joy." This move brought a change of living conditions: No more rainy bivouacs, hunkering down in the dark. He would have a comfortable bed in one of the grand houses that the army had commandeered. He was now on "detachment duty" to the Counter Intelligence Corps (CIC), where he would at last be called upon to put his specialized training to use. The next few weeks constituted both the very worst and, in his newfound friendship with the young writer Robie Macauley, the best of his time in Germany. The "C.I.C. has that great midnight aura of secrecy about it in which our whole family seems to dwell from time to time."[57]

Had his mother been spying for the War Department, he wondered, on clandestine trips to Europe? Intelligence work made him feel more like himself, more connected to his family and his college days, than the grunt work of a rifleman.

The two weeks that Hecht had spent fighting tormented him: "I admit that I felt neither brave nor patriotic. I was profoundly scared." He now carried with him a secret, one of the greatest of his life, one that he never told another soul, save one. When he thought of those weeks, he thought of friends mown down by enemy fire, of mutilated bodies and the breathless terror of night-watching, but he was also nagged by another emotion: guilt. If he thought about it rationally, he realized that those deaths were not his fault; that, if anything, the incompetence of his superiors had put him and his fellows recklessly in harm's way. He knew that to be true deep down. And yet he had not done his part to protect them. The truth was that not once in his engagement with the enemy had he ever shot anyone. When fired on, he did not return fire, or fired over their heads. When fellow infantrymen were hit, he made no counter.

Hecht ultimately admitted as much to his second wife, Helen D'Alessandro. He told her that he *knew* he had never killed anyone—but how, in the chaos of battle, could he be sure? she wondered. He knew it for certain, he told her, and then he told her why. He was not the only soldier to have refused to use his rifle. Some statistics put the number surprisingly high, well over 50 percent. But the fact that he was not alone in this did not relieve his excruciating sense of moral compromise, both in what he was being forced to do and what he refused to do. Ultimately, he was relieved that he never took a life.

As the 97th made ready to march into Czechoslovakia, Hecht was called away from his unit. The division had discovered a concentration camp in a sector of the Bavarian Forest, in the town of Flossenbürg. Founded in 1938 as a camp for criminals, so-called "asocial" individuals, it soon expanded to include political prisoners. During the war it became "an important forced-labor center housing 30,000–40,000 worker-prisoners in the main camp and several satellite facilities."[58] The SS oversaw the camp's operations, which included a granite quarry and a Messerschmitt factory. Later, it became a stopover for Jews being transported to extermination camps in Poland.

Removed from the front lines, Hecht felt that his life had been spared. For the moment, he could let go of the feeling that he or his fellows might be shot or blown up without warning. He had no inkling yet of what the CIC wanted him for, something to do with translating during the interrogation of prisoners. But on the night of April 26, he wasn't asking any questions. He enjoyed his new situation. He sat down in his well-appointed quarters and wrote to his parents of the good news, trumpeting his high spirits with the verse from Isaiah he used to communicate good fortune: "How beautiful upon the mountains are the feet of him who bringeth tidings of great joy."[59] He wrote to reassure them that he was out of immediate danger:

> I must admit that I am not yet permanently situated here—I am working on a basis charmingly termed "detached service." I will, nevertheless, continue to have the highest hopes, for as you know, CIC has been one of those inaccessible nirvanas which I've always hoped for, and because the dissatisfaction of not being in it was heightened by the number of friends I had who did make it . . .[60]

He tried to put behind him the trauma of the last few weeks. No matter how rattled he felt, how shaken by the senselessness of it all, he put his personal feelings aside in letters home, even managing a bit of levity:

> Last night I slept in quarters that were the very paragon of luxury. If the commanding general has any more comforts and conveniences than I had—by God, he is welcome to them; I begrudge him nothing. Though he walk on carpets of concubines, and drink of the nectar of gods, he is no more content than I. I slept on a feather bed of royal cherry wood, beneath a carved wood-paneled ceiling; there was running water and electricity, a radio, the toilet functioned properly, and all the normal facilities of a house, such as walls, floors, a roof.[61]

As welcome as these posh accommodations were, Hecht's greatest uplift came at the prospect of his new assignment. For the first time possibly in years, and certainly since he had arrived in Europe, he was being asked to think, to apply the skills that he had acquired during months of language training at Carleton College:

> You can surely appreciate the beauty of my position when you consider that for the first time since I've been in the Army, I am doing work that interests me. It is a more important phase of the war than I have ever expected to be concerned with, it is a greater responsibility than I have ever been granted in my phenomenal military career. But what intrigues me the most of all is that this is the first time the Army has offered me anything in the way of an intellectual challenge (whose glove I am delighted to pick up). You remember how I complained, even during Basic Training, of the stifling, retrogressive mental atmosphere. My sparkling mental acumen dwindled to a paltry remnant of what it was. O miserere nobis![62]

Most sympathetic among his colleagues in the CIC was Robie Macauley. Macauley and Hecht became fast friends, not only because Macauley had been working in Counter Intelligence for three years already and could show Hecht the ropes, but also because he had the reputation of a rising man of letters back in the States. He had important literary connections, and a knowing way about him. Macauley was a born writer. When he was quite young, his father had presented him with a printing press, and he soon began printing editions of his poems and stories.

Macauley was the sort of serious, committed writer that Hecht aspired to be. He had studied writing with Ford Madox Ford at Olivet College in Michigan, and he regaled Hecht with stories of visiting writers he had met, such as Sherwood Anderson and Katherine Anne Porter. He liked to describe Gertrude Stein and her companion Alice B. Toklas coming to "lecture us in the farmlands of Michigan": "Alice Toklas turned up with a leopard cub, which was a great sensation at Olivet. They'd never seen anything like that before. And we all sat around at Gertrude Stein's feet and heard her pontificate."[63] Macauley was excited when the college sponsored a conference featuring the poet Allen Tate and his wife, the novelist Caroline Gordon.

Macauley looked up to Ford as a mentor, but, after Ford left Olivet, Macauley moved on, too. He enrolled in the famous program in English at Kenyon College in Gambier, Ohio. Macauley's move to Kenyon placed him among a starry circle of poets and writers, and his tales of that place made Hecht wish that he had been there. At that time, the eminent poet and critic John Crowe Ransom was launching *The Kenyon Review*. While at Olivet, Macauley had read Ransom's poems and admired them, finding them "strange, unique, something I had never read before." Ransom was "a kind of role model, a man who divided his career between editing, writing, and criticism, and he was splendid at all three."[64] At Kenyon, Ransom became Macauley's teacher and guide.

Hecht was also looking for role models, and he found one in Macauley. His new friend was tall, lean, and dashingly literary. At Kenyon, he had shared a house with the fiction writer Peter Taylor and the poets Randall Jarrell and Robert Lowell, whose *Land of Unlikeness* had appeared the previous year with an introduction by Tate. Macauley had attended the famous Bread Loaf Writers Conference, long associated with Robert Frost, and graduated from Kenyon with distinction. The following year he joined the 97th Infantry Division in the Ruhr Pocket as a special agent in the CIC, doing the kind of work that Hecht himself hoped to embark on.

The two were alike, both in their shared enthusiasms and general demeanors. Hecht wrote to his parents that Robie had excellent taste in music (Mozart is his favorite composer) and, of course, in literature, and is fully acquainted with contemporary writing. His taste in art is similar to mine, genuine without too much cultivation. . . . He has a sharp quiet sense of humor, is very soft-spoken and well mannered, and is very easily depressed—more easily I think than I. He's tall and lanky, very thin, with amazingly stooped shoulders and it's a tribute to the strength of his personality that the army has never had any effect on his posture.[65] Hecht hoped his parents would meet him someday.

The two friends, who met during a brief hiatus, then weathered together the unspeakable extremes of Flossenbürg. When Hecht walked through the gates of the concentration camp, it was late April. There was fresh snow on the ground. The wrought-iron gate, which now stood open, had *Arbeit macht frei* carved into a stone plaque on one of the granite columns.[66] Hecht had no words for what he saw then: prisoners like "living skeletons" and, beyond them, "mountains of corpses." By the time Army physicians arrived to treat the prisoners, it was often too late to save them: many prisoners "survived their liberation only by a few hours."[67]

A few weeks before, roughly fifteen thousand prisoners had filed out of Flossenbürg on an SS "Death March." They trudged along for days with no food. Those who fell were left to die. Shootings were "continuous." One officer, a Colonel Billings, recalled, "The slaughter continued right up to the arrival of our armor; then the SS guards departed leaving the human wreckage to stagger away; the strongest, taking to the highways; the weak crawling into the woods and barns and other shelter. About 3,000 died on the march; about 3,000 were able to get out of the immediate area where [they were] turned loose; the balance of 9,000 were holed up in the general area."[68] The sheer number of the dead, the bodies and the stench, alerted the 97th to the presence of the camp, near the Czech border where they had been patrolling.

Situated among forested hills in the Oberpfalz Mountains of Bavaria, the village of Flossenbürg dated from the Middle Ages. It lay forty miles east of Nuremberg. The local industry was granite, the quarry there dating from 1875. In the 1930s "the owner of the quarry—also mayor of the village and a loyal Nazi—persuaded Heinrich Himmler to establish a major camp at the site. . . . Between 1938, when the camp was established, and April 1945, more than 96,000 prisoners passed through Flossenbürg. About 30,000 eventually died there."[69]

Hecht's division encountered a nightmare world of the dead and dying:

The Americans learned that thousands of people had died at Flossenbürg from starvation, disease, and at the hands of Nazi executioners. Some prominent individuals were murdered at this camp. For example, pastor Dietrich Bonhoeffer, a well-known Lutheran clergyman and outspoken anti-Nazi, was executed at Flossenbürg about a week before the arrival of American troops. . . . Photographs, transcripts of interviews, and other evidence of war crimes were collected and forwarded to appropriate military authorities. Allied soldiers and the people of the world were beginning to understand the magnitude of the atrocities committed during the period of the Third Reich.[70]

By April 28, the SS had gone, leaving the prisoners to their fates. One inmate, Emil Lažak, a Czech, found a typewriter in the Kommandant's offices and sat down to write the story, in German, of his time in the camp. He produced twenty single-spaced pages. On page ten he paused to type a hairline across the entire page; below the line he typed:

Jet muss ich unterbrechen, die B e f r e i e r sind da !!!!!!! es ist der 23.4.45 10.50 Uhr !!!!!!
[Now I must interrupt; the l i b e r a t o r s are here!!!!!!! It is April 23, 1945, 10:50 A.M. !!!!!!]

He tapped out another hairline, as if to simulate a deck beneath his banner headline, and continued: "I hung out the sign 'Prisoners happy end—Welcome,' which we had already prepared, and immediately gave the first instructions about the hidden weapons. A lieutenant and 4 other soldiers looked at everything and now I can keep writing." Lažak typed all morning, as the soldiers made their way through the camp, arriving at the mortuary, located in the crematorium, stacked with corpses.

One officer wrote home: "It's really the smell that makes a visit to a Death Camp a stark reality. The smell and the stink of the dead and the dying. The smell and stink of the starving. Yes, it is the smell, the stink, the odor of a Death Camp that makes it burn in the nostrils and memory. . . . I can still smell the bodies we found from the Flossenbürg death march. . . ."[71] At the liberation, "only a few thousand prisoners remained. They were dirty, unkempt, ill clothed and appeared to have been starved. Many had welts on their bodies from beatings."[72] Flossenbürg was the main camp of a network of ninety or so subcamps in the region.

As Hecht would learn, Russian prisoners of war were treated the worst. In June 1942, some two thousand Russians were held at the camp. Each day, throughout the winter, they were rousted from their barracks and marched, without their wooden shoes, to the quarry, where they worked barefoot, with scant food. The stone quarry was the site of many deaths by beating and shooting. (Marksmanship was rewarded with furloughs for the guards.) Thousands of French, Polish, Russian, Austrian, and Czech prisoners died there. By the end of 1943, or the beginning of the year following, of the two thousand Russians only eighty or ninety remained alive.[73]

Half of the sixteen hundred political prisoners in the camp were sick from typhus. Hecht put the death toll at five hundred a day, while the C Company action report put it closer to eighty, and then, after the Medical Corps intervention, around thirty. What the GIs saw was hard for them to explain:

> Bodies of once healthy men were now skeletons of bones covered with taut, yellowish colored skin. Many had died with their eyes wide open staring into space as if they were seeing over and over again all the torture the Germans had put them through—their mouths open, gasping for that last breath that might keep them alive. All of them were nude and as they died fellow prisoners carried them through the fence to the incinerator where they were stacked. The stench was unbearable![74]

It was Hecht's job to interview those, like Emil Lažak, who had survived:

> Since I had the rudiments of French and German, I was appointed to interview such French prisoners as were well enough to speak, in the hope of securing evidence against those who ran the camp. Later, when some of these were captured, I presented them with the charges leveled against them, translating their denials or defenses back into French for the sake of their accusers, in an attempt to get to the bottom of what was done and who was responsible.[75]

The 97th Division performed a number of duties: tending to the sick, burying the dead, and gathering evidence against former camp officers and guards to be used at trial. Robie Macauley later described his work: "As a young Counterintelligence Corps agent in 1945, I entered some concentration camps the day we liberated them—the most horrifying days of my life. My job was to interview survivors. Most of the bodies I saw had been stripped and it was impossible to tell which were those of Jews and which of Christians. Nazi murder was a great leveler, fully ecumenical. . . ."[76]

The testimony that Hecht and Macauley collected was later used as evidence for the prosecution of the Flossenbürg cases at the Dachau Trials. The trials, which ran from June 12, 1946, to January 22, 1947, weighed charges against German civilians, camp guards, and SS and medical personnel accused of war crimes. They were conducted by the US on the site of the Dachau Concentration Camp in a northern suburb of Munich in Bavaria. Forty-six former staff from Flossenbürg concentration camp were tried "for crimes of murder, torturing, and starving the inmates in their custody. All but five of the defendants were found guilty, fifteen of whom were condemned to death, eleven were given life sentences, and fourteen were jailed for terms of one to thirty years."[77] Unlike the indictment of the twenty-three major war criminals by the International Military Tribunal at Nuremberg, the US Army's charges against German defendants adhered to a single model based on "violation of the Laws and Usages of War." Numerous charges could be alleged against individual defendants under this heading. In the concentration camp cases, for example, defendants were accused of participating in a common plan to commit war crimes through beatings, assaults, killings, tortures, starvations, abuses, cruelties, and mistreatment of camp prisoners.[78]

The Danish-American novelist Ib Melchior worked alongside Hecht and Macauley. Like Macauley, he was a career intelligence officer. He wrote of his time in Flossenbürg with an unflinching candor; "the guards at Flossenbürg had a reputation for being exceptionally cruel, sadistic, and inventive in their atrocities."[79] The surviving prisoners told the CIC interviewers that it was there that the "X-game" originated:

This is how the game is played: The players formed two teams, and each team sent one of its members into the camp barracks to pick one inmate for use in their game. He was called "the pawn." The playing field was the size of a tennis court with a sort of cross beam gallows, looking like a miniature goalpost, erected on each end. The two "pawns" were stripped naked and hung by their wrists from the top beam of each gallows, legs spread out and anchored to the bottom of the upright posts. High in the air he hung, spread-eagled, forming a human X. The two teams would gather in the center of the field, each team with its favorite guard dog, usually a big German shepherd. Specially trained. At a signal from the SS referee, the two dogs would be turned loose. Cheered by the players, egged on with shouts and whistles, each dog would race for the opposing team's gallows posts and jump and snap at the spread-eagled "pawns" hanging above them.

The winning team? That team whose dog first ripped off the testicles of the opposing team's "pawn."[80]

The Flossenbürg game, as Melchior calls it, was so popular that it spread to other camps. A May issue of *Stars and Stripes* described how the dogs received training for the X-game and how, after the camps were liberated, the dogs lay dead beside their kennels where the liberators had shot them.

Hecht's regular correspondence to his parents trailed off during this time. What could he possibly say to them about what he had witnessed? And then on May 8, VE Day, he wrote to say that he had made it through:

> This letter is written primarily to inform you that the war is over, and I have come through it unscathed. You had probably guessed as much by this time, but I am sure that my own confirmation can clinch the matter more firmly than anything else. Unscathed, of course, does not mean unaffected. What I have seen and heard here, in conversations with Germans, French, Czechs, and Russians—plus personal observations—combines to make a story well beyond the limits of censorship regulations. You must wait till I can tell you personally of this beautiful country and its demented people.[81]

In truth, Hecht was not yet out of danger. On May 24, he composed a letter from a town "near Bamberg," his family seat. Having survived the ETO, his division was being sent to Japan, as the army originally intended. The last divisions to arrive in Europe were the first to go. As it turned out, "only one war was over"[82] for the men of the 97th. Hecht had performed well in the CIC and was praised by his commanding officer, Capt. Grimes, for his smarts and his work in "taking part in such CIC work as interrogation, screening, investigation, and arrests. He was particularly useful as a linguist as he has an excellent knowledge of French and German."[83] Before shipping out for the next posting, Hecht headed home to New York on furlough, a surreal reentry into his old life that only made his next deployment that much more painful.

After VE Day, his unit of the CIC dissolved, and he returned to C Company. In the rare instances that he spoke publicly about Flossenbürg after the war, Hecht referred to it as an annex of Buchenwald. In fact, it was a primary camp, with its own network of subcamps. In 2001, the producer and director Mel Stuart filmed *Anthony Hecht: The Poet's View* for the Academy of American Poets. Shown walking though the handsome, sunlit rooms of his house in Washington, DC, Hecht says that among the chief influences on his poems is the fact that he "was one of the first Americans to enter the German concentration camp of Buchenwald."[84] The camp he entered was both "an extermination camp and a slave labor camp,"[85] but it was not a death camp on the order of Buchenwald or Auschwitz. And yet executions by shooting and lethal injection became widespread enough at Flossenbürg that, in 1940, a crematorium was built on site to expedite the disposal of dead workers. Hecht's mistaking of Flossenbürg as a subcamp of Buchenwald is no great matter; it didn't change what he saw there.

In the last year of his life, Hecht spoke about Flossenbürg to a group gathered at the Museum of Jewish Heritage in New York. He told the story of Abraham Malnik, who witnessed the burning of the Kaunas ghetto. Malnik was captured and sent to Dachau and four other concentration camps. At the liberation, Malnik recalled, "The barracks had three floors and through a window I saw a Russian tank with its insignia. I had to slide down the stairs, stair by stair; my body was nothing but bones. I crawled on my feet and pushed the gate open and held on to the tank. I asked in Russian for a piece of bread and crawled back and gave it to my father." Hecht concluded, "That, ladies and gentlemen, is what the war was about," and he sat down in silence.[86]

4. "Now the quaint early image of Japan . . ."[87]

In late June 1945, Hecht arrived back in New York City, awaiting deployment to Japan. It was a strange in-between time. In one sense he was home, surrounded by family and familiar sights, but he would not be staying long—one short month. He made the trip north to see Roger at Bard and stopped in for a visit with President Gray, with whom he had kept in touch. He met with William Shawn at *The New Yorker,* and he corresponded with Robie Macauley about the possibility of finishing out his time in the service as a member of the CIC. He applied to the Manhattan-based newspaper *Yank: The Army Weekly.* None of these prospects panned out.

His anxiety over what was coming next caused "frequently irritable moods."[88] He dreaded going back to that "imbecilic" and "servile" life; after briefly tasting normal life again he could not "be satisfied with this animal existence,"[89] as he deemed it. But there was no avoiding it: he left for the West Coast, where he would sail for Japan. As soon as he left New York, he regretted the way he had acted toward Roger and his parents. He wrote to them to apologize for spoiling their few weeks of time together. The trip, by Pullman and troop sleepers from Fort Dix to Fort Bragg, brought back grim memories: Bragg had "the depressing aspect of looking very much like Fort McClellan, where I spent my most unhappy days in the Army." It was as if he was moving further away from, not toward, the day of his eventual release.

Hecht watched and waited for several weeks as the war progressed overseas. He boiled it down to a series of headlines for "the Kids": "The Atomic bomb, Russia's entry, the Jap proposal, our counter-proposal, the false report of acceptance, the great delay of communication." And then on August 14, as he was lounging in his barracks, a great cry went up:

[I]nstantly everyone seemed to be shouting. It was like spontaneous combustion, as though everyone had heard the news simultaneously. People rushed out of the buildings and stood around shouting, shaking each other's hands and patting one another on the back. . . . I was caught with the excitement of the great crowd around me, and I went over to one of the men in my company and shook his hand warmly. We stood grinning at one another for some time and could think of nothing to say.[90]

A band played in the street. He realized that, while he would still be heading to Japan, he would no longer be in danger of dying: "All I know is I've lived through the war. This should be enough I guess."[91] But it was not enough to lift his mood as he left for his next deployment.

The steamer to Japan took over a month. He arrived at 3 A.M. in Yokohama on September 25 in dismal spirits. Before leaving, he had had a visit from Robie, who delivered further discouraging news about Hecht's prospects in the CIC. His assignment, in the end, was to compose articles about the 97th for the army's public relations unit, which would then be farmed out to Stars and Stripes and newspaper outlets in the States. He found his work as a reporter congenial and his colleagues more companionable than the grunts in his combat unit. To the Kids he wrote in a breathless tone that must have surprised and pleased them: "The work is fascinating, the company is delightful, the conversation intelligent, witty, provocative, ribald, and thoroughly enjoyable. . . . this is almost the first time since I've been in the army that I've had access to such a fund of sensible and entertaining talk." He now worked in an actual office and composed his letters on a typewriter.

There was not much to report on, however. Occupation duty proved uneventful: "The only troublesome occurrences reported during the early months of the occupation were a few isolated attempts by individual Japanese to steal food, fuel, or clothing. These cases were dealt with immediately and firmly, and there were no undue complications. Considering the overall circumstances, the relations between the Japanese people in the six prefectures and the occupation force developed remarkably well," states one history of the 97th.[92] Hecht's office routine worked wonders for his peace of mind. He befriended the well-known Jewish pianist Leo Sirota, and even tracked down a grand piano in a nearby brothel for him to play a concert for the troops. Sirota had been a student of Busoni in Vienna, and his extensive repertoire included all of Chopin. In a letter signed "Vincent," Hecht chortled to the Kids: "One of the greatest living pianists is to give a recital on a whore-house piano."[93]

Casting about for suitable subjects to report on, he followed a lead from Robie, who helped him by feeding him intelligence from the CIC about a Nazi spy ring that had been uncovered in the town of Karuizawa. Hecht's byline eventually appeared in Stars and Stripes with a pared-down version of his report. It read like something in a John Buchan novel: "Out

of this isolated little resort town up in the hills of inland Japan has come
one of the most unusual stories of the occupation. Karuizawa is not only
a picturesque mountain spa and the home of Empress Dowager Sadako
('the mother of God'). It was, even after the defeat of both Germany and
Japan, as thoroughgoing [a] bit of Hitlerite Germany as one could find
outside the Third Reich." The town had its own SS, Hitler youth, propaganda machine, Staatz Polizei—all the trappings of the Vaterland, Hecht
reported. He was excited and proud of the byline. Not since his poems
and reviews in the *Bardian*, which seemed worlds away, had he published
anything. He tried to work into his journalism writerly touches that might
elevate it above the hackwork of a beat reporter.

With time on his hands between articles, his correspondence proliferated. He even got around to replying to Kathryn Swift, the family friend
who had written him several letters while he was in Europe, and to whom
Hecht always responded via his parents. When at last he overcame his
long silence, which may have bordered on rude from her point of view,
he teased her about her literary taste. About her stated admiration of
Amy Lowell, he joked: "What was Amy for? Now there's a question. Especially if you consider her size. . . . Gross wasn't the word. Mammoth.
Gargantuan. A bloated behemoth. She lacked every physical quality of
femininity. . . . She must have been acutely aware," he concludes, "that
she was not 'acceptable' as a woman when she started smoking cigars."[94]
Was he affecting the roguish man of letters? Did he intend to amuse
Kathryn? Quite possibly both.

By the new year, any charm and interest that Japan might have held,
with its light-infused exotic architecture, was wearing off. More than
the Germans, the Japanese were truly the Other. To the young GI, they
seemed a people made insane by war and political corruption:

> *Human endeavor clumsily betrays*
> *Humanity. Their excrement served in this;*
> *For, planting rice in water, they would raise*
> > *Schistosomiasis*
> > *Japonica, that enters through*
> > *The pores into the avenue*

> *And orbit of the blood, where it may foil*
> *The heart and kill, or settle in the brain.*
> *This fruit of their nightsoil*
> *Thrives in the skull, where it is called insane.*[95]

The disease Hecht names in his poem "Japan," a poem in complex stanzas "after the manner of John Donne or George Herbert,"[96] was native to the area around Hiroshima. Without treatment it impaired physical and cognitive development, due to the migration of schistosome eggs to the brain. Illness and insanity were hard to avoid in 1946. The war had brought the country low, and Hecht felt it had brought him low as well.

Hecht had been in the ETO for two and a half months and in the Pacific for roughly six. He arrived home on March 3 and was honorably discharged the following week. Back home a different battle began. Like his friend the poet Louis Simpson, and J. D. Salinger, who had also worked for the CIC, Hecht struggled greatly after the war. All three soldiers suffered nervous collapse. Hecht later agreed with Paul Fussell that the Atom Bomb had been necessary to bring about the end of the war. In fact, he felt that it saved his life and the lives of his fellows. He saw the Japanese defenses that had been prepared against an American invasion and believed he would not have survived the attack.

In an attempt to cheer himself, he salted his letters home with quotes from Shakespeare. To Roger, for example, he wrote: "How's the old petty pace coming along? From day to day?" He quoted *Hamlet,* the play he knew best, to enunciate his blackest moods: "I have that within me which passeth show / These but the trappings + the suits of woe."[97] Hecht understood that he was "a 'depressive' type," as he told Philip Hoy, "without even the consolation of enjoying intervals of manic highs. This is not a condition in which I pride myself, or for which I think myself entitled to pity. I have seen enough suffering in the world—in my own family, as well as during the war—to know that others have lived far worse lives than mine."[98]

After the war he measured his recovery in part by his ability to enjoy Shakespeare again:

> I emerged from the war sound, and, if not sane, at least not stark raving mad, to no one's astonishment more than my own. And the best index

I think I had of the recovery of my balance, my humanity, and my most valuable faculties, was the gradual recovery of the pleasure of reading Shakespeare. That pleasure has continued and grown richer ever since. I like to believe it has had a subtle and strengthening influence on my own poetry.[99]

Strengthening, to be sure, though not especially subtle. Hecht would become the "most Shakespearean" American poet of the twentieth century.[100]

5. "I am there. I am there."[101]

There is much about [the war]," Hecht admitted to Philip Hoy, "that I have never spoken about, and never will."[102] Geoffrey Lindsay, in his account of Hecht at war quoted above, encapsulates Hecht's painful response to trauma: "In a world neither reasonable or just, Hecht would spend a lifetime trying to find words that could never reconcile, but must attest to, the terrible schism in the fabric of our reality and to the fragility of order, stability, and beauty that is a necessary sanctuary against the underlying terrors of destruction and the void at the heart of human experience."[103] His worldview and moral fabric were in tatters when he returned to the States in March 1946. "What is ultimately shocking," he wrote years later, "is the blinkered naivety of a society that can take young men, transform them into unfeeling monsters, and then, if they survive, expect them to return to civilian life as though nothing had happened. There is a cool detachment to which frontline troops must aspire to survive, what [Paul] Fussell calls 'a severe closing-off of normal human sympathy so that you can look dry-eyed and undisturbed at the most appalling things. For the naturally compassionate, this is profoundly painful, and it changes your life.'"[104]

The terror that Hecht felt in combat recurred as night terrors at home. A few months before he died, he described this entropic feeling with great lucidity:

Fear is a curious emotion. It is very unpleasant; it exists largely beyond rational control. It resembles paranoia in that it's not easy to know when and whether or not it is justified. You look about you and you wonder if these other men who exhibit not the least sign of being troubled are simply braver and better in command of themselves than you, or, as might be possible, simply foolish and unimaginative. And probably these men are entertaining the same bewilderment about you.[105]

This same fear frequently grips military veterans, as they revisit, against their will, earlier traumatic episodes, what clinicians of post-traumatic stress disorder (PTSD) call "re-experiencing." Depending on the person, involuntary memory—the sense that one has not merely re-called a feeling but is *having the feeling in the present*—can extend to a range of darker emotions: hate, anger, dread, guilt. Re-experiencing can take the form of nightmares, flashbacks, and other involuntary memories, or "intrusions." Certain stimuli—a sound, a smell, a particular image or word—will cause an instant reawakening of the traumatic event: in a flash the person finds himself back in the scene, awash with anguish. Dr. Neil Weissman, a psychologist practicing in Maryland, who works regularly with veterans of Vietnam, Afghanistan, the Gulf War, and Iraq, describes it this way:

> The trauma never gets placed in the past; it's always in the present. In re-experiencing, [one] is not able to say, "That happened then; this is now." There's a loss of the sense of the temporal dimension. It's being felt now, and oftentimes [veterans] see scenes that occurred in the past in the present. . . . It doesn't feel like a memory; it feels like an event.[106]

The experience of involuntary memory—along with other symptoms of PTSD such as "avoidance" of the trauma and "hypervigilance," the sense of being constantly on guard—figures in several poems that Hecht wrote about the war.

Hecht admitted to suffering from PTSD, a condition that often becomes more pronounced after the veteran returns to normal life:

> I had what in those primitive days was called a "nervous breakdown," and which today would be styled "post-traumatic shock syndrome." It was arrogant and foolish of me to have supposed that my war expe-

riences could be smoothly expunged by a couple of weeks of heavy drinking. I returned to my parents' home in New York and entered psychoanalysis.[107]

PTSD, what Hecht calls "post-traumatic shock," has been known variously as "soldier's heart," "shell shock," "combat fatigue," "gross stress reaction," "war neurosis," and "combat neurosis." It was added to the standard manual of mental disorders after Vietnam, but the condition itself, some have argued, finds expression in Shakespeare and as far back as Homer.

The symptoms, according to the US Department of Veterans Affairs, include, among other telltales, negative changes in beliefs and feelings, difficulty sleeping, and avoiding situations that remind one of the traumatic events. Hecht's wartime trauma mingled with childhood trauma, one amplifying the other, in poems such as "Apprehensions," "The Cost," "Rites and Ceremonies," and "'It Out-Herods Herod. Pray You, Avoid It,'" to name only a few. As for interrupted sleep, Hecht's nightmares about the war caused him to wake up "shrieking." Only at the very end of his life did these episodes abate.

Hecht depicts "involuntary memory" starkly and dramatically at the end of "Still Life," from *The Venetian Vespers* (1979). The poem begins with the natural world, the description of a lake at dawn, ringed with dew-covered grass:

> *Everything's doused and diamonded with wet.*
>   *A cobweb, woven taut*
> *On bending stanchion frames of tentpole grass,*
> *Sags like a trampoline or firemen's net*
> *With all the glitter and riches it has caught,*
> *Each drop a paperweight of Steuben glass.*
>
> *No birdsong yet, no cricket, nor does the trout*
>   *Explode in water-scrolls*
> *For a skimming fly. All that is yet to come.*
> *Things are as still and motionless throughout*
> *The universe as ancient Chinese bowls,*
> *And nature is magnificently dumb.*

Why does this so much stir me, like a code
   Or muffled intimation
Of purposes and preordained events?
It knows me, and I recognize its mode
Of cautionary, spring-tight hesitation,
This silence so impacted and intense.[108]

Dawn acts as a trigger, returning the speaker to the terror of combat:

As in a water-surface I behold
   The first, soft, peach decree
Of light, its pale, inaudible commands.
I stand beneath a pine-tree in the cold,
Just before dawn, somewhere in Germany,
A cold, wet Garand rifle in my hands.

This jump at the end of the poem from the present to a simultaneous, historical present (note the verb tense of "stand") captures the strange disruption of re-experiencing. Hecht is instantly transported—in the interstices, without transition—back to the war:

That poem, first of all, was probably as near to being a direct personal account as anything that I'd written. The poem begins with a description which is meant to be as serene and calm and beautiful as it possibly could be. The astonishing thing that I never was able wholly to realize at the time, though it kept coming back to me afterwards, was that at certain moments in the war, in periods of actual combat, there would be these moments when nothing was happening, and you could just see nature in its innocence and its beauty and then find that you're there in the midst of it not out of any desire of your own, not because you're a tourist, but because your intention is to protect yourself and kill somebody else. This was something that I have still not really entirely come to terms with. The description that I began with—that lake with the trout and so forth, the spider web with water on it—is not a recollection of an actual scene in Germany, but it certainly could have been a German scene. There were many such mornings.[109]

"The rifle, I think, is the determining thing," he told Langdon Hammer. "I don't believe there's any redemption in the poem at all."

According to the National Council on Disabilities, a veteran may be overrun not only with horrifying images but also with sounds and other sensations of the traumatic event. The poet Alan Dugan, a contemporary of Hecht's, writes about the sound of rifle fire returning to him out of nowhere in "Family Scene: Young Vet and Relatives": the soldier home from war "hears, if he stops dead for a moment, / the hate hawked on every corner of his suburb / and the sound of the gun he thought silent." In Hecht's "A Hill," a mysterious rifle crack disrupts the silence. It has an eerie, unnerving effect in the poem, which begins in a sunlit market of the Campo de' Fiori, over which the Farnese Palace looms down Via dei Baullari, and shifts abruptly to a desolate winter landscape and back. The "vision" overtakes Hecht completely and reads like a textbook flashback:

> And then, where it happened, the noises suddenly stopped,
> And it got darker; pushcarts and people dissolved
> And even the great Farnese Palace itself
> Was gone, for all its marble; in its place
> Was a hill, mole-colored and bare. It was very cold,
> Close to freezing, with a promise of snow.
> The trees were like old ironwork gathered for scrap
> Outside a factory wall. There was no wind,
> And the only sound for a while was the little click
> Of ice as it broke in the mud under my feet.
> I saw a piece of ribbon snagged on a hedge,
> But no other sign of life. And then I heard
> What seemed the crack of a rifle. A hunter, I guessed;
> At least I was not alone. But just after that
> Came the soft and papery crash
> Of a great branch somewhere unseen falling to earth.
>
> And that was all, except for the cold and silence
> That promised to last forever, like the hill.

Then prices came through, and fingers, and I was restored
To the sunlight and my friends. But for more than a week
I was scared by the plain bitterness of what I had seen.
All this happened about ten years ago,
And it hasn't troubled me since, but at last, today,
I remembered that hill; it lies just to the left
Of the road north of Poughkeepsie; and as a boy
I stood before it for hours in wintertime.

The poem combines the description of rapid psychic transport with a deep reading of landscape that embeds traumas of both childhood and the war. Bard College lies north of Poughkeepsie, and his career there was cut short by the war. It was also at Bard where he was confronted yet again with his father's erratic behavior in a possible attempted kidnapping. This bizarre event coincided with the shuttering of Melvyn's over-the-counter securities business at 111 Fifth Avenue. The partnership of Kempshall and Hecht Inc. was among a handful of concerns forced out of business by order of the National Association of Securities Dealers.

"A Hill," Hecht wrote in a letter to his friend, the poet and librettist J. D. McClatchy,

is the nearest I was able to come in [*The Hard Hours*] to what Eliot somewhere describes as an obsessive image or symbol—something from deep in our psychic life that carries a special burden of meaning and feeling for us. In my poem I am really writing about a pronounced feeling of loneliness and abandonment in childhood, which I associate with a cold and unpeopled landscape. My childhood was doubtless much better than that of many, but my brother was born epileptic when I was just over two, and from then on all attention was, very properly, focused on him. I have always felt that desolation, that hell itself, is most powerfully expressed in an uninhabited natural landscape at its bleakest.[110]

That the boy stands there "for hours" is a curious detail and recalls an exchange Hecht once had with W. H. Auden in Ischia. Vagaries irritated Auden: "How can anyone say 'I have watched for an hour'? Poetry must be accurate," he suggested. In Auden's terms, then, the boy standing there "for hours" would seem an irresponsible hyperbole, until one understands how an image can root itself in the psyche, reasserting itself, unbidden, and ever-present. Hecht unpacks the image for Hoy: "My therapist had a lot of theories about ['A Hill']. Anyway, when you ask, 'why would a boy stand for hours in front of a scene of great bitterness,' the answer is, of course, that he does not do so willingly; he is compelled to. And he is compelled to because no one comes to take him away from all this bitterness."[111] Once lodged, the trauma is, in an emotional sense, present not just for hours but indefinitely. McClatchy perceives how experiences of childhood and the war become linked in Hecht's poems:

> We know from other poems that this scene strangely duplicates scenes described from Hecht's childhood, where we find the lonely boy staring blankly out of the window, or standing paralyzed in front of a hill in winter. In other words, his wartime memories—of sickening fear or helplessness—serve to focus earlier, deeper memories [of childhood], and the way they each recall and reinforce the other is part of the force of a Hecht poem.[112]

Hecht often employed what John Ruskin, in *Modern Painters*, termed the pathetic fallacy—the method by which landscape is perceived under the "influence of emotion." He worked at "catching images of landscape and weather—certain slants of light, in Emily Dickinson's phrase—which have had pronounced effects on me."[113] Frequently favoring indirection, he encoded traumatic memories into his descriptions of nature, as with the trees in "A Hill" (like "old ironwork gathered for scrap / Outside a factory wall"). In his essay "The Pathetic Fallacy" from *Obbligati* (1986), Hecht takes, as an example of this, one of his most beloved passages from Shakespeare (also quoted in letters home from the war):

> *Sweet are the uses of adversity,*
> *Which, like the toad, ugly and venomous,*
> *Wears yet a precious jewel in his head;*
> *And this our life, exempt from public haunt,*
> *Finds tongues in trees, books in the running brooks,*
> *Sermons in stones, and good in everything.*[114]

"The very act of description," Hecht notes, "is in some degree meta-
phoric, and when Socrates tries to say what the Good is, the nearest he
can come is to say it is like Light."

Hecht embeds trauma in the landscape with carefully chosen, loaded
diction. In his autobiographical "Apprehensions," a child sits at the window
of a Lexington Avenue apartment building "studiously watching." The
scene is glimpsed through a wrought-iron window guard, like a prisoner
looking out between the bars. A similar bleak sky and iron railing find their
way into "The Venetian Vespers":

> . . . the sight, on a gray morning,
> Beneath the crossbar of an iron railing
> Painted a glossy black, of six waterdrops
> Slung in suspension, sucking into themselves,
> As if it were some morbid nourishment,
> The sagging blackness of the rail itself,
> But edged with brilliant fingernails of chrome
> In which the world was wonderfully disfigured[115]

And in "Death the Whore," the ghost of a former lover rises as a wisp of
smoke in the speaker's consciousness:

> Some thin gray smoke twists up against a sky
> Of German silver in the sullen dusk
> From a small chimney among leafless trees.
> The paths are empty, the weeds bent and dead;
> Winter has taken hold. And what, my dear,
> Does this remind you of? You are surprised
> By the familiar manner, the easy, sure
> Intimacy of my address. You wonder
> Whose curious voice is this? Why should that scene
> Seem distantly familiar? Did something happen
> Back in my youth on a deserted path
> Late on some unremembered afternoon?
> And now you'll feel at times a fretful nagging
> At the back of your mind as of something almost grasped

But tauntingly and cunningly evasive.
It may go on for months, perhaps for years.[116]

Why make it *German* silver if not to bring to mind smoke from the crematoria? In another winter scene that haunts the speaker for months or years, the flora, again, are bent and dead.

It took Hecht some time to find ways to write about the war; he disparaged his earliest attempts, which could be dreamlike and poeticizing. His most accomplished war poems deal with the moral compromise and helplessness associated with combat and the Holocaust. But even when he's not writing explicitly about the war, trauma inheres in the imagery. Words and phrases such as *gray, iron, German silver, leafless trees,* and *smoke* allowed him to access his war experiences without invoking them directly—a pain he wished to avoid. Using the pathetic fallacy, Hecht allowed landscape to imply the situation.

FOUR

MR. RANSOM IN OHIO, MR. TATE IN NEW YORK
(1946–1948)

1. "I had to go back to school"[1]

Home in New York in the spring of 1946, Hecht felt stalled. He had moved back in with his family on East 81ˢᵗ Street. It was April, and in nearby Central Park the forsythias and magnolia trees were beginning to bloom. Roger was up at Bard, finishing his freshman year. Dorothea, who kept up with news of the war and its aftermath, liked to read the headlines to her son in an attempt to draw him out, while Melvyn quietly smoked his pipe in another room. But Hecht answered their mild solicitations with a heavy silence. There was little he could tell his parents about what he'd experienced. How could he? He thought of the many dead he'd seen, of the friends he'd lost: "I stayed in that numbed state until long after I was discharged, having seen over half my company killed or wounded in action."[2]

Rattling around the apartment or holed up in the 3ʳᵈ Avenue bars, Hecht was haunted by what he'd seen: the granite quarry, the abandoned airplane factory, the rows of barracks, the bare hills. He had walked the muddy path to the crematorium, with its tiny concrete cells and unforgettable stench. He worked repeatedly but unsuccessfully to blot them out and met his mother's knowing queries with avoidance and a far-off stare. He self-medicated with whiskey and retreated into himself:

> I was consistently drunk for well over two weeks. My parents were particularly forbearing and indulgent about this. They kept me in full supply of booze. I think I drank day and night, and I fell asleep most nights on the floor of their New York apartment. The drink must have served

as a sort of narcotic for everything unmentionable that had happened or
that I saw during those years.[3]

It must have caused his parents a certain amount of pain to see him in
such a state, but they did what they could to support him. In their finer
moments, they were patient and compassionate. Dorothea was at her
best in extremis. She could be a doting nursemaid in the right circumstances, and perhaps for the first time she gave to Tony some measure of
the sympathetic care he had lacked as a boy. Melvyn appreciated tobacco
and strong drink for its curative properties in alleviating his own upset
and depression. If Tony wanted to pass his evenings drinking and chain-
smoking cigarettes in the dive bars of the East Side, then that was fine
by him; he had earned the right. Melvyn, as was his wont, said nothing.
Hecht acquired a taste for strong drink from Melvyn, though he usually
imbibed in modest amounts: "I have drunk, probably too much, ever
since then, and to this day [in 1988] I get jumpy and restless in the evening
if I have nothing to drink."[4]

Reentry was painfully slow. He felt strung out and wary. Even going
about everyday activities was fraught. Sitting on the subway, one afternoon, he noticed a stranger staring at him: "Usually I would just bury my
head in the book I had, but I decided I would just stare back at him. I was
a combat vet. I wasn't going to look away." The man, who was much bigger than Hecht, continued to glare, until it almost came to blows. Hecht
"looked at him and looked at him," refusing to back down. He had survived Hell, goddammit. He would not cower before this stranger: "The
guy finally got off three stops later, and of course nothing happened.
When I looked down at my book, I saw my fly was open." No wonder
he'd caught the man's attention. He knew in that moment he "didn't
look that tough at all."[5] But he was on constant alert, riled by the kind of
hypervigilance that follows unresolved trauma.

Hecht was stuck, and no amount of drink could free him. He had
no job, nor did he look for one. The New Yorker was, by now, a dead end;
whatever encouragement he had received from William Shawn was long
past. Still numb, he hadn't written any poems in three years, except some
lightverse scribbled in his letters home. But that summer, in a deliberate effort to reclaim his life, he would make a start. More and more,

he thought about writing, though his ambition, slowly rekindling, outstripped his achievement at that point. He had produced only apprentice
work in his college years. He no longer settled for mere finger exercises,
attempting for the first time a sustained gravity in his poems. He thought
more and more about Robie's stories of Kenyon College and its circle—one
is tempted to say *family*—of young writers around the poet John Crowe
Ransom. It was just the sort of place for a poet of Hecht's seriousness and
cultivation, Robie told him.

Hecht "got hold of some of Ransom's work, and read it for the first
time." He found it odd, almost of another era; it "astonished and bewildered" him. "I had read no modern poetry (I don't think I even knew Hardy's work) that so defiantly employed archaisms, elaborate inversions of
word order, and a diction and idiom so alien to modern speech."[6] Despite
these quirks, Hecht came to revere Ransom's poetry greatly, so much so
that he needed to push against it when writing his own poems, so as not to
fall too fully under its influence. He was intrigued by the poems'

> painful anachronisms that endure beyond the hope of resolution: codes
> of outdated morality applied almost laughably to a modern or heedless
> world; lovers torn by an equation of desire and ethics so perfectly bal-
> anced that they are like the proverbial donkey simultaneously attracted
> by two bales of hay, identical in their diametrically opposed distance
> from him and attraction to him, so that unable to choose, he dies of
> starvation midway between them. The effect is both ludicrous and pa-
> thetic, and it is this special emotional cocktail of contradictory ingredi-
> ents, powerful and paradoxical, that forbids a simple response to many
> of Ransom's poems, that continues to puzzle and to charm, and that
> firmly distinguishes him from Hardy.[7]

Despite having only free time on his hands, it was difficult to settle down
to work: "I had no goals or aims," he recalled later, "and would have been
lost had it not been for the GI Bill of Rights that allowed me to return to
academic life, which was the only happy life I'd known."[8]

At Robie's suggestion, Hecht enrolled at Kenyon in the fall of 1946.
He entered as a non-matriculating "special student," a designation common among returning GIs, many, like Hecht, still among the walking

wounded: "[I]t took a longer time to recover . . . than you might think," Hecht admitted. "One didn't just step out of uniform and pick up a copy of Milton and read it again. I had to go back to school."[9]

Gambier, Ohio. The place meant nothing to Hecht: a featureless speck on the sprawling plain of the Midwest. Certainly, he'd *heard* of Ohio. His maternal grandfather, Elkan Holzman, was born in Cincinnati in 1864, and Elkan's wife, Jennie, came from Illinois, two states over. There was, as it turns out, a branch of Midwestern Hechts, but none were of Joseph's line and none were known to their New York cousins. A remote village on the Kokosing River (population 470 in 1940), Gambier held no associations for the recently discharged GI, save one: it was the home of Kenyon, where Robie had taken a degree in English before the war. When Robie described the place, with its Victorian Gothic buildings covered with creepers, his eyes flashed. Hecht must have felt a pang of envy in those moments: here was a community of writers of high seriousness devoted to literature (and each other).

Ransom was at the center of this small but expanding universe. The son of a Methodist minister, he featured prominently among the dozen Southern men of letters who found common cause as "Agrarians" in the 1920s, each contributing an essay to the controversial and, many justly felt, reactionary *I'll Take My Stand: The South and the Agrarian Tradition.* Their association developed out of the group of so-called Fugitive poets at Vanderbilt—including Ransom, Allen Tate, Robert Penn Warren, the sonneteer Merrill Moore, and, in wider orbit, the critic Cleanth Brooks and the modernist poet Laura Riding. Their journal, *The Fugitive,* appeared between 1922 and 1925, when Warren (born 1905) was still a teenager and Tate (born 1899) was in his early twenties. Ransom was the star of their workshop gatherings, a poet and critic of national importance, and, as it happened, increasingly undervalued at Vanderbilt, where they kept pressing him to shore up his credentials with a PhD.

In 1937, Kenyon's new president, Gordon Keith Chalmers, a mere thirty-three years old, arrived from Rockford College in Illinois—hence his nickname "Rocky." Chalmers's first act was to lure Ransom away from Nashville, with a large salary-offer and an invitation to come "write poetry and teach philosophy."[10] Ransom believed he'd have greater freedom there: "I think that at a smaller college I'll have more time for writing. In a large university there are so many demands upon a person's time—committees and curriculum reform and all that."[11] Also, with only lukewarm support from his dean in Nashville, he was wise enough to go where he was most wanted.

Ransom's move from Vanderbilt to Kenyon was a defining moment in twentieth-century American letters. A year after his arrival, he founded *The Kenyon Review,* which would play an important role in Hecht's early career. With associate professor of philosophy Philip Blair Rice (managing editor) and Norman Johnson (secretary) rounding out the staff, it quickly became an outlet for the leading poets and critics of the 1940s and '50s. Envisioned as a successor to T. S. Eliot's *Criterion,* it joined the first tier of literary journals, along with *Partisan Review* and, later, *The Hudson Review.* (When Ransom stepped down twenty-one years later, he passed the reins of the *Review* to none other than his former protégé, Robie Macauley.) The *Review*'s initial number for Winter 1939 featured writing by Macauley's first teacher Ford Madox Ford, as well as Randall Jarrell, Delmore Schwartz, Philip Rahv, R. P. Blackmur, and Yvor Winters. In that issue Ransom proclaimed an Age of Criticism, which he later codified in his book *The New Criticism* (1941), on the work of T. S. Eliot, William Empson, I. A. Richards, Winters, and Blackmur. Ransom's title caught on: The New Criticism's formalist approach to literature—marked by "close reading" and the autonomous nature of the work of art—became the leading critical mode and the one best suited to explicate the particular challenges posed by the modernist aesthetic. The coterie that first banded together at Vanderbilt broadened its reach at Kenyon and, through the *Review,* came to dominate the critical discourse of the day with books by *Review* stalwarts, such as Empson's *Seven Types of Ambiguity* and Brooks's *The Well-Wrought Urn.*

Ransom's genteel manners and soft-spoken affect dispelled the misgivings of his new colleagues. If they had feared an Agrarian firebrand, Ransom in the flesh was benign and beloved by his charges. Students flocked to study with him from around the country, placing tiny, rural Gambier firmly on the literary map. Hot on Ransom's heels, Robert "Cal" Lowell enrolled at Kenyon in 1938, and Jarrell signed on that fall as an English instructor and tennis coach. Ransom installed his two acolytes in the second-floor bedroom of his large house on campus. Meanwhile, at Olivet College, Ford encouraged Macauley to seek out Ransom in his new situation, and after securing a three-year fellowship, Macauley left Michigan for Ohio in 1938.

When rehashing his Kenyon days, Macauley frequently made mention of the writer-crowded Douglass House, where he lived with Peter Taylor, John Thompson, and Lowell. Lowell's biographer Ian Hamilton describes this nestful of fledgling scribes: "The eleven residents of Douglass House—with Jarrell also living in as a chaperon or 'housemother'—had a common interest in Kenyon. Each of them wanted to be a writer, and each considered himself to be a 'Ransom man.'"[12] The years before the war were a Golden Age on the Hill, as the campus was known. When Macauley graduated in 1941, military service had scattered these writers to the winds, but their association was already becoming legendary. Shortly after Macauley's departure, Kenyon hosted a crop of candidates in the ASTP, and military trainees overran the campus, leaving it the worse for wear. After the war, much of the college had to be renovated and restored. The next wave of students to flood the campus included those returning soldiers, like Hecht, continuing their studies on the GI Bill.

When Hecht arrived in Gambier, Robie, of course, had long since moved on, but his brother, C. Cameron Macauley, who went by Chuck, was finishing up his degree. Chuck was a talented photographer and, later, filmmaker. In his freshman year, he hitchhiked to New York City to meet Alfred Stieglitz, whom he photographed. After service in the Navy assembling photographic maps of coastlines around the world, he returned to Gambier as a sophomore. Hecht arrived before him that fall and was anxious for Chuck's company and guidance. To settle his nerves, he popped a few phenobarbital. GIs had overrun the dormitories, so Hecht took up lodging in the home of one Rev. Gribbins, who allowed him to earn his keep by performing odd jobs around the place. When a desk and a pair of rugs arrived from home, along with his clothes and other belongings, he added them to the sparse furnishings—a bed, a dresser, and a wastebasket—setting up a comfortable workspace in the small bedroom.

He paid his registration fee ($65) and signed up for Ransom's Advanced Writing course, Renaissance poetry, and studio painting. With classes set to begin within the week, he sat down alone in his room and began writing again, worried that he might be caught out with very little work to show. He looked to Yeats, a strong influence at this point, for inspiration and guidance: "Yeats, whom, of course I never met, and in whose critical opinions I was not at all interested, served for me not merely as an astonishing model, but as a sort of Zen master, since he was in a position to abide my most pressing questions in total silence."[13] About his early influences, he later told an interviewer: "I played first the role of the sedulous ape, to write in the manner of Eliot, then Stevens, Yeats, Auden, Ransom, Richard Wilbur, Elizabeth Bishop. Each effaced the other, until I became a palimpsest with little bits of all of them—without, I hope, sounding like any one of them in particular."[14] The poems he finished in Gambier signaled a new music and growing maturity. They described an extreme anxiety, a sense of crisis that Hecht had not attempted to express before:

> And seeing this broken landscape tied by the wind together,
> I wanted to drop down on my paper knees,
> And become some wind-bitten plant, and bend in the weather,
> And I wanted to scream.[15]

He showed the poem to Ransom immediately, as a possibility for the *Review,* but heard nothing back. With that first submission to a national magazine, he began his career as a poet, in Rev. Gribbins's house, with empty countryside for miles around—a "broken landscape" that left an imprint on his memory of the place.

Ransom was Hecht's academic advisor and would become his champion. At their first class session, Ransom circulated for discussion material submitted to *The Kenyon Review.* Hecht was delighted by his "magnificent sense of humor" as he read the submissions aloud to the class. After hearing a piece, the group of ten students "analyzed it and tore it apart, put it back together, etc." Hecht was learning three important skills at once: literary criticism, editing, and, most importantly, aesthetic judgment— what to leave in, what to leave out, and the effects the various formal elements of a poem could produce. Outside class, Hecht engaged Ransom in long private conversations, during which Ransom proved "extremely cordial."[16] Ransom liked long hikes and would botanize along the way; he was also a devoted gardener. Hecht took careful note of his observations of the natural world, which resonated with his own inner life.

Robie had counseled wisely: Kenyon was a perfect fit. The Ransom circle past and present became his literary home base, a place of belonging from which to begin writing in earnest. Recalling his longtime friend, the poet Richard Howard observed that "Tony always wanted to be a member of the club."[17] A cryptic remark, at first blush, typical of Howard's barbed observations, but also perceptive. Hecht's search for a literary family to supplant his biological one would occupy him for years, and the fact that he worked best when among friends drew him to seek out sympathetic company. He was wary of strangers, and criticism, even well-meaning criticism, could unnerve him. Unfavorable reviews tormented him, sometimes for years. He desired admission to the literary world and believed he'd earned the right to be there, taking pride in his new associations. From this point on, he would no longer be the shy boy at the margins but a quietly determined writer of promise, among the initiates of Ransom's literary Round Table:

> To have become one of that little group of Kenyon students in the mid-forties was not merely to have joined them under Mr. Ransom's remarkable tuition; it was also to have been assimilated into a hieratic tradition, a select branch in the great taxonomic structure of the modern intellect, in which we were the direct and undisputed heirs not only of Mr. Ransom himself but of all our distinguished predecessors who were his former pupils. These ranged from legendary young men of stunning mental powers who had graduated just too soon for any of us to have met them (about one of these it was affirmed that he wandered the campus reading extremely difficult texts in philosophy from which he tore out the pages and threw them away after a single, hasty, but sufficient perusal) to such as Peter Taylor and Robert Lowell, who were just coming into their fame, and beyond to Allen Tate, Cleanth Brooks, and Robert Penn Warren, who has discernibly changed the course and character of American letters. . . . The responsibility of following in so august a procession we regarded as a difficult, historic burden, just sufficiently mitigated by our private sense of being among "the anointed."[18]

"The religious overtones of these words," Amy Blumenthal writes in a note for the Kenyon alumni bulletin, "recall Ransom's naming the community of poets a 'secular priesthood,' even as they convey a sense of election experienced by those witnessing firsthand the birth of the New Criticism."

The place itself felt like the Oxbridge of Ohio. According to one faculty member's brief history of Kenyon, "The Great Hall was patterned after the dining halls at Cambridge and Oxford, and was designed to accommodate all two hundred and fifty men at the College at sit-down meals. As in the English halls, a High Table was provided for faculty members and visiting dignitaries."[19] Ransom was not the only famous member of the English faculty. With him at High Table sat the renowned Renaissance scholar Charles M. Coffin, whose *John Donne and the New Philosophy* had appeared just before the war. When graduates boasted of their training at Kenyon, they regularly referred to Coffin's tutelage, and he in turn valued their company. He dedicated his anthology *The Major Poets: English and American* (1954) "To the men of Kenyon College who have read poetry with me for many years."[20] There were stained-glass windows alongside portraits of donors and past presidents. Like Bard, the college was founded by clerics; one could easily imagine a fug of incense in the air.

Hecht distinguished himself early in Coffin's 17th-Century Poetry class with a talk on John Donne that ran an hour and a half.[21] Given Coffin's expertise, it was a bold choice, bordering on arrogance. But he followed his passion, and it paid off. Hecht reported home that Coffin seemed "quite impressed with my peroration, told me that he enjoyed the class immensely, and that he had learned a lot from my remarks."[22] In studio painting, he began to make preliminary sketches, and requested his copy of Vasari's *Lives* be sent from home for use in the essays required by the course. He spent six hours a week at the easel—less stimulating than his poetry classes, though still perfectly enjoyable. For fun, he sat in on Philip Blair Rice's philosophy class on the theory of value, which he was excited about in prospect. Rice was an admirer of the philosopher and poet George Santayana and contributed an essay to the *Review* titled "George Santayana: The Philosopher as Poet," and he no doubt shared his enthusiasm with Hecht during one of their numerous bookish colloquies. Hecht came to revere Santayana and even identify with him as an expatriate in

Italy postwar, eventually composing an elegy for him and quoting him in the epigraph to his first book of poems.

Hecht was older and more experienced than the undergraduates, and when an English professor fell ill, he was tapped as a replacement. He interviewed for the position, most likely in Ransom's office, with the "courtly and gentle man" peering out from behind his desk. Ransom "was rather short in stature . . . in his late fifties, his hair already white as swan's down."[23] A natty dresser, he would appear in fine weather in a "powder-blue sports jacket with matching socks with white clocks on them." Ransom loved games—crosswords, golf and other sports—and would invite students to his home for charades. Hecht recalled that, "At the time I knew him Mr. Ransom was an avid baseball fan, an insatiable player of bridge, and if there was any fierceness at all in his character he was said to have expressed it in his playing of croquet." Ransom's writing was as decorous and lively as the man. In his refined prose style, which reminded him of Santayana, Hecht discerned "a subtle, recognizably personal voice—gallant, old-fashioned, deliberate, witty, self-mocking, and generous." In his own prose, Hecht would develop (occasionally to a fault) a number of the baroque qualities he admired in his mentor: "Its rhythmic and rhetorical elegances, its quirky delight in the unexpected word, its worldly and polished skepticism, and its warmth of spirit."[24]

Have you any teaching experience? Ransom asked his solicitous student. He had "an especially beautiful and gently modulated tenor voice, with the special delicacy of his regional Southern speech to which he brought a lilt of his own, characterized by his tendency to end his sentences on a rising inflection."[25] Lowell remembered that "his mouth was large and always in slow perceptive motion, quivering with tedium, or tighter-drawn to repel ignorant rudeness, giving an encouraging grimace, or relaxed, though busy in meditation."[26] His students liked to imitate him reading his poems, contrasting the martial tone of "Captain Carpenter" with his signature mildness. Just before answering in the negative, Hecht recalled that, at Bard, he had been asked to teach solid geometry and trigonometry in a Navy training program for undergraduates. (His then supervisor was a future Nobel Prize winner in economics named Franco Modigliani.) Hecht realized this had little bearing on teaching English, but Ransom was satisfied, "feeling that an interest in literature ought not to be divorced from other kinds of knowledge and experience."[27] And so Hecht's career teaching Shakespeare began by accident, as a replacement instructor of freshman literature. He taught the Bard for the first time—*Hamlet* and *Henry IV*—to students only slightly younger than himself.

Upon his induction into the faculty, Hecht was reminded of the familiar and painful experiences he had suffered at other WASP schools. The dean assured him that there was no problem with antisemitism at the college, as evidenced by "the solitary presence on the faculty of one Dr. Salomon, who taught in the divinity school." "I would have enjoyed punching him in the face," Hecht thought in that moment, but out of respect for Ransom and a desire to teach, he held his tongue. This generosity of Ransom's would greatly affect his future: teaching at Kenyon "started me on the way to my means of subsistence for the rest of my life."[28] He was responsible for teaching an array of classic texts, including *Moby-Dick, A Passage to India,* and *Paradise Lost.*

The unassuming Ransom, in a wreath of sweet tobacco smoke, his pocket full of strike-anywhere matches, felt at ease with the young writers in his orbit. He appeared mercifully ignorant of their admiration, conducting his poetry classes not in sententious pronouncements but with quiet questioning. He expected his students to work along with him, as equals, to tease out the qualities in the poems under consideration. It was a deference born of a deep-seated courtesy of the old school, which Hecht greatly admired. What's more, it soothed him during this anxious time, and reaffirmed the virtues of reason over violence and barbarity. After the inhumanity of the last three years, here was a man who was deeply civilized.

Like Ransom, Hecht dressed well—classic, but with flair. After his trunk of clothes arrived from New York, he could be seen crossing the quad in a "navy blue (formerly olive-drab) shirt and trousers with a char-treuse tie"—"very striking indeed," if he said so himself.[29] In a posed portrait at Kenyon (likely captured by the lens of Cameron Macauley), a dapper Hecht stands beside an immense column, against dark wood paneling with rectangular moldings. With a shaft of light cutting across his face, he looks like a chiaroscuro figure from a painting, a Hamlet brooding in the shadows in a summer sport coat and flannel trousers, rather like how Ransom dressed at that season. He looks young—not like a veteran home from war. Hecht wished to claim Kenyon as part of his story, and this portrait was his proof. In its classical formality, the photo serves as a record of his time there, his starched collar and knit tie announcing him as a Ransom man.[30]

2. "A dangerous influence"

Hecht made friends almost as soon as he arrived in Gambier. He could be tentative in social situations, but an eruptive sense of humor took hold of him when he was in congenial company. He found the other students greatly sympathetic. When it came to his new poems, he was downright bold. After submitting his poem to Ransom and waiting for what seemed like forever (actually only a few weeks), he wrote to his parents with a new resolve: "I have decided to ask Ransom point blank this evening whether he is going to use my poem in the Review. I don't think he'll say 'yes,' and I'm sort of annoyed at the idea of his having kept it this long without coming to any decision."[31] Hecht's first appearance in the *Review* came about only after a bit of confusion. Or it might have been a joke, involving a kind of comic pantomime by Ransom. Hecht remembered every detail of the occasion. He had gone to Ransom's office

> for some help and advice about a class I was teaching. It had something to do with Shakespeare, as I remember, and we were deeply vigorously into it, when I looked past his head to the blackboard where he habitually wrote down the names of the contributors to the next issue of the *Review,* in the order in which they would appear. And there to my astonishment high on the list, and right between Trilling and Bentley, was my name. At this point, Mr. Ransom was being very animated about Macbeth, and all for my benefit, but after a minute or two I could not contain myself, and abandoning all decorum, I interrupted him to ask whether this meant that I was to be in the next issue. He turned around to look at the blackboard and erased the *H* in front of my name, and put down *Br* instead.[32]

After this awkward incident, Ransom—was he embarrassed by their exchange?—published Hecht's poem in the issue for Spring 1947 under the name Tony Hecht. Two things are odd about this. First: While he was known familiarly as Tony and had published under that name at Bard, it was the last time he would appear this way in print. When two more of his poems ("Wind of Spain" and "Dream," both uncollected) were placed next to a poem by Auden in the Autumn issue, he had matured into Anthony. Now that he was publishing in earnest, he needed to decide on the right byline. (A longer, uncollected poem, "Elegy," appeared at the same time in the Kenyon undergraduate magazine *HIKA* under Anthony E. Hecht, after which the E. was jettisoned.) The other curious detail is that, while he mentions giving Ransom only one poem for the *Review,* two appeared—the Yeatsean "Once Removed" and his first poem about the war, "To a Soldier Killed in Germany":

> *Man-eating danger moved to where you stood*
> *Probing the features of the German wood*
> *With a slim rifle. Others than yourself*
> *Hid from the squinting eye that split a hair*
>
> *Among the lenses, plotting your dirty grave.*[33]

Puns, such as the one on "splitting hairs" and "crosshairs," became a feature of many of his mature poems, though here it contributes to what Hecht came to feel was an excess of artifice when writing about the war. Hecht felt that, when he first wrote about the war, he "wasn't able to write about it well. It was just something that scared me stiff. It was like coming out of a horror movie: you know that it makes your flesh creep and that you survived and you're numb. And you don't quite understand what the whole process was."[34] Hecht left the poem out of his first book, though it captures with great force the fear he felt at the time. Another poem, also uncollected, appeared in the Spring 1948 number of Reed Whittemore's *Furioso,* the sonnet "A Friend Killed in the War":

Night, the fat serpent, slipped among the plants,
Intent upon the apples of his eyes;
A heavy bandoleer hung like a prize
Around his neck, and tropical red ants
Mounted his body, and he heard advance,
Little by little, the thin female cries
Of mortar shells. He thought of Paradise.
Such is the vision that extremity grants.

In the clean brightness of magnesium
Flares, there were seven angels by a tree.
Their hair flashed diamonds, and they made him doubt
They were not really from Elysium.
And his flesh opened like a peony,
Red at the heart, white petals furling out.[35]

Also in that issue of *Furioso* was a review by Andrews Wanning, a Renaissance scholar and the dedicatee of Hecht's "The Dover Bitch," whom Hecht later befriended while teaching at Bard in the 1960s.

Hecht saw his parents briefly at Christmas and New Year's, during which his father was convalescing from an unnamed illness which had kept him bedridden in early December. Shortly after returning to Gambier, his poems appeared in *The Kenyon Review*—a promising start to the new year. Hecht was now writing at a great rate, with uneven results but with a fair number of "keepers," which he sent off to magazines. He imbibed Ransom's poetic style, but he was not uncritical of it. "Astonished" by his mentor's elegant prose, he puzzled over his poems' "arrant archaisms, sophistications, and opulent Latinities that contrasted with such shameless, nursery-rhyme simplicities as: 'To me this has its worth / As I sit upon the earth.'"[36] Was this Ransom being ironic? It wasn't clear. In any case, he came to feel that such thudding rhymes and other oddities of diction and tone did not seriously undermine the high rhetoric and suggestive abstractions of Ransom's poems. He and his colleagues at Kenyon became Ransom's advocates and defenders, taking it personally when critics developed a "faulty and trivial" sense of his verse. He took Ransom as a model and gratefully accepted his stewardship, but his natural instinct was to push back against outright imitation.

Hecht expressed a debt to Ransom with his early poem "Samuel Sewall," but he later feared that he had strayed too fully into a style that was not authentically his own. (This was complicated by the fact that the poem was among the most anthologized of Hecht's early work.) Though the subject feels closer to Lowell's New England, the treatment recalled Ransom's historical portraits of Captain Carpenter and the cleric in "Necrological," which begins:

> The friar had said his paternosters duly
> And scourged his limbs, and afterwards would have slept;
> But with much riddling his head became unruly,
> He arose, from the quiet monastery he crept.

With the same *abab* quatrains and loose iambics, an elevated tone, and surprising diction, Hecht worked a similar music, though his humor sings through:

> And all the town was witness to his trust:
> On Monday he walked out with the Widow Gibbs,
> A pious lady of charm and notable bust,
> Whose heart beat tolerably beneath her ribs.
>
> On Saturday he wrote proposing marriage,
> And closed, imploring that she not be cruel,
> "Your favorable answer will oblige,
> Madam, your humble servant, Samuel Sewall."[37]

If "Samuel Sewall" forecasts Hecht's capacity for mischievous wit, more than Ransom typically displayed, then "Alceste in the Wilderness" partakes of a shared darkness and underlying violence:

> Before the bees have diagramed their comb
> Within the skull, before summer has cracked

The back of Daphnis, naked, polychrome,
Versailles shall see the tempered exile home,
Peruked and stately for the final act.[38]

Hecht's epigraph indicts the cowardice of the fashionable set: "Non, je puis souffrir cette lâche methode / Qu'affectent la plupart de vos gens à la mode . . ." In the end, the ranting aristocrat, based on Molière's *The Misanthrope,* returns to face the violence of the Reign of Terror and the guillotine.

Not only was it necessary to resist Ransom's quirks, it was also necessary to sift through his ideas about poetry. More helpful than specific techniques or opinions was Ransom's habit of mind, his close-reading approach to poems, and his personal mildness, which anxiety-prone Hecht valued greatly. He found it

difficult in retrospect to say exactly what it was one learned from Mr. Ransom, to point to particular notions or propositions. One found it possible, and sometimes necessary, to disagree with him—private, interior disagreements about details in interpretation of poems, even of general philosophic premises—without losing any respect for him by such silent dissent. For one learned from him not facts or positions, but a posture of the mind and spirit, a humanity and courtesy, a manly considerateness that inhabited his work as it did his person. And one learned to pay keen attention to poetic detail.[39]

He took Ransom's preference for Eliotic impersonality to heart: "The young man who has just fallen in love is in grave danger if his first impulse is to sit down and write a poem about it. He's in the midst of the experience, and it takes a certain digestion or assimilation of experience to be able to write about it at all, even a kind of remoteness from it."[40] This saying of Ransom's showed Hecht what was missing from his earliest poems. It excused him

from the task of setting down raw and unconsidered emotion: and it suggested a strategy by which to proceed. That is, instead of writing about what left me almost wordless with confused feelings, I could write about situations that no longer disturbed me, from which I had emerged either scathed or unscathed, and I could also write about what happens to others. Best of all, I could write about what happened to me if I disguised myself as someone else.[41]

For this reason, it would be years before he could write about the war to his satisfaction. By his own admission, his first attempts badly misfired: "The first serious poem I ever tried to write was a disaster, and was bad because I tried to express unmediated feelings about one of my father's collapses. . . . I had neither found, nor even looked for, what Eliot called an 'objective correlative' for my feelings."[42] Though he had been home for over a year, when he completed his second (and final) semester at Kenyon, he was still very much "in the midst of the experience"—even more than he realized. The following year this residual trauma caused the first of two nervous breakdowns.

Some of Ransom's cultural and political ideas—particularly those associated with the Agrarians—ultimately upset Hecht, though at the time he was not fully aware of them, beyond the general sense that they were seen by many as "honorable."[43] He read *I'll Take My Stand* only years after Ransom's death and found its reactionary ideas troubling. In his essay in that volume, "Reconstructed but Unregenerated," Ransom comes off as a hide-bound white Southerner who is tone-deaf to the legacy of slavery: amidst his condemnation of capitalism and industrialization, he adds in passing that "Slavery was a feature monstrous enough in theory, but, more often than not, humane in practice; and it's impossible to believe that its abolition alone could have effected any great revolution in society." Hecht notes that Ransom uses "'slavery' or one of its cognate forms, metaphorically and reprovingly, a good number of times to refer to the bondage that industrialism entails, but only once literally . . . in which its faults are declared to be largely theoretical. Reading this was painful to me, and I still find it unpleasant to think about."[44] Lowell, who had been imprisoned as a conscientious objector for several months in 1943, just after his time at Kenyon, observed that "Ransom liked to stand behind, and later off from, the agrarian charge, as if he were an anti-slavery Southern commander with liberal friends in the East."[45] Hecht felt gratitude for all that Ransom gave him—a literary foundation and a home, as well as a platform for his poems—but he never made excuses for him. He cast a skeptical eye on authority figures generally, and the war did nothing to allay this. Quite the opposite, as it turned out.

3. "Unfettered but unfreed . . ."[46]

Following his year as a special student at Kenyon, in the summer of 1947, Hecht avoided a sweltering season at home, cooped up with his family, or rattling around their rental house in Stamford. At twenty-three, he would never again live under the same roof as his parents—except on one occasion under duress. After a few trying weeks at 163 East 81st Street, he concocted a plan with Robie to spend the summer on Cape Cod, swimming, reading, writing, and drinking, in no particular order of priority. What's more: he convinced Melvyn to foot the bill for it. A postcard sent from Truro, MA, of a white-bearded Cape Cod fisherman in oilskins and a sou'wester, supplied a brief but cheerful update: "It's morning; I'm tight already. Beer + sunshine. All in excellent spirits. Have done no work since the paper I sent you—except one line of a poem." The fact that the critic Edmund Wilson lived nearby added to the literary aura of the place, and they kept an eye peeled in the hope of sighting him, to no avail.

Hecht benefitted from Robie's company and from the momentum that their friendly competitiveness generated. Kenyon had been a great equalizer. Hecht and Macauley had both studied with Ransom and both had published work in the *Review*. Hecht was still grappling with his years in the war, with its mixture of boredom and terror; he felt it dogging him, a faint, inchoate specter hovering at his shoulder: "A few things were still hanging in the air," he admitted euphemistically.[47]

It was at this point that Hecht first read Robie's friend Robert Lowell, who was already a famous poet. Lowell's first collection, *Land of Unlikeness* (1944), had been printed in a limited fine-press edition of 250 copies at Harry Duncan's Cummington Press, and was introduced by Tate. His second collection, *Lord Weary's Castle* (1946), won the Pulitzer Prize when Lowell was only thirty. Hecht envied the "seeming self-confidence" that

Lowell derived from his newly espoused Roman Catholicism and, at the same time, mistrusted it: "He was someone who was always interested in power. I must admit that I regarded all such people with considerable distrust, though Lowell himself was always kind and considerate to me. But I had no illusions about him and would never have wanted to become his close friend."[48] Hecht also admired stories in the *Review* by Macauley's and Lowell's friend Peter Taylor, having heard already about his legendary meetings with T. S. Eliot and Gertrude Stein. Hecht felt not a little daunted by it all: "I was genuinely awed by these writers who were already established, and celebrities of sorts."[49] Robie was very much a part of Kenyon's network of new and established poets and writers, and he and Hecht would spend much of the coming year in each other's company, living and traveling together.

Truro was a young bohemian's paradise. There was a play on at the Provincetown Players—Sean O'Casey's *The Plow and the Stars*—which Hecht proclaimed a dud, though seeing a play after years of drought was itself a thrill. Hecht and Macauley enjoyed each other's company, swimming, tanning, and preparing simple but varied meals. They were running short on cash, but a money order from Melvyn was expected to see them both (and a third friend, Fred, a painter) through the summer. The writing came in dribs and drabs, but Hecht hammered away diligently. In late July, Hecht got good news from Paul Engle, director of the famed Writers' Workshop at the University of Iowa in Iowa City. Both Hecht and Macauley had written to Engle in the hope of securing a teaching post for the fall, and both were offered positions, though Macauley's paid a great deal more than Hecht's. (Lowell was also offered a teaching spot that fall but postponed his appointment until later.)

With the Iowa job now in prospect, Hecht decided to accompany Robie in late August to his family home in Michigan, but a trip home to collect his things was unavoidable. Even his brief stay proved too long—he became sullen and irritable, for which he felt the need to apologize to his parents, from the remote safety of the Midwest. He had felt a similar "emotional schism" at the beginning of the summer, as he packed for his vacation on the Cape. The problem seems to have been with his own unease and restlessness. The psychic fallout from the war—

unacknowledged and therefore unaddressed—played on him, fraying his peace of mind.

Even his friendship with Robie suffered. From New York, the pair had driven to Bard to visit friends, and though the college was not in session Hecht met many people he knew and was invited around to drinks on both nights that they were there. The two-day drive north to Albany then west to Hudsonville, Michigan, was stressful: they got lost more than once, in heavy traffic and a blinding rainstorm, and almost missed the car ferry. Robie actively disliked his parents and made "no bones about it." He spoke to his parents very little after their arrival. Robie "told me himself," Hecht wrote to his parents, "that he's been home a total of three weeks since he's been out of the army, and his parents have only the mistiest idea of what's happened to him since then. As a matter of fact, yesterday afternoon, while Robie was away doing something, I had a long talk with Mrs. M. and told her lots of things about what Robie had been doing that she'd never heard before."[50] Hecht received the cold shoulder from Robie's father, whom he suspected felt outdone by Melvyn's recent largesse: "Mr. M. is a rather unsuccessful man. He has tried a lot of things, but never with enough conviction to carry them through."[51] This was a strange thing to write to his parents, as it came uncomfortably close to describing Melvyn, who may not have recognized himself in it. Both Hecht and Macauley were striving to escape the gravities of their families. Robie envied the Hechts' sophistication, and competed with Tony like a sibling to be more "worldly":

[Robie] has become somewhat cosmopolitan in spite of [his parents] malignant provincialism, and quite tolerant in spite of their bigotry. He has felt so superior to them for so long, that he has kept it up as a sort of unfortunate habit, and it crops up ever[y] so often when he's talking to me, in little situations in which it becomes clear that he gives me credit for much less acumen than I have. . . . Robie hasn't the vaguest idea what I'm like, though he seems to think he knows me perfectly.[52]

The days at the Macauleys' family farm near Lake Michigan, Pine Springs Ranch, were airless and hot. Hecht's mood soured. His feelings toward

Robie were comparable to the ways that he both relied on and strove to outdo mentors and friends whom he admired:

> For a good long time I have had the unfortunate habit of selecting some-
> one whose achievements and intelligence (not personality, please note),
> I admire, and of trying to persuade myself that I am his equal. These
> experiences have always been painful, but in every case I have managed
> to come through to my own satisfaction. Whether this is merely a slow
> process of rationalization I have no idea, but I have convinced myself
> that I have advanced beyond [such friends]. . . . Please understand that
> this has not been a process of emulation; I do not desire to be like them
> but better than them, and it has only been through constant and rather
> painful apprenticeships that I have been able to come forward with any
> degree of satisfaction.[53]

Hecht's capacity for clear-eyed self-reflection is striking and also typical. His "habit" of striving to surpass such mentors and friends testifies to his intense, deep-seated ambition for his own writing. Such ambition might even be a necessary engine for a poet. If not, it is, in any case, widely common. Hecht confessed his jealousy over Ransom's fondness for Robie. He felt slighted in comparison: Ransom gave Robie a teaching job at a rate of $3,000, while Hecht received an assistantship paying one-tenth that. The fact that Robie was a few years older made no difference.

What Hecht did not tell Mrs. Macauley during their long talk, and what he could not tell his own parents or anyone for that matter, was what he and Robie had witnessed in those granite hills in western Germany: the mass graves, the crematoria, the abandoned camp, the dead and the dying, the unforgettable stench of it. Robie was the one person who knew without his having to say a word of what he'd been through, but he was also a constant reminder of the things he was working very hard at the moment to forget. Whatever their tensions as summer lapsed into fall, they managed to put them aside as they both embarked on a new chapter at the prestigious Writers' Workshop.

The two took rooms in the house of the Hostetlers, at 533 North Linn Street, within walking distance of the campus. Hecht's room had a double bed and an electric fan, to which he added his furniture shipped from Ohio. For $20 a month each, they also had the use of a shared bath, and Mrs. Hostetler made up the beds each day. He asked his parents to send along his fur-lined gloves, as he'd heard that "it gets down to 20 below here in the winter."[54] His first duties as a graduate teaching assistant involved registering students for classes and attending faculty meetings. He enrolled in three courses, including two in poetry writing, and a third, with Robie, in literary criticism. A photograph from this time shows Hecht in bohemian casualness, poised atop a steamer trunk. His posture is nonchalant—legs crossed at the knee, hands deep in pockets. An unruly shock of thick hair and open collar complete the air of tousled ease. But the eyes betray another mood—hollow, peering up tentatively from raised brows. He looks tired, wan, the side of his face overexposed in sunlight.

It was an isolating and cold winter, as Hecht continued to struggle with his anxieties about the war. Another attempt at writing about combat, "The Plate," which likely dated from this time, exists in a single, fair typescript. It describes a wounded soldier whose skull has been repaired with a metal plate. The second, final stanza reads:

> The body burns away, and burning gives
> Light to the eye and moisture to the lip
> And warmth to our desires, but it burns
>   Whatever body lives
> Into extinction though it wear a plate
> Of armor in it: therefore do we thrive
> In fear of fire, in terror of the ship
> That carries us to fire. A soldier learns
>   To bear the silver weight
> Where in his head the fire is most alive.[55]

The fire in his head became all-consuming during his initial months in Iowa City. The letters home stopped abruptly in October, with a promise to "write again later." There is no evidence that he did. Hecht was shutting down. It became clear to him that he would not be able to continue at Iowa. He needed help. After a brief hospitalization in Iowa City, Hecht returned home to his parents, who started him in psychoanalysis. Hecht didn't speak about his breakdown, even to friends. He masked his upset. His own—inconclusive—treatment lasted two years, on and off.

It says a lot about how scared and desperate Hecht had become that he would live again under his parents' roof. This was a huge step backward in terms of the independence he had staked for himself as a mature writer, in charge of his own destiny. His doctor, Dr. Weitzen, was not hugely helpful:

> My analyst, a good and decent man, but an orthodox Freudian, was not prepared to believe that my troubles were due wholly, or even largely, to the war, so we went ambling back together, down the rocky garden path to my infancy. But I think he must have helped me, as much by his kindness and patience as anything else.[56]

He managed to return to Iowa to finish out the year but left without taking a degree. He continued to be close to Robie, who became his old genial self as soon as he was away from his parents. Robie was seeing another Iowa student, Flannery O'Connor, and Hecht accompanied them on at least one double date, with a girl named Clyde McLeod, called "Pinky," who, Hecht told his parents in a telegram, "says she'll marry me in five years."[57] Robie was "dating" O'Connor (his word) in only the most genteel sense; there was no sexual relationship. In fact, he was engaged to Anne Draper back in New York, a fact which O'Connor knew well. But he had a way of attending to her that she found calming. Mainly they engaged as writers: "I still have vivid memories of sitting out on the porch of the boarding house where she lived," Macauley recalled, "and hearing *Wise Blood* read in Flannery's inimitable accent, chapter by chapter, and talking about it."[58]

In the summer of 1948, Hecht returned to Gambier for the inaugural Kenyon School of English summer program, which brought together poets and critics from across the US and abroad. That year, the "staff" included Eric Bentley, Cleanth Brooks, William Empson (who was flown in from China), F. O. Matthiessen, Richard Chase, Austin Warren, Tate, and Ransom. These renowned writers "had an enormous influence on me, and I was very meek and subordinate in those years and full of unquestioning admiration for them all."[59] Roughly seventy-five students were selected from hundreds of applications, for the three years that the School of English met, from 1948 to 1950. One student, Howard Babb, who was there with Hecht, described the excitement these sessions produced: "I have never before associated with eight men of such brilliance. . . . I honestly believe that I received sufficient inspiration from attending the 1948 session to sustain me in my study of English throughout the rest of my life."[60]

Hecht met a number of his heroes there, including Empson, whom he worked hard to impress. He submitted a "very dutiful essay" on which Empson wrote "a little note at the bottom saying 'You trust the lecturer too much. . . .' Empson was then in the process of working on his book *The Structure of Complex Words* (1951). Many of the chapters of that book he offered as lectures. It was wonderful."[61] He also met the man who would become his champion for years after he left Ohio—Allen Tate. Tate was Ransom's oldest student and near enough in age and accomplishment to be seen as more of a peer. Where Ransom was courtly, Tate was headstrong and brash. His actual head, with a wide, expansive brow, was strikingly large. "I recall that huge cranium, suspended in the air above a limp seersucker suit, like a gathered thunderhead in the summer heat": this was how he looked to Hecht at Kenyon that July.[62] His reputation as a firebrand notwithstanding, Hecht found him to be kind and solicitous, appealingly "ironic" and "always gentlemanly."[63]

Hecht made a strong impression on Tate (who had previously encouraged Lowell, even letting him camp out in a tent on his lawn in Tennessee), and their paths crossed again in New York City, a few months later. Hecht arranged to study with him after his return to New York and took a place within walking distance of where Tate taught at NYU. He met with Tate once a week to discuss his poems at the West Village apartment he shared with his wife Caroline Gordon: "Tate was always the soul of courtesy. He was a very courteous man. He lived in the Village on Perry Street, and I used to find him playing the violin when I came in. He didn't practice enough, but it was nice to hear him playing unaccompanied Bach violin partitas."[64] Tate became a mentor and a model and eventually a friend. Hecht admired him both as an artist and a man. He sensed in him "a fierce and relentless moral passion that is to be seen under other governing conditions in his poetry."[65] Hecht wrote prolifically under his tutelage, sometimes several poems a week.

He remembered one exchange in particular, about his poem "Christmas Is Coming," which Geoffrey Lindsay sees as resonating—with its repeated line "Darkness is for the poor"[66]—with the extreme poverty Hecht saw in Japan. Hecht could be brutal when it came to appraising his own juvenilia:

> The poem floats in some region between raw fact, dream, and parable, in what in the end seems to me a soft impalpable blur. Allen Tate, when I showed the poem to him in draft, asked, "Who are the poor?" I don't know what he meant by the question, whether he was inquiring into my knowledge of a class to which I could not claim to belong, whether I was "affecting" to be one of the unemployed, or whatever. When I answered quite innocently, "Why, we all are," he was utterly silent and without comment.

Hecht floored the Catholic convert Tate with this bit of Christian theology. He later felt that "the sense that I was writing (among other things) a universal allegory is something that to me gravely weakens the poem."[67] After several weeks together, Hecht began to discern Tate's method:

> I came to see that he was telling me about the way a poem's total design is modulated and given its energy, not by local ingredients tastefully combined, but by the richness, toughness and density of some sustaining vision of life—sustaining, at least, throughout the world of the poem, and perhaps with some resonance to it after the poem is done. . . . And what I learned from our conversations was reinforced by my reading of his poems—which we never discussed. It is the sort of lesson one can grasp by intuition and then by the intelligence, and see reaffirmed again and again in every good poem one reads. It is harder to get one's own poems to do it, and I have been working on this ever since.[68]

Tate's comments on Hecht's poems were tactful and generous: "He was very kind to me, and when he got a job teaching in Minnesota, and wanted to leave, he recommended me to take over his teaching job at NYU."[69] After class, Hecht would hang out in the cafés on Bleecker Street or at the Knickerbocker, with live jazz piano, just north of Washington

Square Park. Well in his cups, he'd return to the cold-water flat he shared with Robie and scratch away at a war novel that he had begun working on. Hecht's attempt to write about the war in prose, like his earliest poems on the subject, "didn't pan out."[70] Macauley's stories of the war from this time and after were widely praised by Ransom, Taylor, O'Connor, and Engle—blurbs by these luminaries adorned the cover of *The End of Pity and Other Stories,* when it appeared a decade later. By contrast, Hecht was struggling, squeaking by on a meager stipend, while Robie embarked on an editing job at *Gourmet.* A parade of Robie's friends stopped by whenever they were in town: Lowell and his wife Jean Stafford; John Thompson, who had lived in the writers' house at Kenyon, and others. Flannery O'Connor visited the Lowells in New York that winter, and it's likely that Hecht saw her then.

Hecht felt the precariousness of his situation. Two longer poems came out that fall in *The Kenyon Review:* the symbolist "Fugue for One Voice," whose inner monologue foreshadows poems like "Green: An Epistle," and which Hecht included in his first collection, *A Summoning of Stones* (1954); and "The Private Eye: A Detective Story," which he chose not to collect. Through indirection he hints at his own unease:

> *Monstrous guilt has shrunken into clues*
> *As thin as hair, unstable as an ash,*
> *And unobtrusive as lovers' rendezvous*
> *Or the slight rise of pimples in a rash.*
> *   And the unskilled in crime will let it pass*
> *   As a praying mantis is taken to be grass.*[71]

His own residual guilt from combat—of refusing to fire, of surviving while friends were blown up—was hidden from sight. He alone knew what he went through. His attempts to discuss this with his analyst, whom he took up with again upon his return to the city, largely went amiss, as they plumbed the shadows from his childhood and intimations from his dreams.

The teaching at least was going well: "Like many young teachers, I found it easy to establish a rapport with students not much younger than myself. And I was truly ignited by my subject—that is," he added, "if it

was canonical poetry and literature, as distinguished from the poems written by students."[72] But filling in for Tate at NYU was not a renewable position, and, as the spring of 1949 wore on, the question of what he would do
next loomed. Living with Robie was exciting to be sure, and the revolving
door of literary friends, such as the Lowells, kept life from losing its fizz.
But that arrangement, too, was not a renewable situation, at least not
indefinitely, and when the two friends parted in June, they were never so
close again. With his doctor's approval, Hecht made a move that shaped
the next decade of his life: he sailed for Europe.

FIVE

ITALIAN JOURNEY
(1949–1951)

Just as foretold, it all was there.
Bone china columns gently fluted
Among the cypress groves, and the reputed
Clarity of the air . . .[1]

1. "The most beautiful sight in the world . . ."[2]

Coming into land after more than a week at sea is stirring, particularly so in the wee hours of the morning. Fueled by martinis and lively company, Hecht stayed up all night to witness it. With money saved from his years in the service, he bought a ticket for France and packed his things, including "1 Typewriter," as he later declared to customs. At nautical dawn, with the sun still down, there was a lightening. In near dark, the horizon emerged. Harbor lights marked the thin line of the coast, and the smell of land reached far out to sea. Hecht watched from the bow of a transatlantic steamer as Le Havre loomed into view, a sliver of sun painting the coast of France crimson. A horn announced their arrival: "Came tooting in at about 4 in the morning . . . lights on the water, sky red in the East, blending to ultra-marine just above, very clear, stars all over the goddammed place."[3]

The crossing set the tone for the trip. Steamers of this era featured lavish meals and entertainments, such as costume parties and dancing. Tony and his friend Al Millet, who had suggested the trip, had a high time on board, immediately receiving an invitation through a friend of Al's to drink in the first-class bar: "It is the bar, it is the drink that girds; / Fluid the cause *finalis* of the grape. / Nothing in transit need be done by thirds," he joked in a poem about the journey.[4] On consecutive evenings the two were lavished with caviar on melba toast with chopped egg. They acquired sunburns in the pool, and ate vast amounts, to the astonishment of their disapproving waiter; to tweak him, they ended the trip with "two complete breakfasts, (including creamed chicken and eggs & bacon) before leaving ship in France."[5]

Aboard, Hecht enjoyed the company of a "sculptor friend" of Al's, whom the scholar Jonathan Post (who edited Hecht's letters) identifies as the sculptor Ivan Majdrakoff, the dedicatee of Hecht's shipboard poem, "Seascape with Figures." Majdrakoff's wife, Julia Pearl, a painter, occasioned "A Poem for Julia," which engages works by Hans Memling, Michelangelo, and others. The two poems together illustrate Hecht's psychic movement in his poems away from New York and toward Europe, with its masterpieces of painting and architecture. It was a release into a new freedom, from the old freedom embodied in "Seascape" by the Statue of Liberty, which the passengers leave behind in New York Harbor:

> What, then, is freedom? Merely to be free
> Is nothing. On the seventh day the lights
> Of France's harbor flecked the orchid gloom
> Of early morning, doubled again their glow
> Upon the Channel waters. Raging spume
> Departed from us.[6]

By the time they arrived on "the seventh day," the rage that had been churning in the waters around them had departed. (In fact, the ship encountered a two-day gale that sent some of the passengers to the rail with seasickness: "The sea went black with wrath and there were groans / More sounding than the cold Aeolian gale / Plucked in our rigging.")[7] The poem depicts France as a place of beauty and spectacle.

On shore, the town buzzed with activity: "All the Frenchmen came out in their blue denims and berets and bicycles." The last time he made this harbor, he arrived by troop ship, and part of his elation now was the striking ways that ordinary life had reclaimed the city. He was relieved to be away from New York, referring to the trip in the poem as an "escape."[8] In many ways, Hecht was on the cusp of true independence, apart from Robie and increasingly apart from Roger and their parents, though his family would remain in regular correspondence with him for the next few years. Writing to them was easier than navigating their moods and quiet tensions in person, and he kept up his regular reports.

Roger, having announced his own poetic ambitions, proved a diligent literary secretary, managing Tony's correspondence with editors and magazines while he was abroad. In his letters home, Tony remained the dutiful son and clearly relied on his parents' letters (and subsidies) for support. Still, at twenty-six, he needed sufficient distance to perform a delicate and important negotiation—to begin to live fully as a poet. Like so many former GIs in those years, he returned to the Old World "for pleasure after having to fight a war there." Not surprisingly, he had "no desire whatever" to follow his earlier "movements or revisit Germany."[9] He headed first to Paris.

The typewriter Hecht brought was a talisman. Hecht was not traveling as a tourist but as a writer. In Paris, though he kept a hand in, it seems unlikely that much work got done amidst the whirl of social engagements—long hours in cafés over drinks, dinners out, and a network of American friends and acquaintances to visit. Hecht may not have realized it at the time, but he was part of a wave of Americans heading to Europe. His future colleague at Bard College, Saul Bellow, traveled there a year after the fighting ceased:

> The blasts of war had no sooner ended than thousands of Americans packed their bags to go abroad . . . poets, painters, and philosophers . . . students of art history, cathedral lovers, refugees from the South and Midwest, ex-soldiers on the GI Bill, sentimental pilgrims . . . adventurers, black-marketeers, smugglers, would-be *bon vivants*, bargain-hunters, bubbleheads—tens of thousands crossed on old troop ships, seeking business opportunities or sexual opportunities, or just for the hell of it.[10]

As Hecht walked along the Champs-Élysées or Boul'Mich, he searched for what remained of the golden age of the Lost Generation. When the four-year occupation of Paris ended in August of 1944, it seemed hard to imagine that the city could regain its former glory as a center for artistic and intellectual life. The jails held collaborationists awaiting trial, and the intelligentsia called for the "fair punishment of the impostors and traitors."[11] To Hecht and his set, though, the streets and cafés of Saint-Germain-des-Prés looked much as they had before the war. Simone de Beauvoir proclaimed that Paris endured as a center of infinite possibility for writers and painters. The presses kept rolling as a new generation emerged from the periphery to enliven the scene.

Hecht had recovered well from the breakdown that sent him back home to New York from Iowa—at least by most outward indications. Shortly after arriving in Paris, he attended the engagement party of Ernest Hemingway's son Jack, but begged off attending the wedding. Instead, he holed up at the Hotel d'Islay and wrote to his parents of the crossing he had made. Hecht settled into the cafés, chain-smoking and jotting in his notebook. He relished his newfound freedom and the social whirl going on around him. He had infinite leisure to wander the great palaces of art and the lamp-lit streets of the Latin Quarter. He drifted alone, in a kind of self-imposed exile.

In early August, he asked his parents to check the proofs for two poems that were about to appear in *The Hudson Review*. He had landed his first poems in the *Hudson* earlier that year, and it soon became a mainstay. He was waiting on news from Columbia University, where he had applied for the master's program in English. He hadn't yet decided on teaching as a career, but he was weighing it. Not long after, Dorothea wrote to let him know that he'd been accepted. It was a relief that he had Columbia to look forward to at the end of the summer, and it was also a relief that summer was not yet over. He relished his time abroad and wished to draw out the feeling of liberty that it instilled.

Other American poets were traveling or living abroad that summer—Robert Lowell, John Ashbery, W. S. Merwin, Adrienne Rich, James Merrill. Hecht's fourth-floor walkup at La Villa Saint Germain des Prés, at 29 Rue Jacob, was a stone's throw from Les Deux Magots. He sunbathed shirtless on the banks of the Seine, read Proust, and ate Duck à l'Orange at midnight down the avenue from the Arc de Triomphe. He met old friends and made new ones, including a girl that he fell for with uncharacteristic excitement. Usually cautious when it came to romance, here he adopted a new exuberant tone, though things never got too serious: "We have fallen in love with each other, though not deeply." Her name was Cici Grace, a twenty-two-year-old model and a recent graduate of Smith College. She was "extremely beautiful," so striking that she had already attracted another young admirer.

This would-be rival "was a hulking sort of a guy, with a Charles Atlas torso, of which he was obviously proud, and wore a tight-fitting cerise T-shirt with almost no sleeves to show himself off to best advantage."[12] His name was Marlon Brando, and he had come to Europe chasing movie roles. Brando had played Stanley in the Broadway premiere of *A Streetcar Named Desire* two years earlier but was yet to make his name in films. Now a soft-spoken twenty-five, with longish hair curled at the temples, he slumped in his chair, issuing the occasional grunt. Cici was flirty with Brando, but she preferred Hecht's more refined company. Hecht and Cici began spending long days together, during which they "wandered about the city, sat in the parks and made [chaste] love."[13] When Cici returned from a modeling trip for *Vogue*, the two headed off to Brittany together, where they swam and drank bottles of wine on the beach. Hecht, far from having a type, was yet to engage in a serious relationship with a woman.

Hecht took Cici to *Cyrano* at the Comédie Francaise, where the beau monde filled the stalls in glittering regalia. It was

one of the most vigorous theatrical performances I'd ever seen. Raymond Duncan, Isadora's brother was in the audience in his familiar Greek get-up, toga, sandals, and a band about his forehead. He also wears spectacles, which destroys the effect a bit. The remarkable thing about Paris, however, is that he is not the subject of astonishment or even much notice.[14]

Hecht's French was good, and he followed the verse of Edmond Rostand's play without difficulty. (He later translated poems by a number of French poets, including Rostand and Baudelaire.) At this point, Al had left on a trip to Sweden, and Hecht reconnected with a friend from the CIC, Paul Henissart.[15] Paul helped hatch a plan to travel to the south, stopping in the Alps on their way back to Paris. They never made it there. Instead, they wound up in the magical city of Venice.

2. "An extraordinarily lucky choice"[16]

Hecht found Venice astonishing. His first experience of the Grand Canal and its palazzi inspired an outpouring of detail in a letter to his parents written in mid-August:

> Whenever I come to Europe again I am determined to come here. It is the only European city I have seen, besides Paris, that has a distinctive and individual character and atmosphere all its own, and in some ways, though certainly not in all, it is more charming . . . [T]he buildings are all in delicate pastel colors, deep grape reds, olive yellows, and even the least imposing of them has a charm and loveliness. And the large palaces, like the Doge's, are light in feeling and color, being made for the most part of Greek and Italian marble, sometimes streaked, and sometimes of white porphyry. There is a greater variety of architectural style, including Byzantine (as in St. Mark's Cathedral), Romanesque, Moorish, Gothic and Baroque. . . . There are no real vistas in Venice. Both the streets and the canals are devious, and therefore, because one sees much less of it at a glance, it has a much more intimate feeling. . . . One evening, as we were walking home to supper by way of the Piazza, an orchestra at one of the chic cafés in that area was playing *Eine kleine Nachtmusik*. The effect was indescribable. Even in Paris one cannot stand in the most beautiful part of town with a view of the sea at sunset, and listen to Mozart.[17]

His description is like a self-portrait of his sensibility in miniature: the detailed knowledge of architecture, the interplay of light, the airy strains of Mozart (to whom he nods with his baroque vision of innocence regained in "A Lot of Night Music"). He attended an exhibition in the Doge's Palace of paintings by Giovanni Bellini, who immediately became one of his favorite artists.[18] In his poem "The Venetian Vespers," the speaker describes a view near the mouth of the Grand Canal that Hecht would return to as often as he could throughout his life, with San Giorgio Maggiore across the water and the Basilica di Santa Maria della Salute in the foreground:[19]

Lights. I have chosen Venice for its light,
Its lightness, buoyancy, its calm suspension
In time and water, its strange quietness.
I, an expatriate American,
Living off an annuity, confront
The lagoon's waters in mid-morning sun.
Palladio's church floats at its anchored peace
Across from me, and the great church of Health,
Voted in gratitude by the Venetians
For heavenly deliverance from the plague,
Voluted, levels itself on the canal.
Further away the bevels coil and join
Like spiraled cordon ropes of silk, the lips
Of the crimped water sped by a light breeze.
Morning has tooled the bay with bright inlays
Of writhing silver, scattered scintillance.
These little crests and ripples promenade,
Hurried and jocular and never bored,
Ils se promènent like families of some means
On Sundays in the Bois. Observing this
easy festivity, hypnotized by
Tiny sun-signals exchanged across the harbor,
I am for the moment cured of everything . . .[20]

The portrait of Venice in "Vespers" is of a city and a psyche in decay. Ruskin, quoted in the epigraph, understood the faded glory of the place, but the promise of a momentary "cure," if only as a fleeting respite, is at the heart of the poem and Hecht's love of the place. In later years, and especially after his retirement from teaching, he made an annual pilgrimage to feel again this illusive promise, the promise of wellness as celebrated by Salute itself. Though he came to depict the dark side of Venice in "Vespers," his initial impressions of Italy were infused with awe:

The first effect was really quite like being in love. I was overwhelmed by the majesty and beauty of the place, the beauty of the landscape, quite simply. It took a long time to digest. Many of the things I saw and admired and liked were still as fresh in my mind when I got back to America. I was able to write about them then at a distance without the presence of them which was rather too great. . . .[21]

Completely smitten and vowing to return, Hecht boarded the Orient Express for Paris, where he continued his moveable feast of art and music, attending a concert of the 4th Brandenburg Concerto and taking in an exhibit of Gauguin. The Paris museums, which he had glimpsed as a boy, now drew him with adult ardor. In out-of-the-way shops, he sifted through prints and acquired a few fine pieces on the cheap. His training in art at Bard and Kenyon bolstered his knowledge of a range of media: "We went around to a little art shop that had been recommended to me, and started looking though portfolio after portfolio of etchings, lithographs, woodcuts, dry-points, and water colors of a tremendous and catholic variety of artists." Returning to the shop the next day, he made some admirable selections: "I was able to narrow things down to three prints— 2 Rouaults and a Braque. The Braque was an original signed wood-cut in three colors, limited to 50 copies, of which I had the 40th. The Rouaults were black and white, unnumbered and unsigned. The main thing, however, was that the whole thing came to 50,000 francs, or about $140."[22]

Likewise, he combed the bookshops, stopping at one point in Librairie Galignani at 224 Rue du Rivoli—the shop is still there today—where he acquired a bilingual copy of *Ballades* by François Villon, with translations by Rossetti, Swinburne, Richard Aldington, and others. The most striking feature of this little volume was the fifteenth-century French line engravings that accompanied the poems, very like the poem-etching pairings Hecht would later concoct with the artist Leonard Baskin. All of these—the prints and the poems—Hecht kept for the rest of his life, as mementoes of the new self he was creating, a poet steeped in Continental history and art.

In mid-September, with these artifacts and his typewriter in tow, he left Paris for Cherbourg, where he met the RMS *Queen Elizabeth*. In just over a week, he would be back with his parents and enrolled at Columbia. The intervening school year passed quickly; it was hardly enough time to fully immerse himself in the culture of young intellectuals and writers in Philosophy Hall. In the grand Italianate McKim, Mead & White buildings on 116th Street, he attended Mark Van Doren's famous poetry class and nestled into cubicles in the Neoclassical Butler Library, added to campus between the wars.

The most talented student poets at Columbia were slightly younger than Hecht, and though he came to know them subsequently—a number became close friends—their paths didn't cross at the time. Van Doren was a common thread: he attracted the precocious literary students, teaching undergraduates and graduate students alike, though they remained essentially separate circles. Among the undergraduates was the poet John Hollander, of Eastern European Jewish descent. Hollander's memory of that time does not mention Hecht:

> Most of my classmates at Columbia then were veterans several years older than myself, and they educated me as much as my teachers. Louis Simpson, Daniel Hoffman, Allen Ginsberg, all somewhat older than I was, were all writing poems of what seemed to be vast sophistication; and in 1949 I met Richard Howard, whose talent and literary energies seemed prodigious.[23]

Ginsberg and Hollander became close friends and brothers in the art, though their later styles—beatnik and traditionalist, respectively—could not have been more different. And though they never became close, Hecht liked Ginsberg as well.[24] The intellectually impressive Richard Howard, eventually known for his ventriloquizing dramatic monologues, remembered meeting Hecht in Morningside Heights, and Hecht became something of a model for Howard. Hecht's graduate study in English inspired Howard to do the same. After completing his undergraduate degree, Howard stayed on at Columbia, following Hecht's lead.[25] To these aspiring poets, the faculty, of course, were giants:

> Mark Van Doren was a crucial presence for those of us writing verse, a presence itself fabulous to the degree that precept and example were interwoven in it. Also, Lionel Trilling, Jacques Barzun, Moses Hadas, Meyer Schapiro, the legendary [Shakespearean] Andrew Chiappe— these were some of the teachers who mattered most to the minority of undergraduates in those days of a literary inclination.[26]

Hollander met Hecht at a party in New York, a meeting which Hollander described as dazzling: "I was tremendously impressed by his playing by ear a Scarlatti sonata."[27] Not only was Hecht in his late twenties and a veteran of the war, he was also an established poet. His recent appearances in *The Kenyon Review* and *Furioso* were noted by fellow poets, and he had become a regular of *The Hudson Review*. The Spring issue featured two longer poems, "As Plato Said" and "Japan"; the Fall issue, just out when he arrived at Columbia, contained the multi-part "Songs for the Air, or Several Attitudes about Breathing" and "The Place of Pain in the Universe." These were the fruits of his sessions with Tate, though one hears echoes of other early masters as well. There were Yeats and Stevens as usual, and Auden's influence was becoming increasingly pronounced.[28]

Throughout that fall and into the spring, Hecht attended conscientiously to his studies. The return home, while providing the initial comfort of familiarity, was no long-term answer. In many ways, being under his parents' roof again only made matters worse. New York, in its vastness, provided a kind of anonymity, an opportunity to hide out. Hecht could easily surround himself, in his darker moods, with anonymous drinking companions in bars under the Third Avenue El. He avoided old attachments, finding it difficult to talk with school friends of what he had been through and seen in recent years. Like so many veterans of the war, he avoided speaking of it in social settings. His sessions with his psychiatrist, which continued as before, provided an outlet but no cure for his post-traumatic anxiety.

The main product of his year at Columbia was an eighty-five-page thesis, "submitted in partial fulfillment of the requirements for the degree of Master of Arts, Faculty of Philosophy," titled "Poetry as a Form of Knowledge." Much in the way his youthful poetry showed his influences, his first substantial piece of critical prose owed a debt to some of the same predecessors, namely Ransom, Tate, and other New Critics: "When I first became an avid student of modern poetry and of the few brilliant critics who brought it to life for an inexperienced reader," he later wrote to Hollander, "there was a set of books that were to me almost as valuable as the books of poetry upon which they offered comment. These included *Form and Value in Modern Poetry*, *The Expense of Greatness*, and *The Double Agent*, all by Blackmur; *Axel's Castle* by Wilson, and *In Defense of Reason*, by Winters. Later others, Empson especially, became indispensable."[29]

While Hecht could occasionally be coy about his models, he was completely upfront about his debt to these critics: they "helped me form such critical faculties as I have," he explained with a mixture of modesty and pride.[30] Eliot's "Tradition and the Individual Talent," "From Poe to Valéry," and "The Music of Poetry," Blackmur's *The Double Agent*, Empson's *Seven Types of Ambiguity*, Graves's *The White Goddess*, Brooks's *The Well-Wrought Urn*, and works by Stanley Edgar Hyman and I. A. Richards all serve to bolster Hecht's arguments in his master's thesis about the nature of lyric poetry. There is a sense of urgency, of up-to-the-minute critical debate in Hecht's treatise, expressed in a somewhat breezy, belletristic tone. A number of works Hecht cites appeared in *Kenyon* and *Hudson* only months before. He aligned himself with this literary school.

A bellwether of the New Criticism, Tate was clearly the greatest inspiration for "Poetry as a Form of Knowledge." Hecht quotes liberally from Tate's *On the Limits of Poetry*, a collection of essays that had appeared the previous year. Tate's book contained an essay from 1941, originally printed in *The Southern Review*, titled "Literature as Knowledge," which became a jumping-off point for Hecht's own thoughts on the subject. His argument is also in colloquy with Tate's essays "Three Types of Poetry" (Hecht does one better by outlining four types) and "Understanding Modern Poetry," also from this most recent collection of his essays.

Hecht expands on Tate's observations regarding the rational or scientific approach to literature, lately explored in the writings of Charles W. Morris: "We do not need to reject the positive rational mode of inquiry into poetry," Tate writes; "yet even from Mr. Morris we get the warning lest we substitute the criticism for the poem itself, and thus commit ourselves to a 'learned ignorance.' We must return to, we must never leave, the poem itself. Its 'interest' value is a cognitive one; it is sufficient that here, in the poem, we get knowledge of a whole object."[31] After some elaborate hair-splitting taxonomies, Hecht arrives in the end at a fairly straightforward New Critical view of poetry as expressive of a particular kind of "knowledge," at once beyond but not opposed to scientific knowledge:

If knowledge is capable of being expressed in language, then poetry is the most perfect expression. Words are wild and fugitive, often more powerful than we give them credit for being, and certainly older than people who use them; they are entitled to respect according to their age, their ancestry, and the width and wealth of their experience, and in return for our diligence in this matter, they may be as informative as those distinguished and wise old men, the sages and philosophers.[32]

He enjoyed trying on this new mode, even as he laid claim to his own "school" or lineage. The writers and magazines with which he had recently become associated became badges of his nascent identity as a writer. He found himself, at twenty-seven, in excellent company appearing in highly reputed venues beside leading poets of the age, becoming indeed "a child of the New Criticism." This was not only the way in which he thought of himself (or even positioned himself); it was how others saw him as well.

Columbia was a success, but the threat of failure, as embodied by his father's personal and professional defeats, was never far from his mind, especially during this year in New York. He had a powerful need to succeed in his writing and later in his teaching career, though his main ambition was always for his poems. He kept an eye on worldly success, and never let it slip away for long. But now he had reached a juncture. His master's thesis was written and his degree from Columbia was complete. His next step was not toward a safe haven in teaching but toward an escape into the unknown. He had been thinking of his recent trip abroad all year, and particularly of his time in Venice. As he pondered his options, he might walk to the Frick Collection on East 70th Street, a few blocks down Madison Avenue from his parents' apartment. There he would stand in front of Bellini's large canvas of St. Francis and recall the show he had seen at the Doge's Palace, capturing the moment in a poem called "Anniversary" (later retitled "At the Frick"). Of the Italian landscape, he writes in characteristic blank verse: "it was here he caught / Holiness that came swimming like a school / Of silver fishes to out-flash his lusts," adding that "Now I have seen these mountains." The "anniversary" of the title refers to "The warm Italian winds of one more year" since he stood in St. Mark's Square. The poem appeared that summer,

along with two others, in *The Hudson Review*, with Confucius translations by Ezra Pound, an essay on Lionel Trilling (his former teacher)
by R. W. B. Lewis, and a verse play by Christopher Fry. Though his
thoughts kept crossing the Atlantic, he was slow to commit to another
trip abroad. He required a bit of coaxing, but his army buddy Al Millet
persuaded him.

Millet was living in Amsterdam, courting a Dutch girl there, and he
wrote to Hecht that he had room for him to come and stay. Al was a
painter who had recently studied at the prestigious Cranbrook Academy
of Art in Michigan, not far from where his affluent family lived in Grosse
Pointe. He kept at his painting while traveling, renting a dingy studio in
Amsterdam with room enough for Hecht to set up his typewriter. Hecht
balked at the invitation, complaining of a painful appendix, which Al later
dubbed "psyco-somatic."[33] Finally, he decided, he could afford to get away
for a vacation, living cheaply with Al for the summer. Besides, they had
had a fine (and bibulous) trip together the summer before. There would
be time enough in the fall to make a long-term plan. Hecht plotted his
escape, once again arranging for passage abroad by steamer. Perhaps it
was reading Joyce's *A Portrait of the Artist as a Young Man*, quoted that
spring in his thesis, that inspired him to embrace those Dedalean attri-
butes: silence, exile, cunning. Exactly as he had the summer prior, Hecht
embraced his solitude. He boarded a transatlantic steamer out of New
York Harbor bound for Le Havre. By late July he was back in Paris.

3. Auden in the Mezzogiorno

Having only just arrived in Paris in the fall of 1950, Hecht was already eyeing a trip to Amsterdam to meet up with Al. The rooms
at the d'Islay had nearly doubled in price since the previous summer, but
Hecht's friends from Kenyon, Oscar Williams and his wife, Polly, put
him up in their apartment at 15 Rue de l'Estrapade, not far from the
Pantheon. (This Oscar Williams should not be confused with Oscar Williams, né Oscar Kaplan, the poet and anthologist, who took an interest in
Hecht's work around this time and included him in several popular and
reputation-boosting anthologies.)[34] Hecht's schooling was done; his life

as a writer lay before him; he was happy to turn from academics to his burgeoning career as a poet.

While in Paris, he met Mira Jedwabnik, a friend of Al's from art school, whose family had left Vilna, Poland, for New York just before the war, when Mira was ten. The family was halfway across the Atlantic, on the way to the World's Fair, when the war broke out and they were unable to return home—an extraordinary bit of good fortune as it turned out. Mira had family in Paris and felt at home there. She was younger than Hecht, though worldly and confident. They dated casually, and Hecht's interest ultimately waned. When Hecht headed to Amsterdam, Mira headed home to New York. The two continued to correspond, as friends. A few years later she would marry John Van Doren, the son of Mark, with whom Hecht had studied at Columbia. During their time together, Mira could sense that Hecht was deeply troubled. She knew that he had been in the war, though he never spoke of it. It was clear to her that he had suffered horribly and continued to suffer, though he was too proud to show it.[35] He masked his upset with drink and even one hilarious prank in which he and the Williamses rode the Metro in elaborate getups, with gloves, bow ties, and wigs: Oscar's looked like Olivier's in the film of *Henry V* and Hecht "had one with a bald pate, and blond hair around the edges down to the shoulders."[36] Oscar carried a copy of *Pravda* and Hecht the complete works of Molière, to the astonishment of the other passengers. After a time, mainly because the Williamses had no money, Hecht's stay caused them something of a strain. They were not sorry to see him go, according to Mira.

Arriving in early August at Al's place in the Netherlands, Hecht settled into the small rooms. Amsterdam was "charming" but, like his situation with Al, a bit squalid, having, he later wrote to Richard Wilbur, "more dog turds on its streets and sidewalks than any other place I have ever been to. The city was redeemed largely by its people, who are very agreeable, its good cigars and gin."[37] Al's rooms were tiny, with only a few sticks of furniture and a bath next door, but "enough room for us to work," he assured Hecht.[38] When Al's engagement bogged down, he and Hecht looked for a temporary escape. They searched around for even cheaper accommodations, if that were possible, and wound up going very far afield. A newspaper ad led them to Italy and the remote island of Ischia in the Bay of

Naples, where they decided on the port village of Forio on the windward side of the island.

They rented "half a palazzo" in a poor neighborhood, just up the hill out of town. Forio's cheap rents and languid lifestyle had recently lured another poet, W. H. Auden, who had been estivating on the island since the spring of 1948. Auden took to the place immediately, composing in his first weeks there one of his best poems, "In Praise of Limestone." Hecht likely knew the poem from its appearance that summer in *Horizon,* a magazine he had been following, along with *Partisan Review,* since Bard. Auden's essayistic poem of the Italian landscape became one of Hecht's favorites. Its "posture of mind which lies very conspicuously behind the idea of the *paysage moralisé*" provided an invaluable model for his own landscape poems.[39] Hecht quickly picked up from the locals that the famous poet could be glimpsed in the town square in the afternoons. Still, it would be several months before they met, and only after friends arranged it.

Hecht's trip down to Ischia had been a Grand Tour in itself. He cashed in his return steamer ticket and packed his typewriter and fishing rod for the adventure. Al had picked up an old car in London and brought it back to Holland. By mid-October, the two were winding their way south, making numerous stops along the way, including Orléans, Limoges, Toulouse, Carcassone ("which has a magnificent walled city within it, turreted, crenelated, fortified to beat Hell"), Montpellier, Arles, Avignon, Marseilles, St. Tropez, Cannes, and Nice. They fished for trout in Uzerche, a place recommended by expert fishermen in Paris. Hecht's fine bamboo rod looked impressively Hemingwayesque, but he "got nothing at all" in terms of fish. Monte Carlo was abuzz with the wedding of Errol Flynn, and Hecht won 3,500 francs at the craps table. The nights were thoroughly wine-soaked and the days Edenic: "Down here along the coast, flowers are in bloom, vines with large lavender blossoms, trees with brilliant red flowers on them, palm trees, cactus, cedar, olive, lemon and Cyprus trees."[40]

After stopovers in Florence and Rome, they arrived in Naples by the end of the month and boarded the ferry to the island. Off the port side they passed Capri, and on the starboard side Procida and tiny Vivara.

Behind them Vesuvius towered impressively over the port. There was a "dream-like feeling in Italy" that overtook them as soon as they crossed from the Côte d'Azur to the Golfo Paradiso. Across "the Alban Hills, the Apennines, the pines, the ilex and laurel all suddenly appeared, like props from the background of Renaissance Italian paintings, known to me through reproductions and visits to select American museums."[41]

The island itself was a natural paradise. At its center was a volcano, Mount Epomeo (possibly from the Greek meaning "place with a wide view"), and the subterranean heat it generated gave rise to scalding hot springs that seeped out along the rocky shore into the Tyrrhenian Sea. After his first weeks there, Hecht wrote to Richard Wilbur about the riches of the island: "It's sort of primitive but pleasant here; the weather is rather raw just now, but winter ends in February. Pomegranates, figs, dates, tremendous quantities of grapes (very good local wine), good cheeses, and tiny, brilliantly red tomatoes, the size of ping-pong balls. Lots of olive and palm trees, flowers, especially some strange vine with a violet purple blossom, are still in bloom."[42]

He and Wilbur had recently appeared together in the September issue of *Poetry,* and an admiring note from Wilbur found its way to Forio, along with a copy of the magazine. Wilbur had praised Hecht's "To Phyllis" and "Alceste in the Wilderness" (which ran with an explanatory note, at the urging of the editor Karl Shapiro, about the character from Molière's *The Misanthrope*). In return, Hecht lavished special praise on Wilbur's "Castles and Distances" and "'A World Without Objects Is a Sensible Emptiness'" (with its title adapted from the 17th-century poet Thomas Traherne). Wilbur was well established. His first book had appeared just after the war, while Hecht's would be another four years in the making. Despite Wilbur's head start, the two poets became linked in the eyes of many readers and critics for their shared affinity for high formality. Their voices became more individual as they matured, but there was an obvious stylistic similarity in their early poems.

Ischia in 1950 was rustic and dauntingly remote. Contact with the larger world depended on the ferry to Naples, which might be canceled whenever the weather grew threatening. Return mail from the United States to Ischia took several weeks by ship, and airmail more than a week. Telephones were scarce. But Hecht found this isolation a tonic, relishing, exactly as the Romans had, the salutary effects of the volcanic hot springs. One could soak for long hours, even in the coldest months:

> Romans, rheumatic, gouty, came
>> To bathe in Ischian springs where water steamed,
> puffed and enlarged their bold imperial thoughts, and which
> Later Madame Curie declared to be so rich
>> In radioactive content as she deemed
>> Should win them everlasting fame.[43]

"La Condition Botanique," which Hecht composed that winter, was his poem in praise of "what is called The Life," that is, The Good Life, the Life of Riley, before a haunting image of war intrudes on the scene: "young men in a mud-colored file / March to the summit of their lives, // . . . till they fall in blood / And are returned at last unto their native mud."[44] *Et in Arcadia ego*: even in Paradise, Hecht found death lurking in the landscape; the "condition" of peace in nature to which the poem aspires becomes "our Fool's Paradise."[45]

He took solace in the healing waters. Hecht liked the fact that Ibsen had come there to write, and Toscanini "still took the cure." He admired the handsome houses of Prince Enrico d'Assia, heir to the Italian throne, and, even grander, of the British composer Sir William Walton. He soon fell in with a small crowd of fellow "nameless Americans," a circle of Jewish artists and intellectuals, a few of whom were friends with Auden and his partner, Chester Kallman. The Weisses, Irving and Anne, were closest with Auden. The pair are commemorated in the dedications to two of Auden's poems from *About the House*—"Down There," regarding the cellar (Irving) and "Up There," regarding the attic (Anne). When Auden's libretto for *The Magic Flute,* co-written with Kallman, appeared five years later, it carried a dedication to the Weisses.

Hecht's closest friends in Ischia were the Rosenthals, New Yorkers who had come to live in Italy. Hecht apprised his parents:

> Have met two sorts of "literary" Americans here on the island—that is to say they are in the "literary swim." Name of Raymond Rosenthal and his wife, Elsa. He is writing a novel, has worked as an editor on

"Commentary," a Jewish intellectual quarterly, is a Marxist turned mystic. She studied at the State University of Iowa at the time Leonard Unger and Austin Warren were there.[46]

Elsa, called Elsie, grew up in Brooklyn, where she was a childhood friend of Chester Kallman. She remembered being with Chester the night he met Auden for the first time, at the Poetry Center of the 92nd Street Y on Lexington Avenue. She and Chester were close, and she was made rather jealous when Chester began shifting his attention to Auden after that night. Ray Rosenthal had recently come from Rome, where he'd been studying film in the directors' program at the newly reopened Cinecittà. Still, he was more interested in literature than film. The three had a striking amount in common. After studying at the University of Iowa, Elsa went on to Columbia, just missing Hecht in both places. The two knew a number of professors in common. Ray had been in the war. Like Hecht, he was infantry, and he fought in Italy, in Salerno. He, too, suffered from PTSD. The two men had an unspoken understanding. The Rosenthals' marriage was beginning to falter, and Elsa turned to Hecht with increasing affection, which he gratefully returned. Though it was never acted on, the two felt a kind of love for each other.

Hecht never pressed for it—on the contrary, he must have avoided it to some extent—but eventually an introduction to Auden was made, through Elsa. He already had a great admiration for the older poet, having discovered him as a teenager, counting him alongside the poets that Larry Leighton had introduced him to at Bard, namely Frost, Stevens, Eliot, Pound, Ransom, and Tate. Leighton may well have introduced Hecht to Auden's poems, but once he'd read them the "impetus"[47] was entirely his. Hecht wrote in *The Harvard Advocate*'s memorial issue for Auden that the interest in his work "was mine and was vigorous and constant."[48] Discovering Auden was an event that stuck in his mind:

> I bought his first volume, *Poems*, second-hand (all I could afford) at the Gotham Book Mart [in New York City] in 1940 (it had appeared in this country in 1939); and the second (also second-hand, and inscribed with the name of the poet, Harry Brown) at the Grolier Bookshop in Cambridge. (From then on I managed first-hand first editions.)[49]

Al Millet knew of Hecht's admiration and presented him, as a thank-you gift, with a first edition of *The Ascent of F6*, which Auden co-wrote with Christopher Isherwood in 1936. The inscription read: "To Tony—For being permitted to warm myself by your fire, this frozen idiot is humbly, and affectionately grateful—Al." That volume was also from the Gotham Book Mart, presumably purchased at some point when Al was crashing with Hecht on 81st Street. All of the poets in Leighton's pantheon exerted an important influence early on; Hecht would try on their styles, then actively move away from them, once he had incorporated their qualities for his use. Even more so than Eliot and Stevens, Auden would become a tutelary spirit. Hecht eventually devoted essays to Eliot, Stevens, Ransom, Tate, and Frost (as well as to Wilbur, Bishop, Dickinson, and Keats, etc.), but to Auden he devoted an entire book, *The Hidden Law*, a study of Auden's poetry up through *The Shield of Achilles*.

Before arriving in Ischia, Hecht would have likely purchased and read Auden's *For the Time Being* (containing "The Sea and the Mirror," based on *The Tempest*, which would provide a model for Hecht's sequence on characters from *A Midsummer Night's Dream*, "A Love for Four Voices"), as well as *The Collected Poetry of W. H. Auden* (1945) and *The Age of Anxiety*, which won the Pulitzer Prize in 1948. Hecht may have also read "Ischia," a recent poem with martial notes that would have resonated with the ex-soldier: "There is a time to admit how much the sword decides, / with flourishing horns to salute the conqueror." The island provided a balm for the recent wounds of the war. Hecht shared Auden's gratitude for the natural splendors and companionship he found there. As Auden puts it in "Ischia":

> . . . *my thanks are for you,*
> *Ischia, to whom a fair wind has*
> *brought me rejoicing with dear friends*
>
> *from soiled productive cities. How well you correct*
> *our injured eyes, how gently you train us to see*
> *things and men in perspective*
> *underneath your uniform light.*[50]

Since ancient times, Ischia had been a place of healing. Auden praises the hot springs' ability to soothe the body and "improve the venereal act," as he takes in the long views of Vesuvius and Capri. He praises the local wine and the indigenous "coffee-colored" honey that imbues the traveler there with sweet memories. Hecht, too, found solace there—in the light, the springs, the peace, the friendship, the natural beauty—but he was never completely healed by the powers of the island. He was still racked by the choices he had been forced to make in Germany: as Auden has it, to "choose our / duty or do something horrible."[51] As Hecht saw it, the two were synonymous.

Eventually, through the Rosenthals, he made a date with Auden. Hecht walked the short distance from the piazzetta, with its food shops and fountain, past Maria's Bar Internazionale (where Auden liked to spend his late afternoons), up the hill toward San Vito, to Auden's rented house. Their meeting was arranged around Auden's exceedingly strict social habits. As Hecht recalled, Auden

> was remarkably myopic, and could rarely recognize anyone at a distance of more than ten feet. His clothing, even in the licensed atmosphere of the Italian beach resort, resembled, in his own words, "an unmade bed." His work habits were fixed and inflexible, though set aside on Sundays. He rose around six in the morning and worked for a while before break-fast of coffee, and continued to work, with a brief interruption for a light lunch, until around three in the afternoon. The rest of the day was for diversion, dinner and drinks. But he had a fixed hour of retirement at, I think it was, 10:30, so he could be up and work at six the next morning.[52]

Auden made his young guest feel at home, and their occasional evenings together were wine-filled and gregarious, even including the odd parlor game, a great equalizer among the generations and a pastime Auden particularly enjoyed. One was a version of Desert Island. If each person had one month to live, which novel, lyric poem, painting, and piece of music would he choose to enliven his last days? The game proved revealing about the participants' sensibilities, and pointed up Auden's recent return to the Anglican faith of his childhood and his concerns over the spiritual in art.

Hecht made a mental note of Auden's choices: "The novels of Ronald

Firbank; the paintings of Caravaggio; the lyric poetry of Tennyson; and the overtures (so help me!) of Rossini." For Hecht's part, he preferred Dickens (and, when pressed, specifically *Pickwick*), a choice of which Auden approved. About music—dear to them both—they clashed completely. Auden liked to make outsized, controversial pronouncements, such as, "Anyone who seriously maintains that his favorite music is Beethoven's late quartets," he teased Hecht, "is simply a snob who is putting on airs." It must have seemed to Hecht, at times, that Auden was trying to get his goat. Auden's strictures about the "spiritually pretentious in art" seem to have extended even to Bach, for whom Hecht harbored a "deep devotion." Hecht began to feel that Auden strained rhetorically to defend his own "camp" tastes. But Hecht suffered from a certain soberness in matters of taste, and he was probably right that, on these occasions, Auden found him "far too earnest."[53] Auden, a descendent of preachers, was in the midst of a reawakening of faith, and it permeated both his life and art. Hecht remembered Auden explaining (was he half-joking?) that he, Auden, often wondered at his inability to work past three in the afternoon, until he realized "after he had become a convinced Christian" that the "sense of indolence, loss and depression that came upon him at that hour" was because it was the hour of Christ's crucifixion.[54]

Hecht found Auden to be "a generous man and a shy one" and "reticent, above all things, about his virtues," a winning quality for a famous poet. He demonstrated an extraordinary recall for the poems and prose that he loved, often reciting to the group.[55] He kept whole pages of Henry James in his head, as well as a host of scabrous ditties, including this parody of A. E. Housman, attributed (perhaps wrongly) to Henry Reed:

> *The cow lets fall at evening*
> *A liquid shower of shit,*
> *And, Terrence, you lie under,*
> *And do not mind a bit;*
>
> *Though once you hated it.*[56]

Hecht loved to laugh uproariously (as sad people often do), and he committed the lines immediately to memory. Years later, performing on the same program of light verse at the 92nd Street Y in New York (where Auden appeared many times over the years and Hecht nearly ten), the two traded dirty limericks in the dressing room. A photo by the photographer Jill Krementz, the wife of Kurt Vonnegut and house photographer for the Poetry Center, shows Auden laughing at Hecht's recitation of a spicy bit of light verse.

Outside of these occasional evenings chez Auden-Kallman, Hecht kept largely to himself, cooking, reading, or meeting friends on the beach after a morning's work. His intentional isolation was soon broken by an influx of visitors, including his brother, Roger, who had agreed to make the trip abroad despite his persistent medical issues. Hecht was a gracious tour guide, often meeting guests in Naples and accompanying them back to Ischia on the ferry. Another visitor, Thekla Clark, came all the way from Oklahoma. Her mother was a friend of Dorothea's. Hecht remembered them playing together as children. Spurred on by their mothers, they had recently begun a correspondence. Hecht encouraged her to visit.

In late June, Hecht met her as she stepped off the SS *Conte Biancamano* from the States. It was the first time they had seen each other since the two built sandcastles at the seaside. She mistook him at first, as she leaned over the rail:

> I searched for him among the crowd waiting on the dock. The only obviously non-Italian man I could see was pale, plump, with fluttering hands and dressed entirely in white; my heart sank. At the end of the gangplank, while I was warding off offers of all kinds, I heard someone call my name and looked around to find not the pale, plump young man but a lean, bearded beauty. I felt I had won the lottery.[57]

If their letters had kindled the possibility of romance, it was not to be, notwithstanding their promising meet-cute on the quay in Naples: "The romantic-looking poet fitted in so well with all the other wonders it never dawned on me that he might not be the perfect match for an overconfident Daisy [Miller] with her New World exuberance and vulgarity."[58] This is more or less how Hecht and the Rosenthals came to see her—glamorous and a bit exhausting.

Hecht's Italian was "cautious" but adequate to the necessaries having to do with transporting Clark's luggage and changing dollars to lire. Hecht moved comfortably in the seedy slum-like streets of Naples, the rough underside of which he would render years later with grit and terror in "See Naples and Die." He maintained his cool as he led Clark into an unlit corridor near the docks, which opened into a windowless room lit by a bare bulb with two stubble-bearded men sitting at a table to change currency. He was not robbed, as happens in the poem, but he must have feared he would be.

Their financial business completed, they toured the city. As Thekie effused, Hecht stayed focused on the matter at hand. He talked of the local customs and mentioned in particular the women wearing black for a prescribed period of mourning. Clark later wrote: That detail "should have told me something"—a sign of Hecht's isolating melancholy.[59] Recently widowed, she had left her one-year-old daughter, Lisa, back in America. Clark was sporty, pretty, self-deprecating, and funny. She referred to herself jokingly as the big blonde ("La Biondona"), who liked to talk a blue streak. She actively courted Auden and Kallman, as if collecting them, and she returned in subsequent summers, later hosting them at her house in Florence.

A photo of the group on the beach in Forio from the summer of 1951 shows Hecht much as Clark described him—bearded, thin, tan, and slightly aloof, a brine-streaked Odysseus to her Nausicaa. Another photo taken by the Rosenthals from around this time shows Hecht at the Naples Zoo, again with his new beard, and also a hasty crewcut, courtesy of Al. Perhaps it was his actor training, but Hecht took pleasure in looking the part. As Clark noted, he was the very picture of an expatriate, bohemian poet.

On the ferry ride back to Ischia, Hecht lay his head in her lap, exhausted from a long day in the Neapolitan sun. The sea was glassy on that first day of their meeting and the sun strong, which was fortunate. There were crossings during her stay, however, when they were not so lucky. In bad weather, the ferry ride could be extremely rough:

Custom decreed that once seated the passengers left their seats only to disembark. When necessary they turned their heads aside and threw up on the floor, noisily and cheerfully. Among the regular passengers there was almost a competition: "Aai, was I sick today!" inferred superiority over the less sensitive. Rivers of pasta and asciutta flowed. The crew members would get busy with buckets of sand and extraordinary goodwill. The passengers not actively sick sucked on lemons and groaned.[60]

The two spent a great deal of time together, circling the possibility of romance, but it never materialized. To him, she seemed flighty, and his circumspection only puzzled her. They dined al fresco on pizza or went to the Bar Internazionale Maria, a small but cozy osteria with no windows and two doors looking out on to the street and alley. There they might meet Auden, Chester, and company. Painters, filmmakers, and writers, including the Weisses and Rosenthals, gathered in the evenings around Auden's reserved table at Maria's, with Maria herself, a sort of local celebrity with jet-black hair and a solid frame, presiding. They downed carafes of the local wine (spirits were scarce on the island), as well as coffee, beer, and the rather rough Italian brandy. Chester held court, aping a strong Neapolitan accent to punctuate his riotous stories of local life, before Auden abruptly rose at his usual hour and padded home to bed. Also in the group were Harriet Sohmers, a graduate of Black Mountain College and friend of James Baldwin in Paris, and Bud Wirtschafter, a filmmaker and soundman in whose New York apartment Andy Warhol's *Kitchen* was later shot. These were uproarious and bibulous evenings, and Hecht welcomed the copious drink in particular. When Clark departed Ischia later that summer, she and Hecht said goodbye on the quay, declaring their "serious intentions" to keep in touch, "in tones that neither of us believed."[61]

When his brother was added to the mix in early June, Hecht enjoyed playing the experienced cicerone. During the spring, he had traveled to Rome with the Rosenthals and spent time with Robert Lowell and Elizabeth Hardwick in Florence, before seeing them off on their trip to visit Robie Macauley in Paris. Hecht planned to take his brother on a similar trip, to show him the major sights. (They delayed their trip until after Clark, who threatened to join them, had left Italy.) The initial weeks with Roger in Ischia were hard. Roger was a consummate follower. He was game for whatever Tony suggested, but, left to his own devices, he rarely put forward a plan. Used to having things done for him by nursemaids or governesses, he lacked the will for decisive action. Hecht worried about

Roger's inertia. He loafed indoors and couldn't manage to engage with the books that Hecht recommended as a diversion. Hecht felt an obligation to his brother and helped him whenever he could. To Roger's credit, after his initial bout of inactivity, he began to write poems, getting up to as many as one a day. Hecht encouraged his brother to apply to Kenyon for the fall semester, and he was quickly accepted. Tony sent the news to Tate, with whom Roger had taken a poetry class:

> Roger would have been quite depressed about going back to the States if he hadn't been accepted to Kenyon. He wrote poetry furiously all summer, (generally a poem a day), but he's had bad luck about getting anything accepted. In any case, he must be well occupied at Kenyon now; he's got a heavy schedule, including . . . one [course] with Ransom.[62]

Hecht did not complain of Roger's trailing in his wake, studying with both of his chief mentors, Ransom and Tate. He did note, though, that his brother often had a very difficult time thinking for himself—an observation that hurt Roger's feelings.[63] In time, things did become strained, as Roger's poems seemed to take a number of their cues—including an engagement with the war and the Holocaust—from his brother.

When Hecht mentioned to Auden that he and Roger hoped to hear some music on their upcoming trip, the older poet once again asserted his feeling that music "that had pretentions to ultimate spiritual statements was suspect, along with its admirers." Auden's preference for opera was well known. He had recently completed, with Chester, the libretto for Stravinsky's *The Rake's Progress,* which was shortly to receive its premiere at the Teatro La Fenice in Venice. Hecht recalled that Auden "thought very doubtful my deep devotion to Bach, though he enjoyed playing through the St. John Passion on the piano":[64]

> He was politely but firmly critical of me when I told him I was taking my brother to Rome and that we planned to hear the Bach "Magnificat" in the Roman Forum; for there was to be a performance elsewhere in Rome of Bellini's "Norma" on the same night, and my choice clearly disappointed him.[65]

Awed or shy, Hecht said nothing about his poetic aspirations to Auden; only later did Auden learn from Ray and Elsie that Hecht composed verse. Auden graciously asked to see some poems. He then invited Hecht to the house to discuss them, in an interview that Hecht remembered vividly. Though he was sometimes puzzled by certain of Auden's criticisms, he hung on every word and took a great deal of it to heart. He felt excited and honored by Auden's generosity and attention. Hecht sat across from him as Auden went through each of the poems carefully, handling them with kid gloves yet speaking as frankly as he could. Auden identified him as a poet of the New Criticism, a *Kenyon Review* poet, and even voiced concern that Hecht may have been overly influenced by their theories. He wouldn't have recalled that the two of them appeared in the journal together a few years earlier, though Hecht remembered it well. Auden's musical poem "The Duet" directly preceded Hecht's two poems in the issue for Autumn 1947. (Hecht would have been too diffident to mention it, particularly as he came to doubt the quality of his two poems—"Wind of Spain" and "Dream.")

The meeting was a milestone. Auden was perhaps the greatest poet in English at that time, and the fact that he took Hecht's work seriously and even praised it deeply affected the younger poet. Hecht described the scene to Tate in elaborate detail:

Just before I left Ischia I had a long talk with Auden about my work. The interview, which lasted about two and a half hours, was somewhat tense, due to our not knowing one another very well, and his concern lest I should be wounded by any of his remarks, and my sense of his concern. A few times, when he objected to certain things I thought were defensible, I defended them, and he immediately qualified his remarks almost into oblivion. Our whole conversation was very cautious and tentative. He spent most of the time on specific words and items in the poems, (I showed him about five or six), but his more general comments indicated a certain way about conceiving and writing poems which is different from mine, and which, while I can understand it, does not seem suitable or agreeable for me just now. He remarked generally, for example, that there was an excess of detail in most of the poems which tended to obscure, by their abundance, the central theme or argument of the poem. More specifically, in the "Aubade," (which I believe is out now in the new Kenyon; the title will be changed), he felt the poem could profitably be rewritten in the same number of stanzas, but with each stanza four lines long instead of ten. And perhaps you may remember a rather long poem of mine that Roger showed you last spring, which started out about a Memling painting ["A Poem for Julia"]. Well, Auden remarked that the stories of the Michelangelo incident (about painting his critic's face into Hell), and the business about the Defenestration of Prague were both so familiar as to require only casual reference or allusion in order to recall the whole story, whereas I had devoted an eighteen line stanza to each one. The point here was a little different, though, because it had to do with what might properly be expected of a reader, and tied in with a point he raised concerning an item in another poem called "La Condition Botanique," which should be out shortly in Poetry. There is a reference in this last poem to Simeon Pyrites as the patron saint of Fool's Paradise. Auden recognized the play on Stylites, of course, and knew, in addition, that pyrites was iron disulphide, but could not see what bearing that had on the poem, whereas he apparently didn't know, what I might have expected, that pyrites is fool's gold. What's more, it seems less demanding on the reader to ask him to look up pyrites in the dictionary, where he will immediately come across the familiar nickname, than to ask him to read through the life of Michelangelo for the details of this little incident, which Vasari records, but others may not have bothered with; or to read through a history of the Holy Roman Empire for an account of the defenestration, which I don't believe is even mentioned in the Encyclopedia. But more important than all this is the fact that it shouldn't really make any difference how familiar the story is. The botanical poem, which was the lightest of the group I showed him, he liked the best. Of two poems that had appeared some while back in Kenyon, he said nothing about "Hallowe'en" and remarked about "Springtime," a little translation from Charles of Orleans, that I should make sure I have the archaic spelling right, because it's the sort of thing that scholars will jump on me for. After going over all the poems one by one, (except Hallowe'en), he repeated his comment about the danger of allowing detail to distract the reader's attention from the poem's argument or topic. By way of example, he quoted these lines of Yeats, from "A Prayer For My Daughter":

I have walked and prayed for this young child an hour. . . .

and went on to ask, "Why an hour? Why not twenty minutes or forty-six?"
I think I said something about the use of a conventional language, and the
way it gives the feeling of a distinct, and eventually an individual voice.
But he stuck to his point, and felt that "an hour" was just stuck in to fill out
the line, or rhyme, or something. Anyway, when I objected, he dropped
the point, and turned to something else. It was only very much later that I
recalled his mentioning very favorably Wyatt's "Remembrance" and wondered how he would justify, "Thanked be fortune it hath been otherwise
/ Twenty times better." In the main, though, he seems to think of details
as being illustrative to a thesis, whereas I hope, if I am successful, to incorporate the meaning in the details so that it exists only in them, and not
apart from them. Our mutual shyness made it impossible to be quite open
about all our ideas, but the next day a young couple who have known him
for many years told me that he had told them he liked my work very much
and thought it was better than many of the "younger poets."[66]

Auden could be hugely fastidious and idiosyncratic in his criticism: at one
point Hecht was asked to consider changing his phrase "bachelor oyster"
to "celibate oyster" for reasons "that must have meant more to him than
to me."[67]

Auden told the Rosenthals that he felt Hecht's poems outstripped the
work of Wilbur and Shapiro, both of whom had published a good deal
more than Hecht at the time. Their meeting was cordial, despite the two
not seeing eye to eye on certain fundamental aspects of poetry, a disagree-
ment that went largely unspoken at the time. Younger poets, in order to
become truly accomplished, must hold strong convictions, even if they
later recant them—something that Auden himself must have understood.
He was a perceptive reader, and he quibbled with an aspect of Hecht's
method, which Hecht restated for his parents:

> He feels that details are an ornamental embellishment to verse and should
> never be allowed to distract the reader's attention from the main line of
> discourse, whereas I believe that the details should be made to subsume,
> to contain, to embody, to incarnate the point and meaning of a poem.[68]

Auden liked "La Condition Botanique" best, with its tightly turned lines, loosely informed by the diamond-shaped stanzas of Dylan Thomas's "Vision and Prayer" and the stair-step stanzas of George Herbert's "Aaron" (not unlike those of Wilbur's "Castles and Distances" in the September 1950 *Poetry*).[69] The opening, with its reference to gouty Romans bathing in Ischian springs, an image that chimes with Auden's own "Ischia," would have pleased Auden. Both poets describe the island's natural splendor and allude to its healing powers. Auden admits the power of nature as a corrective to the depredation of "the sword," but Hecht's vision is characteristically darker and deeply inflected by his personal experience of combat:

> But what's become of Paradise?

> Ah, it is lodged in glass, survives
> In Brooklyn, like a throwback out of style,
> Like an incomprehensible veteran of the Grand
> Army of the Republic in the reviewing stand
> Who sees young men in a mud-colored file
> March to the summit of their lives,

> For glory, for their country, with the flag
> Joining divergent stars of North and South
> In one blue field of heaven, till they fall in blood
> And are returned at last unto their native mud—
> The eyes weighed down with stones, the sometimes mouth
> Helpless to masticate or gag

> Its old inheritance of earth.[70]

Hecht had been casting around for ways to write about the war. It continued to eat at him, constantly filling his thoughts and clouding his demeanor. It would take him years to discover an aesthetic strategy that would allow him to capture the menace and violence of what he remembered and continued to re-experience.

For now, he wrote of combat in ornate and highly figured terms, in poems such as "Aubade" (retitled "A Deep Breath at Dawn" in *A Summoning of Stones*). The poem, which Auden suggested in their conference might be accomplished in half the number of lines, appeared in the Autumn 1951 issue of *The Kenyon Review*. Was Auden the angel on his shoulder when, in his copy of the journal, Hecht crossed out the final handful of lines and rewrote them as follows:

> *It is as well the light keeps him away;*
> *We should have little to say in days like these,*
> *Although once friends. We should have little to say,*
> *But that there will be much planting of fig trees,*
> *And Venus shall be clad in the prim leaf,*
> *And turn a solitary. And her god, forgot,*
> *Cast by that emblem out, shall spend his grief*
> *Upon us. In that day the fruit shall rot*
> *Unharvested. Then shall the sullen god*
> *Perform his mindless fury in our blood.*[71]

The light of dawn dispels this ghost from the garden, though the cast-out god Mars (identified by name in the *Kenyon* version) carries on his mindless fury in those who remain. Hecht came to mistrust certain details of the poem, but the presence of the ghost rang true:

> The lines in "A Deep Breath" about admiring a distant view through the shell-penetrated body of a dead soldier who returns as a ghost is too fanciful and unreal, and almost embarrassing. Though not because it involves ghosts. Hardy and Yeats and Eliot wrote about them well enough.[72]

As Hecht looked back on the war from a gulf of six years, his loneliness was complete: the men that he had grown close to in combat were now dead or far away, and in any case, with the exception of Robie Macauley, they would have nothing now to say to one another. (Hecht never corresponded with the men from his company, nor did he attend reunions.) The silence that fell over so many of the veterans of that war fell on Hecht. It was only his ghosts that he consulted now.

When he arrived in Ischia, Hecht imagined that the solitude of a winter there would help him to complete the poems for his first collection. In fact, it would take much longer, as he tore out weaker poems and replaced them with newer work. His first mature poems about the war, included in his second book, *The Hard Hours,* would come a decade after that. He realized the problem even then:

> I knew perfectly well at the time that I wasn't able to do justice to some of the horrors of existence I had reason to know about. That is not to say that I am not modestly proud of the "[The Gardens of the] Villa d'Este" and "[La Condition] Botanique," but that in writing them I was enjoying the challenge of writing "essay poems," wandering discourse that could lead anywhere and stop when it pleased. This was some of Auden's influence. And the more serious poems, "Japan," "A Deep Breath at Dawn" (much Yeats in that one), "A Roman Holiday" (much early Lowell in that one), "Christmas Is Coming," all put the terror of reality at an artistic distance, and were too full of "devices."[73]

Though he included it in *Stones,* "Christmas Is Coming" suffered from these faults: in it "the war has been curiously sanitized by being treated as an allegory."[74] When he showed a draft of the poem to Allen Tate at one point, Tate was puzzled by the allegorizing tendency of the poem. The poem, Hecht ultimately felt, was "a kind of bad dream, with nursery rhyme refrains meant to sound ominous. The poem floats in some region between raw fact, dream, and parable, in what in the end, seems to me a soft and impalpable blur."[75]

Hecht heard something crucial in what Auden said after their meeting: "I think he may be right most of all in saying (as he said to the Rosenthals but not to me) that my verse is perhaps too formal—not in the metrical sense, but in being somewhat impersonal in tone, disengaged from the central emotions of the poems."[76] Hecht admitted as much to Philip Hoy: "In writing these poems I felt I was performing duties that pulled me in opposing directions: one was to honor and commemorate the tragedies and horror of war, while the other was to compose elegant and well-crafted poems in the manner of those poets [e.g. Stevens, Tate, and Ransom] who were still my models."[77] What Auden perceived—this impersonality and distancing of emotion, the penchant for ornamental detail—may well have been a product of Hecht's response to the trauma of the war, of not wanting to awaken the terror of those feelings too directly. Perhaps it was Auden's voice he heard in his head as, a decade later, he pared away the linguistic filigree of *Stones* in favor of the immediacy of *The Hard Hours*.

Hecht was his own harshest critic. His poems continued to enjoy prominent publication, despite the faults he found in them. And he had his champions, who believed in his work and acted on his behalf. If he doubted this fact, a strong affirmation of this reached him in Ischia in early summer: he was awarded the Rome Prize by the American Academy of Arts and Letters. They would pay for him to spend the next year writing poems at the American Academy in Rome, an experience that became a high point of his early career.

SIX

ROMAN HOLIDAYS
(1952–1955)

Sands shift in the wind, petals are shed,
Eternal cities are also undone . . .[1]

1. On the Janiculum

Climbing the Janiculum, the second highest hill in Rome, Hecht could view the entire city, laid out like a model in a museum. To the west of the Seven Hills, across the Tiber, he made his home for the next year. In the distance, he could make out the Forum and the wedding-cake white columns of the monument to Victor Emmanuel II. Just above him on the winding Via Garibaldi, the American Academy in Rome gleamed ochre and white, housed in a handsome turn-of-the-century villa in the Renaissance style, with an interior courtyard of painted stucco and tall cypresses beside an art deco fountain. In fair weather, the fellows of the Academy—architects, artists, musicians, and now poets (Hecht was the first one to be chosen)—took their meals *al fresco* under the ivied portico.

In this cloistered and elegant setting, Hecht must have seemed like a wild man: tanned, bearded, with a hodgepodge of bags in tow, a victrola with classical records, a bamboo fly rod, and "a small cat named Dido."[2] At the center of eleven leafy acres, the McKim, Mead & White building (one of only a few outside the States)—known as the Academy building—takes pride of place. Through the bowels of the building one could access an ancient aqueduct of Trajan. Opened in 1914, it is complemented by the Villa Aurelia and the Casa Rustica.

Hecht had heard about his award in May. It carried a stipend of $3,000, enough to see him through a year of writing, and his anticipation grew over the lazy summer months in the Mezzogiorno. When word of the prize reached him in Ischia, he could not believe it at first. How had this come about? It seemed highly unlikely, a gag even. He wrote to Allen Tate, who had been his champion, in disbelief. Months later, after he was settled in Rome, he wrote again to apologize for being so incredulous, which he worried had sounded the wrong note:

> I want again to send you my most sincere and grateful thanks for your part in my nomination and election to this Fellowship. I'm afraid that when I wrote you saying that my first reaction to the news that I had won, was that the whole thing might be a joke, you perhaps thought I was not taking the prize as seriously as it deserved to be taken. Let me assure you that I meant to express only incredulity; I have never had such a complete and happy surprise in my life. And I feel very grateful.[3]

Residency at the Academy was an honor and an association that Hecht cherished, and his relationship with the place deepened over the years: "The winning of that prize, and the year to which it entitled me," he came to feel, "was one of the most satisfactory of my life. My chief competitor for the prize, I was later to discover, was [his old friend and schoolmate] Jack Kerouac. Rome was to me a revelation; exciting, beautiful, full of infinite complexity."[4] It was the inaugural award to a poet, through a collaboration of the American Academy in Rome and the American Academy of Arts and Letters. He quickly warmed to the heady intellectual atmosphere of the Academy, enjoying the company of scholars and artists—"classicists, archeologists, art and architectural historians"[5]—and his pleasure at their company and the status it conferred spurred a welcome period of productivity. Throughout his career, Hecht would experience stretches—sometimes long stretches—of writer's block, which is to say a mixture of anxiety and depression that kept him from his desk. The anxiety was partly the result of the extraordinarily high expectations he put on himself, an uneasy perfectionism that no doubt contributed to the long gap of thirteen years between his first and second books. Partnerships with other artists and musicians, such as the printmaker Leonard Baskin, with whom he collaborated on "The Seven Deadly Sins," "The Presumptions of Death," a florilegium, and an unfinished series of biblical poems and prints (these last two series included without accompanying images in *The Darkness and the Light*), could knock him from this rut to brilliant effect. Likewise, several residencies in Italy, including stays at Bellagio on Lake Como and Bogliasco, south of Genoa, lent both an occasion and an imprimatur that freed Hecht to write with assurance and even speed. The Academy, to which he would return twice more, was the first such residency. In his studio overlooking the courtyard, with the cat circling his chair, he completed or laid the groundwork for most of the poems in *A Summoning of Stones*.

The brainchild of a group of late-nineteenth-century artists and architects, the Academy was conceived of as a place where younger American artists of promise could study, while deepening their sense of the European past. Chief among this group was Charles F. McKim, who had built Penn Station and the main quads of Columbia University. McKim chose the Janiculum Hill as the site for the Academy building, which commands views of the entire city. Inside the Academy walls, sweeping lawns stretch between garden plots of tomatoes and herbs, and fellows converse on benches or walk the footpaths though the park.

Hecht's letters to his parents reflected his good mood. Roger, as was his wont, performed the duties of Hecht's secretary when he was abroad, and it was through Roger that news came from Tate about the Rome Prize. A brief announcement ran in the *Times,* which made Hecht's parents proud: "The fellowship, which includes $3,000 cash, is in keeping with the academy's furtherance of the arts in this country and its encouragement of younger artists and writers of ability."[6] His father even handed out copies to business associates, much to his son's chagrin. And a piece in The Gray Lady was just the sort of thing that would impress Dorothea's friends. Hecht worried that his winning the Rome Prize might exacerbate pangs of inferiority in Roger, but, for now, the two remained extremely close.

In October, Hecht traveled to the Academy by train, with all of his belongings, leaving Ischia at five in the morning. He knew the route, having made an exploratory trip to Rome with the Rosenthals that summer. He reported on the journey to his folks:

> The whole trip was made without difficulty; even the cat caused no particular trouble (she lives in my rooms, and I take her for a walk in the garden every day), although she was pretty scared by the trip, and being carried in a box the whole way. . . . I have two large rooms, a bedroom and a study, that look out on a beautiful courtyard designed like a cloister, with a garden designed around four beautiful and immense cypress trees which stand at the four corners of a pool, fed by a lazy fountain, and sustaining an immense goldfish.[7]

Hecht found the fellows themselves a mixed bag, all well-dressed and "frighteningly formal." Among them were some "very fine gifted people" as well as "a handful of the stuffiest scholars and crew-cut architects I've ever met."[8] He quickly settled into a routine of work, punctuated by sightseeing trips around the city. From the Academy, he walked or took the bus down the steep path of the Via Garibaldi, with its fine panoramic view of the city, in which Baroque domes mingled with ancient ruins. Not surprisingly—inevitably, even—Rome became his muse.

He later described his first weeks at the Academy to the playwright John Guare:

> For all its ruins, indeed partly because of them, Rome is a city of unparalleled magnificence. A brilliant archeologist took a mesmerized group of Fellows from the American Academy to the Capitoline, shepherding them past Michelangelo's piazza and equestrian Marcus Aurelius, looking suitably meditative, to show us beyond that splendor a sweeping view of the Forum and the Palatine. With care and subtlety he reconstituted the landscape from the rape of the Sabines to the end of the Empire and beyond . . . The city's glories were not merely stratified in geological layers; they lived cheek by jowl in Mediterranean sunlight, open unto the fields and the sky, and a panoramic view of the city from the Academy's height presented an incomparable mix of green and terra-cotta, treetops and ochre slabs, *rus in urbe*. In every nook and cranny, it seemed

to us the more we got to know the city, there were not only concealed beauties but secret lore and the very tread of history.[9]

Ancient temples "stood out as casually as phone booths at home," and churches were "almost too beautiful to permit pious meditation." On the rare days it snowed, the fellows "would flock, in a sort of pilgrimage, to see flakes sift gently down through the great oculus of the Pantheon."[10] It wasn't so much that the city provided him with subject matter, though it did that as well. The subjects to which he was repeatedly drawn— painting and music, Eros, the war—appeared in a new context. As in a quattrocento painting, the Italian landscape and its capital became a backdrop for his recurring subjects, a canvas on which to work. In "A Roman Holiday," written that fall, he depicted the violence of war and corruption, the curses of history that lay beneath the surface of the Old World:

> I write from Rome. It is late afternoon
> Nearing the Christmas season. Blooded light
> Floods though the Colosseum, where platoon
> And phalanx of the Lord slaved for the might
> Of Titus' pleasure. Blood repeats its tune
> Loudly against my eardrums as I write,
> And recollects what they were made to pay
> Who out of worship put their swords away.
>
> The bells declare it. "Crime is at the base,"
> Rings in the belfry where the blood is choired.
> Crime stares from the unknown, ruined face,
> And the cold wind, endless and wrath-inspired,
> Cries out for judgment in a swampy place
> As darkness claims the trees. "Blood is required,
> And it shall fall," below the Seven Hills
> The blood of Remus whispers out of wells.[11]

Hecht found ample correspondences—the blood that cannot be washed away—in Roman history for the wrenching slaughter of soldiers and of innocents in the Holocaust. Church bells broadcast their dark clangor, and *blood* proliferates like a refrain. As he cast about for his poetic voice, ornamental and impersonal, Hecht's subjects announced themselves, growing starkly clear. The blood of Remus is a key: the glories of the classical past, which Hecht prized, were founded on blood—an awareness that never left him. Goethe had had a Roman period, and yet the land that had produced the Great Man of Europe (the land of Hecht's great-grandparents) also produced the Nazis.

Hecht later looked on "A Roman Holiday" and all the poems in *Stones* as the work of an "advanced apprentice."[12] He continued to try out technical approaches, mining the poems of the English Renaissance, as well as the contemporary music of Tate and Ransom. Auden showed a way forward, as did, importantly, Thomas Hardy, in "Spring for Thomas Hardy," with its song-like stanzas and refrain. He also learned from the Dorset poet how to talk to ghosts. Hardy often addressed his poems to his departed wife, Emma, particularly in his poems of 1912–13. The critic Christopher Ricks has noted the extent to which Hecht's poems are "haunted" by the war dead. Hecht saw in Hardy poems such as "Neutral Tones" how one could imbue a landscape with loss.[13]

Hecht worked well that fall. In addition to new poems, he completed seven songs for musical settings by his colleague at the Academy, Leo Smit. He began a long poem (now lost), with a projected four or more sections. In November, he turned to translations. He asked his parents to copy out a poem by Pierre de Ronsard from an anthology in his collection at home edited by André Gide. He began Englishing Ronsard's "Contre Denise, Sorcière," and continued to hone it for many years, before collecting it in his fourth book, *The Venetian Vespers*. Hecht also expressed an interest in medieval poetry and began work on the German minnesinger Walther von der Vogelweide's late poem "Elegy," written in the early thirteenth century. Ultimately uncollected, when it appeared in the Spring 1952 number of *The Kenyon Review*, alongside "The Song of the Beasts," it echoed the isolation and self-recrimination that dogged Hecht after the war:

> *Who danced with me in childhood,*
>   *go agued in the town;*
> *Sweet-broom comes nothing near me,*
>   *the laurels are cut down,*

For that the stream runs toneless
   I fear strange influence,
Hiding that lilt of spilling,
   doth baffle my poor sense.

They pass unkindly by me
   that once sought for my side:
The World is riven wholly
   with wantonness and pride.[14]

In the final line, the poem declares rather abruptly: "Sorrow is mine, and woe." Hecht selected poems for translation with care. He worked on them slowly, sometimes over decades, in quite different versions. The poems spoke to something deep in his psyche and represent a continuity with his original work. No doubt it was too "on the nose," however, to include along with his translation of Charles d'Orleans's "Springtime" in *Stones*.

His reading in Rome was as ambitious as his writing: "Philo, Josephus, Livy, Suetonius, some Roman archeology, Pound's letters, Richard Wilbur's second book of poems (very good), Max Radin (Paul's brother) on the Jews among the Greeks and Romans, and some German poetry." "The Song of Beasts," likely written during his stint at the Academy, includes an epigraph from his reading in Roman history: "According to ancient Roman law, a man convicted of parricide was condemned to be flogged, and sewn in a sack with a cock, a viper, a dog, and an ape, and thrown into the sea or a deep river."[15] (The speaking animals in the poem forecast Hecht's interest in Aesop, which occasioned his collaboration with Leonard Baskin and a series of bestiary poems in *The Hard Hours*.)

While not writing poems, Hecht filled a notebook with dozens of pages about the geography and history of Rome. By recording the Roman past in detail Hecht laid claim to the city, in order to possess it and make it his own. He drew a map of the Seven Hills, and compiled lists of kings and emperors. He made a long list of Roman writers and their works— Ovid, Vergil, Plutarch, Juvenal, Martial, Seneca, and a score of others. He committed to memory battles and edicts, the histories of churches and villas, as he wandered through the ancient city and its environs with his pocket-sized copy of Augustus J. C. Hare's *Walks in Rome*.

The chapter on Tivoli led him farther afield to the spectacular water-works of the Villa d'Este. He wrote a long poem about it, in the vein of "La Condition Botanique," filled with a wistful erotic charge:

> *This is Italian. Here*
> *Is cause for the undiminished bounce*
> *Of sex, cause for the lark, the animal spirit*
> *To rise, aerated, but not beyond our reach, to spread*
> *Friction upon the air, cause to sing loud for the bed*
> *Of jonquils, the linen bed, and established merit*
> *Of love, and grandly pronounce*
> *Pleasure without peer.*[16]

Italy soothed him and inspired him. Without his nearly two years abroad it's hard to know when he would have completed his first book of po-ems. What is certain is that it would not have resembled anything like *A Summoning of Stones*.

At some point during his stay at the Academy, his parents visited, though not together. He later recounted the strange circumstances to Philip Hoy:

> My mother came first. She told me that my father's job (she had by this time demanded that he no longer run his own business, but instead accept a salaried job, and work under someone else's direction) was not "real" in that it was entirely subsidized by her parents, the money being paid to the employer by her own father. She went on to say that she planned to divorce my father, and that immediately his salary would cease. The point was not simply that he would be penniless once again but that the discovery that he had not been holding a real job but was being supported by his in-laws would so humiliate him that he would "probably commit suicide."[17]

His mother revealed all this over drinks in the lobby of the Hassler Ho-tel, not far from the Spanish Steps. She seemed in a "strange state," though she was convinced of the truth of what she had told him. When his father turned up a few days later, Hecht felt obligated to fill him in. Melvyn declared the whole thing to be a fabrication of Dorothea's, "which, it turned out, was the case."[18]

Hecht returned to Ischia for Thanksgiving with the Rosenthals and the Weisses, enjoying an American-style feast of turkey, pumpkin pie, and chestnut dressing. He continued to work on the texts for Leo Smit's songs—seven in all, the cantata ultimately titled "A Choir of Starlings: A Serenata for Four Voices and Ten Instruments." The Academy teemed with birdsong, which found its way into poems and inspired "Spring for Thomas Hardy": "A nightingale that has made his home in one of the cypress trees in the courtyard of the academy" sang "all the time, day as well as night." Putting the finishing touches on "A Choir," Hecht took up another musical collaboration with Lukas Foss, the eminent German-American composer and pianist, who asked him to translate texts from Rilke for a work entitled "A Parable of Death." Music continued to draw him. In January he traveled to Milan to hear Stravinsky and Auden's recently minted *A Rake's Progress* at La Scala. He began a second project with Leo Smit, based on the first named English poet, Cædmon.

When Smit returned from the States, after a triumphant performance of one of his own concertos with Leopold Stokowski, he invited Hecht to join him in Vienna. Hecht eagerly embarked on this musical pilgrimage, cramming his whirlwind visit with performances from beginning to end. He adored the city and told his parents so: "Vienna was marvelous. The food, the people, everything. Heard music every night I was there: Tristan, The Magic Flute, Bach, Hindemith, and the Vienna Choir boys, singing Mass on Sunday morning, and the St. Matthew Passion Monday night." What is striking about this visit is not the pleasure that Hecht took in it but that his account of it included no hint of the city's recent history. He makes no mention of the postwar conditions or that, in addition to its artistic past, Austria had been home to some of the most virulent Nazis. But perhaps Hecht was tired of thinking about the war, or more likely he was still not prepared to come to terms with it. This was true of his early war poems as well: art and artifice provided a buffer that both protected against and obscured the trauma of combat. When he returned to Austria in the mid-1970s, to Salzburg, his reaction could not have been more different. His presence there awakened painful, unsettling memories, which he drew on for his long poem "The Venetian Vespers." But traveling with

Smit, with whom he had struck up a close friendship, and the many hours of concerts no doubt left little time for brooding on the past.

Back at the Academy in midsummer, Hecht could see the end of his fellowship approaching, and he turned his energies to finding a job for the fall. Before Vienna, he had written to Ransom, who said he would keep an eye out for prospective positions in academe. Like Ransom and Tate, Hecht saw teaching as a viable way to make a life as a poet. He wrote to Bard, where he always felt welcome. By August, he still hadn't heard anything back, so he asked Roger to shake the bushes for him. It's not clear how it came about—either through Roger's efforts or a bit of good luck—but Hecht was offered a position in Annandale at the last minute, to his great relief.

On August 21, 1952, he sailed from Le Havre on the SS *Liberté*, steaming into New York Harbor a week later. In his bags was the completed manuscript of his first book. He had gone to Italy as an aspirant and returned as a poet. Things were falling into place.

2. Bellow, Brandeis, Blücher, and a Book

Hecht got back to New York just in time for the beginning of fall term. A few months shy of his thirtieth birthday, he hadn't been on East 81st Street for two years, and everything about New York felt both strange and familiar. If he was having difficulty leaving Italy behind, he had no time to dwell on it. He had never taught full-time before, and he was scrambling to put his courses together.

Not only was he back in New York; he was back at Bard, where he hadn't spent much time since before entering the Army. He had visited since then, and still had a few friends there, but the place had changed dramatically since his student days. In many ways it was the perfect point of reentry for Hecht: it was familiar, remote, peaceful. He had been happy there. An hour's ride on the Hudson River line, it was close enough for him to keep a base in New York City. He could commute weekly to his classes, returning to Manhattan on the weekends. In Annandale, he was reminded of how much the place had meant to him, how formative his experiences there had been. The rolling landscape was the same, as were the woods and stream. Students filled the quads, smoking, laughing, playing music, as they always had. Not long before, he had performed music here, acted, taught math, and declared himself for the first time to be a man of letters.

Bard in those years leaned into its reputation as freewheeling and alternative. It had loosened its ties with Columbia, eventually becoming an independent secular school. Women had been admitted in 1944, just after Hecht's departure for the Army. The campus itself had grown to include the Blithewood Estate, one of the original properties on which the college was situated. Enrollment had more than doubled since Hecht's student days, though it remained tiny by today's standards, with only a few hundred enrolled students. An aura of the unconventional remained, which appealed to Hecht, though the curriculum itself was as traditional as in his day: he taught freshman English, poetry writing, Renaissance poetry, and Shakespeare.

Despite its boutique size and outsider standing, it had attracted a first-rate faculty, many of whom Hecht greatly admired. Hecht befriended Saul Bellow, who was eight years Hecht's senior. Bellow was lean, in excellent shape—a physical prowess that his diminutive physique belied and of which he was proud. His first novels *Dangling Man* and *The Victim* had established him as a young writer of promise, and he would win the National Book Award for *The Adventures of Augie March* the following year.

Hecht only overlapped with Bellow for a few years, but the friendship endured:

> I liked Saul a lot, and I read his work with great attention and pleasure. One of the things that astonished me about it was his very frequent use of the word *soul*. . . . And I was the more struck by this because Saul was not in any noticeable way a religious man. He was pleased with his own Jewish origins, but they were largely cultural ones: they had to do with his taste in food, and jokes, and things of that sort; they had very little to do with any sense of religion at all. . . .
>
> In my case, which is rather different from Bellow's, I felt that I had seen some very bitter aspects of life—the war was only one of these, and blessedness for me was anything that supervened and gave one relief from all the terror that I knew to be really there. I also knew, of course,

that the relief was also there, which was blessedness. I am certainly not someone who feels that they can speak on behalf of any kind of religion, either orthodox or unorthodox. It's, however, a region of experience that I find valuable and important, and I find that the vocabulary makes a kind of sense to me.[19]

Bellow had come to Bard by way of a Guggenheim year in Paris, where he began *Augie March*. Before that he had been teaching at the University of Minnesota, in its renowned English department, where his "main ally" was Robert Penn Warren.[20] Bellow liked to roam the halls of the high-WASP department at Minnesota speaking in Yiddish to his friend Leonard Unger, who referred to himself as a "Jewish Agrarian." When Bellow met Warren, the older writer was completing *All the King's Men*; he had read a typescript of *The Victim* and liked it. The two ate lunch together at the faculty club, and Warren took him in under his protective wing. Their shared fondness for Warren was a bond between Hecht and Bellow.

Bellow, who had been making his way in the academy longer than Hecht, was sensitive to the *goyish* cast of the typical university English department. Even among friends and ostensible allies, manifestations of antisemitism could crop up suddenly. According to his biographer James Atlas, Bellow often quoted from Goethe's *Wilhelm Meister's Apprenticeship*: "We do not tolerate any Jew among us, for how could we grant him a share in the highest culture the origin and tradition of which he denies?" Bellow, like Hecht, was painfully aware of T. S. Eliot's antisemitism—both in the poems and in his treatise on European culture *After Strange Gods*—and of Ezra Pound's in *The Cantos*. Eliot's antisemitism pained Hecht greatly. As Atlas writes, "Bellow [also] pointed to Allen Tate, a self-proclaimed 'Agrarian' from Tennessee who made no secret of his disdain for the predominantly Jewish *Partisan Review* crowd."[21] If Hecht was aware of Tate's prejudice, he was never the brunt of it. Nor, it must be said, did he make a point of his Jewishness as Bellow did, still tending instinctively toward the assimilationism in which he was raised. Even so, he was at times buffeted by an antisemitism that saddened and enraged him. The unspoken biases that had dogged Bellow at Northwestern, Minnesota, and Princeton were largely absent at Bard. The college's forward-thinking ethos, fed by the influx of students from such progressive outposts as the Putney School in Vermont, along with the growing number of Jewish intellectuals recently arrived from overseas, meant that Bellow and Hecht could feel very much at home as teachers and writers.

Another friend from this time, Irma Brandeis, the Dante scholar, arrived at Bard in 1944, after working for the Office of War Information. Brandeis had also spent significant time in Italy, in the mid- to late 1930s, and was known to have been Eugenio Montale's translator and the inspiration for his senhal, Clizia, in *The Occasions* (1939). As another Dante scholar, John Ahern, tells it: "In 1932 in Florence, [Montale] had met a green-eyed, ash-blond American woman with a high forehead, bangs and unruly hair who wore scarfs, jade, and coral earrings."[22] The two read erotic poetry together, including Donne's "The Flea." Brandeis became the unnamed addressee of Montale's "Motets" and, though she did not speak of it, his lover. (She is also likely the model for Domna Rejnev, one of the main characters in Mary McCarthy's novel *The Groves of Academe* [1952], based in part on Mc-Carthy's experience of teaching at Bard.) The poet James Merrill, who had taken a temporary teaching position at Bard in September 1948, found her "an assured, enigmatic single woman," and called her his "Jewish-American Beatrice."[23] Brandeis recalled this magic moment at Bard on the occasion of the establishment of The Irma Brandeis Chair in Romance Cultures: "We shared the company of those good friends whose eminence, then as now, created the durable myth of 'The Old Bard,' a classical academy of the singularly gifted, just north of Rhinebeck . . ." Not long before she died at her home on the Bard campus in 1990, Hecht wrote to her of his nostalgia for the enjoyable days of teaching the two had shared.

Hecht, Brandeis, and the other faculty worked closely together, supervising and adjudicating so-called Moderations and Senior Projects. Hecht learned a great deal from his fellows. With Brandeis, it was her patience with the students that impressed him. She managed a reserve "almost to the point of Roman stoicism," that Hecht himself found difficult to muster, admitting he was "chastened" by her example, "though probably not enough."[24] Beyond the grind of "department and division labors," Hecht welcomed the collegial aspects of the place, "the teas and drinks and opinions" shared by the faculty. With Brandeis he was particularly simpatico and grateful for "the judgments, tastes, and enthusiasms we shared, as well as for occasional joint abhorrences." And, of course, they shared a love of

Italy, which Brandeis seemed to embody for him, a living remembrancer. Hecht felt from the first that Brandeis was

> one of those eminences that established, if not an Athenian, then a Florentine Academy among the apple orchards of the Hudson Valley, and when I think gratefully of those segments of my life that afforded the greatest pleasure and reward they seem to compose themselves of brilliant sunlight on Italian cities, and an American rural landscape filled with good music, woodsmoke, and among many friendly and lively voices, your own, vivid with intelligence, not infrequently ironic, but almost always benign.[25]

A faculty photo of the literature division from the early fifties was straight out of Central Casting: a sea of rumpled tweed, with a few of the faculty affecting more formality, in gray-flannel suits, like those worn by Barzun and Trilling at Columbia. The cohort is standing against a wall of floor-to-ceiling shelves filled with books. Bellow is leafing through a random volume, as others look over his shoulder. Brandeis, between Bellow and Hecht, casts a sidelong glance, amused by the little charade. The overall feeling is relaxed, almost comic, with Bellow the focal point. Still tan and whiskered, Hecht perches on a library stepladder, one knee propping up his left arm, with his cheek resting in the palm of his hand, as he stares off beyond the frame—bored or dreamy? Even in this planned posture of insouciance, Hecht's mien is impeccable, his clothes beautifully made, his tie a tasteful plaid, his hair and beard elegant and slightly roguish.

Bard had welcomed refugees from the war, a number of them Jewish, who formed a bridge between the college and the Old World. Hannah Arendt escaped to New York in the forties and her second husband, the philosopher Heinrich Blücher, began teaching at Bard in 1952. Hecht and Blücher became friends, carpooling from the city to Bard in Hecht's car. Through Blücher, Hecht came to know Arendt as well. Both Hannah and Heinrich spoke with heavy German accents, and while Hannah "spoke wonderfully well," Blücher would occasionally mangle an English idiom, sometimes to comic effect: "When pleased to be done with some unpleasant task, he would remark that it was well to have this 'in the behind,'" Hecht remembered laughingly. Also: in an amusing allusion to

Swift's Yahoo, he would dismiss someone of inferior qualities as "a regular Yoohoo."[26]

In addition to philosophy, Blücher taught a required freshman course called "The Common Course," a section of which Hecht also taught. The Common Course, which later became known as the First Year Seminar, was developed under the direction of Blücher from the time he arrived at Bard. The course was a "great ideas" course and included readings from Plato, Buddha, Heraclitus, the Bible, Homer, and a number of others. Though Hecht was "uncomfortable" with some of Blücher's ideas about these texts, he found the man himself "exceptionally endearing." The two became close on their long car rides together, and they kept each other company up north during the week: "He would visit me every evening before dinner for a drink (most commonly a 'bull shot,' composed of beef bouillon and vodka in equal measure) and then we would meet friends at a local dive for dinner."

In town, Hannah hosted Hecht on several occasions, partly, he suspected, out of gratitude for his generosity driving Heinrich. Hecht thought her "a woman of considerable charm."[27] Born in Hannover, in what is now Germany, she was almost a generation older than Hecht. Her father died when she was seven. She attended the University of Marburg, a student of Martin Heidegger, with whom she also had a brief affair, and took a PhD under Karl Jaspers at the University of Heidelberg. She married Blücher in 1940 and was detained by the French after the Nazi invasion. (She had been imprisoned once before—by the Gestapo in Berlin, where she had gone for research, suitably enough, on antisemitic propaganda.) When Hecht first met Arendt she had recently received American citizenship, and her major work on the Nazis and Communists, *The Origins of Totalitarianism* (1951), had just appeared. A writer of profound moral intelligence, Hannah made a deep impression on Hecht (as she would on Auden, who even proposed marriage after Blücher's death in 1970). Hecht's excruciating poem of murder, coercion, and moral compromise "'More Light! More Light!'" is dedicated to Arendt and Blücher.[28]

As Hecht contrived to make sense of what he had lived through in Germany, Arendt provided both guidance and solace. She had spent her entire life in the crucible of history that only very recently ended with the defeat of Nazi Germany. Hecht admired her enormously for her clarity

and deep understanding of a great range of subjects: "Her learning was almost limitless, or so it seemed to me, and not least because it commanded
regions of scholarship wholly unknown to me." These subjects included
philosophical inquiries into totalitarianism, antisemitism, and the nature
of evil—all of which Hecht ruminated on in his poems, though from an
artist's perspective. Arendt and Blücher prized the arts and poetry in particular. Blücher spoke of art with great intensity in his 1954 lecture on
Homer, in ways that Hecht would have been sympathetic to: "The eyes
of man are sunlike, because art comes and makes them more sunlike. Art
is so mighty because it changes our perception of the world."[29]

Bard students were more casual than their Columbia and Barnard
counterparts. The men wore sport coats and flannel trousers, much like
the denizens of Broadway and 116th Street, but the bucolic influence man-
ifested itself in open collars, with ties the exception rather than the rule.
Broad plaids were popular, as befitted the country-house atmosphere. Blue
jeans with rolled cuffs were seen on both men and women, and pomade
was popular, about to be made immortal by James Dean in *Rebel Without
a Cause*. Bard had come through the war with its progressive values intact.
The college catalogue for 1943 acknowledged that, "While the immediate demands in education are for the training of men for the war effort,
liberal education in America must be preserved as an important value in
the civilization for which the war is being fought. . . . Since education, like
life itself, is a continuous process of growth and effort, the student has to
be trained to comprehend and foster his own growth and direct his own
efforts." The college took pride in its "commitment to global issues of education and democracy." When the anti-Stalin revolution roiled through
the streets of Budapest in 1956, Bard "provided a haven for 325 Hungarian
student refugees . . . Gyula Nyikos, the chief English instructor for these
students, said of Bard's president at the time, 'Jim Case didn't open the
doors; he *flung* them open.'"[30]

Over the past several years, as Hecht worked to write the poems that
would make up his first book, the way was littered with discards—poems,
like a curate's egg, good in parts but not uniformly so. This process of
replacing weaker poems with stronger was finally approaching a happy
conclusion. *Stones* was ready to send to prospective publishers. Hecht
set his sights high, hoping that Macmillan might take an interest, but he

heard nothing in return for half a year, the same after ten months—still nothing. Over the summer of 1953, he may have begun to despair that, despite early affirmations and prominent serial publications, his career as a poet was failing to launch. That fall, in his second year at Bard, he had plenty of distractions from the vicissitudes of the publishing world. He was laying the groundwork for his career as a university professor.

If he was going to be a teacher, the question then became what to teach? Up to this point, he had spent most of his academic life on the receiving end. When he stood up in front of the rows of expectant faces, what would he feel confident saying to them with any authority? Contemporary poetry—he certainly had a deep grasp of it, even in its most arcane modernist forms. That he could teach. He would enjoy introducing students, as he had been introduced by Larry Leighton, to the work of Frost and Stevens, Yeats and Hardy. If he were to make a life of it, he would have to teach what he loved, and, while he had almost no formal training in them, what he loved most were the plays and poems of Shakespeare. It's true: he had lectured on *Macbeth* as part of Freshman English at Kenyon, but he had never before taught an entire semester devoted to the plays. After more than a decade, things had come full circle in ways that must have been as surprising as they were gratifying. He had read and performed Shakespeare as an undergraduate at Bard. Now he would rekindle his love of Shakespeare until it became an integral part of his life as a teacher.

The plays and poems assumed a central role in his writing life as well. For reasons that still lay ahead, Hecht's next book would be even longer in the making than his first—far longer in fact, well over a decade. When they did arrive, his new poems sounded distinctly different—a fact that was widely remarked on—influenced throughout, both directly and in more suggestive, subterranean ways, by his deepening engagement with Shakespeare's verse.

The choice of Shakespeare had a profound personal effect as well. It bore on questions of identity: who exactly would he be, or, rather, how would he present himself to the world? As an actor, he knew that one could project many selves. As the product of a troubled upbringing, he understood that it was up to him to choose what to present. (His father had suggested as much when he recommended Hecht change his name in college.) Hecht became the very model of a modern literature professor: bearded, tweedy, pensive, reserved. In this formula of self-creation, Shakespeare played a leading role. Nothing could be more canonical, more revered and accepted on both intellectual and aesthetic grounds. Stephen Greenblatt writes of the miracle of first teaching Shakespeare:

> It seemed—it still seems—incredible to me that this power [in a speech of King Lear] and the moral intelligence that it conveyed could come into my possession. If I desired it, it was mine as if by birthright, for the simple reason that English was my native tongue. All that I needed to do was to immerse myself in it passionately. And, equally incredible, as a teacher, I could spend my life sharing this passion with my students.[31]

For Greenblatt, the descendent of Lithuanian Jews, mastery of Shakespeare was "like a purchased coat of arms," despite those in his experience who refused to accept such a claim "made by someone of my name, background or religion." Hecht had experienced this exclusion as a student, with his teacher's winking association of Hecht's Jewishness with Shylock, but he would not allow this cruelty to sour him on what he held dear.

On the poetry front, by contrast, he could feel what would become the first great drought of his career coming on. He had written almost nothing since finishing *Stones* the previous summer. As a corrective, he applied for a residency at the MacDowell Colony in Peterborough, New Hampshire, and was accepted. By the first of July, he was ensconced and drafting new work. Each morning he lit out for his writing studio in the woods, "a handsome little cabin, with desks and tables and chairs and a couch, [and] an unnecessary fire-place."[32] From his porch he looked out through enormous pine trees on a mountain range in the distance. All day, he worked in utter silence, and snacked on the lunch that had been delivered to his door.

Hecht was intrigued by the bronze plaque on the front of the cabin, which carried the "pathetic"[33] inscription: "I shall have more to say when I am dead." The line appears at the conclusion of Edwin Arlington Robinson's poem about the American abolitionist "John Brown," whose violent death became an eloquent symbol of the anti-slavery movement. The cabin had been Robinson's during his yearly summers at MacDowell from 1915 to 1934, and his presence still loomed large. One famous story, frequently recounted there, described an exchange between Robinson and a young colonist who, eager to impress the senior writer, declared that he had written several thousand words that day. He piped up: "And what did you do today, Mr. Robinson?" To which Robinson replied: "This morning I removed the hyphen from *hell-hound*. This afternoon I put it back."[34]

Hecht's work flourished in the hothouse environment of the colony, where all practical impediments were replaced by free time, a quiet space, and prepared meals. He wrote to his parents to send his copy of William Empson's *Collected Poems* so that he could reread the poem "Missing Dates." Perhaps it was the close of Empson's poem he had in mind, which bemoans the hardships of a writer who cannot write:

It is the poems you have lost, the ills
From missing dates, at which the heart expires.
Slowly the poison the whole blood stream fills.
The waste remains, the waste remains and kills.

Hecht began work on two poems that July, but he doubted he could finish them to his satisfaction. Despite his fitful momentum, no poems worth collecting appeared until a year later, and then only in dribs and drabs, notably on Roman themes. (Rome remained in his thoughts and he hoped to make arrangements to head back there soon.) That summer at MacDowell, the urge to write about the war remained, but the method eluded him. He was stuck.

Meanwhile, his first collection found a home. It took Macmillan over a year to make up its mind, but once the publisher decided in the affirmative things moved quickly. Early in 1954, Hecht had finished copies in hand. Macmillan had sped the book into production, with handsome results. The slate gray dust jacket sported a sketch of classical ruins—a line drawing of two columns with Byzantine capitals atop a plinth—which was reproduced on the title page. The back cover listed the names in the Macmillan stable of poets, including Robinson, Hardy, Yeats, Marianne Moore, John Masefield, Sara Teasdale, and Edgar Lee Masters. Hecht was thrilled to be in such company. The jacket copy touted Hecht's "disturbing originality" and singled out "Samuel Sewall" as a perfect poem. The book's dedication read simply: "To Roger."

Stones was heralded by a modest but respectable fanfare—fine reviews in two influential journals, *The Hudson* and *The Kenyon*, both of which Hecht admired. Hecht had become closely associated with these two quarterlies over the years, and so he may have had a reasonable expectation of supportive notices, though neither was a puff piece. Joseph Bennett seasoned his notice with warmth, but certain observations seemed to damn the book with faint praise: "One can rejoice in [his] pure professionalism," and "He is a poet . . . who is not afraid to produce a pure exercise."[35] Bennett admired Hecht's baroque effects, "a sort of reflective effervescence in variable mood-keys," which only occasionally bog down in poems such as "A Poem for Julia," in which he displays "a tendency to a moral which seems an appendage to what had been some pretty live language." For Bennett, the best poems were those, like "At the Frick" and "Alceste in the Wilderness," in which "tough subject matter has given his exuberance and vitality considerable bite."

The most prestigious review appeared in the June 5 issue of *The New Yorker*, written by the magazine's in-house poetry critic, Louise Bogan, herself a widely respected poet. The thrill of being noticed in his hometown magazine, where he had roamed the halls pitching stories and soaking up the literary scene, was tempered by certain reservations of Bogan's. She rightly saw it as a young man's book, and, while she readily acknowledged Hecht's "verbal and technical brilliance," she felt that "the shimmer of virtuoso technique" could not mask "that many of the poems have very little content, emotional or otherwise."[36] This wounded Hecht deeply. He frequently felt personally wronged by a bad review, but in this case he may have understood the truth of Bogan's critique.

Bogan speaks of the book, though not in so many words, as juvenilia. This is how Hecht himself came to see it in time. She notes, by way of a thumbnail biography, Hecht's Army service and his Academy fellowship, adding that "The second experience has evidently been more important in his poetic development than the first; he draws more freely upon Italian scenes than upon any background of war." Without knowing the cause, Bogan sensed the truth: the trauma was still too raw.

At *Kenyon Review*, Ransom assigned the book to Arthur Mizener, in a bizarre pairing with a review of Marianne Moore's translations of La Fontaine.[37] Moore receives a lengthy drubbing at Mizener's hands—"Miss Moore's translations are very bad"—while *Stones* comes in for some qualified praise. Mizener announces Hecht as "a poet of great charm, possibly even too great charm," especially when his "witty fancy gets out of control."[38]

Of the "conventional" "La Condition Botanique," he wrote, it is "a poem in which, while apparently making meticulous and even scientifically accurate observations about the obvious subject, the poet gradually builds up a system of assertions about life as a whole. Auden provides all sorts of examples of the kind. . . ."[39] This perceptive bit of criticism foreshadows Hecht's fondness for the pathetic fallacy, for a moralized landscape that is at once external and internal.

A damning review came from the English poet and critic Donald Davie in *Shenandoah*. Partial to poets as different as Ezra Pound and Thomas Hardy, Davie argued that Hecht's style did not feel sufficiently modern. The English poet Dick Davis once puzzled over Davie's critical legacy in a bit of memorializing light verse: "Heir both to Hardy and no less to Pound / At whose address now may you be found?" Davie had a reputation as a hatchet man. Philip Larkin, whom Hecht greatly admired, penned a bit of marginalia, to be sung to the tune of "A Bicycle Built for Two": "Davie, Davie, give me a bad review. / It's your gravy, telling folks what to do." Of *Stones,* Davie wrote that "the poems are full of erudite and cosmopolitan references, epigraphs from Molière and so on; and the diction is recherché, opulent, laced with the sort of wit that costs nothing. Here and there too the poet knowingly invites what reviewers have duly responded with, the modish epithet 'Baroque.'" Davie twisted the knife, offering that a more appropriate term would be "the much less fashionable 'Victorian.'"[40]

Hecht had attracted attention with individual poems published in the *Kenyon* and *Hudson* reviews, but to have a published collection to his name established him as a full-fledged poet. It may well have been that Hecht felt that he was something of a latecomer to the party. Richard Wilbur's *The Beautiful Changes and Other Poems* had appeared in 1947, when Hecht was still struggling to complete his first mature poems. James Merrill, who was three years younger than Hecht, had published *Black Swan* in a private edition in 1946, and in 1951 his *First Poems* appeared from the major New York house of Alfred A. Knopf. Hecht would become close with both poets, their careers intertwining in various ways over the years.

At the same time that *Stones* launched Hecht as a poet, his teaching at Bard began his career in the academy. Hecht's family finances were such that he would always have to work to earn a living. His parents were well enough off, but he was determined not to have to rely on them. He took this responsibility seriously, and, if he wished for any kind of independence, he would have to make his own way. For his brother, this kind of independence was not an option. Roger never left home. He lived simply and required little, but for Hecht this kind of sheltered existence under his parents' wing was out of the question.

3. Marrying Magdalene

Hecht's career was coming together in ways that must have delighted and surprised him. How unlikely and welcome to be back at Bard, this time behind the lectern. He was laying the groundwork for a peaceful life as a university professor, with affable colleagues and summers free to write. Then he met Pat. Hecht had previously avoided serious romantic entanglements, but Pat thrilled him with her allure, her joie de vivre and expansive life force, a powerful antidote to Hecht's fits of melancholy. She would define the next decade and a half of his life, a period marked in the end by acute suffering and another breakdown and hospitalization.

Patricia Harris was a world-class beauty, an aspiring model. Most likely Hecht met her during his first year of teaching at Bard, possibly the summer of 1953, when Pat was only nineteen or twenty. Pat was babysitting for a model friend whom Hecht took out on a date. When he brought the date home, he offered to walk Pat back to her apartment. The physical attraction was strong: to a good degree it was "the consent of flesh" that landed them together.[41] Self-possessed and fearless, she appeared as a diamond in the rough. Young models in the 1950s were associated more with the New York demimonde than with Upper East society, but Hecht rejected such snobbery. He embraced his itinerate bohemian lifestyle of the past few years and wished to be rid of the fussy gentility of his parents' social set. He saw Pat and felt that he could save her, as she would save him from stale convention. He could lend her respectability; she, freedom from stifling mores. With her striking countenance, high cheekbones, and cropped hair, Pat exuded a siren-like sex appeal that drew men to her in any room in which she set foot. Wives pulled their husbands away. Hecht was charmed and felt immediately at ease in her company. She had a frankness about her that obviated the need for formality; they grew quickly intimate. After dating each other for only a few short months they decided to get married. Not everyone approved—including the Bellows, who were dubious of Pat. Some friends, such as the writer and translator Claire White, had the sense that Hecht "thought that he was rescuing her, that she was a sort of waif."[42]

Hecht was riding high on a string of successes, which emboldened him. Still, the marriage, when it came on February 27, 1954, was a tense affair. A brief and tart account of their courtship and wedding can be found in the poet Louis Simpson's scathing roman à clef *North of Jamaica*. Simpson, another student of Van Doren's at Columbia, changes the names—Cape Cod for Fire Island, for example, and Cambridge for New York—but much of what he describes is taken directly from Hecht's life. Hecht appears in passing under his own name (as do the poets John Hollander, Richard Wilbur, Robert Lowell, and others). But Simpson relegates his more detailed portrait of Hecht to the character of Christopher Green.

In Simpson's unflattering characterization, Green is an "epigone" of the New Critics. Like Hecht, he is a successful younger poet, who studied at Kenyon College. There, Simpson purrs, he cultivated an English accent. Hecht's patrician lilt really stuck in Simpson's craw; he later referred to it behind Hecht's back as a speech impediment. Like Hecht, Green knew John Crowe Ransom and Allen Tate. Oscar Williams anthologized his poems. While Simpson includes Green among the promising poets of his generation, he does not care to write like him—too poised, too technically polished. The portrait reveals Simpson's bitchy streak; one suspects it hides more than a twinge of rivalry.

Simpson includes an account of visiting the Hechts' apartment, on the occasion of a party in celebration of Dylan Thomas. (Mira Van Doren remembers attending the actual event.) One senses a level of embellishment here, but the basic account rings true. Simpson arrives ahead of the rest of the party and is introduced by Tony/Christopher to his parents:

> Christopher's mother was a cultured lady who, like her son, had an English accent. I put down my glass on the table and she hastened to slide something between the glass and the surface. I spoke to Chris's father for a few minutes. He was in business downtown and seemed, in comparison with his wife and son, rather subdued.[43]

Simpson picks up on a certain tension between Hecht and his parents:

> When I left the apartment Christopher's mother and father were standing by the door. I said, "Thank you," and added, "You must be very proud of Christopher." "Oh, we are," said Mrs. Green, though with a rather stern expression as though reproving me for having any doubts about the matter.

Green's flaw, the thing that "involved him in all sorts of difficulties" was the fact that he "was lecherous and very attractive to women." Simpson then brings Pat on stage, disguised as Jill, "a stunningly good-looking girl of about nineteen." Jill has "the high cheekbones, straight nose and blond hair of a fashion model, and this, it turned out, was her profession. . . . She looked like the destined companion of South American millionaires. But apparently she was tired of all that, and wanted nothing better than to read poems and literary criticism for the rest of her life." According to the novel, the couple met only a few weeks before they were engaged to be married.

Hecht's head-over-heels attraction to Pat must have fostered Simpson's idea of Green as lecherous. Hecht may well have agreed in hindsight that his libido (and possibly his vanity) had gotten the better of him. This may also have been jealousy on Simpson's part, a besetting foible, one suspects. The sin of lust figures prominently in Hecht's poems in the wake of his troubled years with Pat. At present, though, his depictions of women in the poems tended toward the ideal, though erotically charged:

How she came forward to me, letting fall
Lamplight upon her dress till every small
Motion made visible seemed no mere endeavor
of body to articulate its offer,
But more a grace won by the way from all
Striving in what is difficult, from all
Losses, so that she moved but to discover
A practice of the blood . . .[44]

The woman is more muse than flesh and blood, a figure on which to heap abstraction, in the manner of Stevens's woman who sang beyond the genius of the sea. But there is a dark undercurrent of the carnal in "Double Sonnet." Phrases such as "my unfailing fever" and "trance of lamplight" resolve into Prufrockian defeat: "speechless, inept, and totally unmanned."[45]

A few weeks before their wedding, Hecht published in *The New Yorker* for January 16 another idealized love sonnet, entitled "The Gift of Song":

Wanting her clear perfection, how many tongues
Manifest what no language understands?
Yet as her beauty evermore commands
Even the tanager with tiny lungs
To flush all silence, may she by these songs
Know it was love I looked for at her hands.[46]

If Simpson is right about the compressed timeline of their courtship, the poem, which appears in *Stones* under the title "Imitation," could not have been written about Pat. "Shyness" is not the first word that leaps to mind to describe her. She was outgoing and even frequently rowdy. To Hecht she was "clear perfection," where others like Simpson found fault. The poem is a rousing toast by a young romantic, a compact between poet and muse, which Hecht's relationship with Pat in some sense fulfilled.

Simpson goes on to provide an account of the wedding. The reception took place in the Hechts' apartment, and, according to Simpson, none of Pat's family were present, only a few of her girlfriends, also models (whom Simpson's date identifies as call girls, based on conversations she overhears):

> The wedding reception, with all these beautiful models moving through it, was like a Hollywood scene. The talk was very high-toned, all about where Jill and Chris were going to spend the summer, on the Cape [in fact, Fire Island]. Mrs. Green passed around the room and wherever she had been people seemed to have been converted to Anglo-Saxon Protestants, and most into Episcopalians. Hauteur was rife.[47]

If Simpson has it in for Hecht and his parents, he is positively defamatory about Pat, suggesting that, while she tried to pass herself off as a virgin schooled in a convent, she was in fact a liar who was "far from inexperienced." He goes on to suggest that it wasn't long before Jill began deceiving Chris with other men, until, at last, she left him to become "a *bona fide* countess in a palace on the outskirts of Florence."[48] Simpson is writing his account some twenty years after the event, and he is well aware of the difficulties in the six-year marriage and Pat's subsequent marriage. But initially, at least, Hecht believed all was well. He and Pat laughed together and drank together. (Hecht had what Geoffrey Hill, writing about Ivor Gurney, called "a depressive's gift for clowning."[49]) They were happy and in love, if only for a brief moment.

Given Hecht's teaching schedule and other responsibilities on campus, the pair decided to keep house in Hecht's apartment in Annandale, which—with a thorough cleaning and a few improvements—was ready to receive them at the beginning of March. Hecht wrote to assure his parents that Pat's moving in had gone well: "Everything has worked perfectly. By 1 P.M. today everything was unpacked and put away, the curtains hung, the place swept, the furniture shifted to new places, and we are now all set."[50] The two relished their homey, bohemian existence, grilling steaks in the open fireplace, going for walks through the countryside, and curling up in the cold and early dark of the Upstate New York winter. Claire White, who knew the Hechts in Rome and became close friends with Pat, did not see her as domestically inclined. She was "not the marrying type," it seemed to her.[51] But Pat was giving it her best effort, playing the homemaker and throwing herself into the life of the college. She co-chaired a fashion show to benefit the Bard College Scholarship Fund. According to the short-lived campus publication *Communitas,* old and new wedding gowns were modeled, "showing the changing styles of the last half century."[52] To Pat's credit, she found a niche for herself among the highbrow faculty. Saul Bellow's biographer Zachary Leader observes: "If the style of the students at Bard was bohemian, the style of the faculty was conservative and Ivy League."[53] The faculty seemed like "Castaways from ships that had foundered en route to Harvard or characters who had fallen from grace at Yale," is how Bellow himself put it. His fellows on the faculty were "still refining the airs they had acquired at the great Ivy League centers."[54] Pat was not easily intimidated, however. Her youthful, flirtatious energy must have set the place abuzz. Again she caught the attention of *Communitas*: at a bagpipe concert on the quadrangle, "Bard's contingent of Scotchmen were not to be outdone. Janet Goldenberg and Pat Hecht were doing the Fling with the best of them."[55]

Keeping away from fast-living Manhattan may have been a marital strategy for the couple, like the bon vivants in a Cole Porter song who decide for the sake of their domestic tranquility to "try staying home." Weekends, they kept to the country. Hecht boarded the train to Manhattan only rarely. He read and prepared his classes; she cooked elaborate meals of roast beef and chicken—both of them "still 'cooing' and blissfully happy," as Pat wrote to the senior Hechts in her spiky, slanting hand.[56]

Nothing had intruded on the Hechts' happiness by early spring. With the thaw in the Hudson Valley came not only spring but also what spring promised—the end of the semester. Tony and Pat already looked forward to summer on Fire Island. Then news came in the mail from the Guggenheim Foundation, informing Hecht that he was the recipient of a fellowship beginning in the fall. Hecht dearly wished to return to Rome, "where one could live cheaply and write poetry," he told *Communitas.*[57] He had previously received word from his friend Laurance P. Roberts, the director of the American Academy in Rome, that should he receive the prize he would be very welcome at the Academy, space allowing. He would even receive a special rate for his accommodations. Since Hecht applied for the grant in the fall, he'd gotten married and now needed an apartment suited to a couple. Hecht's salary at Bard was $3,600 (supplemented by an additional $500 from other sources, including his family). He requested $4,500 from the foundation, which (after roughly $500 was deducted for taxes) would "cover all expenses, including travel, for a year spent chiefly in Rome."[58]

In June, he wrote to the president of Bard, James H. Case, to request a leave of absence for the upcoming academic year, having already notified the Literature Division of his good news. He also wrote for some assurance that, following his leave, Bard would have a place for him on the faculty, since the annual appointment letters under which he currently taught made no provision for employment from year to year. He also secretly hoped that the honor that accompanied the Guggenheim would help speed his promotion at the college.

Living within Hecht's means as a college professor, the newlyweds settled for a honeymoon on Fire Island, building up the glamour for their friends of a smart retreat from the heat of summer in the city. Also, thanks to the Guggenheim's largesse, they would enjoy a long trip abroad, which must have seemed to them like the extravagant honeymoon they had secretly hoped for all along. In keeping with the festive spirit of the trip, they booked a shipboard passage in September, likely to Le Havre, with a first stop in Paris. The voyage itself was drab, with "little sun," though calm seas meant that neither ever felt seasick.[59] They "gorged" themselves with rich food and copious amounts of wine, attended all of the "galas" "in First and Tourist classes, as well as our own"—probably the midrange cabin class. They befriended fellow passengers and enjoyed the social whirl of the crossing.

After nonstop partying at sea, their entry into Paris was a harsh one. They arrived by train, very likely hungover, too late to be met at the station by Hecht's friend Paul Henissart, to whom he had written. In his letter, he had asked Paul to make a reservation for them at his old haunt, the Hotel d'Islay, but when they arrived there were no rooms in their name. By now it was midnight, and none of the nearby hotels had any vacancy. Finally, they found one that was close by but "uglier and more expensive." Finances weighed on Hecht generally, as did the responsibility for all of their travel plans. He knew Paris well, and made all of the arrangements for their stay. When anything fell through it was, therefore, his fault—a condition that Pat was not likely to forgive. (The portrait of the emasculating wife in "See Naples and Die," and her disdain for her husband's lack of savoir faire when it comes to foreign customs, may well have begun with a seed planted in Paris. The couple would arrive at Naples later in their journey.) And things had gone awry in a big way: not only was Hecht's friend Paul not there to meet them, but when Hecht inquired, Henissart was no longer employed at his job or living at the address Hecht had for him.

Things might have become bitter between Tony and Pat had their luck not changed in a surprising, almost hilarious way. They ran into a young man who had been Hecht's student at Bard. Despite the fact that Professor Hecht, notorious for his severe grading, had flunked this poor fellow in freshman English, the young man was delighted to run into his old professor. He was currently on leave from the Army and staying in Paris with his aunt at the George V, in the posh 8th Arrondissement, which had become a haven for American tourists in Paris. The next day they all headed off in the aunt's chauffeur-driven Cadillac for a sightseeing tour of Chartres and Versailles. The aunt adored the couple—and here Pat's charm and Tony's striking good looks clearly did the trick. They sang for their supper while their patroness plied them with Champagne for days. On their last night in Paris, wine continued to flow all through dinner at a restaurant in Montmartre, followed by a "very gaudy" nightclub, and several of the aunt's favorite boîtes, until woozy from drink, the two were deposited with their luggage at the station for the night train to Rome.

Such diversions aside, Paris had been dreary, rainy, inconvenient, and, Hecht was now realizing, expensive, despite their meals out with their new friends. On the journey to Rome, his spirits began to lift. As he had during his last time in Italy, Hecht planned to live as cheaply as possible, notwithstanding whatever Pat's expectations may have been for a tonier Grand Tour. He was in charge of making the arrangements and preferred to stretch their funds as far as possible. Fair skies broke through just as their train passed from France into Italy, and there was for the first time since they arrived in Europe the promise of "sunshine and warm weather." Utterly sleepless, they looked out at the Italian scenery with excitement, and Pat, to Tony's relief, found the place "enchanting." The tensions of the trip eased as a rapturous love of Italy—and at the best of times, of each other—washed over them.

When they arrived at the Academy, the Robertses were there to welcome them, gracious as ever. The travelers were now completely exhausted, having only enough energy for a quick meal then straight to bed. The next morning, their renewed enthusiasm propelled them on an all-day sightseeing tour, trekking the long distance from the Janiculum high above Trastevere, across the Tiber to Michelangelo's hilltop Campidoglio. From there they passed the Colosseum and entered the crowded, dusty, resplendent Forum. Through narrow streets, Hecht led the way north, a seasoned guide through the ancient city, to a more out-of-the-way place that he wanted Pat to see—the Church of St. Ignatius Loyola on the Piazza S. Ignazio. There they craned their necks to take in Andrea Pozzo's vibrant painted ceiling, with its towering architectural trompe l'oeil and swirling putti. They followed this Baroque masterpiece with the sober, classical lines of the Pantheon, built for the Emperor Hadrian in the second century BC.

This first day was perhaps their happiest in Rome, perhaps the happiest of their marriage: Tony and Pat standing together under the oculus, illuminated in the shaft of light that descends through the dome onto the floor below. It is a thoroughly Hechtian image, the sun penetrating the darkness, which seems always to be encroaching. When Hecht looked for a way to express his feelings for Pat in verse, he began, as he so often did, with light:

> Hardly enough for me that the pail of water
>   Alive with the wrinkling light
>   Brings clearness home and whiter
> Than mind conceives the walls mature to white,
> Or that the washed tomatoes whose name is given
>   To love fulfill their bowl
>   And the Roman sea is woven
> Together by threading fish and made most whole.
>
> I delight in each of these, delight moreover
>   In the dark skill of those hands
>   Closer to wise than clever
> Of our blind Italian landlady who stands

Her shoes fouled with the lustful blood of rabbit
 Lightly dispatched and dressed
 Fixing it to the gibbet
Of the clothesline where the laundry sails to rest.[60]

Hecht depicts himself in the poem, set in Ischia, as a "furious unicorn / Come to the virgin's lap tethered and tame." It is unclear how far he believed in Pat's virginal facade, but the erotic pull was strong. From their rooms near the Academy, they took in the rhythms of the city, at once fierce and wonderful, ancient, primal, visceral.

With Pat at his elbow, ever seeking new amusements, and the various distractions offered by the activities at the Academy, Hecht found it difficult to settle down. The mood among the fellows was genial, if a bit staid: "On the whole, the group here now is a lot more solemn and less lively than the one I knew before."[61] There were a few familiar faces— two of the fellows he had known previously, though not well—but no close friends. Admittedly, everyone was still testing the waters, but from Hecht's perspective it didn't "look too promising." There was one exception: the Wilburs, Dick and Charlee.

Wilbur cut a striking figure: tanned, athletic, a towering physical presence. He had married his boyhood sweetheart, Charlotte (Charlee) Ward, who was poetry editor of Smith College's literary magazine when Wilbur was at nearby Amherst. The Wilburs were a model of the happily married couple, rare in literary circles, and, despite minor wartime liaisons, they remained devoted to each other until Charlee's death at eighty-five in April 2007. Hecht first met Wilbur in passing one evening in Manhattan, in the lobby of the Algonquin Hotel, whose bar was still a famous haunt long after the heyday of the *New Yorker* Round Table writers. Wilbur rarely made it to New York, so their paths had not crossed again. But now Hecht had reason to look on him with suspicion. By all outward indications, the two poets should have been allies; their mastery of traditional verse set them apart from all but a few contemporaries. Perhaps the editors at *The New York Times Book Review* had this shared affinity in mind when they assigned *A Summoning of Stones* to Wilbur for a review, on April 4, 1954, paired with a book by a poet of contrasting sensibility, Barbara House. Wilbur began with his consideration of House, meting out judicious enthusiasm for her now forgotten book; but his remarks on *Stones,* which rounded out the review, seemed stingy by comparison, both in its praise and the space allotted to it. (One is reminded of the Woody Allen joke that goes something like, A: The food at this restaurant is terrible. B: Yes, and such small portions.) Hecht's book had "much of every virtue except passionate simplicity." And yet: "If he lacks urgent attitudes, if he seems less interested in statement than in felicities by the way, there is a decided personality in this rewarding first book, and any tendency to connoisseurship and preciosity is corrected by gaiety, appetite, and pleasant vulgarity."[62]

When the two poets met at the Academy, Hecht assumed the worst: had Wilbur intentionally stinted on his praise of the book? Wilbur, as it happened, had been feeling bad about the review, not because of his judgments—which in fact were perceptive and ultimately on point—but because of the review's truncated form when it finally appeared. Wilbur had struggled with the tight space he was given, ultimately running over his allotment. The cuts made by the editor "took away my most favorable comments" and Hecht, therefore, had some reason "to feel that I had treated him badly." Wilbur explained this on their first meeting in Rome, and Hecht "believed it right away, and we had from that moment on an entirely warm relationship."[63] Despite certain similarities, Hecht and Wilbur worked very differently. Of Wilbur's work habits, Hecht noted "his deliberate development of an idea into a poem, [which] made him aware that Wilbur composed a poem not by running willy-nilly with an inspiration, but by accreting into it, line by line, ever more nuance, surprise, and significance. Hecht, on the other hand, was proud, though a little wary, of what he called his own 'sailing present tense,' which is on full display in 'The Gardens of the Villa d'Este.'"[64]

A new Italian friend named Dino Rotundi drove the Wilburs all around town, showing them the highlights. (The Hechts' cicerone was the architectural historian William MacDonald, who knew both the modern and ancient city and could regale his pupils with wit and charm.) Rotundi considered one of Rome's crowning glories to be the Pizzeria La Sacrestia, which was known for its famous clairvoyant, who would move among the patrons practicing his occult art. Wilbur's mind was read, and thereafter he persuaded friends to accompany him to the pizzeria, including the Dante scholar Charles Singleton and his wife, Eula. Wilbur's masterly dramatic monologue "The Mind-Reader" is dedicated to the couple. The poem, set in the pizzeria, first appeared in *The New York Review of Books* on July 20, 1972, and may well have served as a model for Hecht's own monologues of the late 1970s, including "The Venetian Vespers," though Hecht's poems, often written in a minor key, could not be mistaken for Wilbur's. Wilbur typically managed a far sunnier outlook and tone in his poems, whereas Hecht's plumbed a darkness that admitted light only dimly and in flashes.

The Wilburs had an apartment in Monteverde Nuovo, where fellows with spouses and children usually stayed, as the Wilburs had all three of their children in tow. The Academy provided them with a cook and a maid. They had a life somewhat apart from the Academy, but even at a slight remove from the social whirl they could tell that the Hechts were unhappy. "Pat was very attractive and flirtatious, and the flirting was very embarrassing and demeaning to Tony. And it became clear to my wife and me that it was not going to last as a happy marriage."[65]

Hecht knew the situation was precarious. When their spirits were high and they could find a way to connect to each other, things were pleasurable, if forever fraught to some degree. When things were bad between them, however, the relationship seemed completely untenable. Hecht saw clearly how widely things swung from tranquil to heated and unpleasant. Alcohol played a significant role in exacerbating the inherent volatility of their relationship. Hecht liked to call their nightly cocktail hour, often co-hosted by the MacDonalds, Fun and Games. These evenings had a built-in sense of exorbitance and bad behavior. (A few years later, Edward Albee would subtitle Act One of *Who's Afraid of Virginia Woolf?* "Fun and Games," in which a tweedy professor and his emotionally volatile wife tilt headlong toward a drink-fueled reckoning. Tony and Pat could have easily performed the roles of George and Martha.)

The fellows' evening routine was quickly established: dinner in the Academy's cypress-tree-lined courtyard or in the grand indoor dining room, followed by more socializing over billiards. After only a month or so, the novelty began to wane. The Wilburs retreated to the seclusion of their residence. In her mind, Charlee Wilbur broke the fellows down into types: "Very young scholars, bearded and predictable"; artists, especially sculptors, whose conversations she found stimulating; prima donnas wary of being upstaged; and "cat haters," who failed to recognize the charms of the city's countless feral cats.[66] To which category did the Hechts belong? Hecht was young, scholarly, sported a beard, but he was far from predictable. No one who followed his convulsions with Pat would have accused him of that. As for Pat herself: she could play the prima donna down to the ground and rarely allowed herself to be upstaged. If the evening began to bore her, she would test out her charms on an unsuspecting, and most likely well-lubricated and married, man in the group. Claire White, a fellow that year, along with her husband, Robert (a grandson of Stanford White, whose firm had designed the Academy building), remembered the kind of hold that Pat exerted over men on these occasions. Charlee, for one, found Pat's behavior a cause for some alarm. She wrote to their friend, the poet John Malcolm Brinnin (who ran the renowned Poetry Center at the YMHA on 92nd Street in New York), that she felt horrible for Hecht, who was clearly suffering as a result of Pat's flirtations and whose "marital problems were attracting gossip and unsolicited advice."[67]

While Wilbur worked away on his translation of *The Misanthrope*, rendering Molière's French alexandrines into limpid pentameter couplets, Hecht tried to work on new poems, but with limited success. In truth, he was distracted. The setting was much the same as during his last, fruitful stay on the Janiculum, but the situation was distinctly different. This time he was a newlywed, and in every decision there was Pat to be considered. She enjoyed the social aspects of Academy life but could not help feeling at a loss. What was her role there exactly, during the long afternoons while Hecht worked in his studio? She wished she could be working as well, and when a modeling job came along some months later, she was greatly relieved to have "a chance to do a little something."[68]

Pat valued her independence, and the modeling work was something of her own apart from Tony. Meanwhile, Hecht shared Charlee's affinity for the sculptors in the group—befriending Dimitri Hadzi and the California surrealist Jack Zajac. Gilbert Franklin did a bronze bust of Hecht at this time, which, when Hecht later owned it, he adorned with a pointed elf's hat. The art critic Dore Ashton and her husband, the painter Adja Yunkers, were spending his Guggenheim year in Rome. Also there that fall were the architect Robert Venturi and the composer Yehudi Wyner.

After a month at the Academy, during which Pat took Italian lessons, the two sought cheaper lodgings. But before they could fully settle into a daily routine of work, sightseeing, and Academy dinners and events, they were dealt a great shock late in 1954: "In spite of all precautions to the contrary," Pat was pregnant.[69]

Enough unhappiness had visited the two in their brief time abroad that Hecht had already begun to suspect that the situation was unraveling. The extent of Hecht's desperation and displeasure can be gauged from the frenzied way in which he sought to extricate himself. He quickly conceived of a coolly practical plan and enlisted his parents' help in carrying it out. Through all the uncertainty and unrest surrounding the situation with Pat, one thing was clear to him: they were in no position, logistically nor in their faltering relationship, to have a child. Hecht had no long-term employment. He still had a vague assurance of a place at Bard, should he wish to return, but nothing was definite. Nor did they currently have a place to live beyond their rented apartment in Rome. They had given up their apartment in Upstate New York and would have to find a new one—presumably with the added expense of an extra bedroom in which a crib could be set up.

Given all this, the thought of raising a child was unimaginable to him at this point, and the pregnancy weighed on them both without respite: "I am chiefly concerned that this should be taken care of first," he confided to his parents by post. "I have told Pat that our return does not mean any alteration in our relationship, though I think that if I had not said this, she would have refused to go home or to have anything done about her pregnancy."[70] What was meant here? Did Pat fear that the two were rapidly growing apart, such that only her presence there could assure her that Hecht still wished to remain together? It seems clear from Hecht's letter that he was having serious doubts in this regard, so much so that he kept his thoughts from Pat so as not to completely explode the precarious dynamic in which they suddenly found themselves. In fact, he had made up his mind that they would not live together again in New York. Tony would need to stay in his old room that he and Roger had shared, at least initially, and he feared the strain that news of the divorce might cause his brother: "I suspect that my return may have a devastating effect on Roger, and I hope this can somehow be taken into account. . . . It is Pat's plan to go back and find an apartment for us, but I am at last certain this is not the solution. However, I cannot say this to her while she is pregnant."[71] He would wait for word from his parents, and for Roger's okay, before leaving for New York.

Hecht acted decisively, almost impersonally, in his own self-interest, though others in his circle at the Academy may have seen it as self-preservation. The Wilburs knew that something was amiss, though it was likely not until later that they learned any specifics. Hecht was now beside himself; he needed to find a way out of this unwanted circumstance, or lose his grip entirely. The gasoline that fed the flames was the fact that he was not writing, and there was no hope of accomplishing anything alone in Rome: "In the frame of mind I'm in, staying here with Pat gone and with other people around me who are and have been working successfully, would only add to my sense of defeat and frustration," he wrote to his parents. The Guggenheim funds, which had been flowing since July, were halfway exhausted, and Hecht had "nothing to show for it"; the "contemplation of this alone" was enough to make him miserable.[72]

Hecht's anxiety was consuming him; he couldn't work and his plea to his parents had bordered on "hysterical," he felt afterward. In his next letter he had "calmed down a bit," even though the situation remained unresolved and at times it seemed even more unmanageable. Pat was struggling, both as a mother-to-be and a recent bride. She changed her mind about terminating the pregnancy. The reason she gave: she was certain he was "asking this of her as a preliminary to leaving her." As it happened, her instincts were not wrong; Hecht was grappling with the question, convinced that such a step was for the best the more rancorous their arguments grew.

Eventually calmed by Hecht's assurances to her about his commitment to the marriage, Pat agreed that it was best to terminate the pregnancy. She began to make plans to fly back to the States and stay with her mother and have the procedure done by her doctor in New York. She had been to see him the previous spring for another operation. Hecht never mentions the type of procedure, though it caused her mother concern. Pat planned to tell her mother that it was too soon after that surgery to have the baby. Hecht worried that, if Pat were home and alone, she might have second thoughts or might be convinced by her mother to go through with the birth, so he proposed an alternative. They would travel together to Switzerland for the abortion, "because it's cheaper there, and I can be with her." She would then fly home to find an apartment and modeling work. Also: "It's legal there."[73] This last point, added almost in passing, was in fact a serious consideration. As Katha Pollitt writes of that time, "Well-connected white women with private health insurance were sometimes able to obtain 'therapeutic' abortions, a never-defined category that remained legal throughout the epoch of illegal abortion."[74] But access to safe abortions had dwindled recently as doctors, wary of prosecution, became more cautious. Hecht confided to his parents his plans: "I suppose I will tell her that I'll follow by boat, though I'm not sure I will. . . . And I'm not even sure I'll tell her that."[75]

Hecht swore his parents to secrecy. As far as Pat knew, he had not consulted them. She still resented him for having confided in them about their "previous difficulties"—presumably culminating in the earlier operation.[76] It is hard to know how the two could have grown so rapidly apart. Simpson's unflattering portrait points the finger at Pat's promiscuity, which, he says, she returned to almost immediately after their wedding. It was clear that Hecht was experiencing extreme emotional and psychological pain; he couldn't think straight. His reaction to the situation was to act dispassionately. He dearly hoped it might all somehow go away.

And then—horribly—it did. Pat miscarried at the end of November. Hecht was upset, naturally, but also enormously relieved, communicating the loss of the pregnancy to his parents as "a God-sent solution to our problems."[77] Pat had continued to be conflicted right up until the end. There was more back and forth, and concern about the danger "so soon after her last operation." Would she have been well enough to go through with it? As Hecht wrote to his parents, both he and Pat were "immensely pleased" that things had worked out as they had, but Pat's miscarriage was followed by (or possibly occasioned by?) an infection in her ovaries. She lay in bed for a week, receiving shots twice a day. The inflammation receded, and she slowly recovered her strength. At last the flurry of doctors and medication eased, though they would have to "lay off sex." Pat was well enough to contemplate again her return home. Hecht still believed that the best solution was for Pat "to go back and get a job in the states, and I ought to stay on here and try to get some work done."[78]

Pat offered to support the two of them with her modeling, so that Tony would be freed from the dwindling support and term of his Guggenheim. But there was another wrinkle that extended Hecht's uncertainty about a course of action: "The medical crisis, like the last one, has brought us sort of together again." Not only were they brought together, but they stayed together, due in no small part, it is possible to imagine, to Hecht's guilt over how he had handled the crisis all along. It was uncharacteristic of him; never before had he acted so calculatingly in what he saw as his own self-interest. To make matters worse, throughout the crisis he had been unable to work. Each day the freedom granted by the Guggenheim waned, and as far as he could tell Pat was at the heart of the crisis: "I feel somehow that if I could get myself away from the emotional complexities that her presence entails, I might be able to get down to work."[79] This need for tranquility had gone unmet during the war and after. Only during his initial stay at the Academy had he found the necessary calm to work in a sustained way on *Stones,* and his current hopes for a renewal of a Pax Romana, so to speak, had gone unsatisfied. This need was absolute, and in future years even the disruption occasioned by a moderate teaching load was enough to prohibit any real productivity where his poems were concerned. He would ask Pat if she would head home without him.

The Hechts celebrated the holidays by going to a round of parties and were even feeling cheerful enough to host a gathering themselves. On Christmas Day, they attended Mass in St. Peter's Square, among the throngs who had come to receive the Pope's blessing. Shortly after New Year's, Hecht thought again of the future, of the year ahead, and he began the "drudgery" of writing to colleges about possible work. Bard would have him back, he knew, but the terms were not ideal. He hoped that another college might take an interest in him and offer him better pay. He didn't hold out much hope, because from his perch in Rome he was asking to be hired sight-unseen, as he would not be back in time to interview in person. Equally remote were his chances of renewing his Guggenheim fellowship, though he applied for one, hoping for lightning to strike twice.

Despite this dreary and nervous-making correspondence, the first weeks of 1955 promised a new start and rising spirits. Hecht was writing again, though somewhat fitfully, and Pat had taken a number of modeling gigs, which would keep her "pretty busy for some time to come."[80] Hecht may have begun to draft his quite personal poem "The Vow" around this time. It appeared two years later in *The Hudson Review* for Spring 1957 (along with another Italian poem, "The Origin of Centaurs"). The tone is by turns tender, ironic, and terrible:

> In the third month, a sudden flow of blood.
> The mirth of tabrets ceaseth, and the joy
> Also of the harp. The frail image of God
> Lay spilled and formless. Neither girl nor boy,
> But yet blood of my blood, nearly my child.
>   All that long day
> Her pale face turned to the window's mild
>   Featureless grey.[81]

As Hecht later explained to an audience at a reading, "a large part of the second stanza, and all of the third stanza is spoken by the ghost of the child who fails to be born":[82]

> And for some nights she whimpered as she dreamed
> The dead thing spoke, saying: "Do not recall
> Pleasure at my conception. I am redeemed
> From pain and sorrow. Mourn rather for all
> Who breathlessly issue from the bone gates,
>   The gates of horn,
> For truly it is best of all the fates
>   Not to be born.

> "Mother, a child lay gasping for bare breath
> On Christmas Eve when Santa Claus had set
> Death in the stocking, and the lights of death
> Flamed in the tree. O, if you can, forget
> You were the child, turn to my father's lips
>   Against the time
> When his cold hand puts forth its fingertips
>   Of jointed lime."

Despite the starkness of the address, the poem ends with hope for the future and a kind of resolution for the couple and their future offspring:

> *Even as gold is tried, Gentile and Jew.*
> *If that ghost was a girl's, I swear to it:*
> *Your mother shall be far more blessed than you.*
> *And if a boy's, I swear: The flames are lit*
> *That shall refine us; they shall not destroy*
>   *A living hair.*
> *Your younger brothers shall confirm in joy*
>   *That this I swear.*

When the poem later appeared in an anthology of poets asked to introduce one of their own poems, co-edited by his friend from the Iowa Writers' Workshop, Paul Engle, Hecht wrote:

> I like the idea of having a child so young as to be yet unborn speak with all the aged, bitter, Sophoclean wisdom of the great chorus in "Oedipus at Colonus." This is not just being tricky or paradoxical; you are meant to feel that the child, being somehow prior to life (in some Wordsworthian realm of glory, perhaps) and also dead, has a source of special knowledge that entitles it to make such formidable pronouncements. It is in a double sense separated from the world of the living. So, there is something very cold-blooded about the way it talks.[83]

Hecht's consultation with his parents had been similarly "cold-blooded," separated from his home in New York by an ocean and feeling cut off from his life as he had envisioned it when setting out for Rome. With Lowell's poem "The Boston Nativity" in the back of his mind, Hecht attempted a more "personal" kind of poem, though he feared that this might be construed as "confessional" and therefore "praised or blamed for the wrong reason."[84] For one thing, the poem alters the facts of the situation to strengthen the expression: Pat miscarried in early December, but Hecht places the event on Christmas Eve, playing on the nativity of Christ. In the war poem "Christmas Is Coming," Hecht makes an even greater leap in time, setting the patrol against a backdrop of a frozen landscape in late December. Hecht himself never fought in this extreme cold, having arrived in Europe in mid-March. By setting the poem at Christmas, Hecht accesses a bitter irony of the promise of Christ's birth: "The lamb is killed. *The goose is getting fat.*" Of "The Vow" he wrote, "Just how much of it is true . . . I take to be my own business, though I think it might be objected that the poem ends on a vow so audacious as to smack rather of hubris."[85] The poem foresees his future children as unmolested by fate; in fact, he swears to it—a prideful claim. But the ordeal had left a deep mark on his psyche; his new poems grappled with the aftermath. Following the miscarriage, there came a reconciliation. The couple were blessed by the Pope on Christmas Day.

Some exciting news provided welcome distraction: his cantata "A Choir of Starlings," which he had written with his Academy colleague Leo Smit, was having its debut at the Metropolitan Museum in New York, and Hecht wrote to his parents to save the date in February. News of the concert, which he was keen for his parents to attend, would have reached him in Ischia, where he and Pat traveled in early March to scout for summer rentals. Two colleges had written that they had no teaching spots open for fall, and the Guggenheim was silent regarding any renewal or extension.

Pat's modeling work was short lived, but it had a great effect on her mood. She traveled briefly to France, and the time away from the usual suspects lurking at the Academy, all of whom had borne witness to her recent trials, renewed her spirits a bit. She met Elsa Rosenthal in Rome, and news of Ischia enticed her. She looked forward to their stay in the south. In March, Hecht reported to his parents that all had been going very well. He had completed a "long poem" titled "Ostia Antica," which had been taken by the small magazine *Botteghe Oscure,* and that poem, along with "Upon the Death of George Santayana," was to appear in Oscar Williams's *The New Pocket Anthology of American Verse.* The poem was the sole product of Hecht's stay in Rome, and for the moment he was uncomplaining, content with the success of the poem itself and with its swift, enthusiastic reception from editors.

Begun before he left the States, Hecht's elegy for Santayana imagines the philosopher's last days in Rome. He had used a quotation from Santayana as the epigraph to his first collection, and a second epigraph launched the poem "Harangue" when it first appeared in *Furioso*. The return to Santayana was a glance backward to earlier concerns and an earlier style, rooted in familiar diction and hammering out an airy, elevated address. "Ostia Antica," too, was more of a retreat than a breakthrough onto new ground. The Academy itself provided the connective tissue: in Rome four years earlier, he had written his first book, and now here he was again writing on an Italian subject and in an essayistic manner similar to "The Gardens of the Villa d'Este" and "La Condition Botanique."

But "Ostia Antica" emerges from a more somber place than "Gardens." Written before "The Vow," it is the first of Hecht's poems to carry the weight of the loss of their first child, for the unborn fetus is a ghostly, though immediate, almost palpable, presence in these poems. As was often the case with situations that were starkly personal, Hecht transforms the experience, cloaking it in a symbolized landscape. Ostia, situated at the mouth of the Tiber where it flows into the Tyrrhenian Sea, was the ancient harbor for Rome. (The name derives from the Latin word for "mouth.") Hecht would have taken the short train ride to the archeological site, which due to silting lay three miles from the coast, its vast network of beautifully preserved ruins clustered beside tall cypresses. The dusty paths resound with birdsong. Besides Pat, it is highly likely that Hecht was accompanied by the MacDonalds, since ancient Roman architecture was Bill's specialty. Hecht commemorated their time exploring the Ancient World by dedicating the poem to Bill and Dale. With Bill, he would maintain a prolific, often jocund correspondence and an abiding friendship—one of his longest and dearest.

Hecht would have visited Ostia's spectacular amphitheater and unique public lavatories, but to get there required walking through Ostia's vast city of the dead. A dense conglomeration of 200 funerary buildings composes the necropolis, which grew along the via Flavia Severiana between the 1st and 4th centuries AD. The tombs are not named in the poem, though a prayer is uttered: "To ghostly creatures, / Peace, and an end to fever / Till all this dust assemble." After a rainstorm that has washed the "ancient stones," the poem seeks to discover the nature of love: it appears transformed into a specter at poem's end: "Then from the grove"—one almost hears *grave* here—"Suddenly falls a flight of bells":

A figure moves from the wood,
Darkly approaching at the hour of vespers
Along the ruined walls.
And bearing heavy articles of blood
And symbols of endurance, whispers,
"This is love."[86]

Hecht had written well in Ischia in the past. Hoping to get some writing done, he headed south with Pat, but its volcanic landscape, hot springs, and beaches provoked no poems. He was blocked again, though seeing friends such as the Rosenthals and Auden himself forestalled his anxiety about his inability to write. The house needed to be set up and a routine established. Tony could again play host, and Pat very much liked what she found there. Ischia was much changed since Hecht had been there half a decade earlier. For one thing, it was more expensive. When the Hechts had driven down by car a few weeks before (with the MacDonalds), they had seen a number of "attractive" houses, but none they could afford: "Most of the people who have any hope of attracting tourists have modernized and extended their houses." Ischia was no longer cut off from the world, a place where telephones were rare and news slow to arrive. Now one could buy the daily Paris *Tribune,* and keep abreast of the latest doings at home with copies of *Time* and *Life.* There were books in English at the local bookseller. While food was still cheap (and with a host of new restaurants and bars more various than ever), the result of all of these "improvements and concessions to the tourists" was that rents had gone through the roof.

With only a small window in which to secure accommodations, Hecht hoped that his old landlord, Trofa, on the Strada San Vito, might be able to let his place, which was Spartan but fondly remembered. Even Trofa had ridden the profitable wave of tourism, upgrading the place with a back porch and an "interior john." He himself had undergone some renovation as well, giving up "his stainless teeth on behalf of more realistic and expensive ones." Trofa had struck a deal with a group of military types, who were moving in at the end of June for the rest of the summer. Tony and Pat could have the place for June, then Trofa would move them out to his place in the hills, which Hecht had visited on his last stay. They left a deposit of L5,000 to hold the place until they returned in a few weeks. They didn't stay long on San Vito, only a few days as it turned out. As they lay in bed their first night on the island, Tony and Pat contemplated the midsummer move—with their steamer trunks and two cats in tow—and the remoteness of Trofa's primitive house, an hour's walk from the nearest supplies.

Having weathered a cold night on the Strada San Vito, they set out to find a better situation, where they could settle in for the duration of their stay. Nothing was very cheap, but they met a man named Silvestri, a well-connected Ischian burgher, who came down a bit in price and could let them have a place through August for a total of L75,000. Though still steep, the price was worth what turned out to be a splendid apartment overlooking Forio:

> The terrace is very spacious with a good view of the town and the sea. On the terrace, which is bordered with flowers and plants, is the well, from which we draw all the water we use. Last and best is the kitchen, which is huge and bright and clean, with a sink, a white tile charcoal range as well as the gas range, and room for six cooks. Every room has two windows except the bathroom, which has one, and the kitchen which has three. The place has clean, whitewashed walls and marble floors. It was already well furnished in all the essentials when we arrived, but we have found lots of fixings to get for it. Of course, there's electricity (24 hrs. a day these days) and we have made some lamps out of wicker lobster and fish traps. Altogether the place suits us to the hilt. We both have fine sunburns already, and I have shaved off my beard, to the bewilderment of the local people and the approval of Pat. I haven't gotten used to the look of myself yet.[87]

Good news continued to arrive: *Harper's Bazaar* wanted to include his work in an upcoming poetry feature and the poet Philip Wheelwright, at the University of California, Riverside, wrote to say that, while they currently had no positions open, he and his colleagues were lobbying hard for Hecht to join their faculty. Pat's modeling career picked up considerably: her photos had appeared in February in the *Sunday Times,* and newsstands currently carried her fashion spread for *Vogue*, all of this recent print work fortifying her bank account by L100,000 (roughly $500). As it turned out, she would need this money in unexpected ways.

As the Hechts began to fit out their new apartment, Tony was drawn into a dispute with Trofa, who now demanded the full rent of L50,000 that he felt had been promised him and sent his demands through his lawyer. Silvestri suggested that Hecht explain the whole situation to the mayor, a personal friend, whom Hecht found to be "a wonderful, stout man, who said the lawyer's letter was ridiculous." There had been no signed contract. Even so, to keep the peace a meeting was arranged at Town Hall with the mayor, Trofa, and Hecht. A small emolument was offered, which Trofa refused with "polite wrath," but the mayor, now left alone with Hecht, reassured him that nothing would come of it. Meanwhile Silvestri quickly made them feel at home, taking the Hechts to visit the homes of his sisters, where they ate and drank "to the point of giddiness." They attended a "little festa in the country on the feast of St. Joseph, the holy cuckold," where they received "endless tumblers of good and strong wine." They had the island to themselves in a way: no other seasonal visitors had arrived yet. An elderly Swiss couple who lived there year-round remembered Hecht from his last stay (with Al and Nel) and invited him for tea. As far as Tony and Pat's feelings for each other, this was a brief good time, a second honeymoon of sorts, though as short lived as the first had been.

Auden arrived in April, and he too would have noted the rising prices on the island. It was to be one of his last summers there. When his landlord learned that Auden had been awarded an Italian literary prize, he decided that he must be more well-heeled than his nonchalant dishevelment let on and raised his rent. Auden decided to seek other summer accommodations, in Austria, from then on. When the end came he wrote a valedictory companion piece to "Ischia," titled "Good-Bye to the Mezzogiorno": "Go I must, but I go grateful (even / To a certain *Monte*)," he wrote, "though one cannot always / Remember exactly why one has been happy, / There is no forgetting that one was."

But this spring he was still embracing the role that the locals had cast him in—the writer—which he accepted without cavil. Seated for his daily coffee at the Bar Maria, he may have been looking over the manuscripts for the Yale Younger Poets Prize, for which he had served as the final judge since 1947. In recent years the winners had included Daniel Hoffman's *An Armada of Thirty Whales,* W. S. Merwin's *A Mask for Janus,* and Adrienne Rich's *A Change of World.* Auden had come to respect Hecht's taste enough to employ him as a reader, and the two spent a long afternoon weeding through the wads of wooden verse. Neither of them, however, found a single publishable manuscript."[88] So exacting were Auden's criteria that no award had been made for the previous two years. To go a third year without a winner would be controversial and a potential blot on the prize itself. Auden reported this unhappy news to Eugene Davidson at Yale University Press, adding that something seemed to be amiss with the vetting process in New Haven:

> I am very worried because, for the second year in succession, I do not find among the mss. submitted to me one that I feel merits publication. It so happens that there is another poet staying here, and I have asked him to read them also as a check on my own judgment. He came, however, to the same conclusion.
>
> What bothers me particularly is that a young poet (John Ashbery) whom I know personally told me he was submitting a manuscript this year. I have reservations about such of his poems as I have seen, but they are certainly better than any of the manuscripts which have reached me. I don't know how or by whom the preliminary sieving is done at the press, but I cannot help wondering whether I am receiving the best.[89]

As George Bradley writes in his introduction to an anthology of Yale winners, Ashbery's "manuscript had indeed been weeded out, along with that of another New York poet, Frank O'Hara. Auden contacted them both and asked that they resubmit their work directly to him. He received the manuscripts in little more than a week and made up his mind within days."[90] The manuscript he wound up awarding the prize to was Ashbery's *Some Trees.*

It wasn't long before tensions flared again between Tony and Pat. By June, Tony wrote to his father privately to say that Pat had left Naples in mid-June on the *Cristoforo Colombo.* They had both agreed on this. Pat would be met by "some girlfriends of hers" in New York and stay with a friend on Third Avenue near Bloomingdale's until she was settled in her own place, with, she hoped, new prospects for modeling work.

The previous month had been a strain for both of them. Hecht's work was stalled, and he decided to double down on his expatriate existence; after all, it had worked before and it could again, with some time away from the frenzy that surrounded Pat. He, too, certainly shared the blame for their current difficulties. His inability to work went hand in hand with his feelings of depression and guilt, which were recently exacerbated by the loss of the pregnancy. When he wrote to Bard giving up his position there, "ostensibly, because I had not gotten a promotion or even a raise," Pat began to feel deeply uneasy about what their life would be like from that point on.[91] The Guggenheim money was gone, and they were dipping into their small savings. She decided that she needed to return to the States to seek psychiatric help. Tony instructed her to get in touch with Melvyn at his office at Parke, Benziger, an export business on Wall Street, to avoid running afoul of Dorothea, who no longer veiled her distaste for Pat.

With Pat back in the States, Hecht had some time to regroup. Pat had overwhelmed him. Her volatility drew him more than he cared to admit, but he was also exhausted by it and needed "a little rest."[92] He hoped he might resume working, and if he could get some momentum going, he would extend his stay into the fall in the hope of keeping up the pace. "But I suspect," he told his father, "that after a year of not writing and after what has happened over here, it may take some time to get back into my stride." In any case he would return to New York later in the fall and "get a job of any sort" to see him through the winter, as he continued to look for teaching work. His uncertainty about his writing and about Pat had a paralyzing effect on him, though he managed to retain a good deal of tenderness toward her: "Please try to be gentle with Pat," he wrote to Melvyn. "She is very sick, and knows it, but tries hard to forget it most of the time. I hope she will want to try to do something about it. If not, something will have to be worked out."[93] Hecht believed the problem lay with Pat, and she for her part seems to have acknowledged as much. In time, he would come to feel that he was equally responsible, and the guilt associated with this failure, and particularly with how the collapse of the marriage affected those closest to him, underlies the poems that would make up *The Hard Hours*.

After Pat's departure a silence set in. Busy with finding work and taking some much-needed time for herself, she did not write to Tony for several weeks, and he grew increasingly "lonely and depressed." He hoped to distract himself, even trying underwater fishing with a spear gun and mask; no longer feeling remotely domestic, he fed the fish he caught to the cats. He was cheered by the news of a new Williams anthology and that Allen Tate was traveling in Italy and would be staying in Rome, where Hecht hoped to visit him. He would certainly see the MacDonalds as well. And he would have another visitor: his father wired to say, GOING ABROAD. CAN WE MEET ROME SEPT. 2ND. *Was it for business?* Hecht wondered. If not, it was a "ridiculously extravagant and absolutely unnecessary" gesture.[94] He wrote to remind his concerned parents that he had "a mind and a life of my own, and know how to take care of myself."[95] His plan was to stay abroad for now until things began to sort themselves a little.

From Rome in early September, he toured briefly in the South of France with the MacDonalds, who remained his closest, most supportive friends in Italy. Poems were coming slowly, one just finished and another begun—a considerable outpouring comparatively speaking. Roger, meanwhile, had landed a poem in *Poetry,* and a copy arrived before the trip to France. Hecht himself received numerous encouragements from magazines and anthologies wanting poems. The well-known German composer Hans Werner Henze, whom he met in Ischia, was writing a song cycle for Benjamin Britten and Peter Pears to tour with, and he asked Hecht to write the libretto. The project was exciting, but by the time he returned to Rome, his writing had fallen apart completely:

The work has been going forward with the greatest difficulty, chiefly because I cannot concentrate. I have no feeling about whether what I am writing is good or bad, and the whole business is totally without excitement and pleasure for me. And I am sure I know the reason. It's that I can't stand leaving unresolved my situation with Pat. I hear from her fairly frequently, asking when I plan to come back, and she knows that I am supposed to appear at the poetry reading in the middle of January. It is not mainly loneliness I feel, though I feel it; but I have been lonely before. It is quite frankly the feeling that nothing is really settled between us, and that in the meantime I worry about how things are going to work out. This has made my work more difficult than it has ever been before.[96]

He decided to leave Italy. He felt miserable, and he was not working, which had been his reason for staying. Pat had been asking when he would return, though she knew that it would be January at the latest, since Tony had been invited to give a poetry reading back in the States. The SS *Constitution* was leaving Naples in the second week of December, which would get him to New York in time for Christmas. He had made a decision: he would reunite with Pat in New York "to see if we can manage to live together successfully. . . . We are both assuming that by returning, we will be trying to find a different basis on which to live."[97] He committed to finding a way to stay together.

SEVEN

"MARRIAGES COME TO GRIEF IN MANY WAYS . . ."[1]

(1956–1961)

1. Mon Semblable, Mon Frère—Leonard Baskin at Smith

Back home in New York, Hecht began the new year in uncertainty—both domestically and professionally. His marriage to Pat remained in turmoil. Could they make a life together, now that they were back in the States, without the novelty of Europe to distract them? Having given notice at Bard, Hecht needed work. His genial circle of colleagues at the Academy comprised professors in a range of disciplines, and it may have been through this academic grapevine that he caught word of an opening at Smith College in Northampton, Massachusetts. As a calling card, he now had *Stones* and its more-than-respectable reception. He sent off an application and a vita, and word came back quickly that he could begin teaching in Northampton in the fall.

After the emotional roil of Rome, Hecht resolved to smooth the waters, to hang on to the marriage if he could. Time away from the city might relieve some stress, he hoped. But would Pat be happy away from New York and any potential modeling work she might land there? Then news came: Pat was pregnant again. That spring they learned they had a healthy baby on the way. In anticipation of the birth, the two attempted to re-form a bond, their common cause propelling them past present hurdles.

Hecht's writing proceeded in dribs and drabs. He found it impossible to work amidst the upsets at home—the bickering and, worse, the heavy silences and recriminations that followed. He regretted his choices and wondered if his own concupiscence—his physical attraction to Pat—wasn't partly to blame for making a bad match. A self-indicting poem,

"The Origin of Centaurs," written that fall, grapples with the dark consequences of lust. (Hecht's sequence from this time on "The Seven Deadly
Sins" includes a gnomic poem on "Lust.") It may well be that the association he made in childhood between sex and disaster still unnerved him. An
epigraph from *King Lear*, in which the mad king rails against the iniquities
of womankind, foregrounds the theme of sexual horror: "But to the girdle do the gods inherit, / Beneath is all the fiend's." Hecht's poem, the
setting of which is more Northampton than Manhattan, works out its dire
argument in poised rhetoric:

> *This mild September mist recalls the soul*
> > *to its own lust;*
> > *On the enchanted lawn*
> *It sees the iron top of the flagpole*
> > *Sublimed away and gone*
> *Into Parnassian regions beyond rust;*
> *And would undo the body to less than dust.*[2]

Hecht includes an echo of another chastening poem, Herbert's "Church-
monuments," which begins: "While my soul repairs to her devotion /
here I entomb my flesh, that it betimes / May take acquaintance of this
heap of dust . . ."[3]

Pat and Tony arrived at Smith at the start of the fall term—the first
of three years there. They ultimately settled in a house at 43 North
Main Street, just over two miles from the Smith campus, which one faculty member recalled as "spreading over a low elevation above the town
center a few miles west of the usually well-behaved Connecticut River
and safe from its occasional flooding." With "less of the picture-postcard
'Ivy' look of so many New England colleges," Smith was "unpretentious
and latitudinarian and 'natural.' The majority of Smith students, like
those in other private colleges for women, came from comfortable and
conservative backgrounds and tended to grow piously tolerant and open-
minded between their freshman and senior years."[4]

Hecht taught freshman English (and nothing else!) during his time at
Smith, a stifling restriction, but one he put up with: he needed the work.
The syllabus for the course, which was taught by other professors as well,

was set by the department. His classes consisted of exposing students to the "analytical study of short-stories, a novel, and a good deal of lyric poetry." He covered the "more or less usual catalogue of poets,"[5] as well as works by Henry James, D. H. Lawrence, Conrad, and Chekhov. Despite the drudgery of what was essentially service teaching, he rose in the ranks from lecturer in his first year to assistant professor for his remaining two. Hecht was pleased with the financial arrangement: "Smith salaries are almost twice Bard's," he advised a friend. "An assistant professor at Smith can get up to $8,000, which is about the beginning of full professorial pay at Bard." Still, it was a slog. His academic duties provided no great intellectual challenges, and grading and lecturing took up all of his mental and physical energy. The teaching load was considerable: "Nine scheduled teaching hours and two additional office hours (in which to make yourself available to any student who would like to see you) and all of this would fall in a block of three consecutive days, either at the beginning or the end of the week. . . . By the time you have been appointed to various departmental committees that beautiful block of four clear days has gotten a little clouded with unscheduled work."[6]

Pat was hugely pregnant as the semester began, and on November 4, their first son, Jason, was born. Her pregnancy had worn her out completely. As Hecht later recalled, not without irritation, during Jason's first weeks at home "his mother got breast fever immediately after the birth, and could not nurse him, or, for that matter, do anything whatever."[7] Hecht handled all of the household chores during that winter. He cared for Jason around the clock, feeding him, bathing him, changing him. The neighbors must have shaken their heads in wonder at the sight of the beleaguered young professor once again hauling a load of freshly laundered diapers to the clothesline and returning in due course to retrieve them, replacing them with another load for drying. In the kitchen, as Pat slept or read, Hecht warmed the bottles of formula, which he administered at all hours of the day and night. On top of this, there was the shopping to do. All of this began to affect his work in the classroom, until the chair of the Department of English Language and Literature, Robert Gorham Davis, called him on the carpet. Hecht's written comments on student work were deemed too cursory, too rushed. Embarrassed by his situation at home—and baffled that the chair of English seemed unaware of his difficulties, since they were openly known—he neither explained nor made excuses. He promised to do better. That's all he could do.

Despite the chaos of the semester, Hecht stole time to welcome his son with a poem. Titled simply "Jason," it begins with the evocation of an unnamed painting of the Madonna and Child:

> *Is it no more than sun that floods*
> *To pool itself at her uncovered breast?*
> *O lights, o numina, behold*
> *How we are gifted. He who never was,*
> *Is, and her fingers bless him and are blessed.*[8]

The poem celebrates the mystery of birth and of life itself, with no mention of present hardships, making good on the promise intoned at the end of "The Vow": "Your younger brothers shall confirm in joy / This that I swear."[9] (The two poems make a powerful pairing, appearing together that spring in a special feature for the *Hudson Review* on "Poets Under Forty," alongside work by W. D. Snodgrass, Donald Justice, William Meredith, Hayden Carruth, Henri Coulette, and others. At thirty-three, Hecht was well below the age cutoff.)[10] Hecht's adoration of his son is at once performative and also wholly genuine, a balance he often managed in his mature poems. Hecht acknowledges that here is a joyful occasion, a cause for hope. It proved fleeting.

As delighted as he was by the birth of Jason, life with Pat remained strained. Hecht would think back on these years at Smith as "a particularly troubled and unhappy period."[11] For outsiders, he put on a brave face, writing to William Arrowsmith of *The Hudson Review,* then in Rome as a fellow of the Academy, that "unto us a son was given" who is "well and happy," adding with a hollow-sounding repetitiveness that "we are all well and happy and find Smith a pleasant but indifferent place."[12] Despite the confiding tone, this was a business letter. Arrowsmith and his fellow editors, Joseph Bennett and Frederick Morgan, were very much taken with Hecht's poems and were eager for him to continue his involvement with the journal. The previous summer, Arrowsmith had commissioned Hecht to write for the *Hudson* a roundup review of fully seventeen books, including works by Richard Wilbur, Tennessee Williams, Conrad Aiken,

John Ciardi, Josephine Miles, Edwin Muir, Reed Whittemore, and a host
of lesser lights. He completed similar annual roundups for the *Hudson* over
the next four years, a vast amount of spadework and reading that paid little
but developed his skills as a critic.

Sensing perhaps that Hecht's talents were being wasted at Smith, Arrowsmith encouraged him to apply for a position at the University of
Texas at Austin, where Arrowsmith chaired the Classics department and
R. P. Blackmur taught English. Though the opportunity never panned
out, Hecht was grateful for Arrowsmith's support. Through Arrowsmith,
Morgan, and Bennett, *The Hudson Review* became a literary home for
Hecht. In addition to contributing poems, appearing regularly beginning
in Spring 1949, he now contributed features and reviews.[13] In 1958, the
editors awarded him a Hudson Review Fellowship, one of several grants
he received while at Smith, including a second Guggenheim in 1959 and
a Ford Foundation Fellowship in 1960. The awards provided a welcome
financial cushion and, in the case of the Guggenheim and Ford fellowships, time away from teaching. In 1966, he became a de facto poetry
editor of the review, recommending pieces to the editor Fred Morgan
and commissioning features.

Hecht was restless at Smith and would have likely gone to Texas if
he were asked. A part of him longed to be back in Rome, and he envied
Arrowsmith his year there. He told him how "nightingales sing in the
cortile in spring, and let go for all they're worth, attracted, no doubt, by
the creative atmosphere of the place."[14] Hecht sent Arrowsmith a draft
of a poem he later abandoned, "Suburb," which depicts a scene as gray as
his mood. It describes a "jungle of houses" as perceived by an insomniac:
"since nothing wakes / Within their draughty halls at sunrise it makes /
No difference[;] nothing slumbers in the dark."[15] Hecht's feelings about
Smith were harsher than he let on to Arrowsmith. He later recalled: "I
was there for only three years, all of them exceptional in their undevi-
ating unhappiness for me . . ." He found his colleagues "pathetic or unpleasant," with the exception of the scholar and literary critic Elizabeth
Drew, for whom he "had the highest regard."[16] The literary critic and
historian Daniel Aaron, later a founder of the Library of America, became a good friend. Aaron could sense Hecht's unease: "I remember his
bleak time there, his cheerless apartment, and his ruefully comic opinion

of the place and its inhabitants."[17] (By contrast, when Aaron later met Hecht in Rome—likely in the late '60s, when Hecht was again living at the Academy—he found him utterly transformed, lively and humorous, blissfully in his element.)

Another colleague whom Hecht admired became a lifelong friend and his most frequent collaborator: the artist Leonard Baskin. Then in his third year at Smith, Baskin was known around town as an outspoken and idiosyncratic visionary. A year older than Hecht, he was born in New Brunswick, New Jersey, and grew up in Brooklyn. Though nearly the same age and from the same city, the two came from quite different backgrounds. Baskin grew up in a family of rabbis. As a boy, he enrolled at the yeshiva, before his talent for the plastic arts led him to break away and follow his own path. His boyhood study of the Torah heavily informed his art, which was steeped in Jewish culture, Holocaust imagery, and the Bible.

Baskin had begun as a sculptor and continued to think of himself as one, even after his prints drew wide acclaim. His typical subjects in both bronze and ink were raptors—owls, crows—birdmen, and hanged men, all starkly and powerfully rendered. His images were dark, both in aspect and tone. In the late '30s, he studied with the Romanian-born New Deal sculptor Maurice Glickman at the Educational Alliance in New York, before entering NYU and then Yale. His military service had been in the Navy, and he had been a runner-up for the Rome Prize before the war. Before coming to Smith in 1953, Baskin studied in Paris and Florence, where he first showed his prints at Galleria Numero. Hecht and Baskin, by now well-established in their respective arts, recognized that, despite their disparate beginnings, they had a great deal in common: Jewish heritage, a deep knowledge of the Bible, a love of Shakespeare and the Greeks, a passion for the fine arts, and a sense of the artist's almost aristocratic role in the life of culture. It seems unlikely that Hecht saw Baskin's two shows at Grace Borgenicht Gallery in New York, in 1955 and 1956—he was in Italy for part of that time—but when the two met in Northampton they quickly recognized in each other a kindred spirit. Baskin invited Hecht to his studio, where he showed him his recent work. Almost immediately they embarked on a number of fertile collaborations, combining Hecht's poems with Baskin's images, in fine-press editions published by Baskin's Gehenna Press.[18]

Known as "Lenny" to his intimates, Baskin commanded a kind of awe from aspiring artists, much in the way Hecht could be intimidating to younger poets. To Baskin's students, "he looked like his self-portraits. . . . He looked like the raptors that he drew. But he would also walk down the streets like he owned them." As the poet Richard Michelson recalls, students could be devastated by him, because "if you showed him your work and he didn't like it he didn't mince words. He would tell you to go back and learn how to draw. He was a difficult man to approach."[19] Michelson, who became Baskin's gallerist in Northampton, assured his wife that Baskin was perfectly nice once you got to know him, to which she responded, "Well, the fact that it takes years to get to know him—that's not the definition of being nice."

Baskin's gruffness was a kind of litmus test of a student's seriousness: "He had to have proof that you weren't just wanting to live the life of an artist but you were willing to work all day, every day. He had to have proof of your moral seriousness. Otherwise, you would be dismissed; he would have no time for you."[20] Baskin himself worked at all hours, often late into the night, even when he was entertaining company. The key was to meet him on his own terms: "I made the mistake that most people make: I approached him with either deference or fear," Michelson remembers. "You had to approach like he was your old Jewish uncle. He didn't mind back and forth. He didn't mind being challenged. He expected that if he gave you your time you had to be as serious as he was, and that meant you had to be passionate and you had to be willing to challenge and you had to be willing to be challenged."[21]

Both men maintained a protective "shell built by a basic insecurity." Hecht was skittish of being judged or excluded, so he developed a carapace. "He came across very much like Baskin," Michelson recalls. "They moved similarly, they had somewhat similar mannerisms, they were the same generation of Jews." Baskin, much like Hecht, "dismissed religion per se, but he certainly took on, without believing in the dogma, the moral weight of the biblical teachings and culture. He took the Prophets to heart, and the Prophets' teachings to him were important. It was quite natural for him to quote Shakespeare, quote Euripides, in normal speech." Hecht's mandarin affect and his immersion in high culture—classical music, painting, and architecture—were attractive to Baskin, who "similarly had airs about him." Baskin felt that the fashionable art of the time was vapid, not engaged with morality, content with surfaces as opposed to engaging more deeply with the human condition. Seen as something of an outsider and a relic by the fashionable art world, Baskin was revered as a master within his own circle. His Gehenna Press produced museum-quality fine-press editions and became widely influential: "Lots of private presses and artists . . . trace themselves back to Baskin, people like Barry Moser and his Pennyroyal Press, and Alan James Robinson's Cheloniidae Press." Museums collect his books, which command tens of thousands of dollars in the rare book trade.

In addition to his alliance with Hecht, the bristly Baskin—"very young, very self-assured of his own standing and his own talent even before he had really done anything"—began a friendship with Ted Hughes, who had recently moved to Northampton. Hughes followed his new wife, Sylvia Plath, a recent Smith graduate who would be teaching for a year at the college, settling in a cramped attic apartment at 337 Elm Street, a few blocks from campus. It was something of a sore point with the couple that Hughes was not offered a position as well. He found a semester's work that January at UMass Amherst as an instructor in English literature and creative writing. Like Baskin, Hughes "thought of himself as a master before he was a master."[22] The two first collaborated in 1958 on a Gehenna Press broadside of Hughes's "Pike: A Poem." Baskin became a lifelong friend of Hughes, even moving to England to be close to him. Page for page, Baskin did more work with Hughes than any other poet, even Hecht—numerous book covers, including two iconic covers for *Crow,* and several book-length collaborations.[23]

Personal hardship may have provided a common bond. Hecht recalled that Baskin

was married to a wonderful woman named Esther who was dying, by excruciating degrees, of multiple sclerosis. Esther was gradually losing her ability to move and, toward the end, even to speak. I used to go and visit very often. During this time, Leonard was preoccupied with his wife's illness, but he was also very industrious and working very hard doing both sculptures and woodcuts on a theme that had to do with death. He was understandably preoccupied with the subject. When Esther was able to, she was still writing books for him. One of them was called *Night Creatures,* a book about gloomy hauntings.[24]

It was apparent to Hughes as well that "Baskin was obsessed by corpses," and a variety of other things attended this obsession, including crows, which he engraved with disturbingly anthropoid characteristics. An invitation from Baskin to Hughes to write a few little poems to accompany his engravings "was the cause of the first Crow poems."[25] Hecht felt at home at the Baskins', which like Baskin's own person was not fussy: "His appearance was rumpled and disheveled. He was not fastidious in his art either. Once he got the power of what he was trying to do—it was that act of creation that was important to him—he might lay the print on the floor and the dog would walk on it." Sculptures were scattered about his house. His studio was huge, and it housed a sprawling book collection. Baskin shelved his library in no discernible order, and yet he knew where every book was and could lay hands on a particular volume in an instant to help make a point. He expected his students to be equally scholarly and curious; "What you don't know could fill volumes," he liked to say. Or: "Before we speak further on this [subject] please educate yourself." Then he'd go to the far bookshelf, "to the third shelf down and the fifth book over, and say read chapter 12."[26] Baskin and Hecht would trade Shakespeare quotes and laugh together, sharing a childlike whimsy as a reprieve from their abiding melancholy: they concocted silly rhymes, a wonderful wordplay where the two "just had fun."[27]

Hecht reminisced with their common friend Eleanor Cook that "even in those days Leonard's interest in mortality was pronounced, in large part because his remarkable first wife was slowly dying of multiple sclerosis."[28] Among many other things, he was "doing eloquent small bronze casts of hanged men." Other subjects were informed by his traditional Jewish upbringing: a fierce portrait of Moses, adorned with traditional horns and quotations from the Bible in Yiddish. A double portrait of a Janus-faced Abraham and Isaac, entitled *Sacrifice of Isaac,* dates from this time. (Hecht's late poem "The Sacrifice," written for a Baskin collaboration that remained unfinished at Baskin's death, treats this subject.)

Another Gehenna edition that would have caught Hecht's eye was *The Auguries of Innocence,* with William Blake's poem accompanied by eight wood engravings by Baskin. Though neither went to temple for the High Holidays after childhood, they both observed Yom Kippur, in their own way. Baskin went into his studio and always "came out with one of his best works. That was his religion."[29] Hecht read Psalms in the privacy of his study. While neither Hecht nor Baskin embraced dogmatic religion, both were drawn to the contemplation of the metaphysical.

For their first collaboration, a German folktale was chosen from *Struwwelpeter,* a series of illustrated children's stories, each a kind of cautionary grotesquery. Hecht adapted the first, eponymous tale into loose-iambic pentameter quatrains:

> *Villainous boys, go bolt the backdoor tightly;*
> *Those in apartments, fear the elevator;*
> *Shiver in bed, endure the nightmare nightly,*
> *Imagining what is left of Struwwelpeter.*[30]

As a boy in Buttenheim, Hecht's great-grandfather Joseph would have known this book of frightening tales, written in 1845 by Heinrich Hoffmann. Hecht had learned from Fräulein about the sadistic strain that lurked in the German soul. Like "A Hill" and other of Hecht's poems, this poem adumbrates the Holocaust in its pointed diction: *sentinel, incinerator, famine, reek rising up.* Hecht's own legacy from the war—insomnia and nightmares—is coupled with parental neglect and abuse at the hands of his childhood nanny. It's a thematic sketch, disguised as children's verse, of what "A Hill" and "'It Out-Herods Herod. Pray You, Avoid It'" work out more fully and horribly a few years later.

In this unfamiliar place, Hecht was happy to welcome familiar friends. He caught up at this time with Allen Tate, as close as he had to a mentor, who

came to give some readings up near where I was at Smith—at Amherst or Mt. Holyoke, or something of the sort—and while he was there he said rather wistfully that "it would be so nice if you could come back with me to Princeton."

My term had come to an end, and Pat and I had a baby boy and a
traveling crib. So, we thought together "why not?", though it seemed
very odd. And the four of us—that is to say my wife and child and Allen
and I—drove to Princeton.

When we got to his house, we set up the crib in one of the bedrooms
next to a set of bookcases. . . . And we put our son to bed in the crib,
and went downstairs to have drinks with him. Suddenly, we heard this
tremendous crash. It was the bookcase collapsing.

The child had somehow reached up and pulled at something. He
wasn't hurt, fortunately, though he was badly scared. And everything
was rearranged very quickly, but the point is that, when we got back to
Smith and we rooted around in the traveling crib, we found there a tiny
votive figure of St. Anthony, which obviously belonged to the Tates. St.
Anthony, by the way, is the patron saint of lost things.[31]

It was some years later that Hecht had occasion to return the statuette
to Tate's wife, Caroline Gordon:

She was teaching at the New School, and I went there one afternoon as she
was about to begin her class. I slipped this little figure in front of her, and
she was just overwhelmed with gratitude. She said she hadn't been able to
find anything since he disappeared, and, much more important, it had been
given to her by Jacques Maritain [who had been influential in the Tates'
conversion to Catholicism]. So, it meant a great deal to her.[32]

Seeing old friends was a welcome distraction from the dead-end feeling of life in Northampton.[33] Nothing about Smith worked very well for
Hecht. The rift between him and Pat grew more pronounced, becoming
a battle of the wills. Pat was a social creature, graceful and a gracious
hostess. Tony could be bibulous and riotously funny in company, but his
melancholy bent meant that frequently the household descended into
silence for long periods, leaving Pat more and more desperate for divert-
ing company.

With the fall semester survived and the holidays behind them, Tony
and Pat reconnected with Bill and Dale MacDonald, friends from the Academy, who had recently returned to the States and were renting a house

AEH as an infant, with his mother, grandmother, and great-grandmother, 1923.

AEH's parents, Melvyn and Dorothea.

AEH with his brother, Roger (center), and his governess, called Fräulein, Central Park, Spring 1928.

AEH with his great-grandmother, Amalie, late 1920s.

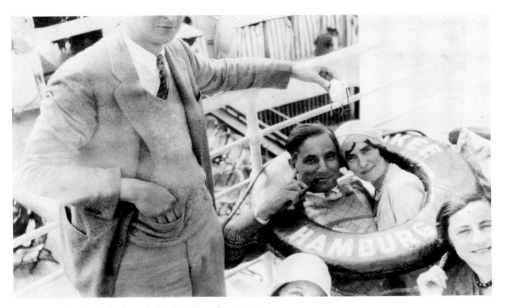

The Geisels aboard the SS *Milwaukee*, 1929.

AEH (right) and
his brother, Roger,
New York City, 1934.

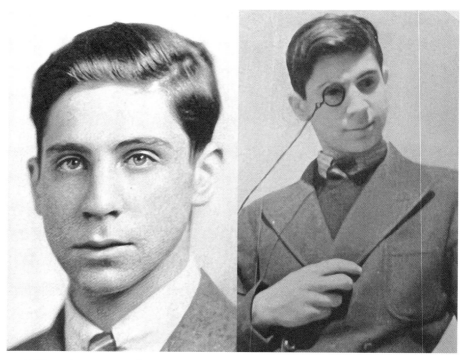

AEH's senior portrait in the *Horace Mannikin*, 1940.

AEH on stage at Horace Mann in Riverdale, New York, 1940.

PFC Anthony Hecht, circa 1943.

AEH, standing, third from left, with C Company's 3rd Platoon on bivouac. The photo is referred to in *"Dichtung und Wahrheit"*: "How, for example, shall I read / The expression on my face / Among that company of men / In that unlikely place?"

The bare hill in snow above Flossenbürg, with its castle ruins, from *Flossenbürg Concentration Camp 1938–1945—Catalogue of the Permanent Exhibition*. (Flossenbürg Memorial/Bavarian Memorial Foundation)

AEH at Kenyon College, 1946.

Thekla Clark (left) and the bearded AEH (right), with Elsa Rosenthal (center), on the beach in Forio, 1951

With Elsa Rosenthal in Rome, 1951.

AEH and Patricia Harris, circa 1954.

AEH at the Villa d'Este, 1955.

Dale MacDonald (with Noah), left, and and Pat Harris (with Jason), Winter 1956–57. The photo is referred to in "Auguries of Innocence."

Roger Hecht and James Wright, in New York City.

AEH with his sons Jason (left) and Adam, April 1969.

Helen and Tony's wedding, New York City, June 12, 1971.

Helen D'Alessandro, in "a pair of bright red sneakers," on her birthday, aged four, 1943. The photo is referred to in "A Birthday Poem."

November 6, 1967

Jill Krementz

AEH with W. H. Auden backstage at the 92nd Street Y, on November 6, 1967. Photograph by Jill Krementz.

Joseph Brodsky holding
Evan Hecht, mid-1970s.

AEH with James Merrill.

Helen and Tony at the Sewanee Writers Conference in Sewanee, Tennessee, as photographed by James R. Peters.

AEH in 1990, as photographed by Nancy Crampton.

AEH at the Library of
Congress, circa 1996,
photographed by Rollie
McKenna.

Tony and Helen at the Hotel Europa in Venice.

in nearby Florence, Massachusetts. A photo of Pat with Jason perched on her shoulder, posing in a wintry scene with Dale and the MacDonalds' young son Noel, later became the inspiration for Hecht's poem of rueful foreboding "'Auguries of Innocence.'"[34] The photo was taken by Bill Mac-Donald during one of their cheerful reunions—Pat and Dale are grinning broadly, though Jason is not. Could this unsmiling child have sensed his parents' difficulties? Even the landscape itself, snowy and sere, seems filled with foreboding:

> The unleafed branches knot
> Into hopeless riddles behind him
> And the air is clearly cold.
> Given the stinted light
> To which fate and film consigned him,
> Who'd smile at his own lot
> Even at one year old?
>
> And yet his mother smiles.
> Is it grown-up make-believe,
> As when anyone takes your picture
> Or some nobler, Roman virtue?
> Vanity? Folly? The wiles
> That some have up their sleeve?
> A proud and flinty stricture
> Against showing that things can hurt you,
>
> Or a dark, Medean smile?
> I'd be the last to know. . . .[35]

The poem hints at Pat's protective shell and at her possible deception—her "wiles" and "gift for guile." In time, Hecht came to feel that she had in fact deceived him, even as he put up a front of domestic harmony:

> A speechless child of one
> Could better construe the omens,
> Unriddle our gifts for guile.

There's no sign from my son.
But it needs no Greeks or Romans
To foresee the ice and snow.

2. Sylvia and Ted and Pat and Tony

Hecht had been teaching at Smith a year when Sylvia Plath joined the faculty. She had been an undergraduate there only a short time before and returned to Northampton from Cambridge, England, where she had been a Fulbright Scholar at Newnham College. In February 1956, she was introduced to Ted Hughes at a party. Their meeting became legendary—with Plath biting Hughes and Hughes violently pulling the earring from her ear. In England she wrote poems, publishing in the *Cambridge Varsity,* and between terms she traveled on the continent. Plath had been a distinguished student at Smith, graduating with highest honors and a thesis titled "The Tragic Mirror: A Study of the Double in Two of Dostoyevsky's Novels." Her father, Otto, excoriated in her poem "Daddy," was an entomologist who taught at Boston University, so she knew something of the academic life she could expect upon her return, as a golden child, to her alma mater.

She and Hecht knew of each other already, though they had never met till now. As an undergraduate intern in 1953 at *Mademoiselle* magazine in New York, an experience on which much of *The Bell Jar* is based, Plath featured five poets, including Hecht, in a two-page spread of photos titled "Poets on Campus," about "five talented young men" who "combine poetry and the classroom."[36] Why did Plath include no women in her roundup? There were fewer women poets in the academy in the early '50s to be sure, though Plath herself would soon begin as a poet-professor. The article also included Richard Wilbur, and Plath was among the first to point to the affinities between the two poets. It was a prescient pairing: Wilbur and Hecht would continue to be linked for their technical mastery, though in the service of quite different sensibilities, for the rest of their careers. Wilbur was at Harvard at this point, having spent the previous year in New Mexico on a Guggenheim fellowship. The *Mademoiselle* photo of Wilbur is distinctly Ivy League, with a blazer and V-neck sweater and a white button-down Oxford open at the neck. Hecht, by contrast, looks scruffier as befits his position at the more "experimental" Bard College. Bearded and brooding, with a T-shirt showing through the collar of his striped polo shirt, he holds a cigarette in his poised right hand. The article highlights Hecht's musical projects, including his translation of Rilke's "A Parable of Death" set by Lukas Foss while at the Academy. The piece was commissioned by the Louisville Symphony Society and was performed there, in New York City, and at Tanglewood, and recorded by Columbia Records. When Wilbur and Hecht met the following year in Rome, Wilbur was significantly further along in his career, though, with *Stones* receiving a wide press, they would have looked on each other as equals.

Plath was a diligent teacher, and she took her responsibilities as a grader in Newton Arvin's lecture course seriously. In private, she and Hughes could be quite catty. Plath recorded in her journal some cutting remarks about Tony and Pat. After she and Hughes hosted the Hechts for dinner, she was put out not to receive a return invitation. The truth is she and Hughes were lonely at Smith and, ironically, so were the Hechts: "Ted and I are aware of a great dearth of invitations, of Tony Hecht even, one might say, owing us a dinner . . ."[37] Sivvy, as she signed herself in letters, had a gimlet eye for character types: "Pat Hecht & serious, pained, wordless baby Jason. Pat pale, studiedly casual in torn sneakers & pleasant as razor blades."[38] As for Tony: "Urbane, hair professionally curled & just barely tinct with grey, as if an outline—he has had three grants to write in Europe & is pocketing his Hudson while continuing to work & teach which galled Ted & me—his taking a year of writing, as it were, from another poet."[39] In retrospect, Hecht blamed Pat for their standoffishness: "My wife simply refused to entertain—in part, at least, because she couldn't cook, and was embarrassed about it." For Hecht, Plath's secret sniping confirmed his "dislike of her as vain, malicious, envious and monstrously self-indulgent. Many people's lives have been far more warped by misery than hers, and without their lapsing into such terrible self-pity."[40] The truth is both couples were suffering. Plath, too, found it difficult to teach and have enough time and energy to write. By mid-1958, after a disappointing year at Smith, she and Ted moved to Boston. Plath took a job as a receptionist in the psychiatric unit of Massachusetts General Hospital and in the evening sat in on creative writing seminars given by Robert Lowell (also attended by Anne Sexton and George Starbuck).

During his short time in Northampton, Hughes formed a bond with Baskin, whose art he found "elect and consecrated. I hesitate to call it religious. It is rather something that survives in the afterglow of collapsed religion."[41] He noted the deep "kinship he feels with William Blake"[42] and the way his "style springs from Hebrew script itself."[43] "The book of Job is like the hidden master plan behind everything he produces," he wrote of Baskin, though it could have easily been written about Hecht.[44] Baskin fairly vibrated with creative energy. He pursued his work at the expense of sleep and society, working late into the evenings. As his guests talked and drank, he toiled away at his drafting table, drawing, carving, testing inks. Baskin had enough gusto for several artists, and his overflow of ideas often inspired the writers in his circle.

Baskin had an idea for Hecht that would lead to an important book for them both. Hecht's "epigrams" for *The Seven Deadly Sins* were published by the Gehenna Press in Northampton in 1958. Hecht later told his son Evan that "one of his desires was to elicit a sentiment of sympathy in the reader about how easy it is to indulge in all of these different sins which are being excoriated, something that he noticed from his own life."[45] The book was further proof that Baskin and Hecht were natural allies. They shared root concerns—sin, death, poetry, the Bible—which occupied them each separately, making their meeting of the minds a natural mingling of their unique sensibilities. Baskin's art fed Hecht's poetry and vice versa. Hecht knew the tradition of Renaissance emblem books, which paired poems and images, and his long-held interest in ekphrasis and the visual arts was apparent in early poems, such as "At the Frick," from *Stones*.

The two also shared an aesthetic, a way of interpreting the world in stark chiaroscuro. Hecht thrived on suggestions from Baskin. A project with set parameters and a loose deadline was just the thing to short-circuit his recurring writer's block. Hecht wrote to Donald Hall of his latest project: "Just finished a collaboration with an artist here, a wood engraver named Leonard Baskin, on a small emblem book called *The Seven Deadly Sins* (the poems intend to justify the sins, not by making them attractive, but by showing that the alternatives are perhaps just as sinful or pointless; the rationale behind this being that the sins are not really deadly till they're really persuasive)."[46] Baskin also served as matchmaker, pairing stark lithographs of raptors by Aubrey Schwartz with Hecht's equally savage poem "Birdwatchers of America."[47] If it weren't for Baskin's urgings, Hecht would not have written as much. It made all the difference that Baskin was not only keen to see Hecht's new work but also taking it as the inspiration for new work of his own. It's hard to say which are starker and more imaginative, the poems or the images, two equal elements, no mere illustrations. The two artists enlivened their sober subjects with a gallows humor very near the hearts of the two men themselves.

Hecht and Baskin served as co-founders and advisory editors of *The Grecourt Review*, named for the college's Grécourt Gates, installed in 1924. Baskin worked on the design of the journal, and an early issue sports a woodcut phoenix intricately worked out inside a red medallion. Supervised by Hecht and Baskin, Volume I, Number 1 contained poems by Plath ("All the Dead Dears") and Hughes ("Groom's Dream"), and the following issue, which appeared in December, with woodcuts by Baskin, featured poems by William Carlos Williams ("The Swivelhipped Amazon"), John Ciardi ("To W. T. Scott"), Robert Bagg (four poems), and the debut of Hecht's "Jason." Plath commemorates her friendship with Baskin in her poem "The Sculptor," from *The Colossus*.

Beyond his new alliance with Baskin, Hecht enjoyed socializing with the classical scholar George Dimock and his wife, Mary. The two couples occasionally vacationed together. Home movies from a trip to Cape Cod show Hecht, lean and lightly muscled, wading in the shallows of a white sand beach. Jason is dipping a toe in the tide, as his smiling father looks on:

> . . . *Slowly the ancient seas,*
> *Those black, predestined waters rise*
> *Lisping and calm before my eyes,*
> *And Massachusetts rises out of foam*
> *A state of mind in which by twos*

> *All beasts browse among barns and apple trees*
> *As in their earliest peace, and the dove comes home.*[48]

With the intricate stanzas of "Jason" and repeated allusions to the Book of Genesis, Hecht sounds a hopeful note for his newborn son. In the home movie, we see him splashing water into the air for Jason's amusement. Hecht laughs as he holds the child aloft in his arms.

3. Jason and Adam

Hecht prized the few friends he made at Smith. He revered the historian Daniel Aaron, who shared Hecht's mischievous sense of humor, and who suggested the title for "The Dover Bitch"—a comic poem on the serious subject of sexual tristesse. The classicist Helen Bacon became a close friend and collaborator. Of all his colleagues, the one whom he valued most on a personal level and who provided some comfort and understanding was the poetry critic Elizabeth Drew, "a friend of Auden's, and the soul of kindness." Auden had recently dedicated to her his poem "Streams," one of the "Bucolics," from *The Shield of Achilles,* published in 1955. The association was a welcome one, and Hecht was pleased to recount to her his time with Auden in Ischia.

Claire White, their friend from Rome, became close with Pat. A poet and graduate of Smith, White was a niece of Aldous Huxley. She married the sculptor Robert White, a grandson of Stanford White, and lived with him on the White estate, Box Hill, on Long Island. Claire and Robert had arrived at the AAR in 1952 and were old hands at the expatriate highlife by the time the Hechts arrived: "It was a time when everybody drank, but it was mostly wine. You couldn't get whiskey or martinis in Rome at the time." Hecht dedicated to Claire his poem "Heureux Qui, Comme Ulysse, a Fait un Beau Voyage . . . ," a translation of du Bellay, which he completed while at the Academy and published in *Voices* in the summer of 1954. In 1955, the four had visited W. H. Auden in Ischia and "things got violent almost." Claire perceived an inherent difficulty in the Hechts' marriage: Tony was "very intellectual, and she was the opposite—very exuberant and fun. She was funny."[49] Claire and her husband got to know Pat "extremely well" after Hecht asked them to bring Pat back to America. Claire found Pat "extraordinary": "She was very handsome, peculiarly charming, Irish, an irresistible creature, but not exactly an ideal wife for Tony, I think. I think there was great tension between them." Claire remained friends with Pat, despite feeling threatened by her: "I had a problem: my husband, Robert White, seemed to like her, like all men did." When Pat was back in the US with Claire and Robert, they took her to meet Robert's father, Lawrence Grant White, who was very elegant, and he "fell for her like mad and his wife got very upset." She "was the only woman I was very much afraid of. . . . She was just so attractive."[50]

Claire visited Tony and Pat at Smith. "As a personality, I liked Tony," she explained with a qualifying tone, "but he was a little bit formal." If he were sitting on the sofa, for example, every time Claire came in the room he would stand up: "That was typical of Tony." He was gracious and also supportive of her literary work: "I had written a book of poems about Rome, *The Navel,* a little chapbook published by the Roman newspaper, and he liked them. . . . I was touched by his encouragement to write poetry." As a confidant of Pat's, Claire was privy to a closely held secret, one that would ultimately drive the couple apart for good. In October 1958, Pat gave birth to a son, Adam. It was clear to Claire, however, as well as to Hecht himself, that the father was someone other than Tony. "The second son was definitely not Tony's," Claire was convinced.[51] The father, whose name is lost, was a young man with a fancy sports car who used to swing by the house to pick up Pat for drives. "Adam's father was 'a sort of society guy,'" according to White. Pat struck White as a Madame Bovary type and not the marrying kind: "I felt sorry for Tony. It was rough on him, his marriage to Pat. . . . It never seemed like a romance. . . . She was something, but I do feel that Tony had the rough end of it."[52] Hecht was aware of the question concerning Adam's paternity but raised the child as his own. As it happened, the marriage to Pat ended shortly thereafter, at her instigation. For Tony, Pat's incapacity to help look after the children caused a great strain: "Immediately after our second son was born she went ice skating and broke her leg, so I had to go through the whole routine—cooking, shopping, laundry, formulas, night-feedings—all over again, and, of course, while teaching full-time as before."[53] It had been a long time coming, but before Adam's first birthday, in the fall of 1959, the two separated, filing for a divorce.

Hecht's epigraph for his poem "Adam," written sometime after the divorce became final in 1961, comes from the Book of Job: "Hath the rain a father? or who hath begotten the drops of dew?" Louis Simpson, in his *à clef* portrait of Hecht in *North of Jamaica*, appears to be in on the secret as well: "Chris must have suffered a great deal . . . ," his pain "hidden in symbols."[54] Simpson portrayed Pat's "old harlotry" in a damning portrait entitled "The Man Who Married Magdalene":

> *Death granted the divorce,*
> *And nakedly the woman leapt*
> *Upon that narrow horse.*
>
> *But when he woke and woke alone*
> *He wept and would deny*
> *The loose behavior of the bone*
> *And the immodest thigh.*[55]

White recognized that in Simpson's "poem about being married to the wrong woman . . . he was talking about Pat." As an example of the impression she left on Simpson and other male writers who encountered her, White remembered Peter Matthiessen exclaiming, "I don't like to stand in line." According to White (and as Simpson himself hinted in his novel), Pat was seen as a creature of the demimonde: "I would say a courtesan. And I think even with Jack Kennedy." Pat worked one summer for the Kennedy campaign and a number of Kennedy men came to visit her on Long Island. According to Adam Hecht's retrospective account, Pat lived in New York for a year after the divorce and was friends with the Kennedys. He remembered seeing the clipping of an article that appeared then, with a photo of Pat, wondering in essence, *Who is this blonde running around the White House?* Pat's joie de vivre was contagious; "by contrast, Tony didn't like to do much; this is what broke them up," Adam later came to believe.[56]

Hecht responded to Simpson's poem with a poem of his own, "The Man Who Married Magdalene (*Variation on a Theme by Louis Simpson*)." Using another biblical epigraph, this one from Jonah, Hecht fires back at Simpson: "Then said the Lord, dost thou well to be angry?"[57] The speaker of the poem drowns his sorrows in a louche bar, striking a note of resignation, an acceptance that comes close to forgiveness:

> *What man shall understand*
> *The Lord's mysterious way?*
> *My tongue is thick with worship*
> *And whiskey, and some day*
>
> *I will come to in Bellevue*
> *And make psalms unto the Lord.*
> *But verily I tell you,*
> *She hath her reward.*[58]

The poem appeared in *The Hudson Review* in the autumn of 1961, just after the divorce became final. The editors of the *Hudson* were unstintingly supportive during this difficult time:

> Fred and his co-editor, Joseph Bennett, had given me, just around the time my wife and I had separated, a *Hudson Review* Fellowship, meant to free me to write. I told Fred candidly that I was not going to be able to use it, and that he would be wise to offer it to someone else. But he refused to reconsider, and the consequence of this was that when my wife departed, she quite literally cleaned me out, taking with her, among other things, my baby grand (though she couldn't play a note), a painting that had belonged to my grandfather, and all but five hundred dollars in our joint bank account, including, of course, the *Hudson* grant.[59]

Of himself at this time he wrote to Donald Hall, who had requested poems for a Penguin anthology: "Smoke, drink, write dirty limericks. Married five years, two children. Am about half-way through a new volume of poems which I hope to finish on my year off from Smith next year."[60] In September, he began a fellowship from the Ford Foundation, working for the next year with a Manhattan theater company. Lowell, Wilbur, and Richard Eberhart were also recipients. William Meredith, who worked with Lowell to study and improve the language of libretti, recalled:

> The Ford Foundation decided it would be interesting to take a group of established writers who had not written plays and attach them to repertory companies and see if they turn out to be good dramatists. . . . Lowell and I expressed an interest in opera and we were accredited to the New York City Opera Company and the Metropolitan for a season. More poets than fiction writers, I think. Anthony Hecht was attached to one of the repertory theaters in Manhattan, Richard Wilbur to the one in Houston.[61]

That winter Hecht resolved to make a change. Like Hughes and Plath, he had grown tired of his treatment at Smith. He sent word to them that he, too, had begun "seething with feelings not unlike their own" about the place.[62] Now back in England, Plath chose Hecht's "'More Light! More Light!'" for *American Poetry Now: A Selection of the Best Poems by Modern American Writers*. The pamphlet appeared shortly after Hecht's poem ran in *The Nation* that March. *American Poetry Now* included work by a number of poets who would become good friends of Hecht over the years: Wilbur, Howard Nemerov, George Starbuck, Louis Simpson, W. S. Merwin, Anne Sexton, and W. D. Snodgrass. Perhaps it was their acquaintance that convinced Plath to include the still emerging Hecht; more likely it was the poem itself, with its brutal imagery and morally fraught dramatic situation. Plath's propensity for extreme, even violent feeling, would have attracted her to the poem's opening, which begins, mid-sentence, with the execution of an English martyr during the Reformation.

In a plot twist worthy of Shakespeare's late romances, during his time at Smith Hecht met the woman who, some fifteen years later, would become his second wife. Like so many first-years, Helen D'Alessandro took Hecht's Intro to Literature course. She was immediately struck by the handsome young professor with the sad eyes and contemplative air: "I fell in love with him when I was a freshman at college. I used to say to my friends, because he was married to Pat, 'I shall never get married because Anthony Hecht is already taken.'"[63] A recent debutante, she had been presented to society at the Gotham Ball. Hecht advised students to read the Classics and the Bible, and she enrolled in courses in both at his suggestion. Later, when she heard his marriage wasn't doing well, she "prayed that everything would be all right, and they'd get back together, because I just wanted him to be happy." For her own part, however, her feelings were crystal clear: "It wasn't a crush. He was such a spiritual person—that look in his eyes just overwhelmed me. And I also remember very clearly thinking to myself—because I'd been going out with a lot of, you know, callow young men—well now at least I know what I'm looking for."[64]

D'Alessandro was a gifted student, graduating magna cum laude. She clearly made an impression on Hecht at that time, though any nascent attraction went unacknowledged. Still, meeting her by chance in New York City over a decade later, he would recognize her immediately. That he had much "sadness and unhappiness in his life, a lot of suffering" was clear to her from the outset; she rhapsodized to her girlfriends, "he's a goddamned Christ figure." It was an outsized, even blasphemous declaration, she knew, and yet she felt as if she had glimpsed his soul. She thought of him often in the years between her college days and their reacquaintance years later. She secretly hoped, when she moved to Manhattan, that she might run into him there.

EIGHT

HARDER HOURS
(1962–1967)

Al that joye is went away,
That wele is comen to weylaway,
To manye harde stoundes.[1]

1. "A different mother tongue"[2]

By the early 1960s, Hecht, nearing forty, was midway on his life's journey, and in many ways the dark surround in which he found himself became pivotal—both in his life and in his poems. But like the tide at Fire Island where he spent his summers during these years, Hecht's fortunes only reversed after they had reached their lowest point. He was drinking more than usual and smoking compulsively, as he had learned in the Army. As his family situation worsened, he began to fear again for his sanity, finding resonance in Lear's plea to the gods: "O let me not be mad, not mad, sweet heaven; / keep me in temper; I would not be mad." The trials of *Lear*—the king's loss of Cordelia, Gloucester's loss of his eyes, the madness on the heath—became touchstones for the poems of broken kinship and incipient insanity that would form the core of his second collection, *The Hard Hours*.

In marrying Pat, Hecht had hoped for a stable home life, which might ground him emotionally and free him up to write. In turn, he had hoped to provide this kind of stability for Pat, to save her from her hand-to-mouth life as a model on the margins of New York society. Pat played at keeping house but never warmed to it. Despite their quarreling, he was deeply attracted to her, and his bohemian side relished the drinks, parties, and the glamour of her flirtatious, wild energy. Quickly, however, the two became like oil and water; there was no peace where, as he put it, "Jewish diligence" met "Irish jest."[3] Free-spirited and headstrong, Pat clashed with the melancholic Tony, who suffered all the more when his work stalled, which it did whenever they were quarreling. And they quarreled much of the time. Pat, for her part, could be aloof and self-preserving, as she continued to follow her own lights. Hecht's long silences provoked wilder and more destructive responses from her. She surrounded herself with old friends and potential suitors, even carrying on liaisons, relishing the attention of men drawn into her orbit.

After the two separated, in the summer of 1959, Pat moved to New York City with the boys, who were still in diapers. She saw a good deal of Claire and Bobby White, and soon moved out to Long Island to be closer to them and to escape the city during the dog days. At first, Pat held out some hope of working things out. As far as Hecht was concerned, this would not be possible without certain conditions. She wrote to him from her summer retreat in Nissequogue, Long Island, not far from Box Hill, to explain her recent behavior and to suggest a middle way forward:

> . . . I know you believe I am unaware of what I'm doing most of the time, but I would like you to know certain things.
>
> I do feel there is *some* hope for us, but I believe we must both change a great deal—maybe more than is possible. I feel that if we had gone on as we were we would destroy each other. The main action for me was to get out of the situation. It was harsh and painful, but I couldn't manage it any other way.
>
> The choice you gave me of seeing that analyst or "fini" I feel was unfair and beside the point. One—even a wife—must decide these things alone. You may still feel this way five months from now (after understanding more about yourself, me, and what we do to each other). At that time your decision will have more meaning . . .[4]

Ultimately Pat moved to end the marriage. According to Hecht, it was she who insisted on it. Lawyers were engaged to settle questions of child custody and support. Hecht left off teaching at Smith—never to return, as it happened. (His contract was not renewed after his sabbatical, and he chose not to pursue it further, joining Plath and Hughes in leaving the place behind.) He began a Guggenheim fellowship—his second in five years—trading Northampton for New York to be closer to Jason and Adam.

That summer he took the boys again for a month to the beach; Adam had only recently started walking. The Ford fellowship in drama, with The Actor's Studio, prolonged his break from teaching that fall. If Hecht produced any texts for the theater during his Ford year, they are lost. In fact, it was all he could do to scratch out the occasional poem, though slowly they were piling up. It would soon be a decade since *Stones,* and his lack of a sophomore collection was not helping his reputation, which at this point still attracted a fit audience, though few: with *Stones* on its way out of print, Hecht felt that he was not "terribly well known. . . . not on any lists and my name does not ring any bells."[5]

In truth, he had amassed a good number of poems toward a new book, and those had found good homes in prominent magazines such as *The Hudson Review* and *The New Yorker,* but he made a conscious decision not to rush things, sensing that some of his fiercest and most wrenching statements, particularly about the war and its aftermath, were still gestating in him. He wrote to Donald Hall, who had requested poems for *New Poets of England and America: Second Selection,* the era-defining anthology he edited with Robert Pack: "I've decided not to go back to Smith next year, and although I could have a book finished by September, I now feel less inclined to rush, and can try to make it as good as I can."[6] Hecht found it impossible to work during periods of upset, and even teaching could sap his energy; he tended to be most productive during vacations and fellowship years. "'More Light! More Light!'" appeared in *The Nation* on March 11, 1961, after it was turned down by Howard Moss at *The New Yorker.* And inclusion in the Hall-Pack anthologies helped to shore up his presence as a leading younger poet. Beyond that, he set himself to translating Baudelaire, his *semblable* and guide as he worked out the darker and more grotesque passages of his own recent poems. Of the clutch of versions he completed for inclusion in New Directions' updated edition of *The Flowers of Evil*—"Duellum," "Cats," "The Swan," "Spleen (I have more memories . . .)," "Laments of an Icarus," "If by some freak of fortune . . ."—he retained only "To a Madonna: Ex-Voto in the Spanish Style" for *The Hard Hours.*[7] The translation is a seamless thematic fit, and even mentions the Seven Deadly Sins, which Hecht explored with Baskin:

> I shall make seven blades of Spanish steel
> Out of the Seven Deadly Sins, and I
> Shall mix my love with murderous savagery,
> and like a circus knife-thrower, I'll aim
> At the pure center of your gentle frame,
> And plunge these blades into your beating heart,
> Your bleeding, suffering, palpitating heart.[8]

There was an immediacy and a violence to Hecht's new poems. They struck Ted Hughes as infused with an "absolute raw simplicity and directness."[9] Life experience found a way into the poems as it had never done before, though not as confession, but in highly charged correlatives and personae. In inventing new voices and situations, Hecht began to introduce a dramatic element to his work, that for all its inherent impersonality was his most personal to date.[10] The two poems to his sons form one of the emotional centers of *The Hard Hours*, expressing a father's love and hope ("Jason," which Hecht once called a "sequel" to "The Vow") and, later, a crushing resignation bordering on despair ("Adam").[11] (A third poem, still in prospect, "'It Out-Herods Herod. Pray You, Avoid It,'" which comes as the last poem in *The Hard Hours* and was one of the last written for it, marries the collection's themes of familial anxiety, Judaism, and the Holocaust.) He saw his boys achingly little after the separation and then not at all. He later explained to McClatchy that

At the termination of five-and-a-half years of a painfully unhappy and unsuccessful marriage, a separation settlement was made, followed by a divorce, which required of my ex-wife that she live within 150 miles of New York City, so that I should be able to see the children on a regular basis. I must add that, while the marriage had been an unhappy one virtually from the start, its failure was a terrible blow to my self-esteem, and it was not I who sought to terminate it. When it was over I

invested all my frustrated familial feelings on the two boys whom I saw,
like most divorced fathers, on weekends, making those days unhealthily
emotional, and completely without any ease or naturalness. In a way, I
resented this arrangement. . . . [I] invested too much emotional capital
in the children. I was the more inclined because I knew their mother to
be completely irresponsible with regards to them.[12]

Hecht hoped to be a positive force in his sons' upbringing. He vowed
to do better than his parents had done, to avoid falling into his father's
habits of feckless jollity and his mother's cool disapproval and neglect.
But his hands were tied by legal wrangling that took years to finalize.
The shame that Hecht felt over his misalliance and the fracturing of his
family inflamed old wounds, until it was clear to those who knew him,
both old friends and new acquaintances, that he was suffering. There
had been a physical toll as well. He had aged visibly; he looked grayer,
tired-eyed.

In the summer of 1960, a fellow New Yorker and former student at
Columbia, Richard Lincoln, became a friend. The two met on the beach
on Fire Island one day, where Hecht was looking after his boys. Hecht was
carrying a copy of the poems of Alexander Pope (whom he had studied
in grad school), and Lincoln, being a literary man—a poet, painter, and
editor at *Commentary* among other magazines—struck up a conversation.
Lincoln had studied for his doctorate in Classics at Columbia, under Moses Hadas. He and Hecht shared a connection to Mark Van Doren, whom
Lincoln considered a mentor during his years in Philosophy Hall, and with
whom Hecht had remained in touch since his graduate school days a decade before. Both had studied Dante with Dino Bigongiari, whose course
in the *Commedia* was renowned. Like Hecht, Lincoln was recently divorced
and looking after his young children—three in his case, along with their
pets, a cat and bird. The two poets were a strange pair of bachelors—like
something out of a Neil Simon play. Both were suffering from depression
brought on by their domestic troubles, and their commiseration deepened
their acquaintance into a friendship. It was clear to Lincoln that Hecht was
"very devastated" by the breakup of his marriage; it seemed to him, at
least, that he was "very much in love" with Pat.[13]

Summers were Hecht's time with the boys. Adam and Jason spent several weeks in July and August with their father in the Pines section of Fire Island and at his new apartment at 415 East 80th Street, which he rented in part as a place for the boys to stay when they visited. "Tony was a wonderful father. . . . He was very devoted to his children," Lincoln observed. Sometimes Hecht would arrive on Fire Island with his friend and drinking buddy, the poet Fredrick Seidel, and his new wife, Phyllis Munro Ferguson, granddaughter of the famous jurist Learned Hand. To distract themselves, he and Lincoln talked about literature, and, typical of men without women, they "talked about girls."[14]

Lincoln's mother, Ethel Solomon, had had a house in the Pines since the '50s, but this was the first summer he spent any time there. Next door lived Natacha Ullman, a "Talk of the Town" writer for *The New Yorker*, who escaped Europe during the war and who published under the pen name Natacha Stewart. She was married to the photographer John Stewart Ullman, who rarely came to Fire Island. Hecht and Stewart began an affair that summer, a relationship that lasted for more than a year. Ullman, whom Lincoln considered a bit of a fool, was away and unaware of the deception. Natacha had two children of her own. As she and Hecht looked on from the sand, their children played together in the shallows. In a love poem to Natacha, "Message from the City," Hecht expresses the wistful uncertainty of their attachment. Back in his New York apartment at summer's end, he addresses her still at the shore: "I think of you out there / on the sandy edge of things. . . ." Their children were a bond between them, but their affair was complicated by the obvious impediments, painful to Hecht:

> *And between us there is—what?*
> *Love and constraint,*
> *conditions, conditions,*
> *and several hundred miles*
> *of billboards, filling-stations,*
> *and little dripping gardens.*
> *The fir tree full of whispers,*
> *trinkets of water,*
> *the bob, duck, and release*
> *of the weighted rose,*

life in the freshened stones.
(They used to say that rain
is good for growing boys,
and once I stood out in it
hoping to rise a foot.
The biggest drops fattened
on the gutters under the eaves,
sidled along the slant,
picked up speed, let go,
and met their dooms in a "plock"
beside my gleaming shins.
I must have been near the size
of your older son.)[15]

Hecht longed for her company in his outcast state, but "conditions, conditions" constrained their relationship from becoming permanent. He did not relish the deception or the moral compromise of the adultery, later admitting to his friend Shirley Hazzard that he had "once involved myself in such a situation," which had caused him considerable regret.[16] The landscape exudes melancholy, with an echo of Auden's "The Fall of Rome": "today the rain pummels / the sour geraniums / and darkens the grey pilings / of your house built on sand."[17]

"Message from the City" appeared in Saul Bellow's journal *The Noble Savage* #5, in January 1962. When several years later Hecht compiled the table of contents for the manuscript that would become *The Hard Hours*, he placed the poem near the beginning, beside "The End of the Weekend" (another poem about an affair, this one based on an anecdote that Ted Hughes told him at Smith). A second poem to Natacha, "A Letter," appears later in the book. It forecasts the end of their relationship by acknowledging their outstanding commitments and their children, whom they did not like to speak of when together:

Others are bound to us, the gentle and the blameless
Whose names are not confessed
In the ceaseless palaver. My dearest the clear unquarried blue

Of those depths is all but blinding.
You may remember that once you brought my boys
    Two little woolly birds.
Yesterday the older one asked for you upon finding
    Your thrush among his toys.
And the tides welled about me, and I could find no words.[18]

"All is not well," Hecht ultimately admitted; try as he might to "continue as before, doing some good," he cannot quiet his attraction: "The endless repetitions of his own murmurous blood." Howard Moss took the poem for *The New Yorker* in June 1961, and it appeared the following year, in the same pages where Natacha's work regularly appeared. As a word of explanation about the poem's discretion, Hecht wrote to Moss: "I hope there will be no objection to the fact that I have deliberately left a few loose ends by way of insisting upon the anonymity of the person being addressed, and the various personal entanglements that set these two apart." Moss, too, summered on Fire Island, near to Hecht, and he knew Natacha well, seeing her occasionally when he was at the beach and even passing messages between Hecht and her. He would have known of their affair and her role as the poem's addressee, but the relationship is not referred to in his editorial correspondence with Hecht.[19] Presumably the anonymity not only suited him fine but was a requirement of publication given the close connection to the addressee.

Hecht had two other significant relationships with women in the '60s, both of them as complicated as his affair with Natacha. In the early spring of 1961, he went to dinner at *Hudson Review* editor Frederick Morgan's elegant Park Avenue apartment, where he was introduced to Anne Sexton. Their meeting was all but inevitable, given the many connections they shared. The year before, Sexton had a brief (but verse-inspiring) affair with James Wright, who counted Roger Hecht among his closest friends. The two young poets were together at Kenyon, and Roger later served as best man at Wright's second wedding, to Anne Runk, in 1967. Tony knew Wright partly through Roger and partly through the Kenyon connection and John Crowe Ransom, a mentor to both poets. Sexton also knew Robert Lowell. She and Sylvia Plath had been his students at

Boston University in 1959, and Sexton continued a correspondence with him. At the Morgan dinner, Hecht and Sexton were instantly drawn to one another and, shortly after, they arranged to spend time together. Writing to Sexton in mid-April, Hecht expressed both attraction and hesitation: "And now what do I say? I love you? Yes, I guess I do. But I feel sort of foolish writing a love letter to a happily married woman. Still, it was a wonderful time we spent together, and in ways that I can scarcely put my finger on, you made me very happy." Hecht recognized immediately a fellow depressive, a sympathy that allowed him to be completely and refreshingly frank with her. At the same time, as alluring and flirtatious as Sexton could be, she was too much like Pat—self-involved, high-strung, a professional model, as well as an "astonishingly gifted and accomplished poet"—to tempt him into a sexual liaison.[20] Under separate cover, as a way to dampen the fire, Hecht sent Sexton and her husband, Kayo, a businessman, a set of wineglasses and asked that they raise a toast to one another and then to him.

With the prospect of sex avoided ("I wasn't talking about 'fucking,'" she wrote to him a little defensively), Sexton became a confidant. In this sense, she was dearer to Hecht during this period than if they had been lovers; dearer, in other words, because they had steered clear of the snares that would have surely brought Hecht more unhappiness.[21] His relationship with Natacha had exposed him to the heartache of falling for a married woman. Hecht confided his affair to Sexton; though he doesn't mention Natacha by name, Sexton may well have caught wind of their relationship, and she certainly knew Natacha's byline. Hecht wrote to Sexton: "I am sad. Because I am in love. But not with you, or, not entirely with you. Anyway, you have a man of your own. The trouble is, so does she. And she feels a kind of mute, Thomas Hardy loyalty to him. But she loves me. I know it." The two traded poems for critique, and Sexton's suggestions were helpful in finishing "Message from the City." Hecht let her know that he thought her "an unbelievably lovely human being."[22] For her part, she relished his kindness. She inscribed to him a copy of her new collection, *To Bedlam and Part Way Back*: "For Anthony Hecht, / With my admiration / for your work and your / face."

That spring he introduced a reading by E. E. Cummings at Smith

College.[23] His student Helen D'Alessandro was in the audience, still starstruck by her professor, whom she'd admired since freshman year: "There was a poignant look in his eyes," which she later ascribed to his marriage breaking up. She approached him to say that she had "decided to honor in English and would he be my thesis advisor. . . . He asked what my field was, and when I replied I didn't know he suggested I decide upon that first. . . . [H]e was probably evasive knowing he would not be returning to Smith."[24]

Meanwhile, through the Whites, Pat met Baron Philippe Lambert, a Belgian aristocrat in the Rothschild line. Not long after the Hechts' divorce became final early in 1961, Pat took the children to live abroad, which left Hecht feeling bereft. Lambert, a banker and art collector and scion of the Banque Bruxelles Lambert banking dynasty, had houses in Brussels and Gstaad, and he rented flats in Paris and London for Pat to travel with the boys. Claire White, whose family memoir *The Elephant and the Rose* begins in Brussels in 1850, was the age of Philippe's older brother, Leon, and she encouraged Pat's attachment to Philippe, since it would mean that Pat would be "taken care of for the rest of [her] life."[25] Claire knew the Lamberts from childhood; their parents had been friends: "We were all immigrants in New York during the war." After Pat began courting Philippe, she proposed renting Box Hill, the White estate on Long Island, which felt cavernously empty after Robert's grandfather, Stanford White, passed away. Claire noted how seamlessly Pat adapted to her new glamorous life: Lambert had given her "a beautiful necklace, because Lambert was rich." Pat campaigned for Jack Kennedy and caught the attention of the Kennedy Boys, JFK's entourage of young apparatchiks. She and Philippe were invited to the White House, where she "made a smash entrance." It wasn't long before Pat removed the boys to Belgium, trading her tiny Manhattan apartment for an Old World castle and ski vacations in the Alps. The news of her plan blindsided Hecht completely:

> Then one day she told me, as I was delivering the children to her at the end of the weekend, that she had fallen in love with a Belgian. . . . So she took the children off to Belgium, and I sank into a very deep depression.

I felt no incentive even to get out of bed in the morning. I don't believe I thought in terms of suicide, but neither did life seem to hold out any attractions whatsoever.[26]

Sexton lent a sympathetic ear, when he told her of his unhappiness:

Yesterday was Adam's birthday (he was three) and next Saturday is Jason's birthday (he'll be five) and very soon Christmas will be here, which means a lot to them and of course to me too, and all these events conspire to force themselves upon my consciousness; and then they'll be gone. You understand that in the long run I am glad that Pat is getting married, and I think it is all for the best for the children. Still, it is hard to be simply rational about these things, and I'm feeling pretty low.[27]

When Pat married Lambert in February 1961, she was already pregnant. She gave birth later that year to a daughter, Johanna. (Her marriage to Philippe eventually dissolved, and she returned with the boys to the States, still presiding over their lives and schooling.) A few days after the wedding, Pat arrived in a taxi to take the boys. Hecht would not see them again before they left for Belgium. To Sexton, he confided that he felt as if he had "been hit with a club . . . I'm only slowly coming out of it now, but it absolutely killed the little spurt of writing energy that took me through the Baudelaire translations and one or two things of my own. Right now I feel as if I will never write again."[28]

Caught up in a whirl of chauffeurs and chalets, Pat wrote from the Chalet Waldegg in Switzerland a note that was breezy with news. It's hard to know which would have pained Hecht more, to hear that his children weren't missing him or that they were. Was Pat's asking for a favor from "your Natacha," who was leaving soon for Switzerland, pure innocence, like her chatty tone? Or was there an undercurrent that further jangled Hecht's nerves:

We're all well and thriving in the Alps.
    I miss New York quite a bit but the children have adapted beautifully. Jason particularly amazes me. He's been so good and seems to like it here in spite of no T.V. Adam has shouted "home" a few times, but is gay as always.

Jason has real skis and poles and looks terribly grown up and compe-
tent on top of the mountain.

We have a phonograph and records in French. Perhaps your Natacha
could bring me some children's story records when she comes as they
don't have any in English here. . . .[29]

Hecht was aware that the separation from his children was not technically legal, but he knew that fighting with Pat would do little good. The
divorce decree required Pat "to live within a certain distance from New
York City," so that Hecht could see the boys regularly. "She told me, 'Of
course, you have a legal right to make me stay here; but if you do, I will
be very unhappy, and if I'm unhappy, the children will be, too.'"[30] Hecht
felt powerless to remedy the situation: "I had asked my lawyer, before
the separation papers were drawn up, whether it would be possible for
me to obtain custody of the children. He told me that it was virtually
impossible, and in those days he was right."[31]

It was years before he could bring himself to write more directly about
the divorce, though always through a veil of impersonality, and naming
no names. "Circles" (from *The Darkness and the Light* [2001]) exudes the
rawness of lived experience:

Many long years and some attachments later
I was to be instructed by the courts
Upon the nicest points of such afflictions,
having become a weakened, weekend father.
All of us in our own circle of hell . . .[32]

The remorse over losing his children mingled in his imagination with his
own childhood trauma, recalling games in Central Park (as does "Third
Avenue in Sunlight") and its "pain-tainted ground":

Where the innocent and the fallen join to play
In the fields, if not of the Lord, then of the Law;
Which decreed that love be hobbled and confined
To Saturday,
Trailing off into Sunday-before-dark;

And certain sandpits, slides, swings, monkey bars
Became the old thumbscrews of spoiled affection
And agonized aversion.[33]

The poem concludes with an image seared into his memory since childhood, and which he now revisits with his own children:

Of these, the most tormenting
In its single-songed, maddening monotony,
Its glaring eyed and nostril-flaring steeds
With perfect teeth, but destined never to win
Their countless and interminable races,
Was the merry, garish, mirthless carousel.[34]

In letters to Pat, Hecht disguised his bitterness. He never betrayed anger or frustration to the boys, but in "Destinations" (from *The Transparent
Man* [1990]) he hints at it through the persona of a divorced man whose
wife has "taken him to the cleaners" in the courts: "thinking of her, he
could recall / Only a catalogue of pettiness, / Selfishness, spite, a niggling
litany / Of minor acrimony, punctuated / By outbursts of hysteria and
violence."[35] Though Pat and Tony never came to blows, the emotional violence of their breakup had a scarring effect. Through another scenario,
reminiscent of Pat and Tony's travels in Italy, Hecht limns a more sedate
but no less forlorn portrait of a broken marriage in "See Naples and Die"
(from *The Transparent Man*). The poem hits close to home:

Marriages come to grief in many ways.
Our own was, I suppose, a common one,
Without dramatics, a slow stiffening
Of all the little signs of tenderness,
Significant silences, self-conscious efforts
To be civil even when we were alone.[36]

Here Hecht adumbrates his own failings in his relationship with Pat—the
long silences and brooding, the isolating bouts of depression that continued to hamstring him. The style is direct and self-lacerating:

The cold, envenoming spirit of Despair,
Turning what was nectar of the world
To ashes in our mouths. We were the cursed
To whom it seemed no joy was possible,
The spiritually warped and handicapped.[37]

Pat could be cold, even cruel, though her manner was upbeat. Hecht was unable to mask the effects of guilt and unhappiness. Many years later, he described to McClatchy what he went through at that time: "My doctor was worried about me, and suggested that I commit myself to a hospital, chiefly, he said, for the administration of medication. It was Thorazine [an anti-psychotic medication], which Anne [Sexton] took, and some other drug [possibly Tofranil] the name of which I no longer recall."[38]

Overwhelmed and exhausted, Hecht spent three months in a psychiatric hospital on the Upper East Side, near the East River. The Thorazine and other medications "were alternative treatments to electric shock therapy more commonly administered at the hospital." In retrospect, Hecht cast his internment in as positive a light as possible: "I met some nice people there, and some that were deeply, frighteningly troubled. (One who had to be subdued with a hypodermic, makes his way briefly into a poem of mine.) I myself was merely depressed."[39] He wrote as much to Sexton:

It's partly the drugs of course, but it's mostly the continued effects of the depression that make me feel that I'm in a trance day in and day out, and that nothing is either going to annoy or please me very much at all. It's like the humming of a single sound in the ear—dull and monotonous yet soothing. But I feel sort of like a zombie, and nothing that happens seems important or interesting.[40]

After his second month at Gracie Square, Hecht was allowed out during the days, and he was grateful for the support of Sexton, who mentioned his situation to Lowell. Lowell's poem describing his stay at McLean's "house for the 'mentally ill,'" "Waking in the Blue," had appeared in *Life Studies* only a few years before. The two poets expressed their struggles with mental illness in different ways: Hecht's indirections contrasted with Lowell's confessions, but it created a sympathy between them. Lowell reached out to comfort a fellow sufferer, inviting Hecht to dinner:

> Lowell was particularly kind to me during this period. The hospital was called Gracie Square Hospital, and there were some public pay phones on my floor, on which incoming calls to patients would be carried. Anyone could pick up the phone when it rang, and then page in a loud shout whomever the call was for. It was the custom of the patients to announce, in a loud cheerful voice, on picking up the phone: "Crazy Square."[41]

After his release, Hecht spent time recuperating (and chain-smoking) at the Guilford, Connecticut, home of Bill and Dale MacDonald, his friends from the Academy. (Bill was teaching at Yale at that point.) Back in New York, Hecht, presumably with his parents' support, saw his psychiatrist four times a week. When he went back into talk therapy is unclear, but it may well have been soon after the separation from Pat. A poem written the year before his hospitalization, "Behold the Lilies of the Field," dedicated to Baskin, imagines a curious overlap between ancient Roman history and the modern psychiatrist's office. Hecht's speaker recounts a scene of extreme violence, the public execution of the Emperor, who is flayed alive

> As slowly as possible, to drag out the pain.
> And we were made to watch. The king's personal doctor,
> The one who had tended his back,
> Came forward with a tray of surgical knives.
> They began at the feet.
> And we were not allowed to close our eyes
> Or look away.[42]

When the gruesome story ends, the doctor urges rest, and the patient complies:

> You must rest now. You must. Lean back.
> Look at the flowers.
> Yes. I am looking. I wish I could be like them.

The speaker wishes to trade his mental anguish for the vegetable world, a life of stasis without suffering. With its title taken from the Gospel of Matthew (6:25), it is an early instance of Hecht's poems that take off from, interpret, or expand on biblical passages, and which compose the lion's share of his final collection, *The Darkness and the Light*. In manuscript, the poem carried an epigraph from the "Heroes" section of Walt Whitman's "Song of Myself": "I am the man. I suffered. I was there." By dropping the epigraph, Hecht chose to mask the personal nature of this portrait of a man in mental distress, though the connection now seems clear. Like "'More Light! More Light!,'" the poem juxtaposes the ancient and the contemporary, employing historical corollaries to reveal the modern psyche. Hecht said of the poem in an interview:

> I don't imagine it's wholly a matter of putting oneself into the past. There are so many contemporary events that seem to have the flavor of that disaster [the flaying]. The modern world is filled with similar illustrations of cruelty. So that in my own mind, and, I should hope in the reader's mind also, this is not merely a poem about something that happened to a Roman emperor, a long time ago, but a vision of the kind of mental process that results in contemporary cruelty and barbarity.[43]

Gracie Square was a surreal place, the walls covered with framed fabric, their geometric patterns meant to soothe, not excite, as might, the staff feared, an actual painting. Then suddenly one day, in the midst of this strangely sanitized world, his father appeared. Melvyn attempted to reach out to his son, with a typically strained and awkward result. Hecht's doctor, whom he liked and trusted

> had forbidden, with my complete consent, any attempt on the part of my parents to visit me—a prohibition my father took pains to violate. I don't know how he got in, but he did, on the pretext of bringing me some toothpaste or cigarettes. He suddenly appeared one day, very briefly, in the hall, and handed me these things. And his grin was terrible, almost triumphant. I was revolted. We exchanged no words.[44]

As with his memories of the war, which he almost never shared, Hecht rarely spoke of his battles with depression or his fears of succumbing to mental illness. He did not hide these facts, but neither did he make heavy weather of them. When they appear in his poems, they appear veiled. The "I" is typically a persona, whereas one associates Lowell's confessional "I" in "Waking in the Blue," for example, with Lowell himself. Hecht's difficulties, his quiet coping and circumspection about loss, led him to question those who wore their struggles on their sleeves:

> I was never very comfortable about the way Anne Sexton exploited her hospitalizations and periods of dementia. I knew her quite well, but this "trait" of hers always made me feel ill at ease. It was clear she enjoyed both the attention she received from therapists and the more general notoriety of being "twelve-fingered," one of her kind. Cal Lowell was quite different, and though perhaps a little proud of his craziness at times (it became a license for recklessness in his manic moods, and seemed to him sometimes the sign of his genius as well as the frailty of his character) he only indulged it to the extent of not taking his lithium when the first manic signs of an attack came on him, chiefly because he felt so good, and, knowing that all the terrible consequences might, perhaps even must, ensue, he could not bring himself to descend from his exaltation.[45]

Following his release, Hecht remained stymied. The next decade—a second bachelorhood for Hecht—was in its way the darkest he endured. Out of this murk came his breakthrough book, *The Hard Hours*. Tellingly, the collection is dedicated "For my sons, Jason and Adam," the tragic loss of whom was at the center of his despair. His poem "Adam" is a cri de cœur from an absent father who fears his son may be too young to remember him. Though Hecht generally espoused a cooler method, here he accesses direct confession:

> *Tell them again in pain,*
> *And to the empty air.*
> *Where you are men speak*

A different mother tongue.
Will you forget our games,
Our hide-and-seek and song?
Child, it will be long
Before I see you again.[46]

He wants to warn his son, to prepare him for imminent and unavoidable hardship:

Adam, there will be
Many hard hours,
As an old poem says,
Hours of loneliness.[47]

These "hard hours" appear in the book's epigraph as "harde stoundes," from the anonymous medieval poem "Ubi sunt qui ante nos fuerunt?" ("Where are those who were before us?"). Hecht had known the poem since his Form 5 English class at Horace Mann, where it was included in his poetry textbook, *The Literature of England*.[48] Hecht kept the book with him and likely relied on it for background for his freshman English course at Smith. (It may have also figured in a graduate course he took in the medieval lyric at Columbia.) The poem, a prototypical *ubi sunt*, recalls better days, wondering where they have gone now that they have been replaced by hardship. Hecht first encountered the poem during a happier time in his life, as an upperclassman at Horace Mann and a freshman at Bard. Those days now seemed so remote, it was almost as if they never happened. Hecht may well have wondered:

Were is that lawhing and that song,
That trayling and that proud gong,
Tho havekes and tho houndes.

[Where is that laughing and that song,
that trailing and that proud going,
the hawks and the hounds?]

His worst fears were realized: he could not protect his sons from suffering, a suffering he had partly caused.

As a way to comfort the boys and to feel closer to them now that they lived thousands of miles away, Hecht sent them stories, typed out in large, single-spaced blocks on blue airmail paper:

> Dear Jason and Adam; Here is a story that I am writing just for you, and I am sure that Mommy, or perhaps your new Nanny, will read it to you when you're all ready to go to bed. Here we go! Once upon a time there was a big, brown Werfel, who lived in a wood, and who was very bad. (A Werfel is a wolf in sheep's clothing; and this Werfel—whose name was Franz—had a beautiful fleece-lined coat that he always wore when he was out being bad.) The thing that Franz did that was worst of all was to keep people awake all night. And the reason he did this is that he was very busy trying to make hay while the moon shone.[49]

Hecht's shaggy dog story, with shades of Ted Geisel, continues at great length. He signed it "with all my love." Being kept awake all night: this was something Hecht knew about. He laments his own insomnia in the uncollected "Ballade for the Small Hours (Acts 20:7–10)," which works one of his numerous turns on the life of St. Paul, here in a somewhat lighter vein:

> *I toss and tumble through the whole*
> *Bedridden torment of the night*
> *Hopelessly distant from my goal,*
> *Blinds drawn and windows shuttered tight,*
> *Trapped in the old nocturnal plight,*
> *Even reduced to counting sheep,*
> *And think with wrath and rising spite;*
> *St. Paul put Eutychus to sleep.*[50]

Hecht had suffered from recurring nightmares since childhood, a condition that was greatly exacerbated after the war, when he would start awake from nightmares. During his divorce, such dreams returned with a vengeance:

I have had recurring dreams betokening anxiety, and usually taking the shape and scenario of finding myself rushing to a depot, a station, or a dock in the hope of getting aboard some vehicle or vessel, and at the final moment, failing. This was a frequent dream when I was young . . . I was always brought awake in a cold sweat. A good deal later in my life, during what was surely a protracted interval of profound unhappiness, in which my first marriage was disintegrating, this early dream pattern combined itself with an image out of a painting by Watteau. The painting, *The Departure for Cythera*, is a lively, seeming joyous representation of crowds of richly fashionable and elegantly clad women, escorted by dapper and cultivated men, all preparing to embark for the island sacred to the goddess of love.[51]

Shortly before the divorce was finalized in 1961, Hecht incorporated this into "Clair de Lune," a dream poem that takes the Watteau as its setting. In the poem,

the ship departs for those sacred regions of unblemished love, leaving behind two persons, a man and a woman, abandoned at some vast emptied estate, and isolated from one another. To be sure, the Watteau and my elaboration upon it serve to disguise strong personal feeling from direct sight of the reader. But this seems what dreams always do. They present us with their truths in elaborate, sometimes indecipherable disguise.[52]

The poem offers another moralized landscape, Hecht's preferred method for encoding turbulent feeling in the visible surround. He took pains to avoid the cheapening effects that can come with bald self-revelation, which smacked of pride, the sin he most wished to avoid. As elsewhere, his diction points to a darkness beneath the surface of the physical world:

> *A gardener goes*
> *Through the bone light about the dark estate.*
> *He bows, and cheerfully inebriate,*
> *Admires the lunar ashes of a rose . . .*

The significance of the dream is driven home to the reader in the final lines:

This is your nightmare. Those cold hands are yours.
The pain in the drunken singing is your pain.
Morning will taste the bitterness again.
The heart turns to stone, but it endures.

Here is another sense of Hecht's "hard hours"—difficult, to be sure, but also petrified, the heart turned to rock by sorrow, as with Lear's "men of stones." The Eliotic impersonality that Hecht constructs is, as Eliot understood, an "escape from personality," an attempt to both express and meliorate personal suffering, a telling measure of the magnitude of Hecht's pain during the dissolution of his family. Though it would arrive eventually, reprieve was not immediately forthcoming. Hecht's hard hours turned into days and then into years.

2. Back to Bard

After two years away from the classroom, funded by grants, Hecht returned, aged thirty-nine, to teaching as his primary means of support. Instead of heading back to Smith, where the relationship with the administration seemed to have cooled on both sides, he returned to Bard in the fall of 1962, commuting each week from his apartment on 80th Street. It was during this stint in Annandale that Hecht began regularly teaching Shakespeare's plays. Shakespeare became his main subject in the classroom, along with surveys of modern poetry, and he carried on teaching *The Merchant of Venice, A Midsummer Night's Dream, Othello, Henry IV, Romeo and Juliet, The Tempest,* and others for the rest of his career, first at Bard and then at the University of Rochester (eighteen years) and Georgetown University (eight years) before his retirement from teaching in 1993. Of his early days teaching Shakespeare at Bard, Hecht wrote in a letter to Hayát Matthews:

I often taught *As You Like It, A Midsummer Night's Dream, The Merchant of Venice, Twelfth Night, I & II Henry IV, Henry V, Richard III, Romeo and Juliet, Macbeth, Othello, Lear* and *The Tempest,* but never, though I have read it ever since adolescence, and read countless commentaries in it,

Hamlet—which still seems to me the most puzzling, amazing, unsettling and defiantly enigmatic play in the whole corpus. There was a time when I knew more of *Hamlet* by heart than any of the other plays. (That later was followed by *Lear* and *The Tempest*.)

As a result of his years of study, Shakespeare seeped even deeper into the groundwater of his sensibility; his next three books in particular are marked by his immersion in the plays and poems.

Following a run of recent acceptances by *The New Yorker,* more good news came from Moss. He wrote to offer Hecht one of the magazine's coveted contracts establishing right-of-first-refusal for Hecht's new poems. Hecht gladly accepted this "first-reading agreement." In return for giving Moss a look at his poems before offering them elsewhere, he received $100 up front (renewable annually) and an increased pay rate over the standard $2.30/line for any poems accepted.[53] Hecht sent back the signed contract with an update on his doings: "I am teaching up at Bard this year, but I have a pretty good schedule, with classes only on Wed., Thurs., and Fri., and I try to get into New York every weekend. Generally, I come in Friday evening and go back on Tuesday morning." He also planned to spend winter break in New York, including all of January and most of February, during which he hoped that he and Moss might meet for dinner (on the magazine, of course).

On February 7, 1963, Hecht made his first appearance as a featured poet at the renowned Poetry Center of the 92nd Street Y, where he would read numerous times throughout his career. Founded in 1939, the Poetry Center hosted readings at the Young Men's Hebrew Association on Lexington Avenue, a stone's throw from Hecht's apartment. Readers included T. S. Eliot, Robert Frost, W. H. Auden, Marianne Moore, and the audience there was celebrated as the most literary and intellectual in the city. It was where, in 1953, then-director John Malcolm Brinnin presented Dylan Thomas's *Under Milk Wood,* and arranged for Thomas's tour of the States. Hecht's debut at the Y was introduced by the polymathic critic John Simon (who liked to boast that he had been John Ashbery's TA at Harvard). Simon, with his silk suit and thick Serbian accent, praises Hecht's method of "seducing" words—as opposed to a platonic relationship to language ("dreary lucubrations") or taking the words by force ("a rape")—a skill, according to Simon, he shares with Richard Wilbur and James Merrill. Simon found in *Stones* "all the charm, all the elegance, all the persuasiveness, all the delightfulness of . . . the master seducer, at work."[54] In Hecht's newest poems—featured recently in *The Noble Savage*, *The Hudson Review*, and the Hall-Pack anthology—Simon sees the poet forging a "wholly new and wholly more profound" relationship with his words.[55] He closes by suggesting that Hecht is one of only a few younger poets from whom readers may expect greatness.

After opening with "To a Madonna" (and claiming Baudelaire as "rather a favorite poet of mine"), he read "The Origin of Centaurs" from a series of animal poems he wrote to accompany lithographs by Aubrey Schwartz. Their fine-press volume entitled *A Bestiary* appeared the year before. Hecht interleaved these poems—"Pig," "Song of the Flea," "Lizards and Snakes," "Tarantula, or The Dance of Death," "Giant Tortoise," "Birdwatchers of America" (produced for an earlier collaboration with Schwartz, *Predatory Birds* [1958])—into *The Hard Hours*. These poems possess a violence new to Hecht's poems, more detailed and realistic than the idealized violence he arrived at in *Stones*. They rail at sin and flirt with madness, and Baudelaire may well be their presiding genius. He read two poems that would be counted among his very best, "A Hill" and "'More Light! More Light,'" the first slyly adumbrating the Holocaust in its imagery of a factory (recalling the Messerschmitt factory on the grounds of Flossenbürg) and the second recounting a scene from Buchenwald, as reported by Eugen Kogon in *The Theory and Practice of Hell*, both of which had a particular resonance with the Jewish audience who frequented the YMHA. Hecht's poem follows Kogon closely:

The Detail leader spied two Jews whose strength was ebbing. He ordered a Pole by the name of Strzaska to *bury* the two men, who were scarcely able to keep to their feet. The Pole froze in his tracks—and refused! The sergeant took the pick handle, belabored the Pole and forced him to lie down in one of the ditches in place of the two Jews. Next he forced the Jews to cover the Pole with soil. They complied, in terror of their lives, and in the hope of escaping the ghastly fate themselves.

When only the head of the Pole was still uncovered, the SS man called a halt and had the man dug out again. The two Jews now had to lie down in the ditch, while Strzaska was ordered to cover them up. Slowly the ditch was filled with soil. When the work was done, the Detail Leader personally trampled down the soil over his two victims.[56]

Hecht strips away the name of the Pole and any features of the Detail Leader beyond his gloved hand and his Luger, creating a horrible facelessness, as if "Much casual death had drained away their souls,"[57] both the victims' and the perpetrators'.

Hecht read the poem in his resonant and elegantly inflected basso, honed by his early experiences as an actor. "'More Light! . . .'" marked the arrival of his mature period, the poems that would make his name, and he delivered them with a humane sonority. Between poems, his disarming modesty and humor invited the audience to engage with the serious subjects at hand. He closed with "The Dover Bitch," a poem that drew an uneasy response. Hecht suggested in his introduction that the poem was a rather "impudent" reply to Arnold's "Dover Beach" and that it should be taken as "lighthearted." Hecht's travesty of Arnold got laughs: "And he said to her, 'Try to be true to me, / And I'll do the same for you, for things are bad / All over, etc. etc." But the tawdriness of the scene is hard-edged and melancholy. Some readers have perceived a sexist tone in the poem, and, indeed, the speaker that Hecht creates can seem crass and condescending. This is a persona, however, and not the poet himself speaking. Written in 1959, at the time of his separation, the poem adopts a callous view of male-female relations, in which the speaker (and, in his own way, the poet) are left very much on the hook:

> I still see her once in a while
> And she always treats me right. We have a drink
> And I give her a good time, and perhaps it's a year
> Before I see her again, but there she is,
> Running to fat, but dependable as they come.
> And sometimes I bring her a bottle of Nuit d'Amour.

The woman has said earlier that the perfume, the big beds, and the French blandishments make her sad. In Hecht's catalogue of characters,

the woman resonates with the "little, paltry Leporello's list / Of former girlfriends" in "Death the Whore." As a "critique of life" (Arnold's
phrase), "The Dover Bitch" concludes (in its scabrous humor) that love
and sex are fallen and inconstant at best and, at worst, woefully sordid.
Hecht's suspicion that he was unworthy of love because of what he had
seen and done in the war and after left him feeling alone and bitter.

He began drowning his sorrows in the neighborhood gin joints. He
often met his friend Fred Seidel at Elaine's in the evening. Seidel lived on
93rd Street. He had met Tony and Pat at a literary event at Mt. Holyoke. Seidel found the couple striking, particularly Pat: "He looked rather formidable, very handsome, with this marvelous-looking woman." Seidel, who
made no secret of his fondness for attractive women, liked Pat, finding
her "lovely, very likable." As for Hecht himself, "there was something very
orotund about him, a magnificence of speech. It was a bit tedious, really,
and about which it was fun to kid him." Hecht's Oxbridge affect lessened as
he grew comfortable with someone: "It seemed to me in the years I knew
him best and saw him most, he was, however gloomy, relaxed—[he] didn't
puff out that way. He quite enjoyed being teased. I was his older brother."
In fact, Seidel made the same initial assumption that many who met Hecht
for the first time fell into, mistaking a defensive hauteur for the man himself: "And he wasn't formidable at all. He was exceptionally nice, rather
subdued, rather quiet." After they became friends, Hecht opened up to him
about his breakup with Pat and his despair at losing his sons: "He had a sort
of breakdown, and he stopped writing, dried up completely, and was very
shaky and dark about himself and about life." Seidel also witnessed his slow
and gradual recovery; he "cheered as time passed."[58]

Seidel, thirteen years Hecht's junior, was the wealthy scion of Russian
Jews from the Midwest, whose family owned Seidel Coal and Coke. In
1962, his first book of poems, *Final Solutions,* was chosen by Robert Lowell, Louise Bogan, and Stanley Kunitz for a prize sponsored by the 92nd
Street Y, but the prize was never awarded; his work was rejected by the
YM-YWHA as "anti-Semitic and anti-Catholic." Hecht defended Seidel's
method in *The New York Review of Books*. He noted that the poems

>   are written in the form of dramatic monologues (in the first person) or
>   as portraits (in the third person). Each poem has its own protagonist,

whom we see at a crucial moment in his or her life; and that moment is often a revelation of meanness, emptiness or vanity. In this sense, the book has the shock of honesty about it, and some of its themes (adultery, frustrated lust) are exposed with an unsparing eye and in their most telling details. There will be those who are horrified by this sort of candor, and who may furthermore make the mistake of identifying the characters' sentiments with the author's. Clearly Seidel has created some characters he does not like, and has given them voice; but even the worst of them invite compassion, and there are in these tough and brutal poems some passages of extraordinary tenderness. Altogether, this seems to me one of the most moving and powerful books of poetry to have come along in years. And if it leaves one with a sense of bitterness, it is worth reflecting that there is a lot in our world to be bitter about.[59]

As for the claims of antisemitism:

The book's title, *Final Solutions*, will remind the reader of Hitler's notorious "final solution to the Jewish problem," and the characters Mr. Seidel delineates with ruthless care have all come to a stalemate in their lives, an impasse which is a sort of "final solution," an annihilating judgment on life. One poem, for example, concerns a refugee from that holocaust, a Jewish psychoanalyst; a woman whose family has been wiped out in the concentration camps. She lives alone on the coast of Maine now, and she sees in the wholesale slaughter of rabbits that are overrunning the neighborhood, "Frail, pink-veined, pale ears, / And pink as perfect gums, / Pink eyes, rose noses, as if / Diseased . . ." a painful analogue of what has happened to all those dearest to her.[60]

Seidel's unblinking grotesquery and violence likely emboldened Hecht in such poems as "The Deodand," "The Short End," and "The Venetian Vespers." Since "'More Light! More Light!'" had already appeared, perhaps it is better to see these poems as following a similar trajectory, fueled by the same moral horror and unafraid of laying bare the atrocities that men and women perpetrate on each other. We hear Hecht's own jaundiced resignation in this bitterness at the world.

Forthright sometimes to a fault, Seidel admitted more recently that, despite their overlapping sensibilities, he was not "such a great admirer of [Hecht's] poetry" in the end, though he felt close to him personally: "I was an enormous admirer of the man. I loved the man. Loved him." He and Hecht "had many very good times . . . during what was obviously a very difficult period for him." Seidel was not disposed to "the filigree and fancy" of Hecht's poems: "I mean, he was not Richard Wilbur, but it was that sort of thing, that sort of delight in intricacies and play and rhyme," whereas he preferred the poems that dispensed with such flourishes. He felt that the honeyed style wasn't Hecht's strongest suit: "Wilbur was much more gifted at that sort of thing." He preferred the "dark and straighter" poems that came after *Stones,* "the best known of which is 'A Hill,'" yet even that he found "theatrical in my ear—overblown, self-dramatizing." Hecht showed Seidel "A Hill" and other new poems in typescript, which Seidel immediately understood: at their core "there was this bleak, blank nothing, and despair."

Seidel was "struck at the time by how disturbed Tony was by his relationship with his parents, by the backdrop of his background. I think he said how analysis had made very plain how troubled he was by what he had come through and what he had come out of, without having *got* out of it." He was ashamed of his father's financial incompetence and frightened by his repeated suicide attempts. His mother doted on Roger and withheld her approval from him. These memories began exerting themselves in the poems, "A Hill" being a case in point: his "therapist had a lot of theories about that poem,"[61] about the "cold and silence" that persisted since boyhood.

Hecht returned to Saltaire on Fire Island for the summer. In Cambridge that June, a friend of Baskin's, Philip Hofer, was finishing his afterword for a new Gehenna Press edition titled *Æsopic.* Hofer had acquired a set of wood engravings by Thomas Bewick (1753–1828) and his studio, illustrating Aesop's Fables. The English Bewick popularized wood engravings throughout the British Isles and "established a school of artist-illustrators who largely displaced the fashionable copper engravers of the eighteenth century by equaling them in refinement." This aspect of Bewick's achievement must have appealed to Baskin, who was himself an innovator of wood-block engraving. Baskin's edition included twenty-four couplets by Hecht, each providing a witty summary of the Greek story, as in "The Tortoise and the Two Crows": "It was a tortoise aspiring to fly / That murdered Aeschylus. All men must die."[62] Hecht included this couplet, along with eight others from the series, in *The Hard Hours,* under the title "Improvisations on Aesop." The titles of the Fables are omitted in this shorter gathering, and one couplet not in the Bewick volume is added as number six: "Spare not the rod, lest thy child be undone, / And the gallows cry, 'Behold thy son.'" Also omitted are the Bewick engravings themselves, which seem quaint (some might say subtle) compared with Baskin's stark emblems. The couplets themselves, however, fit well in the larger scheme of the book. Number four ("The Blind Man and the Lame" in *Æsopic*) chillingly extends the Lear-like "eye imagery" in *Hours*: "The blind man bears the lame, who gives him eyes; / Only the weak make common enterprise." Lurking behind this couplet, Hecht would have seen the beggar Edgar leading his blinded father toward the cliffs of Dover.

Feeling isolated in Annandale, Hecht developed friendships with some of his more sympathetic students. The actor Chevy Chase knew Hecht during his second stretch of teaching at Bard. Chase was on an extended year plan, having "had to wait-through a year [off]."[63] "Everybody re-members Tony for many things," Chase recalls. "He was a very funny combination of proper and improper." Was he mischievous? "Absolutely! He was very funny when he wanted to be." He was a tough teacher, but he "had such a little humorous glint in his eye." Hecht found Chase sym-pathetic, and they would meet for drinks at the pub. If you could "make him laugh a little, he'd let you by," Chase joked. For Chase, Hecht was "a very intelligent, very funny man, who *got* it." But he perceived a dark side as well: "When I knew him he was having some marital issue. . . . I wouldn't have known about it unless he told me. This certainly made one be a bit gentler toward him. And I could see a great deal of anger in him—at what, I couldn't tell. I had no idea he had been through so much."

Chase and Hecht were in a play together at Bard. (Hecht also appears in a short, experimental film by Chase.) Chase recalled: "We staged *Love's Labour's Lost*," and his co-star was Blythe Danner, on whom Chase had a big crush. Chase was no classical actor, but he did the play in order to be around Danner: "I think the only reason I was in it was she was in it."[64] Hecht played Don Adriano, "a fantastical Spaniard" (once played by Paul

Scofield, not unlike Hecht in voice and carriage), the whole production done in the style of Fellini's 8½. According to a student reporter, "The romantic leads were a couple of graduating seniors named Blythe Danner and Chevy Chase." Another of Hecht's students who went on to become a well-known entertainer, Donald Fagen, later of Steely Dan, recalls how he and Walter Becker looked up to Hecht and even tried to emulate him. Fagen, the popstar, was proud of his literary roots, displaying them in such songs as "My Old School" which refers to the train to Annandale, "Deacon Blues," and "Rikki Don't Lose That Number," about the poet Rikki Ducornet, on whom he had a college crush.[65]

In the summer of '65, Richard Lincoln and his new wife, Joan Godshalk, helped Hecht get a place in Saltaire (the Pines having become more of an exclusively gay community). Hecht's girlfriend that summer, Tania Eriksen, was a Scientologist, which his friends found rather boring but which he found amusing. Lincoln recalls how Tania liked to lecture on the faith to anyone who would listen. An art student at Bard, she had gotten pregnant by her boyfriend but couldn't tell her mother. She must have asked Hecht for help, since, after the term was over, he let her stay in his New York apartment. That summer they decamped to Fire Island, where Tania, then six months pregnant, saved one of Hecht's sons from drowning in the Atlantic Ocean.

It wasn't a long-term relationship. Tania eventually moved to England for Scientology training. Hecht addresses her directly in "To Tania: In Pride and Fear," a poem published in *The Listener* in 1968, later removing her name and replacing it with "My dear" when it appeared as the first part of "Going the Rounds: A Sort of Love Poem" in *Millions of Strange Shadows* (1977). It describes the precarious state in which Hecht found himself, in the years after his divorce. Looking down from a commanding height on "all his days," he observes "banners of pride and fear. / And that small wood to the west, the girls I have failed. / / ...But candor is not enough, / Nor is it enough to say that I don't deserve / Your gentle, dazzling love, or to be in love." Despite this, he professes his affection for her:

> *Tania, in spite of this,*
> *And the moralized landscape down there below,*
> *Neither of which might seem the ground of bliss,*

Know that I love you, know that you are most dear
   To one who seeks to know
How, for your sake, to confront his pride and fear.[66]

Hecht's "moralized landscapes" harbor deep, often raw feeling in poems such as "A Hill," "Auspices," "Still Life," and another poem of sexual guilt reminiscent of his feelings for Tania, "Death the Whore." The second part of "Going the Rounds," added to the poem later and set on Fire Island, is very much in this mode—a speaker haunted by a past affair. After Tania has left him "two months later," the speaker is confronted with a landscape that keeps with it a dark memory:

Yet when I dream, it's more than of your hair,
   Your privates, voice, or face;
These deeps remind me we are still not square.
A fog thickens into cold smoke. Perhaps
You too will remember the terror of that place,
   The breakers' dead collapse,

The cry of the boy, pulled out of the undertow,
   Growing dimmer and more wild,
And how, the dark currents sucking from below,
When I was not your lover or you my wife,
Yourself exhausted and six months big with child,
   You saved my son's life.[67]

Trauma brought on by moral compromise can foster the crushing feeling that one is undeserving of love. If Hecht had forestalled this feeling during his years with Pat, it overtook him now, a place of utter desolation where he would remain throughout the composition of *The Hard Hours*.

Bard was small in those days, "fewer than 500 kids," remembered Bill Leonard, a former student: "You basically knew everyone."[68] The college had gone co-ed since Hecht was last there. Teachers were called by their first names. Hecht was Leonard's advisor, and their conferences took place at Hecht's place—"a very private, personal setting, very cozy." Hecht had a little house on the road between the Triangle, which was at the center of

Annandale Village "and consisted of about three houses" and the entrance to Blithewood, an estate that had been absorbed into the college. His living room was sparsely furnished, befitting a bachelor who was only there for half the week, with a couch and a few chairs. Stacks of books lined a bookcase and the floor around it. Sometimes their meetings seemed more friendly than professional. It's possible that Hecht was leaning on his relationships with his students for friendship and camaraderie during a time of intense loneliness. Leonard recalls him as "the typical college-professor-type with the tweed jacket with the patches on the elbow. He was very handsome and, you know, a bit of a snob in some ways. But you could talk to him."

It was a heady time at Bard, the era of the beatnik and the hippy. (G. Gordon Liddy, later of Watergate fame, led a police raid resulting in several drug busts on campus, an event that Fagen alludes to in "My Old School.") Bob Dylan, who was living then in Woodstock, frequently came over to Bard. Leonard made 8 mm movies in the fall of 1964 of Dylan and his friends, Gino Foreman and Victor Maymudes. Dylan was hanging out on campus, "probably looking for girls," riding in on his 1964 Triumph Bonneville motorcycle. He played the upright piano in Leonard's dormitory, Ward Manor. Fagen, too, remembered that piano, on which he wrote some of his first songs. Leonard wanted to write his thesis on Dylan, on whether he was a real poet or not. Presumably dissuaded by Hecht, he ultimately chose the Book of Job for his "moderation"—a period of intense study leading to a substantial essay, which was then reviewed by a committee. Hecht shepherded Leonard through this daunting process, on which the student's career depended. If your paper were approved, students would graduate to the Upper College; if you failed, you might reapply or else you were "out of the school."

Hecht himself was also studying the Bible at the time. In fact, he was always reading the Bible, passages of which he was slowly gathering for the foundations of a long poem, "Rites and Ceremonies," which took him over a year to complete. It was one of the last poems included in *The Hard Hours*. As he wrote to his former Bard colleague Saul Bellow, it had been a while since he had written any new poems. In December 1965, he was granted a fourteen-month sabbatical from Bard, which gave him time to complete the final sections of "Rites." The form of the poem nods to T. S. Eliot's *The Waste Land* (the second section is titled "The

Fire Sermon"), and at one point includes a stanza form borrowed from George Herbert's "Denial," but the subject is the Holocaust.

Lowell remarked on the debt to Eliot, but failed to see the "double-edged" nature of the allusion—"a complication of tone, involving homage but bitterness, and both overlaying the horror of historical fact."[69] Hecht's bitterness was directed at Eliot's antisemitism, which pained him the more because of his great admiration for his poetry. Eliot himself stated to the Reverend William Turner Levy: "I am not an anti-Semite and never have been." "One wonders," Hecht wrote in a late, uncollected essay, "in the face of a great deal of evidence to the contrary, what to make of this denial."[70] Hecht felt betrayed by lines like "The Jew is in the woodpile." Such writing exposed the ugly side of a poetic hero. Eliot was central to Hecht's "earliest encounters with [the] art."[71] But Hecht wondered if Eliot might share a sentiment attributed to Harold Nicholson, which was roughly: "Though I loathe anti-Semitism, I do dislike Jews." "Encountering this bigotry in a poet I regarded with something approaching reverence," Hecht concluded, "was, and continues to be, difficult for me."[72]

Dense with Hebrew scripture, "the whole poem is laden with quotations like tesserae."[73] In 1973 Hecht told *The Harvard Advocate*:

> It's one of the most ambitious things I've tried to write. Its immediate point of origin were certain events in the Second World War, chiefly the concentration camps, one of which I saw as an American soldier. But it took more than a year in composition and it took something like 12 or 13 years of accumulating material, discarding some, rewriting some, tossing things out, and rearranging, so I should think it was a process that was going on, at least unconsciously, for about 12 years, and then conscious writing of the poem for about a year. And it was also an attempt at what not only Hopkins, but I guess a lot of poets have struggled with, the problem of human injustice, and the notion of providence, and its role in the world. I can say that the poem doesn't come to any conclusions on either topic.[74]

In fact, Hecht had been "thinking about the situation for more than twenty years, and about the poem for about 12 before actually writing it," he told Claire White, making notes for the opening section, "The Room," as early as 1954, when they were both at the Academy in Rome.[75]

King Lear, which lurks behind much of the book, makes a cameo appearance in "Rites." As Hecht later explained to the critic Ashley Brown, "To return, for a moment, to a strand that binds *Lear* to my work, they both touch on, not so much madness as the fear of madness." While many other Shakespearean echoes may be discerned in *The Hard Hours,* Lear undergirds the collection throughout. "I would guess that, along with *The Tempest* (which, like [*Oedipus at*] *Kolonos,* is a great play of reconciliation) *Lear* is the play I 'know' best and most carefully; the one I have taught most." Hecht points out to Brown that

> [T]he tragic vision of Lear is actually present in The Hard Hours, in the final part of Rites and Ceremonies. The lines, in quotation marks,

> *"None does offend,*
> *None, I say,*
> *None"*

> is *Lear* IV, vii, 172.

Hecht identifies other echoes from the play, including some "genuine Lear eye-imagery" in the song-like "'And Can Ye Sing Baluloo When the Bairn Greets?'": "These eyes, that many have praised as gay, / Are the stale jellies of lust in which Adam sinned."[76] Of course, we hear Cornwall's lines "Out, vile jelly! / Where is thy luster now?" uttered as Gloucester's second eye is removed by the fiery duke. Further eye-imagery appears slightly earlier in the collection at the close of "Bird-watchers of America":

> *For instance, the woman next door, whom we hear at night,*
> *Claims that when she was small*
> *She found a man stone dead near the cedar trees*
> *After first snowfall.*
> *The air was clear. He seemed in ultimate peace*

Except that he had no eyes. Rigid and bright
  Upon the forehead, furred
With a light frost, crouched an outrageous bird.[77]

Hecht created his most resonant eye-image in the blind gaze at the conclusion of "'More Light! More Light!,'" which more than any other poem in the book adopts the unrelenting negations of *Lear* ("Nor was he forsaken of courage . . . Not light . . . Nor light . . . No light, no light . . . No prayers"). It ends:

No prayers or incense rose up in those hours
Which grew to be years, and every day came mute
Ghosts from the ovens, sifting through crisp air,
And settled upon his eyes in a black soot.[78]

(Another Shakespearean flourish in the poem comes in a voice not unlike the scene-setting Chorus in *Henry V*: "We move now to outside a German wood.") Later in the same letter to Brown, Hecht mentions the contribution he made to the book *Preferences: 51 Poets Choose Poems from Their Own Work and from the Past,* in which the editor, Richard Howard, supplied brief commentaries on the pairings. Hecht was the only poet of the two-score and eleven to select from among Shakespeare's dramatic works, as an accompaniment to his own poem "The Vow." The scene he selected, from the end of Act IV, touches on the horror of impending madness that Hecht refers to elsewhere in his letter to Brown.

If anything, Hecht's regular use of Shakespeare in *The Hard Hours* only increases in his next two collections, *Millions of Strange Shadows* (1977) and *The Venetian Vespers* (1979).[79] Hecht drew on Shakespeare in different ways for his work. Sometimes his Shakespearean epigraphs were late additions, appended to a poem after the fact to provide context. Sometimes Shakespearean quotations constituted multilayered echoes, as in "'It Out-Herods Herod. Pray You, Avoid It.'" Satan in that poem "bestrides" the globe like Julius Caesar. With the epigraph for "The Origin of Centaurs" mentioned above ("But to the girdle do the gods inherit . . ."), Hecht points to Lear's rambling indictment of lust: "There's hell. There's darkness."

Lear, he tells Brown, lurks in the interstices of these poems, and, he adds suggestively, "perhaps elsewhere." One could add the veiled self-portrait of "Third Avenue in Sunlight," with its anxieties about madness, and, importantly, "'More Light! More Light!,'" with its image of eyes filling up with soot.

The dedicatees of that poem, Blücher and Arendt, had become very important to Hecht personally:

> Heinrich made me a good number of gifts of books, including the complete works of Shakespeare in the Schlegel translation (printed, infuriatingly, in old gothic type, which I could only barely decipher). At the end of our association [Blücher died in 1970], we were very close, and I felt the deepest affection for him. I was one of the very few people present (the others were Reamer Kline, the President of Bard, Irma Brandeis, and, of course, Hannah) when, in a private ceremony in their apartment, Heinrich was given an honorary degree by Bard, something which meant a great deal to him since, for some reason, he had earned no degree.[80]

He thought of Arendt's writings on totalitarianism and antisemitism as he finished the last poems for *The Hard Hours.* The book resonates with Arendt's moral seriousness and her clear-eyed anatomizations of human failing.

Another of the last poems written for *Hours,* one of Hecht's most celebrated, was "'It Out-Herods Herod. Pray You, Avoid It.'" Hecht placed it at the end of the collection, perhaps because it knit up so brilliantly, seamlessly, the book's abiding influences and concerns. The title itself nods at once to Shakespeare and the Bible (or, rather, to the Bible through Hamlet's speech to the players). The nursery rhyme music of the poem is forecast in the preceding poem, "'And Can Ye Sing Baluloo When the Bairn Greets?,'" which alludes to a mother singing to sleep a child whose father is away: "Sing bal la loo lammie, sing bal la loo dear, / Does wee lammie ken that its daddie's no here? / Ye're rockin' fu' sweetly on mammie's warm knee, / But daddie's a rockin' upon the saut sea." "'It Out-Herods Herod . . .'" is set during the Christmas season (Childermas, or the Feast of the Innocents, on December 28, commemorates the first-born sons killed by Herod), which he and the boys both loved:

> *For the wicked have grown strong,*
> *Their numbers mock at death,*
> *Their cow brings forth its young,*
> *Their bull engendereth.*
>
> *Their very fund of strength,*
> *Satan, bestrides the globe;*
> *He stalks its breadth and length*
> *And finds out even Job.*
>
> *Yet by quite other laws*
> *My children make their case;*
> *Half God, half Santa Claus,*
> *But with my voice and face,*
>
> *A hero comes to save*
> *The poorman, beggarman, thief,*
> *And make the world behave*
> *And put an end to grief.*
>
> *And that their sleep be sound*
> *I say this childermas*
> *Who could not, at one time,*
> *Have saved them from the gas.*[81]

The poem considers how close he and his sons had come to genocide, in a world where Herod makes the laws. Beginning with *The Hard Hours*, law becomes a leitmotif. Hecht titled his book on Auden *The Hidden Law*, after Auden's poem of that name. In "Peripeteia" he refers to art as "Governed by laws that stand for other laws."[82] These "other laws" put us in mind of Mosaic law, divine law, what Hecht in his contribution to *The New Union Haggadah* calls "divine wisdom."[83] Since the war, Hecht's sense of moral law had been upended, as suggested by his epigraph for "The Book of Yolek": we have a law, and by that law He must die. Hecht became a "seeker after law, / in a lawless world."[84] In his poems—where aesthetic laws point to moral laws—he sought to restore what he had lost.

PART TWO

NINE

LATE ROMANCE
(1968–1975)

Sir, she is mortal.
But by immortal providence, she's mine.[1]

1. Higgledy-piggledy

After a decade of Hecht's groping in the dark, light broke through. Here was a turn, a decisive reversal. It's not that Hecht had been morose this whole time; his affect was more stoic than lugubrious. But there was an underlying angst; he had come to doubt his own worth. He searched in vain for anything in his daily life that might provide an easing of present difficulties. His writing was the constant throughout, which, though at times slowed to a trickle, he never abandoned. Nor did he give up hopes of worldly success. His newer poems, his strongest to date, appeared in leading magazines—*The New Yorker*, *The Nation*, and regularly in *The Hudson Review*—and gave him reason to hope.

Three large events during this time transformed his life completely, affecting his writing, his teaching (still an important means of support), and his personal life. This sequence of occurrences played out over four years, from 1967 to 1971, which, given their suddenness and scope, seemed like an act of fate. The passage he liked to quote in letters home from the war now took on the full-throated expression of a saving grace: "How beautiful upon the mountains are the feet of him that bringeth good tidings, that publisheth peace; that bringeth good tidings of good, that publisheth salvation . . ." Such rising fortunes, compounding suddenly one on another, followed the contours of a Shakespearean "romance," in which the reign of error and pain is transformed into a new conciliatory order, a new set of laws, a reprieve and redemption. A staple of his classroom lectures, *The Tempest,* in particular, took on a deepened personal resonance.

The publication of *The Hard Hours* in 1967 was a signal event, after which his life as a writer was dramatically altered. Also that year, a volume of light verse, *Jiggery Pokery: A Compendium of Double Dactyls,* which he co-edited with John Hollander, garnered a lively response. It, too, was brought out by the renowned poetry editor and book designer Harry Ford, at Atheneum. Ford signed Hecht to a two-book deal, welcoming him to his stable of poets, which came to include James Merrill, John Hollander, Mona Van Duyn, Donald Justice, Mark Strand, W. S. Merwin, James Dickey, Howard Moss, and others. *Jiggery Pokery* had its roots in Hecht's first stay at the Academy in Rome in 1951. In their idle hours over drinks, Hecht and another fellow, the Brooklyn-born classical scholar Paul Pascal, invented a light verse form—the double dactyl—that was a kind of clerihew on steroids. It had been Hecht's ambition early on to "write a poem with a reasonably long line that was one word long, as T. S. Eliot did in 'Mr. Eliot's Sunday Morning Service,' which has for its first line, 'Polyphiloprogenitive.'" Hecht boasted to Pascal and his wife, Naomi, that he had accomplished this in his war poem "Japan," a poem in iambics, with the one-word line *"Schistosomiasis,"* a fatal disease plaguing Japan during Hecht's deployment. Naomi pointed out, to Hecht's chagrin, that the word was not so much iambic (like the rest of the poem) but, in fact, two dactylic feet. She suggested that "perhaps a new form could be devised to which it would be better suited." By the end of that November afternoon, Hecht and Pascal had hammered out the "nature and details of the form."[2]

John Hollander, who met Hecht at a literary party in New York, described being deeply impressed by Hecht's playing of a Scarlatti piano sonata by ear on that occasion—a memorable party trick. Together they solicited contributions by Pascal, James Merrill, Christopher Wallace-Crabbe, Nancy L. Stark, Richard Howard, Donald Hall, Irma Brandeis, Sally Belfrage, E. William Seaman, Eric Salzman, and others. The first examples appeared in the June 1996 issue of *Esquire,* with one of Hecht's own, "Nominalism," placed first. Again, Shakespeare was a likely source, stimulating Hecht's more playful imagination as well as his darker work:

Higgledy-piggledy
Juliet Capulet
Cherished the tenderest
Thoughts of a rose:

"What's in a name?" she said
Etymologically,
"Save that all Montagues
Stink in God's nose."

The *Esquire* feature invited readers to try their hands at the new form, and the outpouring of poems in response led to a follow-up feature in the September issue, though the offerings were frequently marred by shoddy metrics: "It must be firmly pointed out that some of the contributors have been gravely handicapped by tin ears."[3] The tone of the features and of the introduction to the subsequent volume reveal Hecht having a hilarious time. The full volume, produced by Ford, boasted a series of accompanying images by the graphic artist Milton Glaser, who had recently done iconic covers for the Signet Classics Shakespeare series, as well as the famous poster of Bob Dylan (with flowing, particolored hair) included with his *Greatest Hits*. The book, dedicated to Auden (who had chosen Hollander's first collection, *A Crackling of Thorns*, for the 1958 Yale Younger Poets Prize), was featured in *Time* magazine, and an evening of light verse featuring Hecht, Auden, George Starbuck, and William Cole, was put on at the Y in September.[4] (Cole included work by himself and the other three in his little anthology of light verse, *Pith and Vinegar* [Simon and Schuster, 1969], which included an entire section of double dactyls.)

Hecht and Hollander were a good fit, both erudite, refined, steeped in the Bible and classical music. (Hollander wrote liner notes for classical LPs while in graduate school in Indiana.) What's more, they both possessed a crackling sense of humor, which livened their talk and occasionally added a satiric edge to their poems. For Hecht, irony was a serious business: "Irony provides a way of stating very powerful and positive emotions, and of taking, as it were, the bravest possible stance towards some catastrophe."[5] Hollander was an intellectual powerhouse; some even found him overbearing at times. He had a Coleridgean ability to talk without cease about poetry and the arts. With only the slightest prompts he could discourse for hours, hardly coming up for air and veering from Hart Crane to Bach. Hecht and Hollander spent a fair bit of time together during the preparation of *Jiggery Pokery* at Hollander's place at 88 Central Park West, where he lived with his then wife, Anne (Loesser), a historian of fashion and costume.[6]

The friendship between the two poets endured, not without ups and downs, despite their contrasting backgrounds.[7] Hecht's family was German, assimilationist, and well-to-do, on the Upper East Side; Hollander's parents were immigrants from Eastern Europe. He knew Yiddish and salted his poems with Jewish subjects and rituals. He and Hecht never discussed Judaism, except with regard to the Holocaust. Struggling with physical decline late in his life (six years younger than Hecht, he, too, lived to his early eighties), Hollander recalled: "I didn't feel comfortable with American Jews who were isolated from Jewish history. It even had to do with Jewish names." Hollander was not the first to point out that "Tony" was not a typical Jewish name. But Hollander misread one aspect of Hecht's relationship to Judaism. Hecht was never observant, but, after Germany, he wished to be worthy of the suffering he had witnessed. He weathered the stings of antisemitism both as a child and as an adult, but those encounters did not create a direct occasion for poetry. Such painful experiences served as background music in certain poems and, even more so, in several of his essays, perhaps most pointedly in his ninety-page treatise on *The Merchant of Venice*. Hecht ruminated inwardly on his Jewish heritage and his personal connection to the Torah and Psalms—favoring Yeats's "quarrel with the self" over public rhetoric or display. He maintained a deep spiritual commitment throughout his life, drawing on both Judaism and Christianity (particularly as it figured in the visual arts). His poems weigh the cost of sin and the wages of sin—death.

Among the last pieces written for *The Hard Hours* were the sections of "Rites and Ceremonies," a rare instance in his work of verses directly steeped in Jewish liturgy. It opens with "The Room," with its description of the gas chambers. The speaker, herded like one of the beasts on the Ark, calls out to God:

Are the vents in the ceiling, Father, to let the spirit depart?
We are crowded in here naked, female and male.
An old man is saying a prayer. And now we start
To panic, to claw at each other, to wail
As the rubber-edged door closes on chance and choice.[8]

Repeatedly and relentlessly, Hecht revisited Flossenbürg in his dreams, even imagining himself among the murdered:

But for years the screaming continued, night and day,
And the little children were suffered to come along, too.
At night, Father, in the dark, when I pray,
I am there, I am there. I am pushed through
With the others to the strange room
Without windows; whitewashed walls, cement floor.[9]

There were no gas chambers at Flossenbürg. Hecht later read about the gassings at Treblinka, Auschwitz, and elsewhere, in his research into the Holocaust. He had seen the crematorium at Flossenbürg, and he saw the bodies of the dead stacked in heaps, one on top of the other. His subject was no longer combat and the death of fellow soldiers, as it had been in the *Stones* era—poems such as "Drinking Song," "The Plate," "Christmas Is Coming," and "A Deep Breath at Dawn." He now turned his focus to the innocent victims. In a paragraph that Hecht wrote for *The New Union Haggadah*, Hecht describes his mature relationship to the subject:

If it is hard for us to understand such a vast and barbaric annihilation, it is no easier to understand such a complete and miraculous deliverance as tonight we ritually and jubilantly remember and seek for in our own lives. Nor are we entitled to judge how such destruction could come to pass. We, as part of the remnant that survived, are entitled to ask, "Are we among the Saving Remnant? Are we fit for that?" and on this evening, in that hope, to purify our hearts.[10]

This interrogative liturgy, with its rabbinic lilt, expressed Hecht's deepest wish: to live rightly, to acknowledge one's own moral failings, and to see clearly man's inhumanity to man. Once asked if he was a religious person, Hecht replied in a quiet voice: "Yes. . . . I don't normally say that, but I think I am." His spiritual life after the war was gradually shaped by his "understanding of whatever the blessings of life are and a continued reading of the Bible."[11] This lifelong, solitary reading of scripture became his chief religious practice.

In October, *The Hard Hours* appeared, and critics noted the book's stylistic developments compared with *Stones*, which Hecht himself acknowledged:

> The first book was something like an advanced apprentice work—I was still learning my trade. I was still trying to write in the most careful, craftsmanly way that would please me and give pleasure. The subject matter, in fact, didn't have a pressing immediate need for me; I'd write about anything that came to hand. In contrast, many poems in *The Hard Hours* are about things that had enormous emotional importance to me; I was prepared to attack them, whether they came out technically perfect or not.[12]

Hecht would have liked to count himself, as Theodore Roethke did, among the "happy" poets, to "show an affirming flame" (as Auden put it), but his own hardships and compromised worldview drew him toward darker themes:

> I think that Roethke is a fine example because he recognized that the need to affirm something comes out of a desperate sense of how difficult it is to do. I should like to arrive at the same kind of affirmation without denying any of life's awfulness. In other words, *The Hard Hours* wasn't a deliberately depressing book, though it is depressing in some ways, I suppose; the title signifies that. But my first book, *A Summoning of Stones*, had been charming with almost a certain superficial frivolity. *The Hard Hours* perhaps serves as a corrective to some of the rather callow cheeriness of the first volume.[13]

Continuing to hone his craft during his darkest days, Hecht shrugged off the more disconnected ornamentation of *Stones*, learning how to incorporate personal pain into his poems in ways that were not confessional—like Sexton, Plath, Snodgrass, and Lowell—but more in keeping with his New Critical sensibilities. Another protégé of Allen Tate, Lowell jettisoned the New Critical approach, whereas Hecht never really did; instead of personal disclosure he preferred what Eliot called the third voice of poetry, the dramatic voice, which nevertheless closely shadows the personal.

The book was published simultaneously in the US, by Harry Ford at Atheneum, and by Jon Stallworthy at Oxford University Press (OUP) in the UK. The fact that the book wound up with an English publisher at the same time was particularly fortuitous:

> What happened was that A Summoning of Stones eventually went out of print and became very hard to find. In fact, I have only one surviving copy of it myself, and probably wouldn't have that if I hadn't started to inscribe the book to a friend and found that I'd done it up-side-down. . . . Because the book is unavailable, it seemed to my new publisher that it might be made available again. I felt that about half were worth preserving. I don't know why I disqualified others. I guess I didn't like them well enough.[14]

At one point early in the chain of events, Ian Hamilton approached Hecht about the possibility of bringing out a "pamphlet" in England, presumably under the auspices of Hamilton's magazine The Review.[15] There was even talk of a selected poems. But then Hamilton sat on the manuscript for months, during which time Hecht decided to go with Stallworthy, who had inquired separately. When Ford became involved, it was decided that a selection from the out-of-print Stones would append the new volume. Ford, who won an award for the volume's distinctive design, offered to create the plates for the book, which Stallworthy could then print from as well. This procedure continued for most of Hecht's subsequent career.

Hecht's friends and colleagues rallied around him: letters of praise arrived from Tate and Hecht's friend, the poet Philip Booth. Hecht was particularly pleased that "Jimmy Merrill called me just before he went back to Greece and told me it was one of the best books he had ever read."[16]

Reviews of *The Hard Hours* were generally enthusiastic, with a few glaring exceptions. Having praised the book's use of "quiet overtones to transmit the intense emotional experience hidden below the casual surface," Laurence Lieberman wrote in *The Yale Review,* "At times, Hecht's new style grows too flat and prosy, one-toned. All verbal tension is dissipated by the studied dullness of rhythms." And yet, Hecht's new style was capable of exceptional power, in poems such as "'More Light! More Light!'":

> Hecht's most consistently masterful device is to juxtapose stories from history, ancient and contemporary (or scenes from his personal life, present and past, generating a powerful religious and political moral from collision between them). . . . The scissoring movement between story and story provides the reader's nervous system with a series of shocks, a jackknifing of emotions, comparable to that produced by the interplay of plot and subplot in *King Lear,* and in some story sequences of the Old Testament.[17]

For William Meredith, writing in *The New York Times Book Review,* the collection signaled "with dramatic completeness a talent that was only hinted at in *A Summoning of Stones.*"[18] Ted Hughes wrote a note for the program of Poetry International '67, which was printed as an endorsement on the back of both the US and British editions:

> Anthony Hecht's first volume of poems, *A Summoning of Stones,* established him as one of the most accomplished of his extremely accomplished generation. His work was remarkable enough for its classical poise and elegance, but it also had a weight which set it apart. Since then his poetry has come clear in a direction nobody could have predicted. Unlike many of his contemporaries he looked neither toward Lorca nor Éluard nor the Black Mountain poets for suggestions.[19]

Hughes praised Hecht for a kind of bravery in remaking himself, praised him for a fit of inspiration so powerful it remade his style: "The result here has been some of the most powerful and unforgettable poems at present being written in America."[20]

Spring was Pulitzer season: each year the jury sifted the year's top publications to award the prestigious prize. Hecht's hopes for *The Hard Hours* were kindled by rumors about the current deliberations: "I had a dream last night that you were right about what you have been hinting to me—that is about the Pulitzer," he wrote to Philip Booth.[21] Still, this was only far-flung speculation, an idle reverie. Hecht was discouraged not to have made the list for the National Book Award, which went to Robert Bly. "Many an honest Indian ass goes for a unicorn," Hecht joked to Booth, adopting lines from an English madrigal by Thomas Weekes. He joked with Ford that he was on tenterhooks: "Oyster-like with nacreous secretions, I am cultivating a pearl of an ulcer, waiting for that goddam Pulitzer committee."[22]

The year before, the jury, composed of Louis Simpson, Phyllis McGinley, and Richard Eberhart, had reached a tenuous consensus regarding Sexton's *Live or Die*. When the committee deadlocked on Theodore Roethke, who was recently deceased, a devil's bargain was struck. Only Sexton appeared on all three of the judges' shortlists, though she was at the very bottom of Eberhart's and Simpson's. It was a lukewarm, almost grudging conferral. Hecht's award was mercifully different. In 1968, the jury was made up of Louis Simpson (chairman), W. D. Snodgrass, and the Frost biographer Lawrance R. Thompson. Simpson favored James Dickey's *Poems: 1957–1967*, and Thompson lobbied for Marianne Moore's *The Complete Poems* but agreed to back Dickey at Simpson's urging. Snodgrass was strongly disposed toward *The Hard Hours*, and after some preliminary back-and-forth he asked the others to reread Hecht and especially "A Hill," "Third Avenue in Sunlight," "Behold the Lilies of the Field," and "'More Light! More Light!'" Simpson was swayed and Thompson agreed to let the chairman have the deciding vote. In the end, Simpson voted for Hecht, Thompson followed suit, and the vote was unanimous. The book was awarded the Pulitzer Prize in late May 1968.

Simpson's citation aptly characterizes both Hecht's work and the state of American poetry in the late sixties:

Anthony Hecht writes, for the most part, in traditional forms, and for this reason his work has been somewhat neglected in recent years when free verse has been so widely practiced. However, there has been a strong and original development in Hecht's recent poems, particularly

in the poems listed above [Snodgrass's suggested list to the jury]. Hecht
has always had an exquisite sense of diction and his poetry is a pleasure
to read for the control of meter and sound. In recent years, however, a
great deal more has been added, particularly the strength of feeling and
sympathy that strikes the reader in poems such as "Rites and Ceremonies." Hecht is not a polemicist, nor does he have an aesthetic axe to
grind. He is simply a poet who depends on the perfection and strength
of the individual poem. He has never been awarded a major prize. In
honoring Hecht I think that we are honoring poetry itself, apart from
considerations of dogma or literary politics. For these reasons I hope
that the Advisory Board will agree with the Poetry Jury to award the
prize to Hecht.

It is hard to say what Simpson meant by "somewhat neglected." Hecht
was never as famous as Lowell, Hughes, or Plath, but the lion's share of
poems included in The Hard Hours had appeared in leading magazines,
he received prestigious fellowships, sometimes two or more at once,
and he was frequently asked to read from his work at colleges around
the country. (If Hecht was in regular demand before the Pulitzer, it was
nothing compared to the rafts of press and public events in the wake of
the award.) But Simpson's general point was accurate: free verse, long
in ascendance, had become the dominant mode, and poets who availed
themselves of the music of traditional prosody were viewed by some as
crusty and out-of-touch (at best) or anti-Democratic and reactionary. Reviewing The Hard Hours in The Far Point journal in Canada, Marjorie Perloff, a champion of the avant-garde and scourge of the "established style,"
set out to take Hecht down a peg: "I propose to argue here that, despite
his careful control of rhyme and stanza forms, his up-to-date idioms, and
clever literary and mythological allusions, Hecht is not the major poet his
admirers claim him to be."[23]

This demolition smacks of the poetry wars between raw and cooked
that began in the "tranquilized Fifties" and had its battle lines drawn in du-
eling anthologies—The New Poets of England and America, edited by Donald
Hall, Robert Pack, and Louis Simpson (Meridian Books, 1957), and The
New American Poetry, edited by Donald M. Allen (Grove Press, 1960). The
former included an Introduction by Robert Frost and championed Hecht

and other establishment poets, while the latter favored experimentalism, the Beats, and the New York School. Hecht was aligned with the first camp, Perloff with the second.

More good news arrived. Hecht was awarded a residency at the American Academy in Rome and a second Ford fellowship (this one for verse). These foreshadowed two further prizes—the Russell Loines from the American Academy of Arts and Letters and the Miles Poetry Prize.[24] (Hecht's Loines award was championed by Tate, then president of the Academy.) By July, Hecht was in Saltaire, adjudicating squabbles between his sons, who had arrived for their annual stay on Fire Island. Even with a housekeeper, managing the boys took up his days and slowed his writing to a trickle. When the boys weren't exasperating, they could be quite amusing: when he chided them for saying the f-word, Jason, eleven, asked, "Daddy, what does 'fuck' mean?" Hecht "answered in the coolest and most surgical tones that it pertained to sexual relations between men and women." "I know," Jason replied. "Then why did you ask?" "Oh, I just wanted to see if you knew."[25]

After his sons' return to Belgium, Hecht left for the American Academy in Rome. As a Resident that fall, he worked on the translation of *Seven Against Thebes,* which he had undertaken with the classicist Helen Bacon, also a fellow, who taught at Barnard. The two worked well together. What's more, they greatly enjoyed each other's company. It was clear to Claire White, who had returned to the Academy with her husband, Robert, a fellow in visual arts, that they were close friends. Hecht appeared much happier than when he was last in Rome: "That seemed to me the most positive time I've seen him," White recalled. Hecht was "giddy with excitement"[26] to be back in Rome. He was given a handsome apartment, so that his sons Jason and Adam, thirteen and eleven, were able to visit him. In addition to seeing old friends, Hecht finished in his first month on the Janiculum a poem of ninety-six lines in four-line stanzas, a "long vaguely comic thing" called "The Ghost in the Martini," among his best-known pieces, and the first two hundred lines of *Thebes.* A first draft of the play was finished by Thanksgiving. Other poems were beginning to simmer, and as a further affirmation his alma mater, Bard College, awarded him his first honorary degree (which he accepted the following year, when he was back in the States).

Hecht was riding high on the celebrity accompanying the Pulitzer, and Italy was the place he loved best, a psychic home to which he would return more and more in the next three decades. Hecht worked well at residencies, with distractions and mundane tasks at a minimum. He felt bolstered by the imprimatur that they conferred. The Academy itself was pure heaven:

> From the window of the living room in my luxurious suite on the grounds of the Villa Aurelia (which was the Corsini family's summer town residence, and which Bernard Berenson declared the finest villa in Rome) I can look out over my immediate private terrace, with geraniums in terra cotta pots and a quite large bay tree trimmed into the shape of a perfect dome, out through the pines to a clear view of the basilica of Maxentius in the Roman Forum which appears in the middle distance, and much of the rest of the city, littered, as it were, between green branches, to the Alban hills beyond. Freshly cut flowers have been put on my dining room table, and tuberoses on the mantelpiece over the fireplace. I can smell them from here at my desk; they are mildly distracting.[27]

Hecht included this ecstatic passage in a letter to his new boss, George Ford, chair of English at the University of Rochester, where he'd recently joined the faculty. He was mindful that taking a leave of absence after only a year of teaching was a delicate matter, but Ford, keen to accommodate the department's new star, was friendly and supportive. (And he remained so when Hecht, after a brief return to Rochester, took off another year in New York City.) During his time abroad, Hecht spent a couple of weeks with his sons in Switzerland. The trip was unnerving after the *dolce far niente* of Rome. He grew a "rather distinguished looking" beard at their request, which he kept for his return to the States. At the end of his Academy stay, he and Helen Bacon traveled to Greece to celebrate the completion of *Thebes,* visiting Delphi and Epidaurus—Hecht's one and only trip to that part of the world.

Back in Rochester in May, he settled into a "dandy four-room house with a ping-pong table,"[28] while the student protests of 1969 roiled the campus. Though Hecht would never completely warm (surely the *mot juste*) to Rochester as a place, with its arctic winters ("it would take no

Montesquieu to prove that culture could not abide in such a climate"),[29] his new position provided long-term security and a public platform. In addition to giving speeches as the University Orator, he was profiled often in the local papers, each time he received a prize or published a new book. Still, some part of him felt that he had been relegated to the hinterlands, which was confirmed by further acquaintance with the place:

> The Rochester appointment is a permanent one, but I have already heard so many disheartening stories about the climate, that I approach it with a sinking heart and a wall-eyed expression that allows me to scan the horizon for better prospects while at the same time looking thoughtful.[30]

His eighteen-year tenure at Rochester would be the longest of his teaching career, first as an associate professor and then, in 1968, as John H. Deane Professor of Rhetoric and Poetry. Despite his initial qualms, he settled into his duties at U of R, which included oversight of the visiting reader series.

He enjoyed teaching modern poetry, though he had mixed feelings about creative writing: "I would not mind splitting the two semesters with someone who does not mind teaching such a course. . . . I must confess I found a full year of it boring to teach and disappointing in the results."[31] He wrote to Philip Booth about his rocky return:

> I am dazed and unstable. While I was gone the sons-of-bitches put me on a committee that is meant to keep the University from collapsing around our ears, like Columbia. I haven't had time to unpack yet, but I've been up till two or three in the morning, drafting resolutions to be presented at faculty meetings, and we have met several times with trustees and the president and the provost (though not the dean), and, Great Suffering Catfish, I've been trying to teach classes too. It comes as a blow, let me tell you, after all that Roman self-absorption.[32]

About the teaching, he shrugged indifferently: "The local and highly conservative newspapers appear to regard most of my students as being violent and destructive hippy types and a general threat to modern civilization; whereas in truth they could not be a more docile and unimaginative group."[33] Hecht himself was fiercely against the war in Vietnam, which was the focus of student protests, and some of his first poems written after *The Hard Hours* call out the depredations and injustice of the war with scathing irony:

> The President,
> Addressing the first contingent of draftees sent
> To Viet Nam, was brief: "Life is not fair,"
> He said, and was right, of course. Everyone saw
> What happened to him in Dallas.[34]

Hecht spent Christmas in New York and visited with Lowell, whom he considered at that time "a close friend."[35] He invited him to read at Rochester in February, under the auspices of the Hyam Plutzik Reading Series. Lowell was a particularly good choice, given the protests and Lowell's well-known history as a conscientious objector during the Second World War. In the event, the Rochester visit was complicated somewhat by Lowell's nervous energy ("Not unmanageable or disagreeable or top-lofty, but distinctly manic").[36] That summer of 1970, Hecht was shocked to learn that Lowell was in the hospital in London, suffering from a chronic mental condition that Hecht had hoped he had "licked with simple medication."[37]

The letdown that Hecht felt on his return to Rochester after his Christmas in New York was lessened by some good news: he had been inducted into the National Institute of Arts and Letters (later consolidated as The American Academy of Arts and Letters), an honor which pleased him greatly. It signaled Hecht's membership among the top artists and writers of the day. As Richard Howard (whose Atheneum book *Untitled Subjects* received the Pulitzer in 1970) put it, Hecht was sensitive to exclusion, on grounds of antisemitism or otherwise, and valued being part of "the club." He regularly wore the badge of membership, a "gaudy rosette," in his buttonhole: "It turned out that none of my suits had lapel button-holes, and I had to take them all to the tailor."[38] (He was careful to remove this sign of his success in the company of other poets or artists who were not members.) Howard had recently included Hecht in another club: his critical survey of contemporary poetry, *Alone with America*, which affirmed the leading poets including a clutch from Ford's list at Atheneum: Hollander, Merrill, W. S. Merwin, Donald Finkel, Mark Strand, James Dickey, and others. "Atheneum seems to be doing pretty well," Hecht quipped to Ford, after Howard's Pulitzer. It was true: no house boasted a more laurelled roster.[39]

In the fall of 1970, Hecht sent his poem "The Cost," freighted with Shakespearean allusions, to John Hollander for consideration at *Harper's* magazine. Written in the aftermath of the shootings in May at Kent State, Hecht sets the poem in the ancient world, in Rome, beneath Trajan's Column, which depicts the emperor's victory in the Dacian Wars:

> And a voice whispers inwardly, "My soul,
>   It is the cost, the cost,"
>
> Like some unhinged Othello, who's just found out
>   That justice is no more,
> While Cassio, Desdemona, Iago shout
>   Like true Venetians all,
> "Go screw yourself; all's fair in love and war!"[40]

Hecht placed the poem at the front of his next collection, *Millions of Strange Shadows*, though that book did not appear until 1977, after the war was over. It is in fact part of a suite of five poems about war, joined by the death-marked pastoral "Autumnal"; "'Dichtung und Warheit,'" which describes a "clumsy snapshot" of Hecht's infantry company ("those grubby and indifferent men, / Lounging in bivouac, / Their rifles aimless in their laps . . ."); and "A Voice at a Séance," in which a soldier, killed in combat, describes his troubled afterlife:

> It is all different from what you suppose,
> And the darkness is not darkness exactly,
> But patience, silence, withdrawal, the sad knowledge
> That it was almost impossible not to hurt anyone
> Whether by action or inaction.[41]

That one might cause harm by inaction was a thought that weighed on Hecht. His secret refusal to fire his weapon in combat meant that he had not directly caused a death, but the fact that he had let down his fellow soldiers troubled him.

By the beginning of 1971, an *annus mirabilis* by Hecht's own reckoning, he was again on leave from teaching, thanks to a fellowship from the Academy of American Poets, whose founder and longtime president, Marie Bullock, wrote to give him the news. The $10,000 prize was enough to live on for a year, and Hecht decided to return to his apartment in New York. Elizabeth Bishop—whom Hecht had met through a common friend at Rochester, the Renaissance scholar Joseph Summers—wrote to congratulate him on the award. Hecht suspected that she might even have had a hand in his selection: "And of course I'm jubilant about the Academy Award. I assume that the postcard testifies to a partisanship concerning my election, and I couldn't find that more gratifying and flattering." He was particularly pleased to be away from Rochester and his well-meaning but lackluster students: "The award is a way out of this pewter pot," i.e., "the perpetual gloom of Rochester." It proved to be a glorious spring in New York City.

2. "Heureux qui, comme Ulysse, a fait un beau voyage . . ."[42]

Thursday, March 4, 1971, was the day of the National Book Awards ceremony at Lincoln Center—possibly the most fateful day in his life since the war. Hecht was again on leave from teaching and back in his New York apartment for the year. Renowned for generosity, Harry Ford invited him to come to dinner at a good French restaurant to celebrate Mona Van Duyn's win for her Atheneum title *To See, To Take*. Ford was an enthusiastic drinker and set the tone for his bibulous author lunches and dinners, with flowing wine and poets discoursing in rare form. Hecht wouldn't have missed it. He was pleased to attend the ceremony as well, to see Van Duyn receive her award. (Van Duyn and her husband, Jarvis Thurston, became close, longtime friends and the dedicatees of "Antapodosis" from *The Transparent Man*.)

In the throng of overcoated and mufflered literati streaming through the lobby of Philharmonic Hall (later Avery Fisher, now David Geffen Hall), Hecht spotted his former student, Helen D'Alessandro, at the same moment that she spotted him. Having started out at Doubleday, she was now working as the managing editor for the publishing firm Walker and Company. She recalled their encounter in vivid detail:

> I looked around me and thought, "I can't budge. I've got one square foot of space." And then I saw Tony at the far end of the room. I hadn't seen him since my freshman year. He was making his way in my direction. He had his raincoat thrown over his shoulder and was holding onto his overshoes, literally having to push people. I stopped in mid-conversation and said, "Oh my God, there's my freshman English teacher." He came over and said, "I know you, don't I?" And I said, "I certainly know you, Mr. Hecht; you taught me freshman English at Smith." Then everything went blank. He said that he was rushing off to have dinner with Mona Van Duyn and Harry Ford and some other people.[43]

There was a storybook quality to their meeting after so many years, particularly since it nearly didn't happen. The rain had almost kept Helen away, and Ford suggested that Hecht could skip the ceremony and meet up after. But Hecht wanted to support Van Duyn, and Ford graciously sprang for his $15 ticket to the event, a lot of money then. Despite the dislocations of time and geography, Hecht had remained in Helen's thoughts for thirteen years:

> I remembered everything about him, everything I said about him, and I have a terrible memory. Friends reminded me of a time when we were at a jazz club and some guy I was with punched Charlie Mingus. I'd completely forgotten that, all these crazy things in my life, of which I remember nothing. But everything to do with Tony, I remember. Even at Smith.
>   The first time I went home, at Thanksgiving my freshman year, I said to my parents—this is so late-50's—I said, "Now I know what I want to do with my life." My mother looked at me, and said, "Oh?" And I said, "Yes. I'd like to marry an English professor and live in a small New England town." She said, "Don't be ridiculous. You're far too materialistic." I didn't ever think it would be possible with Tony. He was married, and . . . I was a Catholic. Not that my parents would have minded a mixed marriage, but he would have been divorced. I never even went there in my mind; it was just impossible.

And then I moved to New York and got a job at Doubleday, and I remember, for years, walking along the streets, knowing that Tony lived in New York and thinking, "Maybe today I'll run into Mr. Hecht."

If it was love at first sight for Helen, then it was love at second sight for Hecht. He was bowled over by their brief exchange in the theater lobby. Utterly charmed, he acted decisively. In the decade following his divorce, he had felt isolated, with no lasting romantic attachments. Leaving his friends and colleagues in New York only made matters worse. His first year at Rochester had been "intensely lonely."[44] As Helen recalled:

> I went to work at Walker the next morning, and the phone rang. They put the call through to me, and it was Tony. I was just dumbfounded. I said, "How did you know where to find me?" And he said, "You told me last night where you worked." I'd completely blanked on that. He invited me to that famous production of *A Midsummer Night's Dream* [directed by Peter Brook], but I'd already seen it the week before. Besides, I was busy that night and for about a week after.

Meanwhile, Hecht attended Brook's renowned white-box production of *Midsummer* a few days after meeting Helen. As the lights dimmed, he thought of her, dizzy with anticipation of seeing her again at the weekend. He returned to this evening in the theater for the opening of "Peripeteia," a poem about the transformative power of his meeting with Helen (which had also taken place in a theater). In the poem, Hecht swaps *Midsummer* for *The Tempest* and casts Helen as "miraculous Miranda." In melancholy detail, he describes the loneliness that he has lived with for many years, ever since childhood, in fact:

> *But in that instant, which the mind protracts,*
> *From dim to dark before the curtain rises,*
> *Each of us is miraculously alone*
> *In calm, invulnerable isolation,*
> *Neither a neighbor nor a fellow but,*
> *As at the beginning and end, a single soul,*
> *With all the sweet and sour of loneliness.*

I, as a connoisseur of loneliness,
Savor it richly, and set it down
In an endless umber landscape, a stubble field
Under a lilac, electric, storm-flushed sky,
Where, in companionship with worthless stones,
Mica-flecked, or at best some rusty quartz,
I stood in childhood, waiting for things to mend.
A useful discipline, perhaps. One that might lead
To solitary, self-denying work
That issues in something harmless, like a poem,
Governed by laws that stand for other laws,
Both of which aim, through kindred disciplines,
At the soul's knowledge and habiliment.[45]

Though the tone is loftier, more Shakespearean in this poem, the child who looks over the stark landscape is the same boy who, on the "road north of Poughkeepsie," stands frozen before a wintry scene in "A Hill." This boy, however, can imagine a reprieve, as he waits "for things to mend." Then, miraculously, they do. His certainty at the prospect of genuine and deep affection emboldened him to be completely direct with her: "Having known you now for 48 hours," Helen recalled him saying, "I have every intention of marrying you." Her response was equally bold and affirming: "I just ran over to him and sat on his lap and hugged him. And we were happy forever. It was really fortunate—it was meant to be." *The Tempest* provides a figure for their immediate connection:

As in a dream,
Leaving a stunned and gap-mouthed Ferdinand,
Father and faery pageant, she, even she,
Miraculous Miranda, steps from the stage,
Moves up the aisle to my seat, where she stops,
Smiles gently, seriously, and takes my hand
And leads me out of the theatre, into a night
As luminous as noon, more deeply real,
Simply because of her hand, than any dream
Shakespeare or I or anyone ever dreamed.[46]

Hecht resorts to one of his most abiding tropes, the contrast of light and dark, to describe this "miraculous" moment, in which night becomes luminous noon. Hecht wasted no time sharing his good fortune with the Frosts, Alan and Lucy, his friends from his early days in Rochester. In a letter dated March 24, less than three weeks after their meeting at the NBA ceremony, Hecht announced: "I am engaged to be married. . . . The girl is named Helen D'Alessandro; she is dark-haired, shining eyed, soft-spoken, gentle, intelligent and altogether lovely. . . . [W]e somehow contrived to bump into each other in a room the size of a grand ballroom, packed as densely as a loaded elevator. . . . [T]he simple truth is that since I phoned her . . . I have been somewhat dazed."[47]

They met in early March and were married by mid-June. The small ceremony took place in the garden of a townhouse on East 94th Street, where Helen rented the ground floor, just immediate family and a few friends, which pleased them both. Present among the dozen or so guests were George and Mary Dimock, Hecht's friends from Smith. The Rev. John Maguire, whom Hecht had met and liked when reading at Loyola University in Chicago, officiated. Helen's parents, Albert and Helen, had an easy trip down from Bronxville, where Helen had attended high school before Smith. Over the years, Hecht became very close to the elder Helen, who lived nearby, first in Rochester and then in Washington, DC, until her death in 2001, aged ninety-six. The brief notice of the wedding in *The New York Times* mentioned that Hecht was "the son of Mr. and Mrs. Melvyn Hecht, of New York, who is retired from the plastics and metal stamping business." Melvyn, now in his eighties, had not worked for years, but rather than enjoy restful hobbies or other diversions he continued to be plagued by mental health issues, which came to a head again a few years after his son's wedding.

It was no small feat to arrange for the wedding in such short order. Hecht was traveling a good deal now to read from his new collection, largely at colleges and universities in Chicago, Oswego, Syracuse, Indiana, Arkansas, Cambridge, Swarthmore, and elsewhere. An active reader in recent years, he was now regularly "on the circuit." That year he served on the committee for the Pulitzer, along with Louis Simpson and Lawrance Thompson, who voted unanimously for Merwin's *The Carrier of Ladders* from Atheneum.

The Academy of American Poets elected him a chancellor. The celebrity
that accompanied these accolades cheered him. There's a stylish photo of
Hecht from the months of his engagement by the Warhol film star, photographer, and poet Gerard Malanga: Hecht, who always had a theatrical
propensity toward elegant clothes (more richly classic than outright dandyish, as his friend Richard Howard often was), is standing on the sidewalk
wearing a stylish, rather mod, exquisitely tailored suit. Nicholas Christopher
remembers Hecht saying that the photo of him in "Carnaby Street clothes"
(Christopher's phrase) was taken the day that he proposed to Helen.

Helen was impressed by these literary benchmarks, though mostly
it pleased her that Hecht seemed pleased by them. Soon after they met,
"Green: An Epistle" appeared in *The New Yorker*. She recalled "sitting at
my desk at Walker, reading it carefully for close to an hour, and marveling
at its power and complexity."[48] Allen Tate thought the poem truly exceptional: "Unless this old man is much mistaken," he wrote to Hecht after
reading an early draft, "it is one of the great 20th-century poems. It is so
completely and brilliantly finished that I can now only stare at it. It has
all the mystery of great poetry. The last paragraph gives me a *frisson*—so
simple and so strange it is." Still a potent mentor for Hecht, Tate was
not crazy about the title (simply "Green" at that point) and thought it
should be changed to "perhaps a quasi-17th Century phrase." Hecht met
Tate halfway, keeping "Green" but adding the subtitle "An Epistle." As he
described it to Donald Finkel, the poem expresses a "malicious and envious paranoia."[49] He read the poem at the Poetry Center at the Y, where he
appeared in November with Anne Sexton, coupling "Green" ("a sinister
nature poem") with "An Autumnal" ("an innocent nature poem"), which
he presented as "two pastorals," both with echoes of Robert Frost. Hecht
began his rangy introduction—almost as elaborate and suggestive as the
poem itself—by confirming simply that "It's about paranoia." It addresses
an Eliotic "we," the self talking to the self:

> *I write at last of the one forbidden topic*
> *We, by a truce, have never touched upon:*
> *Resentment, malice, hatred so inwrought*
> *With moral inhibitions, so at odds with*

The home-movie of yourself as patience, kindness,
And Charlton Heston playing Socrates . . .[50]

In a scathing catalogue, worked out, as so often with Hecht, in terms of landscape, he enumerates the qualities of a psyche in turmoil. In the decade leading up to the poem's composition in 1970, Hecht had glimpsed his own heart of darkness:

Sequoia forests of vindictiveness
That also would go down on the death list
And, buried deep beneath alluvial shifts,
Would slowly darken into lakes of coal
And then under exquisite pressure turn
Into the tiny diamonds of pure hate.[51]

The poem resolves itself into a weary reprieve. In the event, Hecht's real life reprieve—wrought by his love for Helen, begun in a whirlwind and sustained over a life—was nothing short of astonishing.

Hecht understood this when he borrowed Ferdinand's lines for the dedication of *Millions of Strange Shadows*: "For HELEN 'of whom I have / receiv'd a second life.'"[52] The nature of this rebirth relates to Hecht's innermost sense of himself, which had been dislodged by the war and frayed further, to the brink of madness, in fact, by the breakup of his first family. The self-recrimination and despair that took root during the war was still with him. Oftentimes, in war particularly, "people feel betrayed by the injury to their moral being. They were put in a situation where they have to betray their own moral code, or they feel betrayed by their superiors who put them there to do this." This sense of moral compromise fosters the feeling that one is not worthy of love: "I'm not worthy and you're not safe. I'm not capable of protecting you, and I can't trust anybody."[53]

The effect that Hecht's marriage to Helen had on him was clear to all who knew him. It returned him to himself. Hecht hints at his wonder at this blessed turnaround in "A Birthday Poem," the birthday being Helen's, the date appearing as epigraph: June 22, 1976. Beginning again with pastoral, the poem puts forward an image of pure

innocence (like the one of the little girl spotting daisies in "Green"):
a photo of Helen on her fourth birthday, admiring her brand-new red
sneakers:

You are four years old here in this photograph,

*   You are turned out in style,*
In a pair of bright red sneakers, a birthday gift.
* You are looking down at them with a smile*
Of pride and admiration, half
Wonder and half joy, at the right and the left.

The picture is black and white, mere light and shade.
*   Even the sneakers' red*
Has washed away in acids. A voice is spent,
* Echoing down the ages in my head:*
What is your substance, whereof are you made,
That millions of strange shadows on you tend?

O my most dear, I know the live imprint
*   Of that smile of gratitude,*
Know it more perfectly than any book.
* It brims upon the world, a mood*
Of love, a mode of gladness without stint.
O that I may be worthy of that look.[54]

Here was a restoration of the moral universe, if only glimpsed in passing, like a brilliant yellow taxi gleaming in sun. Everything seemed fresh
and renewed. To one friend, he wrote that he had been "translated, like
Bottom, in *A Midsummer Night's Dream*."[55]

Seeing himself through Helen's eyes allowed him to feel (almost for
the first time) that he was someone worthy of love. Such a relationship,
according to clinicians of post-traumatic stress, can "repair the breakdown of trust and the deep suspicion" that trauma can instill. He had
chosen the epigraph for *Shadows* carefully: a second life. "My real life—
that is, the life that means most to me—only began in 1971; what went

before was either painful or negligible; what followed after became increasingly fine and valuable and happy."[56]

3. "Here in this bleak city of Rochester"[57]

Though Hecht formed friendships with Cyrus Hoy, Joseph Summers, and other colleagues in Rochester, the place itself was frankly depressing: a provincial hub with a horrible climate, on the banks of Lake Ontario. Snowfall, thanks to the lake effect, averaged around 102 inches a year, with abundant cloud cover. "Have you ever been to Rochester?" Hecht asked Helen on one of their first dates; she had not. "Well, perhaps you shall someday," he replied suggestively. She knew in that moment that he was going to propose to her. She accepted, "having been in love with him for most of [her] life."[58]

Rochester was cold and grim by the time they got there in mid-November. Hecht wrote to Harry Ford:

> Rochester is the only place I have ever been where there can be an 85% eclipse of the sun without making any detectable difference in the normal daylight and visibility. . . . To leave it is like emerging from Plato's cave. So what am I doing here? I suppose that like the pious philosopher, I have returned to liberate others.[59]

Hecht channeled his aversion to the place into a mocking sestina, "Sestina d'Inverno," which takes its lead from Auden's sestina "Paysage Moralisé," even sharing a repeating end-word or teleuton ("islands" / "island"). Auden's "cities" is localized into the proper noun "Rochester," which, as it rolls around in subsequent stanzas, takes on a slashing comic effect:

> *The one thing indisputable here is snow,*
> *The single verity of heaven's making,*
> *Deeply indifferent to the dreams of the natives*
> *And the torn hoarding-posters of some island.*

Under our igloo skies the frozen mind
Holds to one truth: it is grey, and called Rochester.[60]

"Paysage Moralisé" (and Auden generally) remained important for Hecht. He continually returned to painterly landscapes, each encoded with past upsets—war and family trauma. When he showed "Sestina d'Inverno" to George Ford, chairman of English, Ford thought it "terribly bold" to have written it, since "it's not regarded as good form to say anything about the weather in Rochester."[61]

Early in 1972, the Hechts enjoyed a brief respite from the Rochester winter. A Fulbright fellowship sent them to Brazil for two weeks, where Hecht represented the United States at a literary conference in São Paulo, where it was midsummer, then on to Washington University in St. Louis, courtesy of the Van Duyns, with Hecht performing light duties as Hurst Visiting Professor. When they returned to Rochester, a week late for the start of term, Hecht wrote to Philip Booth with the news that they had been savoring since summer: "We are expecting a baby in early April."[62] They decided to buy a house to accommodate the new addition, a spacious clapboard at 19 East Boulevard, "a very large, almost manorial house, the likes of which we could neither find nor afford"[63] in a bigger city like New York. Still, like most first-time homeowners, Hecht "felt the mortgage hovering" over him.[64]

On April 5, Evan Alexander came into the world during a blizzard, an event that Hecht commemorated in "The Odds." The poem was also a powerful statement against the Vietnam war:

Like the blind, headlong cells,
Crowding toward dreams of life, only to die
In dark fallopian canals,
Or that wild strew of bodies at My Lai.
Thick drifts, huddled embankments at our door
Pile up in this eleventh year of war.

Yet to these April snows,
This rashness, those incalculable odds,
The costly and cold-blooded shows

> *Of blind perversity or spendthrift gods*
> *My son is born, and in his mother's eyes*
> *Turns the whole war and winter into lies.*
>
> *But voices underground*
> *Demand, "Who died for him? Who gave him place?"*
> *I have no answer. Vaguely stunned,*
> *I turn away and look at my wife's face.*
> *Outside the simple miracle of this birth*
> *The snow flakes lift and swivel to the earth . . .*[65]

As Evan later recounted the story of that cold snap in April, "The day that I was born, there was an unusual winter storm and two feet of snow on the ground. So, things were especially forbidding and hostile in Rochester."[66] This came as a particular shock, since the Hechts hadn't been there long, only two months. To help welcome the newborn, Baskin made up a handsome letterpress birth announcement for the couple.

The house on East Boulevard loomed large in Evan's early memories of family life. He remembered the hush that came over the place when his father was working. He had

> a saint-like dedication to his work and his craft—that was evident to me from a very, very early age. I think as early as three, I understood very real boundaries. My father would need absolute silence and often need to be completely by himself for most of the hours of the day.
>
> When he wasn't actively working, he was reading, often several books at once. There would often be three books out on the bed at the same time, with constant cross-referencing with books in his library. Those images presented themselves at the earliest possible stage.[67]

Hecht was devoted to Evan, who completed their tight family unit. (After Evan was born, Tony and Helen both quit smoking, a habit Tony had picked up in the army forty years earlier.) Growing up with an ineffectual father, a forbidding mother, and an ailing brother, Hecht had longed for ties of true affection; now he was forming them. For Helen's part, there was no question that he deserved all the support necessary to do his work. Her love was an incomparable blessing, and his happiness only increased. In terms of his poems, this newfound feeling of safety and contentment allowed him to delve even deeper into the difficult feelings he had harbored since childhood. Subsequent poems did not shy away from depicting astonishing cruelty in poems such as "The Deodand," "The Short End," "The Feast of Stephen," "An Overview," the war poem "Still Life," and the Holocaust poem "Persistences." The long title poem of *The Venetian Vespers* contains some of Hecht's most graphic writing about combat. His new poems came quickly for a change.

Poetry business proliferated through all of it—the marriage, the move, the birth. Hecht served on a committee that awarded James Merrill the prestigious Bollingen Prize. Merrill was an old friend, since their meeting during Hecht's first trip in Italy. When Merrill wrote to thank Hecht for his part in the selection, Hecht confided a humorous anecdote. The two relished each other's mischievous wit. On his way to Yale to deliberate with the two other committee members—May Swenson and Louis L. Martz, of Yale's English department—he had an encounter. "Dear Jimmy," Hecht began:

Helen and Evan and I flew from Rochester to Hartford, and then took a limousine to New Haven for the event. In the limousine with us was an indisputable hooker, redolent with the scents and gaudy with the embellishments of her trade. It appeared she was destined for the same hotel as we were. I made mention of this fact at the rather literary dinner party (Robert Penn Warren, Cleanth Brooks, Thornton Wilder, Pound's daughter, Stevens' daughter) and said that it occurred to me that she was very likely in the employ of one of the candidates for the prize, and had been sent to New Haven to sway the jury. Thornton Wilder appeared doubtful, [Yale professor] Norman Holmes Pearson seemed prepared to entertain the idea, the wife of the Yale librarian, Mrs. Rogers, was genuinely shocked. Only Eleanor Clark smiled.[68]

Later that month, he wrote to Baskin that he was moving to Leverett House, Harvard, where he would be teaching for the spring term. Hecht was filling in for his friend on leave, the poet and classicist Robert Fitzgerald, and he set up in Fitzgerald's office. That spring, Hecht spent time with Elizabeth Bishop, "who [was] renovating a house on the river near the Aquarium,"[69] and Bill Alfred (the dedicatee of "Meditation"). He saw the Wilburs when they came to visit their daughter. Several of the student poets he taught or advised that term became protégés: Nicholas Christopher, and Brad Leithauser and Mary Jo Salter, who later married.

Back in Rochester, he began a collaboration with his old Smith colleague, George Dimock, to translate *Oedipus at Colonos,* but the project eventually fell apart. Dimock could be an exasperating collaborator at times, but in the end it was his own work that Hecht was unhappy with. (Hecht salvaged two fragments from it—"Praise for Kolonos" in *Shadows* and "Chorus from *Oedipus at Colonos*" for *The Transparent Man.*) Both he and the general editor of Oxford's "Greek Tragedy in New Translations" series, William Arrowsmith, found the language "stilted and unnatural," too much like cut-rate Shakespeare. Hecht put the blame on himself: "No doubt it is the result of my aim at rendering the play in blank verse, which has had, in more places than I can care to think of now, the effect of very inferior Shakespearean rhythms and dictions, and a certain amount of detectable padding."[70] The collaboration had not been easy, for reasons of geography and temperament, and Hecht may have been relieved to let it go.

As for his own poems, Hecht was in the midst of the most prolific period in his life. Much of *Millions of Strange Shadows* was completed, and the long poems of *The Venetian Vespers* followed quickly, with only two years between volumes—a breathtaking pace. These two books together form his middle period, the height of his career. The immediacy of the poems in *The Hard Hours* was, in *Shadows,* couched in a baroque idiom, with no loss of feeling. At the same time, his flair for dramatic voices finds its fullest expression in *Vespers,* its title poem one of his signal achievements. These books solidified his reputation. They are the work of a master poet who has come into his own.

TEN

APPREHENSIONS[1]
(1976–1980)

I look and look,
As though I could be saved simply by looking . . .[2]

1. "Something in the light"[3]

Hecht liked to complain about Rochester. He admitted to his Rochester friend Alan Frost that he'd become "a thoroughgoing Thersites . . . about Rochester weather."[4] To one correspondent he noted that "the city enjoyed only two seasons: winter and the Fourth of July."[5] In regular correspondence with two of the younger poets he met at Harvard, Nicholas Christopher and Brad Leithauser, he compared life on Lake Ontario to a kind of exile: "Banishment up here in the Ovidean wastes of Hither Thrace,"[6] a place where winter slips into spring with no transition "like those squat men that seem to have no necks."[7] It was, he told Christopher, "the worst compromise between a small town (without the rural advantages of such a place) and a city (without the metropolitan vitality and variety of most cities)."[8] Hecht's aversion to Rochester had much to do with his aversion to winter in general. He suffered from frostbite, contracted while in the army: "This is an ailment from which you cannot recover. . . . and it involves excruciating pain in cold weather." As a result, "winter is not something that I look forward to."[9]

But things were not as grim on other fronts. On the plus side, the climate was conducive to work, without the distractions offered by the more "benign climactic conditions" he'd experienced on work trips to places like San Diego, for example.[10] Hecht found the university and his place in it quite congenial: "The English department here at the University of

Rochester is more homogeneous and cordial in its relations within the department itself than obtained" during his visiting semesters at Harvard or Yale.[11] It was, in many respects, the best appointment of his career so far. He wrote to encourage Leithauser, who was trying to decide between a career in academe or a career in law: "I am quite happy here in Rochester and have been virtually since I arrived."[12] Of his reservations about a professorial career, "the note of bitterness . . . in this letter derives from many years of pilgrimage over the academic map." Still, it was always Hecht's plan to make a life in the academy, and, though it may have taken some time for him to find his way to a suitable appointment, it was now working out very well for him. The title of John Hall Deane Professor of Rhetoric and Poetry suited him: "The rhetoric part meant that I was to fall heir to the position of university orator,"[13] delivering speeches at commencement ceremonies and other gatherings. Hecht moved easily into his public role at U of R, becoming a kind of university poet laureate, addressing students and faculty at the annual Yellowjacket celebrations that marked the start of the school year, and hosting visiting writers under the auspices of the Plutzik Memorial Reading Series. Like Hecht, the poet Hyam Plutzik, who died of cancer in January 1962, had been the Deane professor and served in the army during the war. The two poets shared certain connections. Plutzik, too, acknowledged Shakespeare and the Bible as his influences.[14] He began his *Horatio,* a two-thousand-line narrative poem, while stationed overseas, and ultimately published it with Atheneum in 1961. Organizing the Plutzik series, and hosting and introducing the poets, was excellent preparation for Hecht's role in the early eighties as US poet laureate, when he was called upon to host a reading series at the Library of Congress.

Though a poet's place in the ivory tower could be incongruous, Hecht now felt supported by the administration and appreciated by fellow faculty: there are "remarkable advantages," he wrote to Leithauser. "The right colleagues mean right off that you are not taken for a fool simply because you write poetry. And then teaching, while it has terrible routines and numbing exactions, is enormously rewarding when you have good students, and is a wonderfully human[e] and social way to earn a living. And it probably leaves you more time for reading and writing than many other jobs would, quite aside from the long vacations."[15] Hecht's fellow faculty were among the most impressive of his teaching career—Cyrus Hoy, who edited the Norton Critical Edition of *Hamlet*, the Dickens scholar George Ford, and Joseph H. Summers, who joined the faculty shortly after Hecht in 1969. (Summers had also taught at Bard, though he and Hecht did not overlap there.) Renowned for his work on George Herbert, a poet dear to Hecht, Summers was a conspicuous name dropper of literary friends like Elizabeth Bishop and James Merrill. Hecht dedicated "'Dichtung un Warheit'" to Hoy and "House Sparrows" to Summers and his wife, U. T., who was on the faculty at the nearby Rochester Institute of Technology.

A star of the English department, Hecht was often featured in the local papers, which made much of his recent successes. He could teach what he liked, chiefly Shakespeare and modern poetry, both to undergrads and graduate students. He never warmed to leading workshops, preferring to meet promising writers one-on-one, as he had with Christopher, Salter, and Leithauser at Harvard. His course loads at Harvard and Yale had been an exception: he taught writing exclusively, but the student work was of sufficient quality to make it a happy exception to his rule. (He later passed up an offer by the Writing Seminars at Johns Hopkins because of the amount of creative writing they expected him to teach.[16]) Professing poetry to university students was, as he put it in one public address, the fulfillment of a dream that he had entertained as a schoolboy and which was deepened by his own experience as a student at Bard. "The truth is that for many, indeed most, the undergraduate years of college are among the most sustained periods of care-free happiness, intellectual excitement, and self-discovery that you are likely to enjoy in the course of your entire lives."[17]

Helen, a talented decorator, began to populate the rooms of 19 East Boulevard with simple but handsome furniture. The house was an "extremely elegant, large and noble one," Hecht wrote to his colleague John Irwin at Johns Hopkins, purchased "at a bargain price that these days would take your breath away, and on which we pay a 7½% mortgage rate."[18] Evan recalled the cavernous place with nostalgia, and his parents, always warmly indulgent, gave him free rein to explore. Admitted to Hecht's study during breaks in his father's solitary work, he remembered the bust of his father that Gilbert Franklin had made in Rome in the fifties:

We used to make jokes that, aside from Richard Wagner, he's the only person who has a bust of himself in his own study, which he found very amusing. He put a straw hat on the bust that said "Judge" on it, from a cooking competition where [Helen] was a judge. He spun it around and wrote "Judge Not," because he wanted to reference a favorite biblical passage, "Judge not lest ye be judged," which ties into that idea that no one is more sinful than the accusing.[19]

This was telling of Hecht's sense of humor and of his sensibility generally. On the one hand he insisted on formal correctness and a certain gravitas (the Franklin sculpture), which he might then explode with irreverent humor (the hat). In this, he was like his father; fastidiously dressed in Savile Row, while cracking bawdy jokes with his young son. The comic spirit of "The Dover Bitch," the double dactyls, and the self-indicting levity of "Ghost in the Martini" all smack of this antic quality beneath the formal surface. Those who knew Hecht well often saw this lighter side of him.

Not long after the newlyweds were settled, Helen's mother took up residence nearby, conferring a welcome familial warmth he never felt from his own parents. Nineteen East Boulevard was a redoubt, a place of safety. In its sprawling rooms and large silences, Hecht could work more easily than before. Helen was the ideal partner for a poet: smart, patient, and sensitive to her husband's periods of melancholy, though these were fewer since the two of them had met. Possessed of a keen literary sensibility, she was deeply sympathetic to Hecht's work, its accomplishment, its seriousness of purpose, and its place of public importance. She was a gifted cook who wrote cookbooks, and a professional interior designer, with her own clientele. As Adam Hecht recalled of his visits to Rochester, "Helen filled the house with beautiful things." It was clear to him that she was "a very mellow person" and that her demeanor "was good for him."[20] Tony and Helen often remarked on their good fortune, grown almost superstitious about Fate's uncharacteristically gentle hand in their new life together. As a talisman, Hecht saved the printed slip from a fortune cookie that he felt spoke to his current elation: "Nobody will mar your happy future."

This bit of apotropaic magic was eventually pasted into a scrapbook next to a photo of the couple. Both look beatific, their joy clearly deriving from one another as, elegantly dressed, they laugh together on a bed, where they have plopped down in high spirits. *Shadows,* when it appeared early in 1977, was Hecht's love letter to Helen. It contained a number of love poems that reveal Hecht's great powers in this vein—"A Birthday Poem," "Peripeteia," "The Odds," and "Apples for Paul Suttman." Addressing Suttman, an artist he knew in Rome, he wrote:

> *The dearest curves in nature—the merest ripple,*
> *The cresting wave—release*
> *All our love, and find it in an apple,*
> *My Helen, your Elisse.*[21]

This was a new note for Hecht, and he sounded it repeatedly, pleased to announce his newfound love. He became a poet of love's joys instead of love's sorrows. The seamy underside of Eros that found a place in poems like "The Man Who Married Magdalene" was replaced by a healing vision of Agape, full of hope and promise. At the same time, his "dim, weathery ghosts,"[22] particularly those from the war, increasingly took the stage. Out of a new place of safety, he was able to meet them head-on.

Mornings were particularly good for work: the mind

> is both more alert, and, often, profitably the opposite. I mean that in the mildly and pleasantly dazed state I find myself in early in the day after rising—calm and without anxiety, still close to the comforts and suggestions of the world of sleep—I am near enough to unconscious sources, to essential memories, to feel I can call on buried resources in my poems. And after that state, largely passive, is over, my mind is at its most alert.[23]

He wrote out poems by hand, crossing out and scribbling additions and emendations. He would then type them up once he had a working draft. In *Millions of Strange Shadows,* the contrast of light and dark that attends on all of his mature poems is thrown into high relief. Asked by Ford to supply a description for the jacket, Hecht ventured that it is "a collection of poems about the light of knowledge, a sudden illumination, that necessarily casts things into shadow, the shadow of doubt, of ignorance, of what is guilty and hidden. . . . It is about that mixture, *chiaroscuro*, of past and present, of the buried and the recovered, the quick and the dead that constitutes the mysterious doubleness of much of our experience."[24] For Hecht, the darkness was always looming; after his marriage to Helen, he was able to reclaim a vision of the light that he had briefly glimpsed as a boy, a kind of innocence and wonder that in many respects he was experiencing for the first time.

His parents still had the power to upset him. Visits to New York were always fraught. Hecht preferred the greater control he had when visiting them, rather than hosting them in Rochester. Evan remembers that he and his parents always stayed at the Stanhope, across from the Metropolitan Museum. (Hecht had given up his rented apartment at 240 East 82nd, where he and Helen lived briefly after their wedding.) From the hotel, they could easily "make an appearance" at his parents' place on 81st Street, near 3rd Avenue. Roger, as usual, was still living with their parents. Dorothea "was sweet and always very lovely to me and always had presents for me," Evan remembers. "It was all very serious and official. My father seemed to have limited patience for his parents. According to my mother, we'd come over for lunch, and Roger would be there and Dorothea and Melvyn," who would constantly interrupt each other. Hecht would use Evan as an excuse to leave the room, taking him to the living room to play with Legos.

Hecht made no secret of his uneasiness around his parents, even making a joke out of it with Evan: "Whenever Mother's Day would come up, I'd say, 'Hey, Dad, how do you feel about that one?' and he'd just say [in a parody of a New York accent], *Ahhh, Shaddup!!* He didn't have any trouble expressing that he had difficulties and problems with everyone he grew up with." Dorothea was the greatest source of unease, probably because she was more engaged, while Melvyn was content to read or smoke in silence:

He had ultimately more difficulty with her. They were more alike. He took after her more. I know that things that he found fault with in her were curiously traits of his own. She very often would have difficulty, I think, being sentimental or expressing warmth or being vulnerable. I think one might fairly accuse my father of the same traits. Maybe to a much lesser degree. But I thought it was interesting that a lot of the problems he had with her may have been similar to problems that Jason and Adam and myself would have had with him to a degree.

Was Hecht's reserve, his formality, an affect learned from his mother? Possibly so, Evan felt.

During his years in Rochester, Hecht kept in intermittent touch with Jason and Adam. Even at eight years old, Evan had the vague impression that both of his "brothers probably felt that I had kind of replaced them. Things had always been very difficult between them and my father." The relationship with Jason went from bad to worse. According to his brother Adam, Jason never fully recovered from the divorce of his parents. Adam recalls that Jason "was destroyed by the divorce"; he was "never right after that." He felt betrayed and acted out, getting kicked out of schools and having difficulty finding his own way.[25] Jason had a hard time keeping a job and continued to live at home for long stretches. Helen remembered him visiting his father on East Boulevard: "Every time Jason came it was to ask for money. He had some new project or vocation. Tony would write a check, then he'd hear from him the next time he was broke and had some scheme and needed new capital." At one point Jason rode his motorcycle to El Salvador, and it seemed clear to Hecht that he was struggling with substance abuse: Jason "was a mess."[26] Hecht helped Jason financially, but he began to fear that the money only made him more dependent.

For Evan, the visits from Adam and Jason when he "was five and seven and eight" were thrilling. He loved having his big brothers around. In 1980, Adam came to live in the house in Rochester for one semester. Hecht was pleased to have him there, provided he enrolled in Monroe Community College and worked toward a degree. It was Evan's sense that Adam was frustrated with the parenting he had received with Pat and wanted a fresh start: "I think he understood at least implicitly (or it could have been my father making it clear in plain English) that higher education was my father's absolute priority. I think he felt constrained to pursue something like that." But Adam suffered from severe dyslexia. He had a lot of difficulty and then dropped out after the fall semester, which was dispiriting for him and for Hecht. He left Rochester in March, amidst "a lot of tears, a lot of yelling."

Evan was sorry to see him go; he "got along with Adam very well" and had been excited "to have an older brother" living in the house. Adam also taught him

> to ride a bike. He took me sledding. I remember my father very wistfully saying at one point I should be doing these activities. And I remember thinking, *Relax, Dad. I understand this isn't your strong suit.* And it wasn't. My father had a quality about him—and I use this term very loosely, a bit tongue-in-cheek—an almost autistic quality, a sort of emotionally removed, confused, not knowing how to be a dad—that sort of awkwardness, which I think is the same thing he might have experienced with his own mother.

Even so, Hecht doted on Evan and took enormous pride in his accomplishments. (He dedicated his essay collection *Obbligati* [1986] exclusively to Evan "with love and admiration.") He could also be down to earth in ways that surprised his son. Evan remembers his father binge-watching the British television comedy *Blackadder* one winter:

> For Christmas I got him VHS tapes of Rowan Atkinson's *Blackadder*, which he loved. My father was never one to be excessive or indulgent, but all Christmas afternoon he watched six or seven hours in a row; he couldn't get enough of it. So even though he was very mandarin about popular culture and that sort of thing he did like certain things. He liked Monty Python.

For years, he kept a photo of the Marx Brothers on the wall. Hecht prized humor, as a counter to his more febrile emotions. Clearly his new family brought him a real measure of calm and happiness, but he had learned to be superstitious about good fortune. The light does not dispel the shadows; if anything, it delineates and deepens them. But Hecht's newfound peace allowed him to look more deeply and clearly into the well of the past. As a result, he managed to compose a number of his most personal and autobiographical poems to date. Chief among these was "Apprehensions," which returned unflinchingly to the traumas of childhood: Roger's illness, his father's faltering fortunes and attempted suicides, corporal abuse at the hands of his nanny, and the long silences, the sea of loneliness and fear.

In April 1974, James Merrill published a mid-length autobiographical poem in *The New Yorker* entitled "Lost in Translation." Hecht likely heard the poem read aloud at the Bollingen ceremony at Yale the year before, but he had not yet seen it in print. Hecht wrote a fan letter to his friend shortly after it appeared:

> Evan has been allowed to tear up any copies of *The New Yorker* he has a mind to, except the one in which "Lost in Translation" appeared. I can't tell you how glad I am at last to see it before me and to read it at leisure. It is every bit as stunning as when I first heard it, full of tact, splendor and perfectly controlled emotion. It seems to me, more and more, one of the finest poems of our time. I can't think of a poet alive who wouldn't be lucky to have written it.[27]

Merrill's narrative of a young boy left to the care of a nanny would have resonated with Hecht. The poem showed Hecht how one might write a personal, autobiographical poem without subsiding into a confessional register. Hecht composed "Apprehensions," his most sustained and direct memoir in verse, shortly before *Millions of Strange Shadows* appeared in 1977. It was among the very last works he wrote for that book, and for a time, as he assembled the manuscript, it lent its title to the collection as a whole. (The ultimate choice of *Shadows* for the title is telling: Hecht chose a title that pointed toward "miraculous" Helen as the emotional center over his own gleanings and fears hinted at in the double-edged "Apprehensions.") The poem attested to Hecht's aesthetic and aristocratic sympathies with Merrill, but with marked differences in the detail and tone: Merrill's childhood home was a fifty-room mansion called "The Orchard," located in Southampton, New York, while Hecht's was a large apartment on the Upper East Side. Merrill's kindly governess, whom he calls Mademoiselle ("stout, plain, carrot-haired, devout") is countered by Hecht's sadistic Fräulein.

Hecht felt that Merrill's new poem made "all of us, including the Big Names, into Tin-Pan-Alley hacks."[28] To Harry Ford, who published "Lost in Translation" in Merrill's *Divine Comedies* (1976), he admitted an "uncomfortable mixture of envy and admiration," holding Merrill's latest triumph above his own "childish efforts." Merrill's poem may have provided a model for "Apprehensions," but the impetus came by accident, when Hecht discovered at a garage sale in Rochester a complete set of *The Book of Knowledge,* the encyclopedia for young readers he had as a boy. Hecht purchased it, and as he browsed through it in the subsequent weeks, many long-suppressed childhood memories flooded back. Helen remembers that he began "Apprehensions" not long after that:[29]

> *We were living at this time in New York City*
> *On the sixth floor of an apartment house*
> *On Lexington, which still had streetcar tracks.*
> *It was an afternoon in the late summer;*
> *The windows open; wrought-iron window guards*
> *Meant to keep pets and children from falling out.*
> *I, at the window, studiously watching*
> *A marvelous transformation of the sky;*
> *A storm was coming up by dark gradations.*[30]

Like the "ironwork" in "A Hill," *wrought-iron* points to the war (also *guards*). *Ash* often carries a similar resonance in the poems, followed, here, by *funerary greys:*

> *But what was curious about this was*
> *That the sky seemed to be taking on*
> *An ashy blankness, behind which there lay*
> *Tonalities of lilac and dusty rose*
> *Tarnishing now to something more than dusk,*
> *Crepuscular and funerary greys.*[31]

Then light breaks through in the poem, a corollary for the happy turn in Hecht's private life, his love for Helen:

> *The streets became more luminous, the world*
> *Glinted and shone with an uncanny freshness.*

The brickwork of the house across the street
(A grim, run-down Victorian chateau)
Became distinct and legible; the air
Full of excited imminence, stood still.
The streetcar tracks gleamed like the path of snails.
And all this made me superbly happy,
But most of all a yellow Checker Cab
Parked at the corner. Something in the light
Was making this the yellowest thing on earth.
It was as if Adam, having completed
Naming the animals, had started in
On colors, and had found his primary pigment
Here, in a taxi cab, on Eighty-Ninth Street.
It was the absolute, parental yellow.[32]

This exaltation, like an allegro movement in a symphony, lifts the poem out of its tenebrous recesses of memory, before returning to the dark foreboding of the ending, a forecast of the Holocaust.

When *Shadows* appeared, Richard Howard phoned to say how much he admired the book, but he warned "against expecting that, simply because [it] would be warmly admired, it would win any prizes or even be reviewed sympathetically."[33] Howard's prediction was prophetic. When the review by Denis Donoghue appeared prominently in *The New York Times,* it gave voice to a mid-century resistance to received form, what Donoghue calls "the genteel tradition." He called out Hecht's "precision, wit, craft, inventiveness—the virtues which a poet is required to practice in the absence of passion. . . . It is easy to admire [the poems] but hard to keep the admiration from being frigid." He praises "A Letter" from *Hours,* but sees it as a promise that *Shadows* fails to deliver on:

Mr. Hecht is content to be urbane. Not a poet of the incandescent line, he loves the linkages of a stanza, where he has room to move and breathe. If he had lived four centuries ago he would have composed himself by writing madrigals. As it is, he writes long, shapely sentences and sends them through an entire stanza, eight or ten lines for good measure. Fluent without being garrulous, his tone accommodates nearly every effect within the limits of high conversation, including certain excesses of diction which would be offensive on a more informal occasion. In his early poems Mr. Hecht played several five-finger exercises and took pleasure in recourse to the older dictionaries featuring such words as "thew," "flume" (meaning a water channel) and "rondure." When he used the word "umbrage," it was the umbrage given by trees in a garden, not the kind taken by people who choose to be offended. A favorite word of his is "touching," used as a preposition meaning "about" or "concerning," usage which the Oxford English Dictionary, published in 1933, described as "now somewhat archaic." One of Mr. Hecht's poems tells of a dispute touching the taste and color of the Original Fruit, Eve's apple ["Apples for Paul Suttman"]. Another reports that Daphnis sang, on a little snuffbox, "touching love's defeat" ["Alceste in the Wilderness," from *Stones*]. A third begins, "Let men take note of her, touching her shyness," a preposition again, since her shyness is the last thing such note-taking men would touch ["Imitation," from *Stones*]. Like Browning, Mr. Hecht rhymes "rebuke" with "peruke."

It was a devastating takedown. Hecht felt deeply hurt and angry, more so because Donoghue quoted poems from his first collection, published over two decades earlier, against him. Hecht could have admitted such dismissive quips brought to bear on *Stones,* admittedly a work of juvenilia, but Donoghue does not distinguish. Two volumes on, with the plain-spoken intensity of *Hours* and the deeply felt interplay of light and dark, guilt and redemption, worked out so memorably in *Shadows,* this was a crushing setback, an expulsion from the first ranks, and a bitter embarrassment for Hecht in terms of his friends and university colleagues. Edward Mendelson suggests that "Hecht was famously thin skinned."[34] His student and protégé David Mason remembers similarly that Hecht could hold a grudge. But was it thin-skinned to feel that Donoghue's denouncement constituted at best a lack of sympathy and at worst an attack unsupported, it seemed clear to Hecht, by the poems at hand? Hecht acknowledged that poets "are a touchy and easily offended lot, and this reflects the uncertainty of our place in society. . . . [T]here are not many for whom their entire *amour propre* is so intimately tied to their professional careers."[35] The review appeared during Hecht's visiting term at Yale. He picked up the *Book Review,* in the Sunday *Times,* and read the review at the Yale Co-op, and shrank as it "reduced to self-admitted failure, evasion and triviality the labor of ten years . . . in the space of a few paragraphs."[36] An admiring review in the London *Times Literary Supplement* and a sympathetic review by Howard in *Poetry* for November 1977 ("this densely qualified, masterfully varied new volume") could not dull the sting, since the *Times* was *"the one review* that everybody sees."[37] To call the poems mandarin is one thing; to say that they were bloodless and inert, marred by pretentious diction and a lack of feeling, is another. Hecht felt that he had been wildly misread. It was a slight that he could not easily forget or forgive.[38]

2. "Something by Shakespeare"[39]

While at Rochester, Hecht immersed himself in his teaching, delving deeper into the plays and poems of Shakespeare. He hoped to bring the texts to life for his students. "I love the things I teach," he told an interviewer at U of R: "It seems to me one of the great pleasures to communicate that excitement and that pleasure to students."[40] Hecht had long associated passages from the plays and Sonnets with his own complex feelings. Shakespeare's diction and music were finding their way into his poems more and more: echoes and resonances and even outright quotations couched as allusions and epigraphs. Like the dyer's hand, Hecht's own verse was stained with the telltale signs of his trade.

Hecht worked to improve as a professor. His teaching had become a vocation and a source of pride. He demanded a good deal from his students, many of whom found the Early Modern language challenging. During his lonely bachelor years at Bard, he had looked to his more precocious students like Chevy Chase for sympathy and even friendship. Older now and happily settled, he took a more distant, professional approach, acknowledging that he did not "incline socially . . . to mix very much with my students."[41] The Professor of Rhetoric hoped to persuade his students that these texts were "infinitely rich and deep and worthy of considerable interpretation and comment and thought." It was not always an easy sell.

Hecht read out long passages in class with nuance and force. He had relished performing since boyhood. The poet Monroe K. Spears, a long-time editor of *The Sewanee Review* and the author of a book on Auden, singled out Hecht's public readings for praise: "He is among the greatest readers of our time—and, as far as one can tell, of any time."[42] Spears went on to characterize Hecht's ability to play the cascading syncopations of natural speech rhythms across the meter: "Tony has the vocal and musical equipment necessary to enunciate clearly while expressing all the complex interplays between meter and prose meaning. . . . [H]e uses all the resources of art—music, rhetoric, allusion—to deal with the most serious and fundamental questions."

Shakespeare crops up increasingly in Hecht's poetry, quoted in poems, transformed into puns, employed as epigraphs, through numerous echoes, in the very movement of the verse, particularly Hecht's blank verse, as well as in the dramatic nature of his monologues and personae. "I am by now a stubborn, middle-aged university professor," Hecht quipped, "who rejoices in teaching Shakespeare and who mercilessly brainwashes students into believing he is a great writer."[43] J. D. McClatchy even suggests that, with "his solid build and sad eyes, his heraldic grey hair and pointed beard," Hecht himself resembled "a benevolent Shakespearean Duke."[44] With his students it was frequently a stern benevolence—he could be a daunting figure, even to his favorite students. Always a tough grader, Hecht allowed students to improve their grade by rewriting. One freshman, Lisa Cohen, who had been a straight-A student in high school, was devastated to receive a C on her paper on Fate in *Romeo and Juliet*. She grudgingly reworked it, and Hecht lifted her grade to an A−, with one comment: Why hadn't she delivered her best work the first time? For Cohen this became a keystone of her education, a "Meliora moment," as they liked to say at Rochester.[45]

Hecht drew on Shakespeare in numerous ways in his poetry at this time. Nearly half of the poems in *Shadows* contain some echo or reference to Shakespeare, and the long title poem of *Vespers*, echoing themes and images from *The Merchant of Venice* and *Hamlet*, carries lines from *Othello* as an epigraph. Also well worth extended consideration is the Shakespearean (and Wordsworthian and Frostian) nature of Hecht's blank verse in "Vespers" and other of his dramatic monologues.[46] In *Shadows*, allusions come not as single spies but in battalions. Following the quotation from *The Tempest* on the dedication page, the first poem in the book, "The Cost," begins with an epigraph from Hamlet—"Why, let the stricken deer go weep, / The hart ungallèd play . . ."—and Cassio, Desdemona, Iago, and Othello are each mentioned in the poem. A line from *Othello* is adapted to echo the poem's title—"And a voice whispers inwardly, 'My soul, / It is the cost, the cost.'" There are "samphire-tufted cliffs" straight out of *Lear,* and behind "motes," "the mind's eye," and "so much dust" we hear Hamlet's soliloquies. All this by page five. The next poem takes its epigraph from *Titus Andronicus.* And so on. "The Ghost in the Martini"

> is full of quotations from Shakespeare and the Bible and Milton, too, because these juxtapose themselves ironically against the cocktail chatter. But every once in a while one resorts to them because one wants the reader suddenly to expand his own sense of the significance of what's being said. When the reader recalls that something was once said by Job or by Christ or by Henry V, suddenly the poem ceases to be the parochial concern of the poet and becomes something more universal. It enlarges its own dimensions in this way.[47]

"A Birthday Poem," with Helen's birth date as epigraph, quotes from Sonnet 53, and expects the reader to recall two lines from the poem he does not quote: "On Helen's cheek all art of beauty set, / And you in Grecian tires are painted new."

So close to the bone, so intimately felt are Hecht's uses of the Sonnets and plays, they can only be understood as acts of (what T. S. Eliot called) sensibility: an idiosyncratic, internalized expression of the many aesthetic pleasures and revelations that Hecht discerned in Shakespeare's language of elation and despair. As Hecht, toward the end of his life, wrote to the poet David Mason, "As for Shakespeare, he was able to do anything, and he repays infinite study."[48] The plays and poems served as touchstones throughout his life, from the terrifying night watches of the war to the poems written in Italy only months before his death. In his interview with the National Endowment for the Humanities chairman Bruce Cole, published in *Humanities* in 2004, Hecht spoke of Shakespeare as a lifelong revelation, finding his abiding influence again and again.

For example: After reading "a great deal of Shakespeare," he "was able to see that in *Moby-Dick* Melville was strongly influenced by all kinds of Shakespearean idioms, by cadences, by actual images that he borrowed from the tragedies. One can't really read *Moby-Dick* without fully savoring the Shakespearean background, the language in it." The very same thing could be said of Hecht's poems; without an ear for the music of Shakespeare—his rhythms, images, grammar, and syntax—it is possible to miss the full emotional resonance and framework of Hecht's verse. In Shakespeare, he found corollaries for his own themes. A favorite exam question for *Romeo and Juliet* was unmistakably related to his own project: "Discuss the imagery of darkness and light . . ."

3. "He haunts me here, that seeker after law . . ."[49]

If light, in Hecht's cosmology, dispels darkness, it also delineates and deepens it. He remained grateful for his new life with Helen, and they spoke of their good fortune in reverent, almost mystical terms. But nothing could eradicate the darkness or even lessen its threat. Hecht was now better equipped to withstand it—the fits of melancholy, the re-experiencing of trauma that haunted his dreams—but the sources of trauma were still very much present and close to home. As congenial as he found his situation at Rochester, it hid a queasy underside of exclusion: the Rochester English department, he complained in a letter, "is known locally and, increasingly, nationally, for its overt anti-Catholicism and for its covert antisemitism; I have never in all my life encountered so many unabashedly virulent statements about Catholics nor so many surreptitious ones about Jews as I have here."[50] Despite his lasting friendships with Joseph and U. T. Summers and Cyrus Hoy, and with accomplished students such as Jonathan Post and David Mason, Hecht was again made to feel like an outsider, the condition he feared most of all. It clarified and strengthened his sympathies: "I cannot help identifying," he later wrote to the poet David Havird, "with all the Jews who have experienced persecution, for I have felt the effects of anti-Semitism throughout the whole of my life, though not in extremis, and I invariably wince at finding it widespread in Western literature."[51]

In the fall of 1977, memories of the war were rekindled by a trip he made to Salzburg, Austria, to teach in the Seminar in American Studies. On the border of Germany, Salzburg was the closest Hecht had come to Bavaria since his deployment in 1945. It had been his "ambition for many years to take Helen to Europe," and this teaching stint would cover the cost of his travel. The plan was to tack two weeks in Venice and one in Rome onto the end of the trip. Evan, five, would travel with them, and Helen's mother would join them in Salzburg. But he failed to foresee what the trip would mean for him. Salzburg was only 300 kilometers (a four-hour drive) from Flossenbürg. The association overwhelmed him. After teaching during the day, then having dinner in the dining room of Schloss Leopoldskron, he retreated to his room, too depressed to join the other fellows in the bar area downstairs for drinks.

Salzburg still carried the scars of war. During the Anschluss, the town came under the control of the Third Reich. Synagogues were destroyed, and Jews either left or were deported to concentration camps. A camp for Romani prisoners was established during the war that provided slave labor for local businesses. Bombing by the Allied Forces destroyed half the city. After the war, thousands of Jews found a temporary home in Salzburg's transient camps, with as many as two thousand displaced persons entering the camps each day. Hecht had returned to Europe many times since the war—to Paris, Italy, and Greece—but, except for a brief trip to Vienna with Leo Smit, Hecht hadn't heard German spoken since he confronted SS officers with the testimony of survivors. This was his first stay of any length in a German-speaking country since the war, and it caused profound fits of anxiety and depression. To make matters worse, the Seminar that year also featured the novelist John Gardner, whose excessive drinking Hecht had encountered one summer at Bread Loaf: "John got so drunk every night that he had to be put to bed by his students."[52] In the event, Gardner proved even "more foolish than usual."[53]

By the time Hecht escaped to Venice, he was rattled and exhausted. His dark mood imbued the Floating City with the faded grandeur John Ruskin describes in *The Stones of Venice*: "a dying city, magnificent in her dissipation, and graceful in her follies, obtained wider worship in her decrepitude than in her youth, and sank from the midst of her admirers into the grave."[54] To Dimitri Hadzi, Hecht admitted that in "The Venetian Vespers" he appropriates some of Ruskin's language, "especially as regards the initial darkness of [San Marco] when entered from the sunny piazza, and the general clarification of its interior as the eye accustoms itself to the muted light. Also: the lines about the 'dissolute young with heavy-lidded gazes / Of cool, clear-eyed, stony depravity' are virtually Ruskin's own words about the people who hung around just outside the church to pick up tourists."[55] Other sources are "A Wanderer in Venice," by E. V. Lucas, "which supplies the names of Buono and Rustico"; "a cheap paperback guide book, published by Scrocchi"; and "Wonders of Italy," with pictures of the mosaics in San Marco.

Once in Italy, Hecht's spirits were gradually restored: "How splendid, after the wretched gemütlichkeit of Austria, to enter civilization in the shape of pasta and Verdi and pasta verde, to say nothing of Carpaccio and Giorgione, the cathedral, palazzi and sunlight."[56] A new poem quickly began to take shape in his imagination, mingling his impressions of the place with themes drawn from Shakespeare and his copious reading. As he reported to Roger in New York:

> I'm at work on a long poem about Venice, only just begun. By way of preparation I did a lot of reading in the hope of finding things to pil-lage. First, of course, *Othello* and *The Merchant* and *Volpone*. Also Otway's "Venice Preserved," a very strange work of which the first two acts are boring and operatic, but the last three are grotesque and make the flesh creep. Naturally, guidebooks and Baedeker. Peter Quennell on Byron in Venice. Shelley's curious, damaged poem, "Julian and Maddalo," about his visit to Byron in Venice. Mann's story. Studies of Turner and Fuseli. Of course I could have gone on and on—and never written the poem. But I have enough to go on now, I think, and anyway all the pillaging will only serve some background function.[57]

Back in Rochester, a voice, as yet unidentified, began to emerge: "A dramatic monologue in blank verse (shades of Browning) now already over 600 lines long with probably 200–300 to go, set in Venice, but concerning an act of domestic American treachery."[58] The speaker was a patchwork figure, assembled from aspects of several people from his past:

One of them was a man I had met in Italy (though not in Venice) [Ischia, in fact], who suffered a deep and ineradicable guilt because his family history was the family history that's described in my poem. It was appalling. I liked him very much. He was a gentle, kind, decent man, but he had boils, like Job, all the time, a psychosomatic ailment. He was a rigid vegetarian who would not eat eggs unless he could be assured that they were infertile. He was punishing himself terribly and deprived himself of many pleasures. But he was only one of several people who are, as it were, incorporated into that speaker.[59]

Hecht had not been back to Venice since his trip there with Roger in 1951. As he revisited San Marco and the palazzi of the Grand Canal, his brother was very much on his mind:

There is also a component of my brother's suffering in the character I created. It seems to me that man, nameless in my poem, in his illness and stoic resolve was a kind of figuration for the city in its decay, its lingering on from greatness to a tourist attraction, yet with an undeniable dignity and beauty for all that. My intention was to braid these twin elements, man and city, so that the reader would feel them to be appropriately matched.[60]

Hecht harbored a frightening memory from his trip with Roger, grasping his brother's "tongue in my hand as he lay rigid on a street in Venice, attempting to prevent him from further harming himself during a seizure of epilepsy."[61] The speaker had been a medic during the war and was haunted by the carnage he witnessed there. Hecht again drew on his own experience, depicting a friend killed by enemy gunfire: "The top of his cranium like a soft-boiled egg, / And there he crouched, huddled over his weapon, / His brains wet in the chalice of his skull." The anonymous speaker, "a twentieth century infidel/ From Lawrence, Massachusetts," whom the critic John Frederick Nims calls "X," has battled mental illness since the war. Hecht again calls on his memory, in this case of a patient in "the violent ward" at "Crazy Square": "They subdued that one / With a hypodermic, quickly tranquilized / And trussed him like a fowl."[62]

Hecht insisted that X was not him, but rather a patchwork of friends, family, and acquaintances. Yet "the psychological self-portrait is unmistakable," the critic Edward Mendelson has rightly pointed out; "What makes him autobiographical is Hecht's interpretation of him as a son without a father, seeking in the rules of etiquette the same body of laws that Hecht sought in poetry."[63] The dark family history underlying the poem recalls *Hamlet*; X's uncle has replaced his father, who has disappeared. According to Hecht, X has "cut himself off from family life as his father was cut off. He has taken upon himself the penance for all the accumulated guilt, largely suspected, but absolutely unproveable, of what went on when he was a child."[64] The truth of X's childhood is hinted at with a line from *Hamlet* (his uncle is "a little more than kin"), and revealed in the last line of the poem, through an allusion to Launcelot Gobbo from *The Merchant of Venice,* who mangles the adage "It is a wise child that knows his own father."

Hecht's anxiety about his own father colors the poem throughout—a mire of guilt and estrangement. Hecht never mentions him as a source for "Vespers," but the truth was Melvyn was dying: "My father is rapidly losing his faculties, attempting suicide or threatening to, causing my mother and brother constant unremitting alarm, yet they refuse to put him in a home," he confided to Ford.[65] The shame of his father's erratic behavior and efforts to kill himself nettled Hecht. Melvyn is behind the figure of the mysteriously absent father in "Vespers," which draws on the same childhood traumas as a "A Hill" and "Apprehensions." The poem is the apotheosis of Hecht's use of the pathetic fallacy, its visual details and even the act of seeing itself fraught with psychological and emotional pressures.

Though Hecht could be coy about his poems, he does not disguise the intimate nature of "Vespers." How personal *is* the poem, the poets Daniel Anderson and Philip Stephens once asked him. "Oh, probably very personal," Hecht admitted:

You remember that famous declaration by Flaubert: "Madame Bovary, c'est moi." . . . He was saying he knew and felt everything that she went through. . . . He didn't know anything about her. She was not a well-educated woman. The whole thing was a creation of his own imagination, but clearly something that was deeply personal as well. I think that's got to be true of any poem by any writer. There's a great investment of your own feeling and understanding and compassion—and sometimes detestation.[66]

To David Havird he caviled, "the speaker of 'The Venetian Vespers' is *not me*, though I have used some events in my life in the course of the poem."[67] To Hoy he admitted that the poem necessarily included "something of myself."[68] Like Hecht, the speaker's "war experience and his dark family secrets incapacitate him."[69] As background to the long work, Hecht was concerned with the "sins of the fathers as in *Hamlet, Oedipus*, [and] Exodus 34:7."[70] Hecht was in high gear, and the intensity with which he worked suggested the emotional urgency of the long poem that was taking shape:

> I would have to say I was, at the end, trying to write a poem about Venice from a point of view of somebody who was very troubled and perplexed. Venice was as important to me as the speaker was, and every once in a while I wanted to get in some gorgeous descriptive effects of what clouds look like or what a rainstorm looks like in the city, and I wasn't going to let anything stand in the way of those little fanfares of description.[71]

The poem came together rapidly. Hecht considered various titles—"A Passage," "A Passenger," "The Forfeit," "Clouds," and "Vacancies"— before lighting on the Monteverdian "The Venetian Vespers."[72] By the end of the year, it was done. "I want especially in this poem to say what has to be said clearly yet nowhere explicitly, which means very delicate tuning of the dials."[73] Such details are worked out though a morality of seeing, through the classic Hechtian chiaroscuro. First, light:

> *Lights. I have chosen Venice for its light,*
> *Its lightness, buoyancy, its calm suspension*
> *In time and water, its strange quietness.*
> *I, an expatriate American,*
> *Living off an annuity, confront*

The lagoon's waters in mid-morning sun.
Palladio's church floats at its anchored peace
Across from me, and the great church of Health,
Voted in gratitude by the Venetians
For heavenly deliverance from the plague,
Voluted, levels itself on the canal.
Further away the bevels coil and join
Like spiraled cordon ropes of silk, the lips
Of the crimped water sped by a light breeze.
Morning has tooled the bay with bright inlays
Of writhing silver, scattered scintillance.

Then, darkness:

I enter the obscure aquarium dimness,
The movie-palace dark, through which incline
Smoky diagonals and radiant bars
Of sunlight from the high southeastern crescents
Of windowed drums above. Like slow blind fingers
Finding their patient and unvarying way
Across the braille of pavement, edging along
The pavonine and lapidary walls,
Inching through silence as the earth revolves
To huge compulsions, as the turning spheres
Drift in their milky pale galactic light
Through endless quiet, gigantic vacancy,
Unpitying, inhuman, terrible.
In time the eye accommodates itself
To the dull phosphorescence.

Robert Fitzgerald, Hecht's "old and trusted friend," made some suggestions for improvement, which were warmly received: "He gave some [feedback], very sparingly, and it was excellent."[74] After a few final revisions, the poem appeared as the first twenty-five pages of *Poetry* magazine for October 1978. This was the happy culmination of what is widely thought of as Hecht's masterwork; the unhappy culmination came the year before, shortly after the poem was completed. Melvyn, whose often fraught life inflects the poem, died. His death marked a decisive moment for Hecht, after which he began to see his life on the downward slope. In 1979, Dorothea died as well, within a year of her husband.

With long intervals between his first three books, Hecht now had a manuscript nearing completion only two years after *Shadows*. The intensity and speed of his output surprised even him. The hauntings of trauma did not disappear; rather, they became somehow more legible. "Persistences," the poem Hecht turned to immediately after "Vespers," extends the theme of a "seeker after law" in the wake of the Holocaust. Of the specters haunting his dream, the speaker wonders:

> . . . *Are these the apparitions*
> *of enemies or friends?*
> *Loved ones from whom I once withheld*
> *Kindness or amends*
>
> *On preterite occasions*
> *Now lost beyond repeal?*
> *Or the old childhood torturers*
> *of undiminished zeal,*
>
> *Adults who ridiculed me,*
> *schoolmates who broke my nose,*
> *Risen from black unconscious depths*
> *of REM repose?*
>
> *Who comes here seeking justice,*
> *Or in its high despite,*
> *Bent on some hopeless interview*
> *On wrongs nothing can right?*
>
> *Those throngs disdain to answer,*
> *Though numberless as flakes;*

Mine is the task to find out words
  For their memorial sakes

Who press in dense approaches,
  Blue numeral tattoos
Writ crosswise on their arteries,
  The burning, voiceless Jews.[75]

Hecht mistrusted the impulse to speak on behalf of the persecuted, which could easily be an act of arrogance or pride: "One feels that people like Elie Wiesel have a kind of singular title to write with authority on subjects about which I can't write with the same confidence and same moral right. So I've been reluctant to write about it."[76] During the Vietnam Era, he felt that, despite his hatred of war, certain kinds of protest could be both ineffectual and self-serving: "Opposed as I was to every aspect of the war, I was also determined not to rant and rave in public poetry readings on the subject, which was ultimately only a kind of self-promotion." He wrote of the Holocaust in the most searing terms, though rarely. Like Yeats's Ireland, it was a subject that hurt him into poetry.

Given his reticence to speak or write about what he himself had witnessed, he must have found it extremely odd that his brother, Roger, had taken up the Holocaust as a recurring subject. Roger had not been to war, though this was not uncommon: "There are an awful lot of people, even my age, who were not in the war," Hecht explained in an interview for *BOMB*. "They were not qualified for military service. My brother was one of these."[77] Hecht saw his brother clearly: Roger "never had a job, his epilepsy making that kind of work impossible. He lived with my parents all their lives and continued to occupy their New York apartment until his own death."[78] For Roger's part, he remembered a black cloud hanging over Tony as a boy. "Roger thought Tony was doom and gloom," Adam Hecht remembered. From his young nephew's perspective, Roger "wasn't like that; he was mellow and likeable."[79]

The same year as *Vespers*, Roger brought out his volume entitled *Burnt Offerings*. Roger was forty when his first book, *27 Poems*, was published by Alan Swallow in 1966. Four more books followed from various houses, including *Signposts, Parade of Ghosts,* and a limited edition of his selected poems entitled *A Quarreling of Dust.* His poetry appeared in the best magazines, including *The Paris Review, Poetry, The Kenyon Review, Sewanee Review,* and *Voyages,* where he served as an advisory editor. He was friends with Ted and Renee Weiss, colleagues of Tony's at Bard, and the editors of the *Quarterly Review of Literature.* Occasionally, Roger and Tony appeared in the same issue of a journal. People who were surprised that Roger should be a poet like his brother were equally surprised that his poems were frequently quite good.

There is a marked family resemblance, so to speak, between Roger's and Tony's poems. It could be eerie at times—subjects, styles, tones, allusions, and much else are uncannily similar. Personally, the brothers were quite different. For one thing, Roger never went out: "There were problems with his eyes, his legs, his right hand. All these he met with stoical reserve, and often with a truly gallant cheerfulness," Tony remembered.[80] Because of these ailments, Roger had a helper who looked after him. He walked with a cane around the family apartment on 83rd Street and watched sports on TV. (He bonded with Anne Sexton over baseball, and Melvyn would boast of his son's knowledge of stats.) By contrast, Tony had been to war, traveled widely, and risen steadily as a professor in the academy. Still, the two shared an intimate connection: "Such was the nature of our brotherhood and the intensity of the bond between us," Hecht mused, "that [Roger's] life was sometimes disrupted in sympathy with the disruptions in mine. There was a time of great misery in my life which so distressed Roger as to require his hospitalization. And he was not allowed to be released until I had taken steps to resolve my problem. It was not the only time in our lives when I was aware of the perfect harmony of our responses."[81]

While Hecht did not feel competitive with his brother as a poet, he must have felt at times that Roger was nipping at his heels. For *Burnt Offerings,* Roger interviewed survivors who had come to New York after the war and worked these accounts into poems. In the title poem of the collection, the speaker is haunted by the ghosts of murdered Jews. Though he never spoke of it publicly, Hecht's discomfort at such poems—their tin-eared presumption, not to mention their obvious indebtedness—must have been extreme:

> *Now all night long I hear some dead Jews calling,*
> *Calling, calling someone, maybe me.*
> *No, it is no nightmare. All that bawling*
> *Is only what you might call history.*[82]

Roger cultivated a wide circle of poet friends, who sometimes blamed the more-successful Tony for not doing more for his brother profession- ally, to boost his career. It's not hard to imagine the difficulties of such efforts on Hecht's part. To Roger's credit, he has many poems that are far better than the above passage suggests. But it's hard not to feel that he followed his brother's style and concerns too nearly to make his own distinct mark.

Hecht felt low after *Vespers* appeared: "I am undergoing, curiously, and for the first time, a mild post-partum depression, now that the book is delivered." It was "a new experience . . . [and] not a happy one. I feel obscurely discouraged."[83] He consoled himself by planning for summer travel: "A trip to Europe en famille of 45 days to Rome, Florence, Venice, [and] London, beginning in late June."[84] On December 2, 1979, a glowing review of *Vespers,* by Christopher Ricks, appeared on the front page of *The New York Times Book Review*. Ricks was drawn to the images of "dark- ness and light" in the long title poem: "There is much to be said about the illuminations that he gets from light in all its diversity . . . That light is seldom transparent for Hecht [in] this splendid poem of light and dark."[85]

Hecht said little about his parents' recent death, but it greatly height- ened his own sense of mortality. Elegy became the dominant mode in Hecht's next two books, as more of his friends died: "There are certain things that are clearer to me now having to do with age, having to do with the proximity to the conclusion of life."[86] In February 1980, his and Roger's friend James Wright was dying in a hospital in New York. Hecht visited him but could report to Harry Ford only that the "prospects are absolutely black."[87] He sat with Wright's wife, Annie, who was hoping Jim might live long enough to finish his latest book of poems. Betty Kray, from the Academy of American Poets, sent updates: there was little hope that Jim would live beyond the winter. Hecht worried for Roger, "who really has no other friend than Jim."[88]

One hilarious incident with Tony and Jim Wright involved an early morning taxi ride the two took following a poetry reading. As the journalist Amy Blumenthal recounts, to keep them entertained on the long ride to the airport, "Hecht intoned from memory the sonorous and grief-stricken lines of Milton's elegy 'Lycidas,'" but "he recited the poem, nearly two hundred lines, in the voice of W.C. Fields!" As Hecht told Philip Hoy:

> It was my habit . . . to allow Fields a few interpolative comments now and again. I remember that after the lines *He must not float upon his watery bier* / *Unwept, and welter to the parching wind,* / *Without the meed of some melodious tear* I would pause and let Fields observe: "That's very sad— that part about the watery beer."[89]

Wright was so tickled that all he could do was mutter, "Thank you."

Wright's decline upset Hecht: "[I] set aside certain poems I had intended to work on . . . to compose—I suppose rather ghoulishly, since the poor man is still alive—a little elegy for him."[90] Not only was the timing off, but he also realized that the tone was as well. His inchoate feelings of loss were still too raw to produce a suitable tribute. The result was a "rhetorical and stylized" poem that "avoids personal emotion." It was a misfire, a throwback to the jeweled Renaissance idiom of *Stones*:

> *Bring in the sweet o' the year!*
> *The golden pomp is come!*
> *Yet all that glad to hear*
> *Its whisper shall be dumb.*
>
> *Its whisper shall be dumb*
> *Yet shall all sound surpass,*
> *Singing within the tomb,*
> The people is as grass.
>
> Behold *Tibullus* lies
> Here burnt, whose small return
> Of ashes, scarce suffice
> To fill a little Urne.[91]

Hecht sent the poem to Robert Fitzgerald, then wisely tucked it in a drawer. His second attempt, in his later style, is fully achieved and deeply poignant:

> *Dear Jim, I call to you across the darkness*
> *Where we are emptied of all our vanities,*
> *Where none of our pleas is answered. Beyond the slosh*
> *And wet, beyond the salt, tumultuous puzzle,*
> *Beyond millions of deaths, loss and injustice,*
> *The derelict shacks, the bare, neglected farms,*
> *May it please these muscular powers to rehearse*
> *Your pain and whispered words, lavish their tears*
> *On all the waste of which they are the image,*
> *Or else by their own terrible energy*
> *To be lifted out of themselves in a ghostly mist,*
> *Gray, neutral, passionless, and modified,*
> *Where even love or joy ceases to matter,*
> *Beyond the human into that giant calm,*
> *The silent granite of another dawn.*[92]

As further tribute to Wright, Hecht placed the poem in *The Kenyon Review*, where he, Roger, and Wright had all gotten their starts.

ELEVEN

"WAITING FOR THINGS TO MEND"[1]

(1981–1992)

> I stood in childhood, waiting for things to mend.
> A useful discipline, perhaps. One that might lead
> To solitary, self-denying work
> That issues in something harmless, like a poem,
> Governed by laws that stand for other laws,
> Both of which aim, through kindred disciplines,
> At the soul's knowledge and habiliment. . . .[2]

1. Murmurs

A change came over Hecht during his years in Rochester: the depressions he routinely suffered were greatly alleviated. From Helen's perspective, they seemed to lift almost entirely. The two were rarely apart and almost always traveled together, whenever Hecht gave readings or attended conferences. Another regular source of his unease, his strained relationship with his parents, was both alleviated and deepened by their deaths. As well as mourning their loss, he may have felt a certain relief. It was never entirely clear to Helen what had caused his feelings for his parents to cool. Certainly, it had not always been this way: Hecht and his parents

had once had a very close relationship. Letters from summer camp, from college, during the war, and afterwards, when traveling in Europe were completely open, loving, good-humored, and high-spirited. He seemed to hold nothing back, writing as frankly as he would to a close friend of his own generation and often soliciting their advice. He took for granted that they would be amused and non-judgmental and that they would share his literary and artistic, musical, and intellectual interests.

His disaffection must have developed slowly, perhaps partly as a consequence of analysis, when he came to terms with early neglect. But they seemed very supportive from his college years on through the trials of his first marriage. And they always welcomed the college and army friends whom he brought home to visit during vacations and leaves.[3]

He came to resent his father's weakness and his mother's emotional distance. "My father in many ways [was] a shackled and enfeebled man,"[4] he told McClatchy in 1988. Melvyn became Hecht's "natural rival," but because he was "handicapped" by nervousness and an overreliance on charm, Hecht felt he needed always to "pull his punches" with him, to downplay his accomplishments. The same went for Roger, who, because of his epilepsy and other chronic ailments, lived as a virtual recluse.

With Hecht's successes arriving one on the heels of the other, this feeling must have grown acute. Increasingly after *Vespers*, Hecht was acknowledged and honored as a leading American poet. In quick succession, between 1981 and 1984, he was appointed to a two-year term as Consultant in Poetry to the Library of Congress, now the US Poet Laureate, and awarded (jointly with John Hollander) the prestigious Bollingen Prize from Yale. Father Tim Healy, president of Georgetown University, who would later woo Hecht away from Rochester, conferred on him an honorary degree. Another doctorate followed from Towson University in Maryland. He traveled to Milan to accept the Librex-Guggenheim Eugenio Montale Award, with a stay in Venice tacked on the end of the trip. Elected as a member of the American Academy and Institute of Arts and Letters in 1970, he joined the board of trustees of the American Academy in Rome and, in the spring of 1971, became a chancellor of the Academy of American Poets in New York. All these honors, as Hecht turned sixty, cemented him as one of the most celebrated poets in the country.

Ever since the mid-sixties, Hecht had kept up a busy reading schedule, applying on several occasions for time off from teaching at Bard, Smith, and, most recently, Rochester, to go on tours in North Carolina,

New England, Michigan, and elsewhere. After he joined the poetry list at Oxford University Press, he read in London, Oxford, and Cambridge, and toured briefly with Anne Sexton (also reading with her at the Poetry Center of the 92nd Street Y). He read at international festivals such as the "Festival of Two Worlds" in Spoleto, where he was photographed by Horst Tappe with Ezra Pound, at "Pound's last public reading."[5] While in Rome for AAR board meetings, he met with friends like Joseph Brodsky and Mark Strand. In Venice, he enjoyed the company of David Kalstone, who was staying at the Palazzo Barbaro, where Henry James wrote *The Wings of the Dove*. These heady excursions were typically followed by "restless and unprofitable" weeks back in Rochester.[6]

He now regularly appeared in the most prominent venues in New York City. Brodsky, whom he'd met at Harvard, introduced him at a "black-tie poetry reading" at the Morgan Library on Madison Avenue. Prior to the event, there was a dinner at the Colony Club, hosted by Academy of American Poets president Lyn Chase, who sent out engraved invitations.[7] In his introduction to the reading, Brodsky called Hecht "the best poet writing in English today."[8] In Upper Manhattan, he appeared with J. D. McClatchy at the Y, an equally celebrated venue, with a devoted following among the New York literati. On these visits to New York, Hecht would lunch with Harry and Kathleen Ford at Lutèce or another elegant East Side restaurant.

If Hecht doubted his place in the ranks of living poets, this was the time of greatest assurances. His was a name to conjure with in American letters, and yet there were roadblocks and betrayals that gave him cause to fret. He was taken aback by Louis Simpson's duplicity, which he only recently discovered and in the most roundabout way. When the poet Henri Coulette proposed Hecht for a series of readings in California, Hecht learned that

> Louis Simpson, representing Berkeley, demurred. He explained that I suffered from a very pronounced speech defect, and that it would be a kindness not to expose me to public terror and humiliation that a poetry reading by me would certainly entail. Since Simpson was the only one of the [organizers] who could claim to know me personally, his

word on the subject was final. Henri explained that when I answered his phone call, he was astonished and pleased to find I could talk without difficulty.[9]

Was Simpson referring to Hecht's "affected"[10] pronunciation, his mid-Atlantic vowels? Was this what Simpson considered a speech impediment? Hecht suspected it was just Simpson being vicious. And for no good reason. This was particularly galling since Hecht had "always thought Simpson a friend."[11] Louis had chaired the jury that awarded him the Pulitzer, and the two had served together on the jury that awarded the prize to Merwin's *The Carrier of Ladders* in 1970. Simpson had asked Hecht for advice in getting reading engagements and for a recommendation to the Guggenheim Foundation, which subsequently awarded him a fellowship. Simpson's possible resentment first reared its head in his portrait of Hecht as Christopher Green in *North of Jamaica* and in their exchange of Magdalene poems, but this was treachery of a new sort.

On the writing front, Hecht was at the height of his career. Helen, too, was thriving, having recently delivered her latest cookbook, *Cold Cuisine*, to Atheneum. Hecht was a happy passive collaborator on the book, having tested with her "over 200 recipes of splendid hot-weather foods": "I can testify to its merits as one who savored every last one of them." No doubt Hecht's parents, had they been living, would have responded positively to his latest accolades, though Hecht was familiar enough with his father's flightiness and his mother's grudging praise to not have expected much. His memories awakened feelings of nostalgia, guilt, affection, and disappointment all at once. The older generation had passed; he was now the eldest. Death took center stage:

> There are certain things that are clearer to me now having to do with age, having to do with the proximity to the conclusion of life. . . . I found myself writing about people who are suffering from terminal diseases, who have had to come explicitly to terms with the idea of their own death. This is not to say this is not a subject that I didn't know about before.[12]

In "The Short End," from *Vespers*, a fire claims the female protagonist. Harry Ford was less than enthusiastic about this squalid tale set in "a hapless rural seat,"[13] but Hecht wanted to balance "Vespers" with "the sleazy instead of the opulent, America instead of Europe, a woman as central instead of a man," and also "to make a character almost entirely unprepossessing, a fat and slovenly drunken woman with garish and vulgar taste, and to try to win the reader's sympathy for her by the time the poem was over."[14] Hecht worried to Brad Leithauser that "nobody seems to like [the poem], though I continue, with slackening confidence, to think it's good."[15] Hecht was relieved when his colleague and friend, Joseph Summers, wrote to praise the poem:

> The epigraph from "The Phoenix and the Turtle" and the "Century of Progress" pillow seem to place it as a shattering account of the death of Love and Constancy, the degradation of even death as well as the landscape and dreams, in the brutal and seductive world of "mid-America" . . . the most repulsive landscape that anyone ever invented (I think it makes Eliot seem relatively jolly—and Browning's not quite so sick as I'd remembered).

Another of Hecht's dramatic voices took shape shortly after *Vespers* came out in 1979. It was based in part on his old friend from Iowa, Flannery O'Connor. Hecht had been reading her letters: "They are absolutely marvelous," he wrote to Brad Leithauser in the winter of 1980.[16] He embraced the challenge of creating a character with "a new credible voice."[17] He had also grown tired of critics associating his speakers too nearly with himself. In part to underscore their fictive quality, Hecht began writing monologues in the voices of women, beginning with "The Grapes" from *Vespers* and now in "The Transparent Man":

> The speaker in "The Transparent Man" dies of leukemia, not of lupus; and I went out of my way not to make this woman a southerner, a writer, or any of the things that Flannery so importantly was. But there was something about Flannery which was unbelievably gallant. It was that gallantry in her I admired and wanted to produce in my poem. It

was the capacity to regard the imminence of your own death and feeble-
ness with a kind of detachment which I thought was quite wonderful.
This was what I was aiming for in that poem.[18]

Over the course of a decade, Hecht lost several friends—the poet
L. E. Sissman, James Wright, and David Kalstone. Each received an
elegy in the final section of *The Transparent Man,* which concludes with
"Murmur" and the line "Through the great crowds: 'Remember you are
mortal.'" In writing these elegies for friends, Hecht was also writing
one for himself: "You have stumbled upon some gross fatality / There in
the void—quite possibly your own," he reflected.[19]

Taken together, the poems in this section, including the title poem,
form a kind of *memento mori.* The most affecting of these, also one of
Hecht's most powerful poems of the Holocaust, is "The Book of Yolek,"
a sestina in which the terminal letters are an acrostic of Yolek's name
(along with the letter *p* which appears on Jewish gravestones as part of
"here lies").[20] Hecht takes as epigraph a line from the Gospel of St. John
in Martin Luther's translation:

> *Wir haben Ein Gesetz,*
> *Und nach dem Gesetz soll er sterben.*
>
> *("We have a law. And by that law he must die.")*

It is the answer given by the Pharisees to Pontius Pilate after he suggests that the charges against Jesus are baseless. The quotation echoes
the state-sanctioned genocide of the Jews during the Holocaust, and he
chose Martin Luther's translation of John's Gospel deliberately. Hecht
was thinking of Luther's violent antisemitism and his assertion in *On the
Jews and Their Lies*:

> we are even at fault in not avenging all this innocent blood of our Lord
> and of the Christians which they shed for three hundred years after the
> destruction of Jerusalem, and the blood of the children they have shed
> since then (which still shines forth from their eyes and their skin). We are
> at fault in not slaying them.[21]

Here Hecht recalls the "blood libel," which he expands on at length as the key for unlocking *The Merchant of Venice*, in his long essay on the subject in *Obbligati*. (A great admirer of Bach's music, it's likely that Hecht first came upon the passage in the libretto to Bach's St. John's Passion, which sets Luther's translation—yet another example of how the highest achievements of European culture, and German culture in particular, contained the seeds that flourished under the Third Reich into the horrors of the 1940s.) The poem ends:

> *Whether on a silent, solitary walk*
> *Or among crowds, far off or safe at home,*
> *You will remember, helplessly, that day,*
> *And the smell of smoke, and the loudspeakers of the camp.*
> *Wherever you are, Yolek will be there, too.*
> *His unuttered name will interrupt your meal.*
>
> *Prepare to receive him in your home some day.*
> *Though they killed him in the camp they sent him to,*
> *He will walk in as you're sitting down to a meal.*[22]

"No one else knows where the mind wanders to," the speaker reflects at one point in the sestina, in which *camp* doubles as a summer camp from childhood and a concentration camp. The speaker's mind is impelled to a summer day in 1942 and a Home for Jewish Children, who are being rounded up for transportation to the death camps: "How often you have thought about that camp, / As though in some strange way you were driven to." Hecht doesn't write that "No one knows where the mind wanders to" but, rather, no one *else* knows. This sense of aloneness, of no one understanding or sharing thoughts of trauma, is consonant with the isolation experienced by traumatized veterans. The other phrase that jumps out is "as though you were driven to." The agency lies not with the speaker, but beyond the speaker, in the power of the memory itself. Yolek may walk into the middle of daily life at any moment. One must set a place for him, as for Elijah at Passover. The first stanza Hecht wrote for "Yolek" began with "The fifth of August, 1942."[23] He moved it down to the third stanza, to allow for a walk in the woods and the memory of summer camp to open the poem with contrasting innocence.

After the war, Hecht "read widely" in Holocaust literature, until eventually he "could no longer separate my anger and revulsion at what I really saw from what I later came to learn."[24] He "came to feel an awed reverence for what the Jews of Europe had undergone, a sense of marvel at the hideousness of what they had been forced to endure. I came to feel that it was important to be worthy of their sacrifices, to justify my survival in the face of their misery and extinction, and slowly I began to shed my shame at being Jewish."[25]

The poem is a concrete memorial in the vein of George Herbert, who relished shape poems and other visual wordplay.[26] The deaths of "The burning, voiceless Jews" continued to tear at Hecht's conscience and imagination: "I think that my experience of the Second World War confirmed my identity as a Jew after having seen what I saw," he told an interviewer a few months after "Yolek" was written in late summer 1981. "And it has made what would otherwise have been a not very strong part of my background become more important to me, and made me identify with the life of the Jews historically and particularly in modern times. And to feel that I must bear witness and be a spokesman."[27] The working titles for the poem underscore its commemorative nature: "The Law," "Memorial," "Via Dolorosa."

Even the most baroque and sprightly poems in the book, the sequence "A Love for Four Voices," has a dark undercurrent. Its four sections, echoing the four-part structure of Haydn's String Quartet in F major, Op. 77, No. 2, compose a kind of masque reminiscent of Auden's "The Sea and the Mirror." The lyrics in the sequence are divided among the four lovers in *A Midsummer Night's Dream*—Lysander, Demetrius, Helena, and Hermia, with the occasional tutti section. The voices are meant to correspond to the two violins, viola, and cello of the standard string quartet. Through its reimagining of the relationships of the four young Athenians, darker shades emerge from comedic byplay. As he wrote to his colleague Joseph Summers, in response to a kind word about the poem, which had grown on Summers with time:

I am particularly pleased by your revisionary assessment of "A Love for Four Voices." Your varying views of the "colors" of the poem perfectly reflect my sense of the curious coloration of Shakespeare's play, which, while undeniably a joyful and indeed gleeful celebration of love, is nevertheless ever so cunningly hedged about with peripheral omens and reminders of the imperfection of life. The mother of the page that Titania and Oberon fight over had died in childbirth; there are raw jokes about venereal diseases; the infidelity of the fairy couple remembers the promiscuity of Theseus and Hippolyta, with whatever suggestion this may provide regarding the future of their marriage. And indeed the very oscillations of the young couples in the course of a single night does not bid fair for the future. The "Pyramus and Thisbe" play is a joke, but a joke with a bitter taste, and there's a good deal throughout the play to remind us of our mortality. It's been my hope in some way to suggest these same glimmerings or penumbras while still keeping the poem essentially light-hearted and cheerful; and your kind comments persuade me that I've succeeded.

Hecht's sweet tooth for elaborate figures is on full display in the poem, possibly the last extended instance of the Hechtian Baroque (or as Jonathan Post has rightly termed it in this case, Rococo). Hecht's sense of Eros, seen in "The Origin of Centaurs" and "The Man Who Married Magdalene," still occupied him in his mid-fifties. "I found myself . . . this past year writing love poems that were very explicitly erotic and that may very well have come from somebody who is in his twenties or early thirties."[28]

It was this stirring mixture of affection and threat, love and bitterness, light and dark, that enlivened his reading of the play:

> All the great Shakespeare tragedies are the richer, the more persuasive, for providing this double vision [of comedy and tragedy]. But it is also there in even so seemingly taintless a comedy as *A Midsummer Night's Dream*, where a possible sentence of death may be imposed on Hermia if she disobeys her father regarding the choice of her husband. And this is only the beginning of fearful omens. The marital hostilities of Oberon and Titania are anything but a cheerful portent for newlyweds. Mention is made in the course of the play of venereal disease and women's death in childbirth [. . .] And the

complications of comedy and tragedy not only end but begin the play.

Any modern critic who blithely assures us that "the play is a comedy, and. . . . nothing fatal, irreparable, or unforgivable will occur to disturb our pleasure and our laughter" has missed all the anxious notes of contingency and conditionality that hedge the play about.[29]

The poem was published in the April 1981 issue of *Poetry* by the editor John Frederick Nims, who had given "The Venetian Vespers" a home a few years earlier.

That spring, Hecht was weighing a new prospect. Earlier in the year, he had received a call from the Library of Congress, letting him know that he had been chosen to succeed Maxine Kumin as the twenty-sixth Consultant in Poetry at the Library, the position later known as US Poet Laureate. The move to Washington was not without its logistical challenges, but after a little back-and-forth, Hecht resolved to make it work, embarking on a path that would lead him away from Rochester for good.

2. "O ye laurels . . ."

When the call came from Associate Librarian John C. Broderick, it was necessarily provisional. Broderick was inquiring on behalf the librarian Daniel J. Boorstin: if Hecht were offered the consultancy, would he be willing and able to accept it? The duties were light enough: a poetry reading in the fall and a lecture in the spring, the term running from October to May. The Consultant also organized a series of public events throughout the year, readings and lectures offered under the auspices of the Gertrude Clarke Whittall Poetry and Literature Fund. As Hecht explained to *American Arts*: "These readings are given in a public auditorium where they are both video and audio taped and become part of the archives." Beyond this, the Consultant "has a diplomatic and ambassadorial responsibility to institutions in the neighborhood which he obliges by attending classes, giving little talks, reading his poems, or being useful in some other way," though these duties were loose and largely undefined.[30]

The real issue was not so much the workload as the relocating. For eight months a year he would need to be in residence at the Library. The appointment was for one term, which was frequently renewed, but Hecht felt that it would be too disruptive, particularly with Evan in grade school, to uproot for just one year. The Library made assurances of an extension at the outset: "By mutual agreement with the Library on this, it was virtually understood in advance that [he] would be [in Washington] for two years, rather than one year on a probability basis, which would possibly, or possibly not, lead to a second year." With the timeframe settled, he negotiated with the dean at Rochester for the time off and a financial arrangement that would make his leave possible. He gave his inaugural reading in Coolidge Auditorium on October 4. Hecht had been there before, recently for a memorial tribute to Archibald MacLeish, and first, in 1971, at the invitation of William Stafford. At the reception after his reading on that occasion, a woman approached him and said, "If you write any more poems in the future, try to make them more cheerful."[31] When he told this story at his first reading as Laureate, the audience roared with laughter.

Hecht intentionally chose a "more benign" program for his debut as Consultant. His characteristic wit was on full display in poems for friends—"Recyclings" (later retitled "Antapodosis") for Mona Van Duyn and Jarvis Thurston and "House Sparrows" for Joe and U.T. Summers, its "very modest and humble" subjects inspired by their Christmas gift of a guide to birds of the Northeast. Hecht had undergone a sea change in his life and work since his reading in 1971. The melancholy in the poems had not lessened, but now it was tempered with something like joy—a strange and unfamiliar note. He marveled at his good fortune, for which he was hugely grateful, almost superstitiously so. The ameliorating power of love in "A Birthday Poem" and measured public tones of "The Cost," with which he concluded the reading, become even more striking, set against the backdrop of historical events in the poem: horrific battles, the Atomic Bomb, "Jews / Gone down in blood," and My Lai.[32] These poems were written before Hecht took up the Consultantship, but their outward gaze on current and historical events harmonized with his increasingly "public" role.

Hecht donned his new robes with modesty and a certain gravitas. When asked by the Library *Newsletter* if poets were "the unacknowledged legislators of the world," he replied, "I remember discussing this matter with Allen Tate, who was once Consultant in Poetry of the Library of Congress, and Allen, who was a very witty man, said that the statement is perfectly true if enough emphasis is put upon the word 'unacknowledged.'" Hecht was slightly wary of the institutional aspect of his role. For Hecht, a "consultancy" was better than a "laureateship": "For one thing, the laureateship [was at that time] for life. England, while very literate, is also comparatively small, whereas this is an enormous country with many cultures, both regional and ethnic. A great many of these might be represented if the term of each consultancy remains brief. With a laureateship, however, if some wretched, long-lived person like Wordsworth gets in, he can run through administration after administration."[33]

His office looked out over the Capitol, a view commemorated in "View of the Capitol from the Library of Congress" by Elizabeth Bishop during her tenure there in 1949–50. "It's the best view in town,"[34] Hecht told a reporter from *The New York Times*. Though Hecht's own poems shared qualities with those of Auden and Philip Larkin (the English poet "whose style mine most resembles"),[35] he touted the domestic product. "We are no longer in the cultural shadow of England," he told the *Times*. Modern American poetry has been "extraordinarily rich and diverse and accomplished, in dramatic comparison with the 19th Century."[36] Looking out from that office across The Mall to the Washington Monument, he thought of the friends and colleagues who had come before him: Bishop, Tate (1943–44), Lowell (1947–48), William Meredith (1978–80), and others he had known over the years.

Another change, this time in appearance, coincided with Hecht's public duties. As a young man, Hecht was, at times, a fastidious dresser, like his father. But in the woolly 1970s it was not the fashion for a poet to be too polished. At Rochester, Hecht had sported an open collar and a mop of unruly graying hair. In Washington, he traded his tweeds for a smart double-breasted blue blazer with a tasteful pocket square. He came to prefer a natty bow tie to the workaday four-in-hand. He grew back his beard, pointed and "aristocratic." In private, of course, he was typically casual, though elegantly so. Helen's studied eye for style may have had some influence. He and Helen found a convenient place to rent in Chevy Chase: "A modest brick colonial style, and perfect for us for the two years, at 110 East Lennox Street." According to Helen, they "looked at some furnished houses, but I knew I couldn't stand it. They were all so awful. So, we rented unfurnished and shipped a few things we could spare from Rochester and just bought the rest. It was a small house so it wasn't a big financial outlay."

From the lectern at the Library, he spoke with warmth and authority, introducing events and readings. He delivered two lectures of his own—on Robert Lowell and the Pathetic Fallacy—both of which were published by the Library as pamphlets and became centerpieces of Hecht's first essay collection, *Obbligati*, published shortly after his term concluded. "The Pathetic Fallacy," which leads off the collection, became a touchstone of Hecht's aesthetic, of his ability to map deep feeling and personal experience onto the natural world: commenting on Psalm 19, he argues that "This eloquence of the physical universe, this demonstration on the part of the natural world, amounts to a revelation to all who are not blind and deaf. . . . The world as holy cipher and mute articulator can be found not only in medieval texts and Shakespeare but in those emblematic or symbolic poems by Herbert and Donne and Herrick that are among the greatest achievements of their age."[37] The following essay in *Obbligati*, on Auden's "In Praise of Limestone," expands on this notion of the *paysage moralisé*, a "conceit" that "fascinated him throughout his career": "It presents to us a climate, and, by extension, its characteristic landscape, which corresponds to, or even induces, certain moral qualities of human behavior, personality and character traits."[38] John Gross, reviewing *Obbligati* for *The New York Times*, praised Hecht's work as a critic ("not only stimulating but beautifully written")[39] and perceives the personal stakes that underlie the essays: "His essays reflect many of his own interests as a poet, and something of his poetic temper. He relishes formal elegance, but only when it is sustained by authentic emotion." Gross singles out Hecht's take on Auden: "He is unashamed, too, in his taste for the baroque. One of the few tetchy moments in *Obbligati* is when the dismissive comments of an architectural historian provoke him into speaking up on behalf of the Spanish Steps in Rome, with their 18th-century 'illusion of freedom.' It occurs in the course of an account of W. H. Auden's 'In Praise of Limestone,' a meditative poem on the interplay between nature and culture that he is particularly well qualified to expound."

The title of the book "refers to a complex set of obligations undertaken by these essays—obligations to the works and poets they deal with." Hecht was also thinking of the function of criticism, likening it to "a musical obbligato; that is, a counterpart that must constantly strive to move in strict harmony with and intellectual counterpoint to its subject."[40] The longest essay in the collection, *"The Merchant of Venice*: A Venture in Hermeneutics,"* expresses a complex response to Shakespeare's great play of love, hate, and money. Getting singled out in grade school for being of Shylock's "race and religion" was still vivid in Hecht's mind.[41] In the essay, he makes it clear that it is not Shakespeare he is taking issue with: "I am not claiming that Shakespeare wrote this play in order to express private biases and bigotries of his own. The ideas in this drama were popular, current, much in the air of the times. . . ."[42] Hecht delves deeply into the history of Judaism and antisemitism, and thanks his colleague at U of R Rabbi Abraham Karp for his "generous and valuable advice and encouragement." Despite many attempts to place the essay in periodicals, its sheer length and quite possibly its querulous tone put editors off. Hecht claimed that his take on the play, which had never been fully understood, was "apodictic," that's to say irrefutable and definitive. The force of his conviction on this point lends the essay an obsessive quality: for Hecht, the biases and bigotries of the play had become intensely personal.

During his stints in DC, between which the Hechts would retreat to their more spacious house in Rochester for summers and the Christmas holiday, he was approached by Father Timothy Healy, the president of Georgetown, about making a permanent move to Washington. "That wonderful, admirable man . . . made honorable overtures to me by way of trying to persuade me to take up teaching duties at his university," Hecht recalled with pleasure.[43] The two had met in Rochester, when Healy led a group of academics who were reviewing the U of R for the purposes of accreditation, and again when Healy conferred an honorary doctorate on Hecht the year before his first term as Laureate: "From the first we got on famously. He loved poetry and was devoted to Donne."[44] Hecht was keen to escape the Rochester winters, which were literally painful because of his frostbite. Then there was the "undeniable lure of the National Gallery of Art, the Phillips Collection, the Library of Congress, the Folger Shakespeare Library, too many museums to mention, the beautifully landscaped public places, the dandy restaurants (Rochester had virtually none) which grew dandier and more numerous with time, and the comparatively easy accessibility to New York, the shuttle flight."[45]

Helen recalled it this way:

Tim Healy had studied under Dame Helen Gardner at Oxford, and she was the one who told him about Tony's poetry. He was a very literary man and taught English literature while he was still president of Georgetown. He would always have students up to his office and then he would teach the class there.

Tim at one point said to Tony, "You know, if we could ever get you to Georgetown, you'd be really welcome there." Tony always said I'm very happily situated in Rochester and never considered it seriously. Those were the days when one got lots of offers in the academic world from different universities. Then we came [to Washington], and after a year at the library, we both looked at each other because it made us miss New York terribly. We remembered what being in a real city was like. Before then we'd been focused on our tiny family so we never gave it another thought. By our second year at the library, Tony spoke to Tim (we saw a lot of him while we were here) and said I'm willing to talk terms. Although Tim wanted the English department to approve and appoint him, he was made a university professor. He arranged for Georgetown to have the mortgage on the house. He thought it would be easier to find a house before we left for Rochester, so we found one in the spring.[46]

The house, where Hecht remained for the rest of his life, was at 4256 Nebraska Avenue, NW, in Tenleytown, not far from the National Cathedral. It was purchased for $375,000 in 1984, and the Hechts moved in the following year (after a final year of teaching in Rochester). The Rochester house sold for $142,000, so there was a considerable difference to make up in the mortgage. "There was no possibility of buying the house out-right," Helen explained.[47]

During his tenure at the Library, he arranged a celebration of the Academy of American Poets over two evenings with fourteen poets, in-cluding six former consultants, who read to packed audiences in Coolidge Auditorium. He hosted appearances by Shirley Hazzard, Joseph Brodsky, Bernard Malamud, Richard Ellmann, Reed Whittemore, and Northrop Frye. At the end of his second term, Hecht's good friend Robert Fitz-gerald was appointed as his successor at the Library, but by late summer Fitzgerald was seriously ill and unable to assume his duties. Whittemore, a former consultant, became interim laureate. Hecht began teaching at Georgetown in the fall of 1985, and kept up a full reading schedule. Even with his duties at the Library behind him, it was a busy time. Later that year, he served as a reader of grant applications for the National Endow-ment for the Arts, on a committee with Robert Hass, Robert Creeley, and Larry Levis, demotic and experimental poets of a very different stripe than his: "I can't say I feel altogether at home in this crowd,"[48] he confided to his publisher.

Hecht's public persona as Laureate was sober and erudite. To Hass and Levis, both younger by a generation, Hecht may have appeared stodgy. With friends, however, he cut a very different figure. He loved to laugh and drink. "He was a wild man in those days," Nicholas Chris-topher recounts. "He'd have his martinis. At the Algonquin, I remember having two martinis with him, and we went and had dinner somewhere nearby. He said, 'Well, we'll have a third, and then we can really talk.' . . . I never thought of him as formal, though he'd have a bow tie on, and he had that voice. To me that was his natural voice."

The house on Nebraska Avenue was an impressive, columned af-fair, with comfortable guest rooms on the third floor. Brad Leithauser's brother, Mark, an artist and curator at the National Gallery, and his wife, Mary Bryan (known as Bryan), were among the Hechts' closest friends in their new city. Poets visiting the area would come to stay, and the Hechts' guest book records many such happy visits from James Merrill and his then partner, Peter Hooten; Mona Van Duyn and her husband, Jarvis Thurston; Derek Walcott; and Joseph Brodsky, of whom Hecht was

especially fond. They had become good friends while Hecht was working on a number of translations of Brodsky's poems, two of his longer
poems—"Cape Cod Lullaby" and "Lagoon"—appearing at the end of
Vespers. Hecht admired his work and trusted his literary taste and like-
minded sensibility. He kept a photo of Brodsky in his study, next to Saul
Bellow and Derek Walcott.

It was particularly distressing, then, when Brodsky didn't care for one
of Hecht's new monologues. Brodsky had solicited a poem by Hecht for
possible inclusion in a pamphlet he was assembling, but when Hecht sent
"See Naples and Die," about a marriage in turmoil, Brodsky demurred.
He tried to soften the blow by claiming that any advice from him about
Hecht's poem would be like the "Russian proverb about eggs trying to
teach the hen." But, except for the fourth section, the poem seemed to
him to be "seriously flawed. It meanders and promises far more than
it delivers . . . the verse has escaped the narrative." Brodsky continued:
"The story itself, it must be said, doesn't warrant the length it has been
put to," and he advised Hecht to "ditch this piece altogether" [MARBL].
Other friends like J. D. McClatchy and Mary Jo Salter liked the poem, and
Harold Bloom later called it "a major American elegy for one's self, as figured in the emblem of one's earlier marriage."[49] Hecht wrote to Brodsky
to defend and explain the deeper themes behind the piece, at once raw
and personal: "My poem is intended as a *commentary* on the events in *Genesis*: the temptation, the fall, and the expulsion. It is also a commentary
on the epigraph from Simone Weil. It is mainly, however, an account of
the visions of paradise and of damnation that are glimpsed in the course
of mundane affairs. The speaker is one of the damned; and one who has
failed to understand what has happened to him."

Brodsky's subsequent apology helped to redeem the painful exchange
somewhat and salvage the friendship. Brodsky deeply admired Hecht's
poems, and made no secret of his admiration, stating in his *Paris Review*
interview from 1982 that "if I were born [in the US] I would end up with
qualities similar to Hecht's. One thing I would like to be is as perfect as
Hecht and Wilbur are. There should be something else, I presume, of my
own, but insofar as the craftsmanship is concerned one couldn't wish for
more."[50] But Hecht was deeply rattled by his take on "See Naples and Die."

Summer trips to Italy became more frequent as Hecht approached retirement. He felt elated there, pleased to be free of his academic duties. It's no surprise that these trips inspired new poems, such as "Meditation," a rumination on Old Master paintings: "'Meditation' was written in the garden of the Hotel Cipriani in Asolo in northern Italy, where I visited with my family just after a stay in Venice. The Venetian sojourn had of course involved going to the Accademia to see paintings, and again I was struck by the stunning beauty and serenity of those great altar pieces by Bellini and Carpaccio and Cima da Conegliano."[51] Hecht included "Meditation" in the anthology *Ecstatic Occasions, Expedient Forms: 65 Leading Poets Select and Comment on Their Poems*, edited by the poet David Lehman. Italy had been the site of ecstatic occasions for Hecht, ever since the icy vision of "A Hill," and it would continue to crop up in his late poems, including those that he wrote in the last years of his life.

Hecht was close to completing *The Transparent Man,* which would be eleven years in the making by the time it appeared (along with Hecht's *Collected Earlier Poems*) in 1990. In the meantime, he took on a side project, a selected volume of George Herbert's poems in The Essential Poets Series from Ecco Press. Auden had edited a selection of Herbert in the 1970s, and the Welsh-born cleric had come to mean a great deal to Hecht and his work. He composed a brief introduction, but clearly he had more to say on the subject: "My little edition of Herbert will be out, they tell me, in December. I hope that as time goes on the publishers will allow me to extend my notes on the poems considerably. For the present, the only thing that seems at all original is a gentle indication of Herbert's debt to Donne, often in the form of taking Donne's secular love poems and 'converting' their conventions, and even their metaphors, to pious ones."[52]

From Herbert, Hecht borrowed a stanza from *The Temple* for his Judaic liturgical poem, "Rites and Ceremonies," and the more recent "Gladness of the Best" refers directly to Herbert and his house in Bemerton. Another of Hecht's occasional poems, "Gladness" was written

for a friend of mine who became a rector of a church in New York City. He's now the Episcopal Bishop of Missouri; his name is Hays Rockwell. For his installation as the rector of St. James Church in New York I wanted to write a poem. As a student at Oxford, he'd written a thesis

on George Herbert, and he and I both greatly admired Herbert. So, I
wanted to write him a Herbertian poem, which meant that it was going
to be in fancy metaphysical stanzas, and be direct, on the other hand,
and yet elaborately conceited too, as sometimes Herbert is.[53]

As *The Transparent Man* neared completion, Hecht's output slowed
again to a trickle. "As for my own work," he wrote to Jacky Simms, Jon
Stallworthy's successor as poetry editor at Oxford University Press, "I
confess with humiliation to a blockage that has gone on, alas, far too
long, and which I am struggling to overcome."[54] This difficulty came at
an inconvenient time: "I have something like two thirds of a new book in
hand," he explained to his English publisher, "and need to write the final
third before turning it in. But I have been procrastinating and have been
writing prose (mainly criticism) instead."[55]

For *The New York Review of Books* he reviewed A. L. Rowse's *The Poet
Auden: A Personal Memoir*. At the same time he was putting the finishing
touches on his lengthy *Paris Review* interview, conducted by J. D. McClatchy,
and excavating some of the background material of *The Waste Land* for a
conference in St. Louis where he was giving a paper. All this meant that he
clearly wouldn't "get much done in the way of poetry this summer, and I
normally can't write any during the teaching year." He took the spring term
off from teaching, in hopes of finishing the book of poems. He looked
forward less and less to teaching, and his students at Georgetown were
something of a disappointment. (As an example of their poor writing, he
included this excerpt in his commonplace book: "The concern which is
held about the briefness of this life tends to be doing so because of their
focus on its end.")[56] With the exception of Elias Mengel he made no friends
on the faculty to rival the strong bonds and collegiality that he enjoyed in
Rochester. By the spring of 1989, he wrote to Brad Leithauser that he was
"just about unshackled and freed from academic bondage for the year."[57]

In the fall of 1989, he wrote a long letter to Roger with the latest
news, including his departure from his publisher Atheneum and his move
with Harry Ford to a new house:

Knopf, which is to be my new publisher, will bring out two books of
mine, both in May. One will be the new book of poems, to be titled *The*

Transparent Man. The other will be a collection of my earlier books published by Atheneum, and now out of print: *The Hard Hours, Millions of
Strange Shadows*, and *The Venetian Vespers*, all gathered into one volume.
I'm very pleased and heartened by this. The new book, though it was six
years in the making (rather speedy for one with my track record) seems
to me decidedly more "shapely" than any of my others, with clear formal resonances despite a wide variety of tone, setting, and material. But
experience has taught me that such considerations are never noticed by
reviewers, and all the plotting and planning we take such pains with are
largely a waste of time.[58]

I am back at teaching again this fall, and I am now old enough to
feel I can say without embarrassment that the charm of it has begun to
pall. . . . Lots of men have retired by my age, but I am determined to see
Evan through college before I let my family slip back to a much-reduced
income.[59]

But this past year, as regards income, I was very lucky, and won three
prizes that carried much more money than éclat. The result of this is
that we have been able to expand what had been a ridiculously small
and constricting kitchen by knocking down a wall that gave on our back
lawn, and adding a capacious glass-walled-and-ceilinged conservatory.[60]

Hecht's letter to Roger was prompted by news of Roger's ill health.
After the death of their parents, Roger relied on a caregiver, Mary Carr,
who "looked after him daily during the last years of his life."[61] Then, quite
suddenly, while sitting in the bath, Roger died of a heart attack on March
5. Hecht was floored: "It was shock more than anything else that so
stirred me. I knew at once that the loss was almost entirely symbolic,
though the knowledge did not in the least diminish my Gordian knot
of rage, guilt, and other violent emotions that I had thought pretty well
buried for good."[62]

In a letter to Nicholas Christopher, he admitted to being in "very low
spirits just now. Earlier this month my brother, who was nearly three
years younger than I, died very suddenly and unexpectedly. His death has
shaken me severely."[63] A memorial event was held at the New York Society
for Ethical Culture at the end of April. Clearing out Roger's apartment
was upsetting as well. The apartment smelled of old books, which were

scattered everywhere. It appeared as if it had been ransacked (by whom wasn't clear), and Hecht worried that it might have been a robbery:

> I have been unable to forget the vivid sense of shock, and of violation, I felt at seeing the manifestly *vandalized* condition of Roger's apartment. I don't know whether you realize that, as a boy, and later in my youth, I lived there myself, sharing what was to become Roger's study with him as a double bedroom. Cabinet doors ripped from their hinges, all the family silver (much of it with family monograms) vanished beyond trace, even the sheets and the linens disposed of—all this fills me with serious doubts. For Roger would not have disposed of any of these things on his own initiative. . . .[64]

Hecht spoke warmly of Roger at his memorial in April, while acknowledging the complications of their relationship over the years:

> There are some of you here who saw more of Roger and knew him better than I did during his last years. Jobs and a geographical destiny, which was not always to my liking, kept us apart from one another. And yet we were brothers, the children of the same parents and our closeness was of long standing and of greater intimacy than anyone can guess at, though there are few outward and visible signs of it.
>
> For example, we are both poets . . . a bond so close as to trouble both of us from time to time. But however troubling, the closeness, the sense of intimate identification, remained. . . . I was for years the helpless witness to those afflictions and remember grasping his tongue in my hand as he lay rigid on a street in Venice, attempting to prevent him from further harming himself during a seizure of epilepsy. And that affliction was not his only one. There were problems with his eyes, his legs, his right hand. All these he met with stoical reserve, and often with a truly gallant cheerfulness. In fact, cheerfulness, strange as the circumstances make it seem, was one of his strongest and most endearing characteristics.[65]

Hecht knew firsthand how brave his brother had always been in the face of his many infirmities. He admired and loved him for it.

There were further losses that year: Irma Brandeis died, and Howard

Nemerov was in the hospital for surgery. It seemed to Hecht that, at sixty-seven, he had reached the age where such news arrived with increasing frequency. Hecht kept up a number of regular correspondences. He exchanged letters frequently with the novelist and *New Yorker* fiction editor William Maxwell, who expressed enormous admiration for Hecht's poems. Maxwell wrote to Hecht that "Vespers" was one of the finest poems of the twentieth century. Theirs was one of the most prolific correspondences of Hecht's life, running to hundreds of letters. (His correspondence with William MacDonald was its only rival.) Hecht, in turn, admired Maxwell's sharp eye for painterly detail and his ability to describe "the flayed landscape of the western prairie" in *Time Will Darken It* (1948) and elsewhere. "There is an amplitude of sympathy" in Maxwell's fiction that Hecht thought "almost Russian. He presents few characters unworthy of sympathy."[66] Maxwell was equally sympathetic in his letters and in person, and they enjoyed seeing each other at the Academy of Arts and Letters. It was through Maxwell, in 1988, that Hecht learned of the death of his former lover Natacha Stewart, who was living in Gstaad; the "news . . . is indeed haunting," Hecht replied, in a state of shock.[67]

Hecht had also stayed in close touch with Sandy McClatchy after their work together on Hecht's *Paris Review* Writers at Work Interview. McClatchy was a brilliant reader of Hecht's poems and one of his greatest champions. His own poems showed an affinity with Hecht's work and with Merrill's, and he was their most talented protégé. (Hecht later asked McClatchy, an editor as well as poet and librettist, to serve as his literary executor.) He kept up with former students such as the poets Brad Leithauser and Mary Jo Salter, Jonathan Post, Nicholas Christopher, and David Mason, whose dissertation on W. H. Auden's long poems he helped supervise at Rochester. Leithauser, in particular, had become a confidant, responding thoughtfully and sympathetically to Hecht's "panic" over Brodsky's rejection of his Naples poem. Leithauser's praise for the poem (along with encouragement he'd received from Ford and Merrill) had talked him down from the emotional ledge he found himself on after Roger's death: "Joseph's letter should doubtless not have had so disturbing an effect, and probably wouldn't have had, but for the fact that I have been deeply distressed by the death (at first from unknown causes, and, as it was finally determined, a heart attack) of my only and younger brother, Roger, in early March. Merely because he was younger, I had always expected him to survive me."[68]

In September 1990, one of Hecht's longest friendships, with the historian of Roman architecture William MacDonald, abruptly ended. Their outpouring of raucous letters had grown into a friendly competition, each attempting to outdo the other with elaborate letterheads obtained for the purpose. Since their first meeting at the Academy in Rome in the fifties, they had remained close as they raised families and made their separate ways as academics. At dinner at the Hechts' one night in Washington the conversation came around to discussing Trajan's Column, erected in Rome around AD 113. Roman architecture, MacDonald's specialty, was a subject in which Hecht, too, took a great interest. Hecht had made the column, and its depiction of the Dacian Wars, a centerpiece of his poem "The Cost." Hecht had sent the typescript to MacDonald for comment prior to its publication in *Horizon* in 1971. MacDonald now took the occasion to correct Hecht's poem, which ends with a crushing irony: the Dacian Wars' "fifteen-year campaign / Won seven years of peace." In fact, the wars had lasted only a couple of years, a historical fact that made a nonsense out of Hecht's argument in the poem. According to Helen, Hecht had asked MacDonald to check the poem's accuracy. When asked why he hadn't corrected the error before it was collected in *Millions of Strange Shadows* in 1977, MacDonald quibbled that it was not a historical study but "only" a poem with a looser set of standards for factuality. This enraged and disappointed Hecht, who felt both betrayed and condescended to.

The friendship, one of Hecht's longest and closest, lapsed into silence the next day, after an acrimonious phone call between the two. For years, the two had challenged and amused each other with long, lively letters, composed under wacky pseudonyms: for MacDonald, "Orville Rong," "Tigellinus," "Onopodius of Nicea," etc.; for Hecht, "Billy Graham, the Chilly-Assed Chiliast," "Epictetus," "Timon of Akron," etc. The letters arrived on ornately decorated stationery filched from places like "New Omayad Hotel," "The Byzantine Institute, Inc.," "The Helmsley Palace," and postcards from around the world. They exchanged satires of erudition that suggested true erudition, outdoing each other in outrageous invention.

Hecht felt embarrassed after MacDonald's correction. "The Cost" was a poem of great seriousness, in its anti-war theme. As a more graphic and immediate caution against war, "The Deodand" considers the mutilation of a French Legionnaire:

> *In the final months of the Algerian war*
> *They captured a very young French Legionnaire.*
> *They shaved his head, decked him in a blond wig,*
> *Carmined his lips grotesquely, fitted him out*
> *With long, theatrical false eyelashes*
> *And a bright, loose-fitting shirt of calico,*
> *And cut off the fingers of both hands.*
> *He had to eat from a fork held by his captors.*[69]

MacDonald's irritation at Hecht's accusation was so strong that, years later, when Hecht attempted a reconciliation, he was met with a chilly reply from MacDonald. MacDonald had been dismissive of Hecht before.[70] Helen recalled a luncheon that included MacDonald, the former director of the Academy in Rome Laurance Roberts, his wife, Isabel, and others. When the subject of fractals, which was then in the news, came up, Hecht brightened, and asked what it entailed, having heard about it before. MacDonald replied, "It's nothing you would understand." It's possible to imagine that beneath the hauteur, MacDonald was jealous on some level of Hecht's successes as a writer. In any case, their permanent rift left Hecht feeling angry and low.

Some good news early in the new year bolstered his spirits. The Pulitzer committee selected *The Transparent Man* as a finalist, awarding the prize ultimately to Hecht's press-mate at Knopf, Mona Van Duyn, for *Near Changes*. Pleased to be nominated, Hecht was becoming rather philosophical about prizes: "Praise doesn't mean a thing," he told one interviewer. "You've only to win an award to know how empty it is. I mean this. The best thing to hope for as a writer is to win the approval of friends you respect."[71] Meanwhile, he had made no real strides toward a new collection, devoting himself to criticism, and in particular to a lengthy study of the poetry of W. H. Auden. He had planned it as a "shortish book,"[72] but, as he wrote to Brodsky, a fellow admirer, "I have so much to say I'm almost scared of the sheer abundance."[73] The 700-page manuscript, begun in May 1990, came together with lightning speed; in July of the following year he wrote to David Mason to say that he had completed a draft. He then took the manuscript with him that summer to Venice and Asolo to complete some needed revisions, and by the last day of the year the book was done.

Dedicated to Father Healy, who had brought him to Georgetown, and to Roger's memory, *The Hidden Law* is Hecht's most sustained work of criticism by far. His connection to Auden was both literary and personal. The book acknowledges Hecht's long-standing debt to the older poet as both a stylistic and moral example: "Both in his writing and in my acquaintance with him, one of the things that most impressed me about him was his sense that perhaps the most common everyday run-of-the-mill sin of modern people is their tremendous preoccupation with themselves, their utter egotism. He wrote a description of prayer: 'Prayer is our absolute undivided attention to something other than ourselves.'"[74] Hecht proceeds book by book through Auden's work up through *The Shield of Achilles* (1955).

While working on the book, he took on a further prose assignment, a series of lectures on poetry and the arts for The A. W. Mellon Lectures in the Fine Arts at the National Gallery of Art in Washington. The series was founded "to bring to the people of the United States the results of the best contemporary thought and scholarship bearing upon the subject of the Fine Arts."[75] Poetry was again placed on the back burner, with vacations and leaves of absence devoted to the Auden book and Mellon Lectures; "In both cases, they took up time I might otherwise have tried to use for poems. I can't do both kinds of work at the same time."[76] Taken together, these two books of "laws," along with "The Book of Yolek" (originally titled "The Law," and echoed by the epigraph from John "We have a law and by this law he must die"), point to Hecht's questioning of the principles, both just and unjust, that circumscribe earthly existence.

That summer he and Helen decamped during their home renovation for two weeks on the Cumberland Plateau in Tennessee for the annual Sewanee Writers Conference. For several summers, Hecht became a member of the conference faculty at the University of the South, co-teaching workshops with Mary Jo Salter and others. Hecht had always avoided teaching workshops, preferring instead to lecture on Shakespeare and modern poets such as Yeats and Auden. As congenial as the surroundings were at Sewanee, he was reminded of his aversion to the workshop format: to Dave Mason he confided that "I detest giving courses of this kind, and no longer give them at Georgetown or anywhere else."[77] He found it too hard-going to wade through the lackluster verse of most students.

The Mellon Lectures ran on five consecutive Sunday afternoons at the National Gallery, beginning in October and ending in mid-November. Hecht found the audience attentive and appreciative. He wrote to B. H. Fairchild, another younger poet he had championed, that he was "rather sorry they [were] over. I enjoyed myself both in preparing [and] delivering them. . . . They were a very pleasant thing to look forward to every Sunday afternoon for a month and a half. They kept me quite cheerful through that term."[78] After term was another matter. The reviews of the lectures, published as *On the Laws of the Poetic Art,* were decidedly mixed. A positive notice in *The Sewanee Review* was outweighed in Hecht's mind by a scathing review in *Kirkus*: "It's difficult to imagine these academically complex sentences and paragraphs were ever read aloud. . . . too often poetry seems the farthest thing from the writer's mind." The reviewer declared the lectures full of "dry analysis reminiscent of high school English classes."[79] This came on the heels of a prominent pan of *The Hidden Law*: "I still haven't wholly recovered from the review of my Auden book that was published in *The New York Times Book Review*." This review, "written by one Emily Eakin in 316 meanly chosen words," found the book marred by "eccentric interpretations and lackluster style."

He let Fairchild know that the fall would be his next-to-last term of teaching before retirement. The policy at Georgetown enforced retirement at seventy. Hecht was concerned about the loss of income, but he welcomed his departure from the classroom. It was time. He was ready. He had had the sense in the last few years of teaching's diminishing returns. He took on more prose projects, such as an introduction to the Cambridge edition of Shakespeare's Sonnets, and signed on as the poetry columnist of *The Wilson Quarterly*. He also hoped to begin a new book of poems, though he had yet to find a clear way forward. Then, out of the blue, he heard from his old friend Leonard Baskin, who had a new collaboration in mind, the first of several, as it turned out. An assignment from Baskin was one of the surest cures for writer's block, and most of the poems in Hecht's final two collections were written with Leonard in mind.

TWELVE

PRESUMPTIONS
(1993–1998)

Among these holiday throngs, a passer-by,
Mute, unremarked, insouciant, saunter I . . .[1]

1. Leaving Academe

Roger's sudden death affected Hecht more than he'd anticipated. As he expressed in his eulogy, he and his brother had been extremely close on a level that was not easily apparent to outsiders. Hecht may well have felt at times that Roger was shadowing him too nearly, copying him in effect, but, if so, he never confronted him with it. The New York apartment, where the boys had shared a bedroom, was not just empty now; it was a shambles. The family housekeeper had kept things in order while Roger was alive, but the apartment had been broken into and looted after his death. The collection of family books, many of them first editions, had been sold off by Roger (including books that Hecht had wished to keep), compounding the sense of effacement: the record of his early life had dwindled to a pile of photo albums and some boxes of letters home from summer camp, the war, and his first years in Italy.[2]

Quietly, perhaps without even fully acknowledging it himself, he was in mourning. Characteristically stoic, he made no public shows of grief; it was not his way and he took no comfort from such displays. To Francine du Plessix Gray he wrote that he had no "need for the comforts of ritual grieving for others: there have been too many, beginning well before my front-line combat infantry service in WWII. I have felt no inclination to police my grief, or to formalize it though public acts of piety. But this does not mean any less respect for the rituals of mourning. . . ."[3] It was his habit to keep his sorrows to himself.

Hecht thought of Helen and Evan, now in his early twenties. As his career in the classroom wound down, he worried about making ends meet on "a fixed retirement income during an on-going inflation and providing for Helen and Evan as well."[4] As for the teaching itself, he had become disillusioned with the students at Georgetown. He painted a grim picture of the climate on The Hilltop, as it was called:

> I didn't used to feel so resentful of my academic work, but I confess that my students at Georgetown have been a serious disappointment. At first, I was unwilling to admit this, even to myself, though I could see that I was being more or less forced to inflate my grades over the sort I used to give at Rochester. But things have not only not improved—they seem to have worsened. And this term in my Shakespeare class of 41 students there were fifteen F's. There are to be sure a few good ones, but not enough to make blithe the heart.[5]

And it wasn't just the students who fueled his disappointment: "All things considered, the students were better than my colleagues. There were only two fellow teachers in the English department that I held in esteem and affection, and they both died well before they were due to retire."[6] To make matters even worse, his hearing had begun noticeably to deteriorate, and he "found it increasingly difficult to hear students when they asked questions. It was humiliating to have to ask them to repeat what they had just asked, both for them and for me."[7] As a result of all these factors combined, when the time came, Hecht was "able to face retirement with equanimity."[8] Come May, he hung up his mortar board and gown "with joy in my heart and glad cries on my lips,"[9] finally free of the "demanding, and sometimes, demeaning, routine" of academic life.[10]

Despite the harsh review of *The Hidden Law* in *The New York Times*, from which he had not "wholly recovered," his book was into a second printing and was selected for a Readers' Subscription Choice that fall. Working now on his lengthy introduction to a volume of Shakespeare's Sonnets, he had never written prose at such a clip, whole volumes as well as occasional essays that would be collected later, but there was a trade-off. It had been several years since *The Transparent Man* was published, and he had written virtually no poems since. If it wasn't writer's block outright, then no inspiration or impulse toward poetry pushed back against the sea of prose. Fortunately, a new collaboration with Baskin, *The Presumptions of Death*, which as usual paired images and verse, had him working on poems again and working quickly and well.

Which came first, the poems or the pictures? Langdon Hammer asked him. "In this particular case, the pictures," Hecht explained:

> It was Leonard who proposed the whole project: title, topics, every-thing. . . . In the first part Death is represented as speaking *in propria persona,* engaged in "sauntering about," playing Peek-a-Boo, "riding into town," being hypocritical or demure. In the second part he "adopts" the persona or voice of various different people, including an Oxford don, a scholar, [a whore], a justice, a knight, an archbishop, a Mexican revolutionary, a Punchinello, film director, and circus barker. There are twenty-two in all.[11]

Hecht's text provides a seamless counterpoint to the images. Both are witty, scathing, melancholy, stark, elaborate, whimsical, and haunting by turns. Baskin urged Hecht to "write what gets set off in you, long or short, serious or humorous, pedantry or doggerel. I entirely trust you. More than that, I entreat you to be your brilliant poetic self."[12] *Presumptions* was more collaborative than what Hecht had told Hammer. In the end, some of Baskin's suggested titles fell by the wayside (a queen, a fat financier), and Hecht added several of his own: death as analyst/patient, as Cain, as ghost of a lover, though not all of them made the final cut. Hecht and Baskin elaborated on older models, which evolved out of Guy Marchant's *Danse macabre* of 1485. Baskin called it his "mixed-up Toten-tantz." The sequence, Hecht wrote to Daniel Albright, is

> a rather deliberate variation on the medieval "Dance of Death." Accord-ing to the traditional formula, Death invites persons of all ranks, ages and fortunes to dance with him—Schubert, Ransom, and Mussorgsky are all in this line. The idea of the "Dance," I gather, arose out of the 14th-century plague of death from ergot poisoning, in which the victims went into violent seizures and epileptic fits (resembling some sort of wild dance) just before death. In the traditional version, Death remains

the same indomitable figure and only his victims vary, and this makes
for a certain limitation in terms of a reader's expectations. It was, I felt,
essential to overcome this handicap insofar as it was possible. And the
result was to have Death play all possible human roles (reserving to himself only his secret, ultimate purpose) and this would allow a great variety of "voice," however insistent the central theme, as, for example, in
Lydgate's [15th-century] *The Dance of Death*.[13]

Death adopting various personae, his "presumptions" as Baskin termed
them, gave Hecht "a chance to write dramatic monologues of one sort
or another."[14] Hecht had touched on the subject a quarter-century earlier,
in *The Hard Hours,* with "Tarantula, or The Dance of Death." It's possible
that this poem gave Baskin the idea, though he himself had taken on
death as a subject in his art since his earliest works. In this sense, the two
artists could not have been better matched.

It's no surprise that Hecht was increasingly drawn to death as a subject
the older he got: "The fact that I am now in my seventies gives the topic
a certain pertinence in my case, though my acquaintance with it began
fairly early. . . . [A]t my age not only many of my contemporaries but not
a few of my juniors (including my own brother) have predeceased me."
He was quick to add that the subject was not merely a personal obsession
but a perennial and even generic concern of poetry itself. Indeed, death
may well be poetry's most abiding subject, in one guise or another. It also
found its way into the classroom. As a professor, Hecht had come "to grips
with a good number of elegies, as well as religious poems about Death, an
astonishing abundance of mortuary materials. Finally, I think it pertinent
that this book is a collaboration with an artist (Baskin) who has himself
been seriously preoccupied with the topic."[15]

By midsummer, Hecht was back at the Writers Conference in Sewanee, where he reconnected with Walcott and Brodsky. He began making notes on Baskin's letters and hoped, he wrote to Baskin, "to cover the
grounds you propose, with perhaps some forays of my own. . . . I will
make a list of the titles you outlined and take them with me to Italy."[16]
Hecht had been awarded a residency of five weeks at the Villa Serbelloni
at Bellagio on Lake Como. He took the project with him and made rapid
progress: "The setting is as wonderful as any I know. We were quartered

in a medieval tower attached to the Main Villa, and my study in the tower adjoined our ample bedroom."

A program of the Rockefeller Foundation, the Bellagio Center sprawls over fifty acres on the peninsula between Lakes Como and Lecco in Northern Italy. It began receiving residents after 1959, when Ella Holbrook Walker, Principessa della Torre e Tasso, gave the property to the Foundation. Among the scholars, artists, writers, musicians, and scientists in residence for Hecht's four-week stay was the novelist and memoirist Edmund White, who recalled their time together with fondness: "He had a kind of English accent, and he was terribly refined." They had known each other slightly through Sandy McClatchy and James Merrill, and White had been to lunch at the Hechts' on Nebraska Avenue, in their sort of "White House-type house" with its columned portico. White felt warmly toward both Tony and Helen: "They were extremely nice. As a gay man, I always felt that they were with me."[17] White felt that both of the Hechts were wonderfully self-created, he as a kind of English gentleman, refined and highly civilized, and she as an elegant fashion plate "who was accomplished at everything."

While at Bellagio, Hecht put in a word to the director Pasquale Pesce for a residency for Brodsky, which was met with enthusiasm. To Brodsky himself he recommended the place but warned him about the amount of mandatory socializing involved: "In certain moods I find myself disinclined to exchange banalities with complete strangers."[18] Awkward cocktail hours aside, Hecht worked well during his weeks on Lake Como, completing several poems toward the "Presumptions" sequence. He sent them along to Baskin with two suggestions for further poems (neither of which made the final cut): "As you know, I want to do a sestina, and a shaped poem in the form of a skull."[19] "Death the Whore" was another early installment (which Hecht at one point titled "Ghost"). It is one of Hecht's most affecting dramatic monologues, again in a woman's voice, and it weaves together a sense of guilt at Eros and its consequences with encoded images of the Holocaust. Like "'More Light! More Light!,'" it ends with the image of smoke, a callback to the "thin gray smoke" with which the poem opens, bringing the poem full circle, a recurrent haunting:

Oh yes, my dear, you thought of me; I know.
But less and less, of course, as time went on.
And then you learned by a chance word of mouth
That I had been cremated, thereby finding
More of oblivion than I'd even hoped for.
And now when I occur to you, the voice
You hear is not the voice of what I was
When young and sexy and perhaps in love,
But the weary voice shaped in your later mind
By a small sediment of fact and rumor,
A faceless voice, a voice without a body.

As for the winter scene of which I spoke—
The smoke, my dear, the smoke. I am the smoke.[20]

Prose deadlines in the fall intruded on his progress with the Death dance, along with a crowded schedule of readings from New Hampshire and Michigan to the Miami Book Fair. In New York, he gave an introduction for Wilbur and a reading at the Century Club on 43rd Street, where he was a member.[21] His speech, later collected under the title "Richard Wilbur: An Introduction," concluded with the poem "Ballade of the Salvaged Losses," with the envoi:

Prince, though you seek both high and low
For all death's covetous amerces—
The fountain's leap, the ember's glow—
They're all in Richard Wilbur's verses.[22]

Hecht had written about Wilbur's poems on more than one occasion, and he included his introduction from the Morgan in *Melodies Unheard*. He sometimes wondered in his more insecure moments why Wilbur had never written about him, given their long association. Wilbur did however return the tribute of a ballade, in which he shows a deep appreciation for Hecht's poems, as well as for his light verse ("The Dover Bitch" and double dactyls) and translations (Baudelaire, Voltaire, Brodsky). It begins:

Who is the man whose poems dare
Describe man's inhumanities,
And count our deadly sins, and bare
Such truths as cause the blood to freeze,
Yet in whose darkest verse one sees
How style and agile intellect
Can both instruct and greatly please?
I speak, of course, of Tony Hecht.[23]

Hecht was a polished reader of his own poems, and he took seriously his charge to please an audience. A lecture and reading from around this time, sponsored by Mary Jo Salter at Mt. Holyoke, was typically well-attended: "His lecture on Auden brought a full house, and at his reading the next day there was standing room only."[24] His critical appraisal of Auden was "so allusive and dense that even someone well-acquainted with Auden found it hard to absorb all of," though there were "many nuggets of insight." He focused on an aspect of Auden that had taken deep root in his own work, "where Auden praises the faculty of *attention.* . . . part of Auden's larger point of trying to forget the self." Again, he quoted Simone Weil about "the ability to pay attention is the essence of prayer." At dinner after with the Baskins, they looked over a first unbound edition of *The Presumptions of Death.*[25]

"It's a beautiful book," Salter said, struck by the fine workmanship typical of the Gehenna Press.

"It's a *gorgeous* book," Baskin replied, correcting her in his typical curmudgeonly fashion. It had come together quickly. Whether it was the familiarity of the "death" theme, the camaraderie of the collaboration, or the fact that an admired friend had been awaiting his new work, is unclear; likely it was a combination of these. The sequence was completed in a year, and, together with Baskin's accompanying prints, formed the lion's share of *Flight Among the Tombs* (1996).

The day after his meeting with Baskin, Hecht read several poems from the sequence at Mount Holyoke College, including the longer monologue "Death the Whore," in which Salter detected shades of Hecht's first marriage. Pat was very much on his mind at the time, since she was living in nearby Northampton. It made Hecht uneasy. He felt he was in "enemy territory." In the twenty years that Salter had known him, Hecht never spoke of his first family. They were for different reasons lost to him. In Northampton, Pat had become an eccentric, almost a "bag lady."[26] Old friends barely recognized her. Jason had moved to Guatemala, where he continued his repeated pleas for money. Adam was well-adjusted, diligent, and good with his hands, with a family of his own, but the question of his paternity remained an open wound for Hecht.

On his second day in South Hadley, he had lunch with Brodsky. Brodsky came into the restaurant like a whirlwind, twenty minutes late, rattling off questions about poetry and belief that dominated the conversation. He wanted to know, When a man holds a creed, does that enlarge his soul or limit it? He spoke of "Wystan" and the finer points of English prosody. As Salter recalls:

> Throughout lunch the Nobel Prize winner deferred to his friend's knowledge and opinions, with the air of a college student who has managed to take up the whole office hour of his distinguished professor. Every subject Joseph brought up was clearly of burning, urgent interest, something he'd been carrying around in his head with the frustration that nobody around him had been smart enough to entrust with it—and now, in Tony, he had found someone smart enough. . . . They talked about the later chopping up of the psalms into hymn stanzas vs. following the lines of the Bible exactly as they appeared and extending the line to fit it.[27]

Brodsky attended the reading that evening "but left suddenly just as Tony began his final poem." Salter's then-husband, Brad Leithauser, got the sense that Hecht was "clearly unnerved by Joseph's departure." No doubt he flashed on Brodsky's criticism of "See Naples and Die," and he may have worried that Brodsky's slipping out was a response to "The Transparent Man," with which he ended the reading. Whatever the case, Brodsky made no move to congratulate Hecht before he departed Holyoke the next day, leaving Hecht to suspect the worst. Brodsky's opinion continued to carry enormous weight with him.

Hecht distracted himself with work. Back at his desk, his most pressing assignment was his introduction to G. Blakemore Evans's edition of Shakespeare's Sonnets. Once the introduction was drafted, he had only the finishing touches left for the Mellon lectures. Meanwhile, a suite of six "Presumptions," without the images, were given pride of place as the leadoff feature in *Poetry* magazine in August 1996.[28] Without his academic duties, Hecht's output—both prose and poetry—increased. He was enjoying retirement enormously. He had a room dedicated to his poetry library and a study for his correspondence and prose writing. Helen had overseen the renovation of the kitchen into an airy solarium (nicknamed "The Crystal Palace"), where they took their lunches together most days. There were events in the evenings and dinners out, as well as his own readings, which he gave around the country. The Hechts entertained regularly in their beautifully appointed dining room, and their guest book of overnight visits was filled with whimsical notes and doggerel by Brodsky ("I am a heathen / in all respects. / I crave no Eden / with its effects. / Since I have eaten / and slept at Hechts'")[29] and Walcott; Leithauser and Salter; William Meredith; Mona and Jarvis; James Merrill and Peter Hooten; David Kalstone; Jon and Jill Stallworthy, visiting from Oxford; Sandy McClatchy and his partner the renowned book designer Chip Kidd, who drew in a picture of Batman saying, "Holy Hospitality!"; Philip Hoy, who had conducted a book-length interview with Hecht by fax machine from his home in North London; Alfred Corn; Annie Wright; William Gass and William Arrowsmith; Robert Fitzgerald; Christopher Ricks; Dimitri Hadzi; Lyn Chase; Nicholas Christopher. As with all their date books, phone books, and diaries, the Hechts' guest book included friends who had died. Kalstone had passed a decade earlier, at the shockingly young age of fifty-three. William Arrowsmith went in 1992. That winter the Hechts learned of the death of James Merrill, a particularly hard blow. The roster of the dead seemed to be growing all the time.

Summers consisted of a convivial session of the Sewanee Writers Conference in Tennessee and a late-summer fortnight in Venice and Asolo, in the Veneto. Sewanee could leave him feeling drained; particularly in later years he found the more lackluster student work dispiriting. By contrast, Italy was his paradise, his annual trips there the highlight of his final years. In Asolo, the Hechts stayed in the deluxe Cipriani hotel, housed in a villa once owned by Robert Browning. (The town was also home to a historic Jewish Quarter, the site of a sixteenth-century massacre of ten Jews by a mob.) In Venice, Hecht wandered from the Europa, where they stayed, to the ends of the city, admiring San Marco or the Tintorettos at the Scuola Grande di San Rocco or Bellinis at the Accademia. There were drinks in the evening on the terrace of the Hotel Europa, with its views of Santa Maria della Salute and, across the wide mouth of the Grand Canal, San Giorgio Maggiore—negronis or martinis, the latter misted with French vermouth from a Venetian atomizer that Helen kept in her purse for such occasions.

Hecht always referred very specifically to the times in his life when he was happiest: at Bard, at the American Academy in Rome, in Venice. His years with Helen were certainly chief among them: the joyous peripety of his later life. The two of them doted on their son, Evan, now an adult, a kind soul and a student of philosophy. But by his middle seventies, Hecht's qualms about the future manifest themselves in the world around him: "The changes in the light of day as inklings of mortality have been rung with great effect by a good many poets, and one thinks right away of Dickinson ('There's a certain slant of light') and Hardy ('The Darkling Thrush' and many more)."[30] To Danny Anderson, a poet he knew from Sewanee who had interviewed him for BOMB, he confided some persistent misgivings about his poems: "There are always doubts about oneself. They do not disappear or diminish with age. You do not get used to them, the way some actors habituate themselves to stage-fright, and in the course of time seem to overcome it. . . . Very often what seems naked vanity (as in Jim Dickey) is a mask for anxiety of this sort."[31] Hecht's circumspection was offset by his confidence in his most recent work, his poems for Baskin and a new suite of elegies: "I've grown out-of-love with almost all my earlier work. . . . About to conclude my seventy-fourth year, I genuinely feel that my poems are as good as, if not better than, ever."[32]

2. Deaths in Winter

Hecht's introduction to the Sonnets was his third foray into Shakespeare criticism, after his essays on *Othello* and *The Merchant of Venice* collected in *Obbligati* ten years prior. Like the *Merchant* essay, the introduction to the New Cambridge Shakespeare edition of *The Sonnets* grew to an almost ungainly length. His work with the editorial staff at

Cambridge did not go smoothly: "It was one of the most infuriating experiences I've ever had with any publisher," he wrote to the poet Dana
Gioia, venting about Cambridge's "editors modeled on George S. Patton."[33] Length was a point of contention: "First I was told I would be
confined to 10,000 words. I told them I couldn't possibly do it in less than
50,000. Curiously, they gave in to that, but at the same time asked me to
furnish a complete history of the sonnet form, and a general discourse
on prosody." In the end, Hecht found himself "obliged to compromise
in ways that still pain me." Hecht completed a "history" of the form, but
it was not included, appearing a year later than the introduction in *The
Antioch Review* for spring of 1997.[34]

For Hecht, the Sonnets were, in Shakespeare's hands, fundamentally
dramatic: of all the Elizabethan sonneteers, Hecht argued, "Shakespeare
was beyond question the most penetrating. He was also the one who
seemed perfectly able to adapt the form itself to his analytic or diag-
nostic and deeply dramatic purposes."[35] Shakespeare's Sonnets speak
with "powerful, rich, and complex emotion of a very dramatic kind,"
and it was in the tensions between the characters—speaker, addressee,
and often referent—that the Sonnets came to life for him.[36] The sonnet
form itself frequently provided the stage on which his dramas played out:
"Shakespeare often seemed to think of his sonnets in terms of the Italian
division, including the dramatic or rhetorical relationship of octave to
sestet," the dialogic nature of thesis and antithesis creating a dramatic
tension in the poems.[37]

In Sonnet 138, Hecht discerns the drama brought about by mutual
deception and self-deception: "When my love swears that she is made of
truth, / I do believe her, though I know she lies . . ." The poem is a private
rumination on "love as illusion, as self-deception, as bitterly unreal—in
ways that remind us that the world of *A Midsummer Night's Dream* is not
altogether as taintless as it might at first appear."[38] As Hecht puts it in a
short prose monologue of Lysander's in his pastiche of *Midsummer,* "A
Love for Four Voices": "It is sheer fantasy confers such powers: I vote her
beautiful out of my need. Her grace is in the gland of the beholder. This
is plain masturbation thinly disguised, in which I dub her my sea-born
Galatea, and she brightly replies, 'Baby you're aces.'"[39] Hecht discerned in
Shakespeare's comedies how playfulness often concealed darker themes.[40]

In the winter of 1996, Hecht learned of Brodsky's passing in Brooklyn, NY. He was fifty-five. It came "almost exactly a year after Merrill's death," he wrote to Gioia. "Both Merrill and Brodsky were my juniors, and I regarded them both as good friends."[41] Hecht had not seen Merrill for some time when he died in February of 1995; indeed, no one had. He had been sick for several years and "betook himself to a remote and unfamiliar place in the southwest to pass his last days out of public view."[42] For his absent friend, he wrote "An Adieu," placing Merrill among the first rank of poets:

> *You are now one of that chosen band and choice*
> *Fellowship gathered at Sandover's sunlit end,*
> *Fit audience though few, where, at their ease,*
> *Dante, Rilke, Mallarmé, Proust rejoice*
> *In the rich polyphony of their latest friend,*
> *Scored in his sweetly noted higher keys.*[43]

The loss of Brodsky was even harder to bear. He was perhaps his closest poetic ally, and his death left Hecht "truly stunned for a while, and then demanded some sort of elegy. I have worked on that for some time setting everything else aside." For weeks Hecht attempted to express his love and admiration. Sandy McClatchy sent him two other elegies that had recently appeared, but Hecht put off reading them, replying:

Many thanks for sending the Brodsky elegies by Heaney and Muldoon. I opened the envelope boldly, and as soon as I had identified the contents I stuffed it right back again as though it were a notice for jury duty. The fact is that I am myself engaged in writing an elegy for Joseph, and I feel superstitious about reading one by anyone else till my own is finished. For two reasons that I am aware of. The first is an honest desire not to be influenced by another poet; the second is a nervous fear that my own as yet unfinished poem will suffer so greatly by comparison that discouragement will prohibit continuing. I'm not sure that either of these reasons is the real one. Since Heaney is trying to echo Auden [in "Audenesque"], and I am decidedly not, that cannot be a great danger. And perhaps I could immunize myself from danger of Muldoon in something of the same way. My poem tries (with whatever success must be judged by others) to appropriate Brodsky's own poetic resources, including extravagant personifications, metaphors drawn from time and space, many foreign settings, etc. Call it plain superstition, but I will still set aside those poems you sent until I have finished my own.[44]

"A Death in Winter" acknowledges Brodsky's heroism in mastering personal pain, a quality Hecht greatly admired and worked to achieve in his own life. It ends:

> *Reader, dwell with his poems. Underneath*
> *Their gaiety and music, note the chilled strain*
> *Of irony, of felt and mastered pain,*
> *The sound of someone laughing through clenched teeth.*[45]

Hecht revered many of his colleagues from the Academy of American Poets and the Academy of Arts and Letters, but he felt a special affinity with Merrill and Brodsky; they were his "chosen band and choice / Fellowship," the "club" (as Richard Howard had termed it) to which he most wished to belong. With them gone, Hecht felt a good deal more alone and his efforts to write poetry of lasting value ever more solitary.

Hecht sent his elegy for Brodsky to Harry Ford, as a late inclusion to *Flight,* choosing Baskin's wood engraving for "Death the Poet" for the cover. The collection's title is taken from Christopher Smart's "Jubilate Agno," with this passage serving as the book's epigraph: "Let Mattithiah bless with the Bat, / who inhabiteth the desolations of pride / and flieth amongst the tombs." Along with Mark Strand, Tomas Venclova, and others, Hecht read at Brodsky's memorial service in March at St. John the Divine, near Columbia University. He chose a short poem of Auden's.[46] (In 1973, he had read poems at Auden's memorial service in the same cathedral.) The three poets subsequently appeared on *The Charlie Rose Show* to remember their friend. Hecht spoke slowly, with deep feeling. It was clear that he was still grappling with the loss:

> He's unquestionably one of the greatest poets of modern times. I can't bracket him among the Russian poets because I'm not sufficiently acquainted with them, but he clearly admired Akhmatova and he must

certainly be a part of her tradition. . . . [She wrote letters] in his behalf
when he was a prisoner, as did Shostakovich and a great number of non-
Russians, writing to see if they could get him relieved from the five-year
sentence to Archangel that he had been committed to. And he was—he
had an extraordinarily difficult life even before he was sent to prison. His
parents were poor. His father had been in the navy and wasn't promoted
because he was Jewish, and Joseph dropped out of school . . . in ninth
grade, and had more than a dozen jobs, including working in a morgue
to help subsidize the meager family income. And it was during this time
that . . . Akhmatova noticed his poetry and encouraged him and wrote in
his behalf after he was sentenced. It was an extraordinary career.[47]

Hecht's elegy for Brodsky ran in *The New Yorker* on November 4, 1996.

Even with the poem added to *Flight,* Ford worried about the brevity of
the book. He asked if Hecht had any possible additions. Ford must have
realized that his request was something of a long shot given how slowly
and deliberately Hecht worked, but as luck would have it he did have new
poems, thanks again to Baskin's prompting. Fast on the heels of "The Presumptions," Hecht had turned his attention to "flower poems" for what
eventually became the deluxe folio edition of *The Gehenna Florilegium.* This
new series afforded Hecht a great deal more flexibility in terms of tone and
subject, so long as each poem included the mention of a specific flower to
accompany a Baskin print. Two such poems had already been included in
Flight—"Sisters" (cyclamen) and "A Pledge" (thistle). Hecht sent Ford a third
touching on his beloved Baudelaire entitled *"Là-bas:* A Trance." Early in 1997,
he wrote to Eleanor Cook about the state of the collaboration: "[Baskin] has
done 15 beautiful woodcuts and I have so far turned out about four poems
to go with these. . . . I've got one about sunflowers that has been written
since [*Flight*] appeared." Hecht enjoyed the assignment in part for its loosened parameters: "The key to writing about flowers, I find, is to approach
them very indirectly."[48] In a note accompanying *"Là-bas:* A Trance" in a letter to Baskin, Hecht informed him that "It's the first of the flower poems."
Hecht's scholarly side also engaged with the sequence: in his research, he
"discovered a nice Renaissance item. The Elizabethan herbalist John Gerard
informs us of the sunflower that 'the buds . . . boiled and eaten . . . after the
manner of artichokes . . . surpasses the artichoke far in producing bodily

lust.'" The flowers began to take on personalities and associations, which Hecht wove into the poems.[49]

With recent publications in both verse and prose, Hecht attracted lengthier overviews of his work from distinguished critics. John Bayley, writing in *The New York Review of Books,* took stock of Hecht's recent work, finding a common thread in Hecht's impressive scholarship and fluency with the poetic tradition:

> The elegiac note is everywhere in this, perhaps Hecht's best, collection [*Flight Among the Tombs*], from the poet who gave us the masterly *Millions of Strange Shadows* and *The Venetian Vespers* twenty years ago and has standards of craftsmanship and erudition higher than those of most of his contemporaries. The timeless element in his work is partly owing to his learning, which is amply demonstrated in *The Hidden Law*, his fine study of Auden's poetry published four years ago, and in his more recent Mellon Lectures, *On the Laws of the Poetic Art.* For Hecht learning is a part of poetry, as much an aspect of it as cadence and meter, which themselves bring many echoes from the past.[50]

Dozens of notices of Hecht's latest books poured out from leading literary reviews, small magazines, and national newspapers. The Mellon Lectures, published by Princeton in a lavishly illustrated edition, received a positive review from Robert Beum in *The Sewanee Review*, but other critics found the book hard going. For William Logan in *The Washington Post,* it was "not a distinguished addition to a series that engendered Kenneth Clark's *The Nude* and E. H. Gombrich's *Art and Illusion.*" Logan's mixed review of *Flight,* under the title "Old Guys," stung Hecht, for whom the din of adverse criticism drowned out a number of glowing positives: "*Flight Among the Tombs* contains little of Hecht's best work, his acidic lines on human nature (nature nature, too), his astringent, moral colloquy with history. But in a long and magnificent career he's written dozens of poems I've nearly read the ink off of, have taught and quoted with pleasure."[51] Hecht felt that the *Times Literary Supplement* "grotesquely misread my Mellon lectures out of what may be a medley of indifference and malice. This has rather depressed me . . ." He took cold comfort that

"The *TLS* was far kinder to me than [Helen] Vendler"[52] was in *The New York Review of Books*. He worried that Vendler, who served on the committee to award the Academy of American Poets' Gold Medal for Distinguished Service to Poetry, had blocked his nomination with candidates of her own, poets such as John Ashbery and A. R. Ammons, part of her personal critical canon, whom she had championed in the past.

His letters from this time make mention of his disappointment, and there was another subject that began to creep in that would remain in one form or another for his remaining years: his failing health. Hecht had been suffering from disabling back pain, which had recently worsened and prompted him to seek help from doctors. "The discs in my lumbar region have altogether worn away," he wrote to Harry Ford. "After nearly two years of inability to walk any distance, or to stand for any length of time, I have determined to put myself in the hands of a surgeon."[53]

With his new collaboration with Baskin underway, he became impatient with his condition, which prevented him from making progress on the *Florilegium*. He began to dread public functions in which he would be required to sit for long periods of time: "My back now makes it difficult to sit comfortably in the standard folding chairs"[54] at the annual Academy of Arts and Letters ceremonial, in which the members are arranged on risers on stage. He confessed to Baskin that, as a result, he was not writing poems and was hoping that treatment might alleviate the pain sufficiently so that he could return to work: "I would very much like to return to the flower poems as soon as I can."[55]

In addition to the debilitating sciatica that plagued him for over three years, he suffered from serious dental issues, "both protracted and painful,"[56] which kept him from working. Hecht joked ruefully with Philip Booth that he was succumbing "to some of the indignities of age."[57] Hecht's back surgery early in the year provided something of a reprieve from pain, but not completely. The good news was that he was well enough to travel, and he and Helen looked forward to what had become their annual trip to Venice. They had made a reservation at the Hotel Europa, Hecht told John Malcolm Brinnin, despite his continuing "dental and spinal deterioration."[58] Their trip that summer spanned two and a half weeks in July and August.

With work stalled, Hecht fretted that he was falling behind in his collaboration with Baskin. That fall, however, he enjoyed a wonderful bit of good luck, thanks to Sandy McClatchy, who had become one of his closest friends and allies. (At the time it was published in fall 1988, McClatchy's *Paris Review* interview with Hecht was the fullest autobiographical account of Hecht's life and work, surpassed since only by the book-length interview he embarked on with Philip Hoy a decade later, in 1998.) McClatchy had recently joined the board of the Bogliasco Foundation, which ran a Study Center for writers and artists in a villa south of Genoa. McClatchy urged Hecht to apply and planned to overlap with them during their time at the center. It proved to be an ideal place for Hecht to return to the flower poems.

The coast of Liguria near Genoa, dotted with fishing villages along the rocky coast that climbs steeply to surrounding hills, is known as the Golfo Paradiso, and the Study Center was a paradise for Hecht as he worked to complete the poems for the *Florilegium*. He and Helen were given a room in the main house, the Villa dei Pini, with splendid views of Camogli to the east and the Med stretching out to the west, over which each night a fiery sunset drew the gaze toward Genoa. After stints in his studio, Hecht took meals of local specialties with Sandy McClatchy and the other fellows. There was good wine, and cocktails in the parlors before and after dinner. Bogliasco offered a productive balance of leisure and stimulation, with weekend trips to Rapallo and the densely populated *caruggi* in Genoa's *centro storico*. Hecht returned again twice in subsequent years and always produced a significant amount of writing. And on this first visit he had real cause for excitement: by the time he and Helen returned to Washington in late October, he had completed eleven of the sixteen poems for the Baskin project. By the end of October he wrote to John Hollander that the project was complete, though the work on Baskin's end of producing the prints was still ongoing. In his letter, he thanked Hollander for his elegant review of *Flight* that had recently appeared in *Raritan,* in which he commended Hecht's "ringing tones of the voice of the speaker in Ecclesiastes. It is also there in his moral rage. Nietzsche says somewhere that 'all truths for me are soaked in blood'; for Hecht this is true of many of his tropes, even as his poetic art is soaked in truth."[59]

Baskin worked quickly, producing the proofs of the *Florilegium* by the end of the year, though the finished book, one of Baskin's most deluxe productions, wouldn't arrive until June of 1998. Now in his later career, Hecht had received many of the top prizes, and he kept an eye on ones he had not yet received, such as the Academy of American Poets' Gold Medal and the MacArthur, for which Hollander had nominated him unsuccessfully, "though many of my juniors, and not a few of my inferiors have received it."[60] His luck changed dramatically that fall when he was awarded the Dorothea Tanning Prize (now the Wallace Stevens Award) from the Academy of American Poets, which "recognizes outstanding and proven mastery in the art of poetry," and carried a purse of $100,000. Increasingly, Hecht's career was being celebrated for its contributions to American poetry that spanned a half century. Critics were taking the long view, providing career surveys, as Hollander had for *Raritan*. The timing was perfect, then, when Philip Hoy, an English publisher, approached Hecht about doing a book-length interview. McClatchy had brought out a sterling conversation about the life and work in *The Paris Review* interview from 1988, but this new exchange would be even more in depth and wide ranging, bringing Hecht's story up to date with the last ten years, including all but his final book of poems. Conducted by mail and fax machine, the interview grew into Hecht's longest and most important autobiographical document, spanning his family history, the traumas of childhood and the war, his friendships and academic posts, as well as the background to many of his greatest poems. Hoy's invitation came at Christmastime and the two-year project began in earnest early in 1998. To George Core, editor of *The Sewanee Review*, he wrote: "I have spent my time recently being 'interviewed' long distance by a man named Philip Hoy (no relation [to Cyrus], I assume) in London. He began by introducing himself with just such an interview he'd conducted with W. D. Snodgrass, and, with my consent, sending me 93 questions. They are very good questions, indicating that he had read long and carefully."[61]

The Hoy interview caused Hecht to take stock, not only of his life and career but also of his legacy. He and Helen began to assemble his archive of letters and news clippings, family photos and manuscripts, with an eye toward selling them to a library that would catalogue and preserve them. It was another way in which he confronted his mortality, the reality of which was more and more brought home to him by the death of friends and his own failing health. He had aged noticeably in his early seventies, though mentally and creatively he was very much his usual self. But he was slowing down. Never one to suffer fools, he no longer hid his irritation at the inanities of the poetry world. Very much his mother's son in one regard, he picked up a habit of writing letters to the editors, weighing in on issues and correcting errors, particularly where literature and Shakespeare in particular were concerned. He could be taciturn in unfamiliar settings, and even longtime admirers and friends found him formidable. All these common marks of age were inevitable for Hecht—a poet in late career, increasingly alone, missing friends who had gone. He took enormous comfort in Helen and Evan. Helen's long-term project to renovate and decorate the Washington house had made their home a place of calm and beauty, with quiet, sunlit meals in the solarium kitchen and bibulous gatherings around the long, stately dining table. He felt an incredible tenderness for Evan:

> The morning's perfect blue imparts
>   Coolness of water-freshened cress,
> And shallow flagstone pools repeat
>   A della Robian cloudlessness.
>
> Motionless, happy, striped in blue,
>   A boy surveys the sunlit field.
> Something about him stops me dead:
>   His presence, and what lies concealed
>
> In light shifts of the afternoon,
>   In dwindled palettes of the dusk.
> He stands immobile, played upon
>   By morning and the roses' musk,
>
> Stands as he stood there years ago,
>   The ineradicable boy,
> Pitted against all marshalled griefs
>   And ranked antagonists of joy.[62]

As Hecht felt his circle growing smaller, his ties to Helen and Evan became the center of his world. They were his source of joy, his stay against confusion, against the marshalled griefs that were always with him: the estrangement from his elder sons, the guilt that clung to him after the war. As he did often elsewhere, he cast his griefs in military terms: *marshalled, ranked.* From Helen and Evan, he felt forgiveness and love, patience and understanding. From the safety of their home together, he could find a space to write, to address the hardest parts of his past without being overwhelmed by them. The haunted memories persisted, but he refused to shy away from them. By turning them over in memory and committing them to verse, he hoped he might find peace.

THIRTEEN

BOTH ALIKE TO THEE
(1998–2004)

1. A Midrash for Baskin

Hecht's seventy-fifth birthday, in January of 1998, was a joyful event, a tonic for recent health concerns and a welcome respite from the elegiac poems of *Flight*. The occasion—a party in New York, at the elegant Mark Hotel on East 77th, and a Festschrift of light-hearted birthday wishes from friends going back years. Most of the poets wrote poems, with Richard Wilbur's daisy chain of clerihews a highlight:

> *Anthony Hecht*
> *Does Milton in dialect,*
> *Rendering the phrase, "and hath not left his peer"*
> *With a Fields-like trombone smear.*

And, more earnestly, from Wilbur and his wife, Charlee:

> *Anthony Hecht*
> *Is one of the elect.*
> *We think him the choicest of choices.*
> *Here's a love from our two voices.*

There were notes and verses from dozens of faithful friends: the Fords, Mona Van Duyn and Jarvis Thurston, a gorgeous crow by Baskin, William Maxwell, Sandy McClatchy, Brad Leithauser and Mary Jo Salter, Dave Mason, W. S. Merwin writing from his home in Hawaii, and younger poets he'd befriended in recent years—Joseph Harrison and Greg Williamson. Amid the jovial quips and teasing, the thoughtful tribute of Cyrus Hoy, his old friend from Rochester, must have pleased him greatly:

Since we are near contemporaries in age, I recognize something of the moral landscape that has taken shape during the years of our lives, heightening and haunting our imagination, looming over our moral consciousness, and I have long admired the precision with which, in your poetry, you have created language for prefiguring these impressions, for bearing witness to them. . . . [Your work] has assumed the richness and the variety of a complex theatre of our world, with a unique repertoire of figures who give voice in a range of responses—ironic, grotesque, banal, lyrical, sometimes deluded and sometimes alarmingly clear-sighted—to the conditions amid which they dwell.

Plans for the party and the letters were overseen by Helen, with RSVPs going to Helen's mother in nearby Chevy Chase to ensure secrecy. Hecht was abashed and delighted by the event, of course, but most affecting, perhaps, were Helen's thoughtfulness and loving handiwork. Tolstoy must have been mistaken in his claim that that all happy marriages were happy in the same way: the way the Hechts complemented each other was fortunate and rare. Helen embraced life and took real pleasure in living. Her optimism and hope boosted Hecht's spirits, and in her company, he felt his true self. Like the figures in Yeats's "Lapis Lazuli," he could look on life's tragic aspects with equilibrium and patience.

The year, beginning on a high note, continued in the same vein. There was an evening of Poets Laureate with the Clintons at the White House. After some nettlesome delays on Baskin's end, *The Gehenna Florilegium* arrived in early summer, and it exceeded Hecht's imaginings. He praised his friend for creating "a thing of overwhelming beauty."[1] He described it to Pete Fairchild, a younger poet he had met at Sewanee, now a friend, "Everything, from the shade of linen of the cover boxing, to the sumptuous, Italianate gold figurations, and the spine, the paper in two colors, the whole rich composite, is wonderful to behold, and I rejoice in it, as Helen does."[2] The folio-sized book included fifteen colored woodcuts signed by Baskin, printed from maple blocks and hand-bound in peach gilt-stamped Morocco and pale green, with a tooled spine and deckle edges. An edition of fifty was printed on handmade paper by the letterpress of Arthur Larson. Traditionally, a florilegium was a treatise on flowers dedicated to ornamental rather than the medicinal or utilitarian plants covered by herbals, with botanical illustration as a genre dating back to the fifteenth century. Again, Hecht's and Baskin's preoccupations seamlessly aligned, prefigured by "La Condition Botanique," "The Gardens of the Villa d'Este," and "Behold the Lilies of the Field," which Hecht had dedicated to Baskin three decades prior.

Hecht was proud of the final product, and he earmarked his flower poems for inclusion in his next as-yet-unnamed collection. He was pleased, too, that Baskin's commission had provided him with the impetus to write a new group of poems in short order; it had lent a kind of permission. Having completed it, Hecht was again without a project, and his pace of production slowed. He found the way forward in Englishing the poems of others: "[When] I find myself stalled in writing my own poems, I turn to translation," he wrote to Robert Beum, who had recently given his Mellon lectures a favorable notice in *The Sewanee Review*. He included on the verso a translation of Baudelaire's "Le Jet d'eau," "a poem that has haunted me for years," he told Beum, "and which I have tried my hand at before. This is the nearest I've come to the pure magic of the original."[3] It begins:

> *My dear, your lids are weary;*
> *Lower them, rest your eyes,*
> *As though some languid pleasure*
> *Might take you by surprise.*
> *The tattling courtyard fountain*
> *Repeats this night's excess*
> *In fervent, ceaseless whispers*
> *Of murmur and caress.*

Hecht paired this retranslation with another Baudelaire poem, "The Ashen Light of Dawn," that comes so close to Hecht's own preoccupations, it almost seems as if he had written it himself. It begins:

> *Reveille was bugled through army camps*
> *As a soft dawn wind was fluttering streetlamps.*
>
> *It was the hour when smooth sun-tanned limbs*
> *Of adolescents twitched with unlawful dreams,*

When, like a bloodshot eye beside the bed,
A nightlamp soaked oncoming day in red,
When, weighted beneath a humid body's brawn,
The soul mimicked that duel of lamp and dawn.

Dawn was a persistent subject. "A Deep Breath at Dawn" (originally titled "Aubade") was among Hecht's earliest published poems, and the subject continued to exert a hold on him and would even in his very last poems. It was where the darkness and the light met, and mingled, and vied. It was a figure for the moral dramas that continued to grip him both waking and in his still-recurring nightmares, though they were less frequent now.[4]

Health issues persisted, and Hecht was put on strict orders by his doctors: "I've been obliged to allow my routines, duties, pleasures and obligations to lapse, and, consequently, to pile up ominously (even pleasures can be ominous) because of a medical procedure I recently underwent. They implanted a steel stent (a tubular wire mesh that distends a blood vessel) in the right artery of my heart." Released after more than a week in the hospital, he was "now obliged to eat very carefully."[5] As upsetting as his hospital stay and surgery must have been, Hecht counted himself lucky. He had friends who were worse off. Several friends had recently been diagnosed with cancer, including Kathleen Ford, who died later that year.

By summer, things were on an upswing again, and Hecht began in earnest on his book-length interview with Philip Hoy. The questions arrived in July, with a request to have them completed by the end of the year, if possible. Hecht worked diligently on his responses, replying to Hoy with his answers by September, despite his annual trip to Venice and Asolo. With Hoy's prompting, Hecht put into words, often for the first time, the terrors of his childhood and of combat, while asserting that there were some experiences of the war that he would never talk about. He prepared his answers carefully, drawing portraits of Dorothea and Melvyn, of Roger and Auden. He spoke about individual poems, including "A Hill" and "The Venetian Vespers," unlocking a number of their underlying concerns. He wrote of PTSD and of his stint in Gracie Square. Hecht found the work to be "a pleasure . . . I've found it possible to be somewhat more candid about my life than was possible before."[6] There was a summary quality to his responses, of setting the record straight for posterity. He was thinking about his legacy in other ways, as well. In November of 1998, an assessor of his personal papers came to look through forty-six "disorderly" cartons. This number grew to fifty-six and beyond, as Hecht prepared his papers for sale to a library.

In November, Jacky Simms at OUP telephoned to say that Oxford, which had been bringing out the British editions of Hecht's books since *The Hard Hours,* was dropping its poetry list. This was headline news in England and a devastating blow for the poets who had been cut loose. It was particularly discouraging for Hecht, who was "about halfway into the next book of poems."[7] He now had a clear vision for completing the book, thanks again to Baskin, who had recently proposed another collaboration, perfectly tailored to Hecht and engaging their common preoccupation (almost an obsession) with the Bible. Baskin would create images to accompany Hecht's poems based on Old Testament figures, such as Haman, Esther, Judith, Susannah (from the Apocrypha), Samson, and others—ten in all.

The year ended with the Hechts' usual holiday festivities. Hecht had always loved Christmas, and Helen made the house into a splendid holiday idyll out of Dickens or *Fanny and Alexander.* Hecht painted the scene for Hoy in rich detail: "Our very ample and well-shaped tree is all in place, lighted and decorated; the house is garlanded and full of flowers; red and white poinsettias, white roses, baby's breath, and a fine smell of balsam."[8] It was a time for family and high spirits, and Hecht relished the occasion. Evan returned home for the holidays, and Helen's mother came to stay on Christmas Eve. Happy to make his gratitude known, he dedicated his last two books "To Helen and Evan."

The biblical poems now occupied him full time, and when Sandy McClatchy proposed another Italian residency, Hecht knew that he had a project that would benefit from the structured hours that the Centro Studi in Liguria afforded. He returned to Bogliasco in the fall of 1999, and though he was excited to focus on the Baskin collaboration (his fifth!), he was slightly anxious and depleted: for back pain and syncope (fainting, or perhaps, in Hecht's case, something akin to vertigo) his doctors had prescribed "befogging" medications.[9] His initial trip to Bogliasco had yielded good work, and with a new project underway, he was anxious to get as much done on it as possible by the end of October. He needn't have worried. The work flowed easily and well. During his stay at Bogliasco, he "got more poems written than I dared to hope, including a suite of ten on Old Testament themes."

The book was nearly done: "I am within my aim for perhaps two or three more poems to feel that I will have a substantial book collected. But I am daunted by the prospect of turning it in."[10] The reason for his hesitation was that Harry Ford, his editor since *The Hard Hours,* had died earlier in the year. As he put it in "Sarabande on Attaining the Age of Seventy-seven," "The dramatis personae of our lives / Dwindle and wizen."[11] Deborah Garrison would succeed Ford, though for the moment Hecht felt as if he was without an editor; "Now that Harry Ford is no longer my editor at Knopf, I feel obscurely abandoned."[12]

The biblical poems were a culmination of Hecht's lifelong reading of the Bible, which he studied continuously.[13] biblical passages, subjects, and allusions salt his poems from the beginning—sometimes throughout, as in "Rites and Ceremonies," "Death the Archbishop," "The Seven Deadly Sins," "'And Can Ye Sing Baluloo When the Bairn Greets?,'" and "The Man Who Married Magdalene"; sometimes in part, as in "The Feast of Stephen," "Upon the Death of George Santayana," "The Book of Yolek," "Riddles," "'More Light! More Light!,'" and "'It Out-Herods Herod. Pray You, Avoid It'"; sometimes in passing, as in "Birdwatchers of America"; and sometimes as an underlying source, as in "See Naples and Die." The Bible was part of a shared sensibility with Baskin, and, also, with Brodsky. Brodsky had been deeply sympathetic to Hecht's poetic project, which Hecht described as a kind of hermeneutics: "I remember our conversation many years ago," Brodsky recalled, "when you said something to the effect that all what we do in our profession is essentially a commentary to—'making sense out of' you've said—the Holy Book."[14] Another basis of Hecht's friendships with Baskin and Brodsky was their shared experience of Judaism, a "grave sadness," as Hecht put it, "somehow Jewish in spirit."[15]

The fate of his new manuscript was still uncertain, though, by the end of the year, it had a title—*The Darkness and the Light*—a phrase from Psalm 139:12: "The darkness and the light are both alike to thee," the full verse serving as the title for the final poem in the book. Hecht took time out from his careful cataloguing of personal papers to work on poems: "I find

myself, curiously, in a happier version of the situation I was in when preparing my first book of poems. I would keep adding new ones, but each
new one convinced me that it was better than some of the old ones, and as
I added new material I would delete at as fast a rate, so that I seemed never
to end with a complete book. Today I feel less need to eliminate—though
a good editor such as Harry might well persuade me to cut things out."[16]
Three weeks at the Atlantic Center for the Arts in Florida in January 2000
was enough for Hecht to put the finishing touches on the manuscript; he
sent it to Knopf in February, with three late additions: "Mirror," for Sandy
McClatchy;[17] "The Ceremony of Innocence," a scene of torture that resonates with "The Feast of Stephen" and "'More Light! More Light!'"; and
"Chromatic Fantasy," which was ultimately omitted.

Old ghosts, perhaps stirred up by his interview with Hoy, prompted
Hecht to delve again into childhood and the war. The three-part "Sacrifice," a late masterpiece, juxtaposes two lyrics in the voices of Abraham
and Isaac with a longer narrative of a French family during the German
retreat from France. The German soldier holds a mother, father, and son
at gunpoint. The father has hidden the family bicycle in a tree to keep it
from being stolen by enemy soldiers:

> He looked at the frightened family huddled together,
> And with the blunt nose of his rifle barrel
> Judiciously singled out the eldest son,
> A boy perhaps fourteen, but big for his years,
> Obliging him to place himself alone
> Against the whitewashed front wall of the house.
> Then, at the infallible distance of ten feet,
> With rifle pointed right at the boy's chest,
> The soldier shouted what was certainly meant
> To be his terminal order: BICYCLETTE!

In this moment, everything stalls, and the world goes still. The father
does not give up the bicycle despite the danger to his son:

> It was still early on a chilly morning.
> The water in the tire-treads of the road

Lay clouded, polished pale and chalked with frost,
Like the paraffin-sealed coverings of preserves.
The very grass was a stiff lead-crystal gray,
Though splendidly prismatic where the sun
Made its slow way between the lingering shadows
Of nearby fence posts and more distant trees.
There was leisure enough to take full note of this
In the most minute detail as the soldier held
Steady his index finger on the trigger.

It wasn't charity. Perhaps mere prudence,
Saving a valuable round of ammunition
For some more urgent crisis. Whatever it was,
The soldier reslung his rifle on his shoulder,
Turned wordlessly and walked on down the road
The departed German vehicles had taken.

There followed a long silence, a long silence.
For years they lived together in that house,
Through daily tasks, through all the family meals,
In agonized, unviolated silence.[18]

Hecht imagines the hidden cruelties and deep, unspoken guilts that can mark a family forever. Family secrets: Hecht was familiar with such "dark and Cabalistic" mysteries.[19]

Hecht's biblical poems are a midrash: they interpret the ancient narratives in a modern context, in contemporary language, in ways that shed light both on the original verses and on their meanings for a modern reader. Midrash is an interpretive act, written by rabbis, that seeks "answers to religious questions (both practical and theological) by plumbing the meaning of the words of the Torah." The more narrative strain of midrash, the Aggadah, often occupies "the meeting ground between reverence . . . and creativity" and frequently addresses "the concerns of its authors."[20] This was certainly true of Hecht's Bible poems, which touch on the challenges to morality in wartime, the Holocaust, the tensions arising between fathers and sons, depression, lust and murder, memory, and, his flood-subject, death. A biblical poem that Hecht composed in the early '90s, then left uncollected, "Cain the Inventor of Death," considers the famous fratricide in Eden:

> And I was the first child.
> For me the sun arose
> And the flung grain of stars
> Attended my repose.
>
> Later a brother came.
> In rivalry we fought,
> Or romped, tumbled and raced,
> Wrestled and strove in sport.
>
> And once I hit him hard,
> Perhaps by some mistake,
> Hit him so that he slept
> And slept and didn't wake.[21]

The debt that one brother owes to another had always occupied Hecht since early childhood, and even after Roger's death a few years before "Cain" was written, he continued to examine his feelings of resentment, guilt, and deep love.

Midway through the project, Baskin received a shock; his kidneys were failing, and he was placed on dialysis. In the following months he went quiet, and Hecht feared intruding on a household in crisis. That summer of 2000, Baskin "died after a long and intermittently painful illness. He was unable to complete the book we were collaborating on. And then, within a week of one another, Emily [Maxwell] first, and then William Maxwell died."[22]

At the American Academy of Arts and Letters annual dinner meeting, Hecht remembered his friend's fiery personality:

> It can be admitted that Leonard Baskin was a man with enough self-confidence to seem brash, and, to some, even vain. He wrote that after his first frail efforts as a sculptor, "I learned to carve, and it is not conceit

to note that I learned to carve exceedingly well." . . . He was, I think, not
vain, but joyfully sure of himself. And he was undeniably opinionated;
indeed, many of the artists he cherished were precisely opinionated—
which is to say, committed, *engagé*, imbued with social concerns, militant,
hortatory.[23]

He celebrated Baskin's late flourishing, even as privately he might have
wished that their final collaboration had come to fruition.[24] Deeply affected by these deaths, Hecht wrote to Francine du Plessix Gray about
the looming possibility of his own: "It seems to me as I approach my
seventy-eighth year that I have been acquainted with death from very early
in my life; and by acquainted I mean intimately acquainted. I no longer
have much fear as regards my own death, though I dread the possibility of
preliminary pains that may precede it. I am much more distressed by the
thought of the misery that my death will give to my family."[25] In addition
to Helen and Evan, there was Helen's mother, now in her mid-nineties,
and still going strong, free of the kinds of ailments that plagued Hecht: "I
feel rather more feeble and infirm when I compare myself to her."[26]

Hecht had had a scare earlier that year, which was successfully treated
with surgery. To the poet Agha Shahid Ali, he disclosed the grim details:
"They were mining for pancreatic cancer, and while what they found
was benign, in the course of disemboweling me they relieved me of ⅔s
of my pancreas, as well as the whole of my gall bladder and duodenum.
So I am a much altered man."[27] (Hecht had recently been appointed to
the Pulitzer Prize jury, and he let Ali know that he was high on his list.
The irony is that the widely beloved Ali, too, joined the procession of
untimely deaths the next year, dying of brain cancer at fifty-two years old
in December 2001.) During Hecht's recovery from surgery, Helen "happened to overhear some dreadful raving of mine when I was altogether
out of my mind."[28] Helen was terrified and "genuinely feared I had lost
my wits forever."[29] Fortunately he was soon himself again, though, after
two weeks in the hospital, a somewhat reduced version, he joked ruefully: "One of the things I still miss is strong drink, though I am allowed
wine for the present, which I enjoy."[30]

In general, Hecht was able to keep his spirits up. The Poetry Society
of America awarded him their lifetime achievement award, The Frost

Medal. At the ceremony, Hecht gave remarks on Frost's "The Wood-Pile," before reading a selection of his own poems.[31] Certain irritations, however, became too much for him, particularly where it involved any rough handling of Shakespeare. He participated in an evening of Shakespeare readings by poets at the Unterberg Poetry Center of the 92nd Street Y in New York City, titled "Shakespeare and the Poets."[32] Afterward, he wrote to the Poetry Center's director Karl Kirchwey, thanking him for the invitation but criticizing the reading styles of a number of the participants. He reiterated these objections in a letter to Richie Allen, a former student from Bard:

> To answer your question about the ineptitude of the poets who tried, with marked lack of success, to read passages of Shakespeare, the problems were multiple. They often could make no sense of the meter, they often had a poor grasp of the meaning of the words, they almost always were deaf to the music of the poetry, and lacked all sense of drama. Except for these few failings, they were great.

Hecht could not resist taking on the role of custodian and defender, firing off epistolary attacks at both the ignorant and the brazenly mendacious. When the Easton Press advertised "THE GREATEST SHAKESPEARE LIBRARY EVER" (Hecht typed it out in disdainful capitals), with "peerless illustrations and textual fidelity," he sent a pointed corrective: "You cheap and bogus frauds. . . . [Who is the Easton editor] Herbert Farjeon as compared with such Shakespeare scholars and critics as Kittredge, Dover Wilson, Harrison, Evans, Hotson, Baldwin, Chambers, Kermode and a good number of others?"[33] The Easton Press website still lists its volume of the complete works for a princely $460.

Readers of *The Washington Post*'s "Letters to the Editor" were often treated to Hecht's withering condemnations of sloppy Shakespeare scholarship and any imprecisions regarding his works. It wasn't that he combed the paper looking for such things. Home with the flu or housebound in a snowstorm, these errors would catch his eye, and he could not help but send a stern clarification.

Hecht was self-critical enough, particularly regarding the sin of pride, to know that such controversies and quibbles were counterproductive on some level. He wrote to Rebecca Armstrong with some hard-won observations about the pitfalls of resentment. He had seen it claim other poets, like Plath in her journals, which he found "rancorous, scornful, envious, and at times quite vicious." He took Ruskin at his word that "The emotions of indignation, grief, controversial anxiety and vanity, or hopeless, and therefore, uncontending, scorn, are all of them as deadly to the body as poisonous air or polluted water . . ."[34] He was painfully aware near the end of his life of the time he had wasted in these states. Now more than ever, he understood the brevity of life, and he aspired to affirm what Wordsworth called "that best portion of a good man's life, / His little nameless, unremembered, acts / Of kindness and of love."[35] He admired this same aspiration in Auden, still a moral and poetic guide. As Auden had done for him, Hecht performed acts of kindness for numerous younger writers.

Hecht devoted considerable energy at this point in his career to championing the work of younger poets—Mary Jo Salter, Brad Leithauser, B. H. (Pete) Fairchild, David Mason, Ron Rash, Greg Williamson, Timothy Murphy, and many others—"encouraging them in private, recommending their books to publishers, and declaring for them in public, not just with blurbs but with sometimes lengthy introductions to their books," as Philip Hoy has noted.[36]

Another reminder of life's impermanence came that summer. Helen's ninety-six-year-old mother suffered three heart attacks in rapid succession. Hecht was very fond of her, and loved her as the thoughtful, patient mother he never had. He and Helen visited her every day without fail for months until her death in October, at which time

> it fell to Helen to tidy up all the practical matters—closing her mother's apartment in Chevy Chase, disposing of the furniture, closing her bank account, paying whatever bills were due, dividing valuables with her sister [Carol], arranging for the funeral and interment. Helen and her mother were unusually close, and from the time Helen and I married her mother lived near us, both in Rochester and DC, and visited us every week and on all holidays.[37]

That Christmas, she was deeply missed. The Hechts spent the holiday in New York, the loss being too closely associated with their annual festivities on Nebraska Avenue and "too deeply felt for the occasion to mark any gladness for us."[38] They hoped that being back in New York might help to distract them.

Visiting New York in past years, returning to the streets where he grew up, had been fraught for Hecht, particularly while his parents were alive. Now the city seemed more benign and welcoming. With the sale of his papers to Emory University in late 2002, he could afford the "long-standing dream of a pied-à-terre"[39] and purchased a small apartment on the Upper East Side, on 93rd and Lexington, a block from the 92nd Street Y, in Helen's old neighborhood. New York, he explained in an interview for *The New York Sun,* "doesn't resonate with all those childhood traumas anymore for me. In fact, the apartment we now have is a block from where my wife used to live just before we were married. . . . I have many friends there. So, it's a place that I think of as altogether friendly."[40] So many of his poems over the years had been about confronting the past; now he wished to put it to rest to whatever extent he could.

In "'The Darkness and the Light Are Both Alike to Thee,'" the last poem in his last published collection, he aspires to a condition beyond the vicissitudes of light and dark, good and evil, sorrow and joy. He took the poem's title from Psalms, which he read each year on Yom Kippur as a private act of atonement. Pete Fairchild, whose poems Hecht had championed, felt that Hecht "knew not simply the indelible presence of history's brutalities or the tragic weave of the cosmos somehow isolated and apart, but the old interdependency of light and dark, their collusion from the very beginning."[41] Hecht imagines life as an all-night vigil in which sunrise is both a birth and a quietus:

> Like trailing silks, the light
> Hangs in the olive trees
> As the pale wine of day
> Drains to its very lees:
> Huge presences of gray
> Rise up, and then it's night.
>
> Distantly lights go on.
> Scattered like fallen sparks

Bedded in peat, they seem
Set in the plushest darks
Until a timid gleam
Of matins turns them wan,

Like the elderly and frail
Who've lasted through the night,
Cold brows and silent lips,
For whom the rising light
Entails their own eclipse
Brightening as they fail.[42]

With an echo of the opening of Donne's "Valediction Forbidding Mourning," the dying fade almost imperceptibly away. From his earliest poems, Hecht had considered death as a subject. Now, more and more, he was confronted with his own.

2. Il Golfo Paradiso

In the two years before his final illness, Hecht was busy as ever, with trips planned to England and Rome. He traveled to New York on several occasions, staying in the new apartment, which he thought of as "the chief and most luxurious innovation of our lives."[43] Health issues persisted, however, putting paid to his trip to London and Oxford, though after heart surgery he felt "in better shape than I've enjoyed for decades."[44] The following summer, he was fêted at the West Chester Poetry Conference, in an evening arranged by its co-founders, Dana Gioia and Michael Peich. Hecht enjoyed seeing George and Susan Core from Sewanee; Philip Hoy, who had traveled from England; and the critic Gregory Dowling, who traveled from Venice. The poet Norman Williams led a three-day critical seminar on Hecht's poetry, one of a "series of special programs . . . planned to celebrate my eightieth birthday." Hecht spent his time there in "a blur of happiness and pleasure."[45]

Two crowning volumes appeared: *Melodies Unheard* in May 2003, with essays written since *Obbligati*, and, in the fall, *Collected Later Poems,* with twenty-two woodcuts by Baskin. He was proud that the Baskin images were included and proud of the book generally—"a good way to celebrate my eightieth year."[46] Despite his prediction that his health would keep him from seeing Rome again, he traveled there to give a handful of readings, including on the Janiculum at the American Academy and at the Keats House in the Piazza di Spagna.[47] To Eleanor Cook he wrote that "the city never fails to astonish and overwhelm with delight."[48] A "serious infection of the blood" in the late summer landed him back in the hospital, but in general he was relieved that his health was not worse.[49] In September, he was honored with an eightieth-birthday celebration at the Poetry Center of the 92nd Street Y, with readings and remarks by Nicholas Christopher, John Hollander, Richard Howard, Elizabeth Spires, Brad Leithauser, and Sandy McClatchy. Richard Wilbur, who was caring for his ailing wife, Charlee, sent along his celebratory birthday ballade for Hecht. The Hechts spent Christmas in New York, with Evan, who was living in Brooklyn.

In many respects, Hecht was riding high in his final year. His *Collected Later Poems* received the *Los Angeles Times* Book Prize, and he and Helen delayed the trip they had been planning to Bogliasco by a week to fly to LA to attend the ceremony, replete with its "fake Hollywood Academy Awards glamor." Hecht was amused by LA's "curious inferiority complex about its intellectual/literary status," which, he joked, it "fully deserved."[50] He spoke briefly but movingly at the event, before heading to Italy via New York. By the time he and Helen arrived at Bogliasco, his travels and illnesses had taken their toll, and he began again to ruminate on his diminished abilities, both physical and, he feared, literary as well.

A long hiatus from writing poetry, begun after the publication of *The Darkness and the Light,* began to fill him with "a not completely latent anxiety." He wrote a letter of commiseration to his friend Dimitri Hadzi, who had been hospitalized for depression, feeling "the more distressed for having gone through such a hospitalization myself at one time."[51] Hecht wrote as one who still grappled with such debilitating and disorienting moods. He was anxious about the trip to Genoa. His previous residencies at the Centro Studi Ligure in Boglasco in 1997 and 1999 had been gratifyingly productive. Now with Baskin gone, there were no new collaborations in the works. Hecht worried that, if the writing didn't go well, the weeks at the study center would stretch out interminably, spoiling the memories of those previous visits.

His fears were quickly allayed. The balmy air and wide Tyrrhenian views calmed him. He wrote rapidly and forcefully, touching in fresh ways on familiar themes: Shakespeare, Judaism, and his love for Helen. Despite the salubrious climate, appetizing Genovese fare, and ample cocktail hours, Hecht sensed that his health was declining. There was nothing concrete, no formal diagnosis, merely a tacit suspicion that he was not out of the woods as far as doctors and hospitals were concerned. He voiced this creeping anxiety in "Declensions," with its Shakespearean epigraph: "And every fair from fair sometime declines." Shakespeare provides three epigraphs for his final poems, a further suggestion that he sympathized with Keats who wrote, "I felt rather lonely this morning so I went and unbox'd a Shakespeare—'There's my comfort.'" Like Keats, Hecht's quotations from Shakespeare give "the impression of being called upon because they have become part of the texture of [his] thought; they have been adopted by him, and assimilated to the vigorous metabolism of his imaginative life."[52]

Hecht confronted loss in several guises: loss of the past, loss of friends, and, as in his earlier poem on John Clare, "Coming Home," loss of mental faculties. He acknowledged that he was preparing for death. Like a late installment of "The Presumptions of Death," the grim reaper in the new "Declensions" appears as Death the Thief:

> *Eyesight and hearing fade:*
> *Yet I do not greatly care*
> *If the grim, scythe-wielding thief*
> *Pursue his larcenous trade,*
> *Though anguished by the grief*
> *Two that I love must bear.*[53]

At breakfast during their three-week stay, the Hechts were fortified with freshly brewed espresso and fruit from the local market. After a morning of work or reading, the fellows gathered for lunch—radicchio salad, focaccia de queso, orecchiette with olives or pesto. Afternoons were perfect for walks into nearby Nervi, a former spa, with its museums, parks, and trompe l'oeil facades. The sea spanned the horizon, with a steady traffic of ships heading in and out of the port of Genoa to the northeast.

From their rooms in the Villa dei Pini, Hecht watched each morning the gradual lightening of the sky over the hills above Comogli. He saw the horizon emerge from the darkness. Waking up early, with Helen asleep beside him, he thought again of the anguish his death would cause her. (When Hecht changed the title of "Aubade" to "A Deep Breath of Dawn" in *Stones,* he could not have foreseen that he was saving it for the title of one of his last poems.) He drafted a new "Aubade." Dawn, he told Ada Fan, had impressed him at a young age

> because of the way the light fell. I was very sensitive to light, and mornings—the very earliest part of the day—seemed hopeful, promising. I found infinitely depressing the light of three to four in the afternoon. . . .
>
> Mornings are more golden, afternoons more apricot and rust: a sad brick-like color of absolute desolation. And if you take sunrises and sunsets as intervals of time, rather than static instants, it's either always getting lighter or getting darker. . . .
>
> The child's experience is bound to be visual . . . He doesn't know how the world is put together; he just looks. And his visual impressions may stay with him and profoundly affect him; but he may not be able to find language precise enough to convey these impressions until much later.[54]

The poem in full reads:

> *How shyly dawn slips out of its own absence*
> *Into its first pearl self, a nacreous birth*
> *Welcomed by silent stones—as though the world*
> *Somehow was cleansed of all hostilities.*
> *The wards of hope in every hospital*
> *Brighten ever so slightly. A pale gray,*
> *A gray full of unearthly tenderness*
> *Visits the window's curtains, those random folds*
> *And soft wrappings of light. But what's to come*
> *Is as foreordained as Beethoven's Great Fugue.*
> *It begins delicately with apricot*

Tinting the steeple tops and cornices
Of the municipal facades, and swells
In volume and complexity that turn
Into varieties of lemon, leading
To formal gladness, indisputable gold.

If the heart leaps at this usual miracle,
If the music figures its own destiny,
Think how I feel each day lying beside you,
Watching the easy cadences of your breathing
As you lie gilded in the advancing light,
Recognizing in each familiar feature
A fund of goodness, a calm dormant beauty
That in accord with Galilean laws,
With braided melody in trellised parts,
Rouse with the rising light to blessedness.[55]

"Aubade" was his valediction, his final love poem for Helen, she who had brought him back to himself and through whose eyes he came to see himself as worthy of love.

At Sewanee that summer, Hecht attended a panel on his work and gave a reading, featuring "Aubade" and other new poems. He stood without assistance at the podium, though friends noted that he had begun to look visibly ill. It was Hecht's final reading. Despite his gaunt appearance, Hecht delivered his poems with characteristic aplomb, receiving a standing ovation.[56] The reason for his weight loss and physical weakness was explained by his doctor in Washington that fall: it was cancer. Hecht began treatment immediately: "a series of chemotherapy sessions that last eight hours and recur at intervals of three weeks. This is likely to take me as far as late November."[57] He hoped to work around readings at Kenyon and Colorado College, but in the end they had to be canceled.

The last weeks were hard; he became "mildly depressed by the lassitude, banality, and torpor of the 'ideas' that drift idly through my mind at virtually all hours in this, my third-plus week of chemo, which leaves me bored; and for one who has long had an active mental life, this is disagreeable. But it may also be that these episodes of lumbering infelicity are serving some benign purpose, and dissipating some unhealthy morosities of thought."[58] At home on Nebraska Avenue, he was occasionally able to sit up and talk with visitors, though mostly he slept. He had imagined his end often, confronted death and its presumptions. The negotiations were over. He knew it was time.

3. Among the English Poets

Hecht's burial in the cemetery at Bard College in April 2005 took place among family and a few friends, a simple affair, though marked by a certain ceremony. Two of Shakespeare's Sonnets, numbers 74 and 79, were read. The setting was poignantly appropriate: Hecht first seriously engaged with poetry at Bard, and it was there that he fell, as an actor and a reader, "transposingly" in love with Shakespeare. His professors in Annandale were Hecht's first champions, having "no doubt of his talent—either for poetry or for the stage."[59]

His illnesses in his last years had been a trial, but even at his weakest he wished to acknowledge his gratitude for the good fortune that came to him after the traumas of his youth, the way that tragedy sometimes resolves unexpectedly as comedy. He was grateful for his literary successes and for his happy marriage to Helen. He believed that in a very real sense she had saved his life. He had been thinking of his own death for some time, and it's possible that in the months before his diagnosis, before he became visibly frail, he had intimations of the illness that would overtake him. On New Year's Eve, in the last year of his life, he wrote a letter to Fr. John McGuire, the cleric who had performed their wedding, at the address Hecht had for him from thirty years before:

> I thought it worth the risk of trying to reach you at the tail end of a troubled year with some good news. You were good enough to marry my wife and me in June 1971. The event took place on the terrace-garden of her home in New York. You inaugurated a marriage that can have few equals. I am as happy today as I have ever been in my life. We have a son, now 31, who lives in New York and to whom we are devoted. All this was begun by you, and it seemed worth trying to let you know.

The letter came back "return to sender," but Hecht had expressed his gratitude, as it were before God.

Beyond his transformative love for family, a miracle given the troubled ties and dark secrets that had marked his childhood, Hecht had one thought: he hoped his poems might live. From the day it had dawned on him to become a poet, he had been faithful to this vision of himself. Despite periods of doubt, when the writing wouldn't come, he never lost his defining purpose and identity: he was a poet, and, he dared to hope, an important one. Echoing Keats again, he said to Helen at the end: "I pray I shall be among the English poets." Keats's words to his brother George were more assured: "I think I shall be among the English Poets after my death." Hecht's prayer is in the subjunctive mood, expressing faithfully, without pride, an intimate wish. A worthy member of that pantheon is all he ever wanted to be. These were his final words, after which he drifted off, for the last time, to sleep. In the issue of *The New York Review of Books* for October 21, 2004, "Aubade" appeared. It's unlikely that Hecht saw it in print. He died the day before, aged eighty-one, at home in Washington, DC, with Helen beside him.

In his obituary for *The Wall Street Journal,* Benjamin Ivry compares Hecht's struggles to Lear's: "The eldest has borne most."[60] But how was Hecht able to bear it? The music of Shakespeare brought him back from desolations after the war, and the music of the Bible sustained him through emotional and spiritual crises. As Ivry suggests, Hecht (like Auden before him) discovered in language the "hidden law" that bestows an implicit order on the world, without which, like Lear, we "shall go mad." Brodsky felt that, if Hecht's "poetry is tragedy, and to me it is, it is necessarily so, and not only because it comes from this world but because it echoes the world beyond this one . . . I think that he simply talks back to the language, of whose beauty, wisdom, sensuality, inevitability of form, irony and everlasting nature this poet is the clearest mirror."[61] A mirror held up to nature: it's an echo that would have pleased Hecht well.

/

ACKNOWLEDGMENTS

Throughout the writing of this book, I have benefitted from the guidance and support of a great number of colleagues and friends, chief among them Anthony Hecht's widow, Helen, who has been a tireless custodian of her husband's legacy. J. D. McClatchy, who served as Hecht's literary executor until his death in 2018, was my teacher at Columbia and a generous mentor, whose wisdom and example I benefitted from more than I can say. He remains the most perceptive critic of the poems and was a close friend of Hecht's for decades. After Sandy's passing, Helen took on the role of executor. Her experience as a literary editor and her deep knowledge of her husband's life and work has been indispensable. She tirelessly read several versions of the manuscript, pointing out errors of fact and filling in missing details, while never inhibiting my characterizations and interpretations of Hecht and his work. I am deeply grateful to Deborah Garrison and Alfred A. Knopf for permission to quote from Hecht's poems.

I received valuable encouragement from Michael Anderson and Ernest Hilbert, who read the chapters as they were written and urged me to keep going. Without them, I might have flagged in my efforts to tell the story through to the end. I was extremely fortunate to receive detailed notes on the finished draft from my colleague Andrew Motion, who, in addition to his brilliance as a poet and biographer, is an editor of extraordinary insight and skill. What's more, he wields a red pencil deftly and unsparingly without shedding a drop of blood.

It is a far better book for the careful reading and painstaking feedback of the two most knowledgeable Hecht scholars—Philip Hoy, editor of Hecht's *Collected Poems*, and Jonathan F. S. Post, a former student of Hecht's who produced the first book-length study of Hecht's work, *A Thickness of Particulars* (2015), as well as a selection of Hecht's letters. Their comprehensive knowledge of Hecht's life saved me from a host of errors of fact, and their insights into the work were bellwethers that guided my inquiries. Douglas P. Warwick worked tirelessly to compile a genealogy of the Hechts going back to Germany in the mid-nineteenth century. I am hugely indebted to him for his expert sleuthing.

Others who have contributed to the book in a variety of ways are Jonathan Aaron, Daniel Anderson, Madison Smartt Bell, Diann Blakley, Gerry Cambridge, Barbara Connolly, George Core, Gregory Dowling, Benjamin Downing, Kevin Durkin, Dana Gioia, Jonathan Gondelman, Langdon Hammer, Erin Harris, Jeffrey Harrison, Edward Hirsch, Natalie Charkow Hollander, Lauren K. Hall, John Irwin, Brian Kelly, Roger Kimball, Karl Kirchwey, David Landon, Herbert Liebowitz, Charles Martin, Joshua Mehigan, Edward Moran, Francis Morrone, Arthur Mortensen, Wade Newman, Michael Peich, Debra Pemstein, Edward Perlman, Wyatt Prunty, Lawrence Rhu, Lilly Rudd, Bernard Schwartz, Don Share, Willard Speigelman, Elizabeth Spires, Ernest Suarez, Liz Van Hoose, Greg Williamson, Ryan Wilson, and Christian Wiman.

I was fortunate to have the opportunity to interview many of Hecht's colleagues, friends, and relatives, all of whom generously relayed their memories and impressions: Harold Bloom, Chevy Chase, Nicholas Christopher, Denis Donoghue, Frederick Fierstein, B. H. Fairchild, Dan Goldwater, Kenneth Gross, Joseph Harrison, Adam Hecht, Evan Hecht, Helen Hecht, Edward Hirsch, John Hollander, Richard Howard, Philip Hoy, Brad Leithauser, Richard Lincoln, David Mason, Jonathan F. S. Post, Tita Rosenthal, Mary Jo Salter, Frederick Seidel, Mark Strand, Mira Van Doren, Rosanna Warren, Dr. Neil Weissman, Claire White, Richard Wilbur, Norman Williams, and Anne Wright.

I am grateful to the librarians and institutions that made available documents and letters from their archives, particularly Kathy Shoemaker at Emory University, where the Anthony Hecht Archive is housed in the Manuscript and Rare Book Library at Emory University (MARBL). Thanks, also, to Teri Cross Davis and Dr. Georgianna Ziegler at the Folger Shakespeare Library; Olga Kazarov at Smith College Special Collections; Sebastian Hierl at the American Academy in Rome; Arielle Moreau, Ivana Folle, and Valeria Soave at the Bogliasco Foundation; and Bernard Schwartz at the Unterberg Poetry Center of the 92nd Street Y.

To the members of the critical seminar "American Master: Anthony Hecht" (West Chester University, June 6–8, 2019), co-led by Jonathan Post, I wish to extend my thanks for their informative presentations, which included papers by Professor Post, Richard Aston, Gregory Dowling, Moira Egan, Robert B. Hass, Michael Healy, Anne Higgins, David Katz, Janie McNeil, Mark Myers, Peter Vertacnik, and Ryan Wilson.

I was afforded time to write by residencies at Bogliasco and at Jesus College, Oxford, where several chapters were drafted, and by sabbaticals given by the Writing Seminars at Johns Hopkins University, which allowed for travel to Germany, Italy, and France, on the trail of the subject. To my wife, Sarah Harrison Smith, I owe my fullest debt of gratitude. Unwavering in her faith in the book and my ability to see it through, her belief quieted my hesitations and doubts. Without her, this book could not have been written. Our children, Susannah, Harrison, and Nicholas, provided regular encouragement that kept me moving forward. Adults now, they were little when the book was begun; they have been patient with their father during his decade of Hecht.

NOTES

When quoting from Anthony Hecht's letters, I have corrected spelling and typography (e.g., replacing underlined text in typescript letters with italic text) whenever such changes had no bearing on the sense. Unless otherwise noted, quotations from AEH's correspondence and other documents are taken from The Hecht Archive in the Manuscript and Rare Book Library at Emory University (MARBL). A generous and expertly edited edition of AEH's letters, with extensive biographical and critical commentary, was compiled by AEH's former student Jonathan F. S. Post. I am indebted to this work as well as to Mr. Post's excellent critical work, *A Thickness of Particulars,* the first full-length appraisal of AEH's poetry.

I have relied heavily on two autobiographical sources and two biographical sources. The first two are interviews that AEH gave during his lifetime—*The Paris Review* Writers at Work interview conducted by J. D. McClatchy (McC) ("The Art of Poetry 40," *The Paris Review,* Issue 108 [Fall 1988], pp. 160–205) and *Anthony Hecht in Conversation with Philip Hoy* (Hoy), edited by Philip Hoy (Chipping Norton, Oxfordshire: Between the Lines, third edition, expanded, 2004; second edition, October 2001; first edition, June 1999). This volume also includes an extensive bibliography of AEH's work. The third source is an unpublished journal of recollections written by Helen Hecht. The journal comprises 107 handwritten pages and was mainly composed between January 2006 and 2011 (HHJ). Many of AEH's memories of childhood and later, as told to Helen over the course of their marriage, are recounted. The fourth is a genealogical history of AEH's family going back to Buttenheim, Germany, in the mid-nineteenth century, compiled by Douglas P. Warwick in 2012 (W).

Works Cited

Poetry

A Summoning of Stones, 1954 (SS)

Collected Earlier Poems, 1990 (CEP)

Collected Later Poems, 2003 (CLP)

Criticism

Obbligati: Essays in Criticism, Atheneum, 1986 (OB)

The Hidden Law: The Poetry of W. H. Auden, Harvard, 1993 (HL)

On the Laws of the Poetic Art (Andrew W. Mellon Lectures in the Fine Arts), Princeton, 1995 (LPA)

Melodies Unheard: Essays on the Mysteries of Poetry, Johns Hopkins, 2003 (MU)

Introduction

1. *Anthony Hecht in Conversation with Philip Hoy,* ed. Philip Hoy (Chipping Norton, Oxfordshire: Between the Lines), p. 26. [Hereafter Hoy.] As Hecht (hereafter AEH) tells Hoy in this invaluable book-length interview, he suffered from PTSD (what he refers to as "Post Traumatic Shock Syndrome"), which has a wide-reaching impact on his life and his work. In the interview, Hecht says that his sleep was troubled in this way "for years." In fact, as his widow, Helen, explained in an interview with the author, he suffered from these disruptive nightmares on and off for the rest of his life. In his last years, he reported that he was no longer troubled by bad dreams.

2. "Anatomies of Melancholy," by J. D. McClatchy, from *The Burdens of Formality: Essays on the Poetry of Anthony Hecht,* edited by Sydney Lea (Athens, GA: University of Georgia Press, 1989), p. 191. [Hereafter BOF.]

3. Letter to Ashley Brown, 4.18.78, MARBL.

4. Letter to Father Timothy Healy, 2.14.81, MARBL. When "Sestina d'Inverno" appeared in *Millions of Strange Shadows* (1977), AEH wrote, "some colleagues found it expressive of disloyal and traitorous sentiments. They have dropped those accusations this winter." The severity of Rochester's winters became a recurring subject of playful grousing in his letters. According to Jonathan Post, the Rochester English department subsequently took to reciting the sestina at their graduation ceremony.

5. Ted Hughes, from his program note on AEH for the Poetry International '67 festival, in London.

6. *The Tempest,* 5.1.195. Hecht places this line and the preceding line of Ferdinand's as epigraph to his collection *Millions of Strange Shadows* (1977).

7. In his introduction to his *Paris Review* interview of AEH, J. D. McClatchy dubs him "an aristocrat among poets."

8. "Anthony Hecht," by Ada Fan, *City Newspaper: A Journal of Urban News and Opinion*, Rochester, New York, Vol. 11, No. 21 (February 18–24, 1982), p. 8. [Hereafter Fan.]

9. A number of newspaper articles from the sixties and seventies refer to him mistakenly as speaking with a British accent.

10. Nancy Lewis, interview with the author.

11. "The Art of Poetry No. 40," an interview by J. D. McClatchy, *The Paris Review* (Issue 108, Fall 1988). [Hereafter McC.]

12. The title that AEH chose for the first chapter of his book on W. H. Auden, *The Hidden Law* (Cambridge, MA: Harvard University Press, 1993). [Hereafter HL.]

13. Fan, p. 8.

14. Letter to Daniel Halpern, 5.17.77, MARBL.

15. Ibid. AEH spoke of W. H. Auden in similar terms in the preface to his study of Auden, *The Hidden Law*: "Poetry has long been thought of as a sort of code, and more than that, a shibboleth: a device to prevent any invasion of the domain of occult knowledge and understanding by those who are deemed unworthy. And poets exhibit varying degrees or strategies of reticence," p. viii.

16. Letter to David Bromwich, 2.12.82, MARBL.

17. Hoy, p. 58. All quotations from this book-length interview are from AEH, unless otherwise indicated.

18. *Collected Later Poems* (New York: Knopf, 2009), p. 123. [Hereafter CLP.]

19. *Collected Earlier Poems* (New York: Knopf, 1992), p. 65. [Hereafter CEP.]

20. CEP, p. 211.

21. Edward Mendelson, "Seeing Is Not Believing," *The New York Review of Books* (June 20, 2013). Mendelson points to a number of autobiographical threads in "The Venetian Vespers" having to do with AEH and fatherhood (hereafter Mendelson).

22. Letter to David Lehman, 2.4.91, MARBL.

One: Hecht & Sons

1. Quoted by AEH in "Beginnings," an interview for the Borzoi Reader online, February 2001.

2. The title of a poem from "The Presumptions of Death" sequence in AEH's *Flight Among the Tombs*.

3. Hoy, p. 19.

4. In fact, the suicide rate during the Great Depression was lower than legend would lead one to believe. Still, Winston Churchill saw from his room at the Savoy-Plaza Hotel a man jump from the fifteenth floor, causing a crowd to gather and the arrival of fire trucks.

5. Hoy, p. 19.

6. McC, p. 183.

7. Hoy, p. 19.

8. Hoy, p. 17.

9. The building had three addresses: 140 East 89th Street, 1327 Lexington Avenue, and 141 East 88th Street; Melvyn & Dorothea preferred using 140 East 89th Street.

10. "Apprehensions," CEP, p. 156, first appeared in *Millions of Strange Shadows* (1977). In a letter to the poet and Johns Hopkins professor John Irwin (9.29.76), AEH referred to it as "a longish poem about the stock market crash," though clearly it was much more personal than that. It is one of AEH's most directly autobiographical poems.

11. AEH wrote about his fascination with nursery rhymes in "First Loves" in the Poetry Society of America's publication *Crossroads* (Spring 1998), pp. 17–8. [Hereafter First Loves.]

12. "Apprehensions," CEP, p. 154.

13. CEP, p. 155.

14. From Helen Hecht's journal, p. 5. [Hereafter HHJ.]

15. "Apprehensions," CEP, p. 154.

16. "Apprehensions," CEP, p. 159.

17. Helen Hecht, interview with the author.

18. HHJ, p. 13.

19. First Loves, p. 17.

20. "Beginnings," a brief memoir written for *The Borzoi Reader* online, Feb. 2001.

21. "Apprehensions," CEP, p. 155.

22. "Peekaboo," subtitled "Three Songs for the Nursery," from "The Presumptions of Death," in *Flight Among the Tombs* (1996), CLP, p. 95.

23. From *The Hard Hours*, CEP, pp. 66–7.

24. It would not have been lost on AEH that his family business was the same as Shakespeare's. John Shakespeare dealt in hides and was at one time a prosperous glover and whittawer or tanner.

25. Stephen Birmingham notes the use of this phrase in his important study *Our Crowd: The Great Jewish Families of New York*, which characterizes the assimilationist ideal the Hechts themselves aspired to, though they fell short of the level of financial success enjoyed by the most prominent members of the Jewish upperclass in New York.

26. "History of the House of Hecht," *Hide and Leather: The International Weekly*, Vol. 58, No. 9, August 30, 1919, p. 33.

27. AEH's typescript "Note's on AEH's family," MARBL.

28. Ibid.

29. HHJ, p. 15.

30. Other prints owned by AEH and hung in his home in Washington, DC, were woodcuts by Leonard Baskin, Samuel Palmer, Tiepolo, Mark Leithauser, Dimitri Hadzi, Piranesi, Rembrandt, and Lucas von Leyden, several of which he and Helen purchased as gifts for one another over the years.

31. This division that Stephen Birmingham identifies in his book *Our Crowd* is

elaborated upon in his succeeding companion volume, *The Rest of Us: The Rise of American's Eastern European Jews* (1984).

32. Hoy, p. 17.
33. Ibid.
34. Hoy, p. 18.
35. Hoy, p. 15.
36. "Apprehensions," CEP, p. 154.
37. HHJ, p. 1.
38. Ibid.
39. "Memory," CLP, p. 169.
40. McC, p. 168.
41. Hoy, pp. 18–9.
42. Hoy, p. 17.
43. From AEH's eulogy for Roger Hecht, delivered Saturday, April 28, 1990, at the New York Society for Ethical Culture on West 64th Street in New York City, MARBL.
44. McC, p. 168.
45. AEH, interview with the author. The quotation appears in a profile for *The New York Sun* titled "The Baroque Mastery of Anthony Hecht," Sept. 24, 2003, p. 16 (hereafter Sun).
46. McC, p. 168.
47. HHJ, p. 12.
48. McC, pp. 166–7.
49. McC, p. 166.
50. "Efforts of Attention: An Interview with Anthony Hecht," by Langdon Hammer, *The Sewanee Review*, Vol. 104, No. 1 (Winter 1996), p. 90. [Hereafter Hammer.]
51. McC, p. 159.
52. Ibid.
53. HHJ, p. 6.
54. Ibid.
55. HHJ, p. 8.
56. CEP, p. 237.
57. CEP, p. 238.
58. J. D. McClatchy in an introduction to a reading by Hecht, with Joseph Brodsky, at the Unterberg Poetry Center of the 92nd Street Y in New York, December 22, 1991.
59. CEP, p. 185. The poem is set at least two decades after AEH's childhood trip to the Alps, though the memories of that trip were a likely source.

Two: "An Education for Which I Received No Grades . . ."

1. "St. Paul's Epistle to the Galatians," *Melodies Unheard: Essays on the Mysteries of Poetry* (Baltimore: Johns Hopkins University Press, 2003), p. 250. [Hereafter MU.]

2. CLP, p. 79.

3. Letter to Jon Stallworthy, 9.12.67, MARBL.

4. Annie Wright, interview with the author.

5. HHJ, p. 3.

6. "The Short End," from *The Venetian Vespers* (1979), CEP, p. 196.

7. HHJ, p. 4.

8. *A Handbook of Summer Camps: An Annual Survey* (Third Edition) (Porter Sargent, 1926).

9. *The History of Camp Kennebec,* by Frances Fox Sandmel (North Belgrade, ME, 1973). This typewritten document provides background on the camp used throughout this chapter. The Camp Kennebec archives are housed in the Special Collections Research Center, Temple University [hereafter Sandmel].

10. Undated letter from Hecht to his parents from Camp Kennebec (likely July 1935).

11. Sandmel, p. 15.

12. *The Kennebecamper 1935,* camp yearbook, pp. 49–50.

13. Ibid.

14. *The Kennebecamper 1936,* p. 49.

15. Sandmel, p. 10.

16. Letter to his parents, 7.5.36.

17. Undated (1938?), marked "Private / For Dad," MARBL.

18. Sandmel, p. 12.

19. Undated letter (1938?), MARBL.

20. Letter to his parents, 6.3.38, MARBL.

21. Letter to his parents, undated (Summer 1935), MARBL.

22. McC, p. 166.

23. Letter to his parents, 6.3.38, MARBL.

24. *The Kennebecamper 1938.*

25. Sandmel, p. 41.

26. From "The Pathetic Fallacy," a lecture given at the Library of Congress on May 7, 1984, later collected in *Obbligati: Essays in Criticism* (1986), p. 12 [hereafter OB].

27. OB, p. 26.

28. "Songs for the Air, or Several Attitudes About Breathing," from *A Summoning of Stones,* p. 27. The comparison of a cloud to a whale recalls *Hamlet* III.ii, among the countless Shakespearean echoes Hecht employed in his work.

29. "Once Removed," *The Kenyon Review,* Spring 1947, published (perhaps mistakenly) under the name Tony Hecht, the only time his nickname appears as a byline. Hecht enunciates this same desire to trade the shocks of animal existence for the insentience of the vegetable world in several mature poems, including "Behold the Lilies of the Field."

30. For much about New York private schools of the period, and particularly

Horace Mann, I have relied on *Citizen Newhouse: Portrait of a Media Merchant,* by Carol Felsenthal (Seven Stories Press, 1998). [Hereafter Felsenthal.]

31. Interview with the author, 8.28.2003.

32. *The Merchant of Venice,* I.iii.98.

33. "St. Paul's Epistle to the Galatians," MU, p. 250.

34. *The Stranger in Shakespeare,* by Leslie Fiedler (Stein & Day, 1973). Fiedler considers the role of women, Shylock, Othello, and Caliban.

35. "Horace Mann—The 1940s," by Daniel Rose. Though this memoir by the well-known real estate developer and philanthropist Daniel Rose covers the 1940s, the school was much as it had been before the war, when AEH was there: "World War II left us essentially untouched," Rose writes. [Hereafter Rose.]

36. Felsenthal, p. 30.

37. HHJ, p. 19.

38. Evan Hecht, interview with the author.

39. Felsenthal, p. 31.

40. Hoy, p. 20.

41. Rose, pp. 6–7.

42. Nicholas Christopher, interview with the author.

43. Felsenthal, p. 41.

44. "Eulogy at the Funeral of Alfred Baruth," by Daniel Rose (https://www .yumpu.com/en/document/view/11423751/eulogy-at-the-funeral-of-alfred -baruth-daniel-rose).

45. Ibid.

46. McC, p. 164.

47. McC, p. 163.

48. Interview with the author.

49. The play appeared in their English textbook, *The Literature of England: An Anthology and a History—Volume Two: from the Dawn of the Romantic Movement to the World War,* which the boys underlined and carried around as their script.

50. Of his early study of the piano, AEH later wrote to W. D. Snodgrass: "Back in my youth one of the earliest pieces of music a beginner was given was Mendelssohn's 'Spring Song,' which lodged in my mind so firmly that though with the passage of time I became acquainted with a lot of other Mendelssohn, that early tune seemed not only unalterably associated with spring but with a very early and moderately cheerful time of my life" [2.24.94, MARBL].

51. A letter from Kenneth Lynn to AEH, 6.23.97, MARBL. AEH wrote to W. D. Snodgrass in 1999: "Once, long ago, I used to go out with a girl who hated Vivaldi. She was a concert pianist, came from a very wealthy family (her mother was the president of the Museum of Modern Art) [Grace M. Mayer was in fact a curator of photography] and eventually went to marry a composer/conductor. . . . Our relationship was neither long nor happy. She was

impossibly spoiled, owning a large apartment in the Dakota building on Central Park West, with two grand pianos in her living room" [9.2.99, MARBL].

52. Letter to Kenneth Lynn, 6.25.97, MARBL.

53. Ibid.

54. *Horace Mannikin 1940*, p. 48.

55. *Subterranean Kerouac: The Hidden Life of Jack Kerouac,* by Ellis Amburn, p. 45.

56. *The Quarterly,* Summer 1940.

57. McC, p. 172.

58. Hoy, p. 21.

59. Letter to his parents, 9.10.40, MARBL.

60. HHJ, p. 71.

61. Bard Archive, Interview with Richard F. Koch, 5.27.2000.

62. Adviser's semester summary, Spring 1941, registrar's files, Bard College.

63. Adviser's semester summary, Fall 1942, registrar's files, Bard College.

64. Letter to parents, 10.20.44, MARBL.

65. Hoy, p. 23.

66. Hoy, p. 21. One imagines Leighton lingering over the lines later in Gaveston's speech where he describes "a lovely boy in Dian's shape, / With hair that gilds the water as it glides, / Crownets of pearl about his naked arms, / And in his sportful hands an olive tree, / To hide those parts which men delight to see. . . ."

67. Ibid.

68. Hoy, p. 22.

69. "A Matter of Formality: Distinguished Man of Letters Anthony Hecht Remembers Teaching and Learning at Kenyon," by Amy Blumenthal, *Kenyon College Alumni Bulletin,* Volume 26, Number 1 (Summer 2003). [Hereafter Blumenthal.]

70. Hoy, p. 22.

71. Letter to Evan Hecht, 1.7.02.

72. McC, p. 165.

73. *Kennebecamper,* Summer 1941, p. 7.

74. Hoy, p. 17.

75. Hoy, p. 19.

76. Paul Morrison, Adviser's Semester Summary, Fall 1942, Office of the Registrar, Bard College.

77. Hoy, p. 24.

78. Ibid.

79. Paul Morrison, Mid-Term Report, Fall 1942, Office of the Registrar, Bard College.

80. Letter to Frank Glazer, 2.16.94.

81. Letter to Beum, 12.7.98, the date, the anniversary of Pearl Harbor, marked "(the day of infamy)."

82. Hoy, p. 24.

Three: "Ghosts from the Ovens"

1. "'More Light! More Light,'" CEP, p. 65. In writing about AEH's Army service, I am particularly indebted to two essays by Geoffrey Lindsay—"Anthony Hecht, Private First Class," *The Yale Review*, Vol. 96, No. 3 (July 2008), pp. 1–26 [hereafter GL1]; and "Anthony Hecht in Occupied Japan," *Sewanee Review*, Vol. 119, No. 4 (Fall 2011), pp. 641–55 [hereafter GL2].

2. Letter to Jon Stallworthy, 9.12.67, MARBL.

3. The Hecht archive at Emory identifies this photo as c. 1914, though it is not clear how this date was arrived at. In that year, Melvyn would have only recently left Harvard to manage his father's business. It seems more likely that he was drafted in wartime, a few years later, rather than enlisted so soon after taking over his father's affairs.

4. McC, p. 169.

5. Hecht's proposed senior project, a series of poems, was never realized. Instead, he submitted this explanatory limerick entitled "A Poem" as "not merely a brief outline, but my complete Senior Project": "In a frenzy of virtue and verve / I entered the Army Reserve. / But this valor, I heard / Today, has incurred / A premature summons to serve" (registrar's file, Bard College).

6. Letter to parents, 7.26.43.

7. GL1, p. 5.

8. From the website of the National World War II Museum in New Orleans, https://www.nationalww2museum.org/.

9. "Battleground," the typescript of a talk by AEH at the Museum of Jewish Heritage in New York City, given at a screening of William Wellman's film of that name on March 17, 2004, p. 5, MARBL [Hereafter B]. In this talk, AEH included extended passages from his interview with Philip Hoy. Clearly, he felt that what he wrote on that occasion remained a true expression of his war experience.

10. B, p. 4.

11. Ibid.

12. Ibid.

13. Ibid.

14. Letter to parents, 7.26.43.

15. Letter to parents, 4.26.44.

16. Letter to parents, 7.26.43.

17. Letter to parents, 5.23.44.

18. McC, p. 170.

19. "Abiding Questions: An Interview with Anthony Hecht," by Lawrence Rhu. *Harvard Advocate*, CVII 2/3 (Fall 1973), pp. 21–2. [Hereafter Rhu.]

20. McC, p. 169.

21. McC, p. 170.

22. Ibid.

23. McC, pp. 169–70.

24. Rhu, p. 22.

25. McC, pp. 170–1.

26. As quoted by Paul Fussell in *The Boys' Crusade: The American Infantry in Northwestern Europe, 1944–1945* (New York: Modern Library, 2005) [Hereafter Fussell].

27. McC, p. 171.

28. Letter to parents, 4.26.44.

29. Ibid.

30. Fussell, p. 68.

31. Fussell, p. 67.

32. Fussell, p. 98. (Lindsay's use of this quotation and others from Fussell powerfully supports his portrait of AEH at war.)

33. GL1, p. 8.

34. Hoy, pp. 24–5.

35. Letter to parents, 10.12.44.

36. AEH's FOIA Army file consists largely of dozens of hospital forms from Camp Callan hospital.

37. Letter to parents, 10.12.44.

38. Letter to parents, 8.21.44.

39. Letter to parents, 11.22.44.

40. Letter to parents, 9.28.44.

41. V-Mail to parents, 2.27.45, marked "at sea."

42. V-Mail to parents, 3.4.45.

43. Letter to parents, 3.25.45.

44. Letter to parents, 4.6.46.

45. This account, included among AEH's papers (MARBL), dates from his time in Japan, where he closed out his service just after the war. The typed account, emended in his hand, may have been prepared as a submission to *Stars and Stripes,* though it's condemnations and accusations were not a likely fit for that official outlet. The passage in brackets in the penultimate paragraph is a handwritten emendation to the typescript.

46. GL1, p. 15.

47. Company "C" 386th Infantry Action Report, MARBL [hereafter CoCAR].

48. Hoy, p. 25.

49. Undated typescript, MARBL.

50. "Welcome to the 97th Infantry Division—The Trident Division: Information, history, and photographs about the 97th Division in World War II," webpage [hereafter W97].

51. *Battle for the Ruhr: The German Army's Final Defeat in the West,* by Derek S. Zumbro. Quoted in Lindsay, GL1.

52. Ibid.

53. GL1, p. 18.

54. Hoy, p. 27.

55. Hoy, p. 26.

56. CLP, p. 79.

57. Letter to parents, 4.26.45.

58. W97.

59. Letter to parents, 4.26.45, MARBL. The whole verse from Isaiah (52:7) in the King James version reads: "How beautiful upon the mountains are the feet of him that bringeth good tidings, that publisheth peace; that bringeth good tidings of good, that publisheth salvation; that saith unto Zion, Thy God reigneth!"

60. Ibid.

61. Ibid.

62. Ibid.

63. Thomas E. Kennedy, "A Last Conversation with Robie Macauley," *Agni*, No. 45 (1997), p. 180. [Hereafter Kennedy.]

64. Kennedy, p. 181.

65. Letter to parents, 5.24.45, MARBL.

66. *Flossenbürg Concentration Camp, 1938–1945: Catalogue of the Permanent Exhibition*, Christina Schikorra, et al., editors. Flossenbürg Memorial / Bavarian Memorial Foundation (Braunschweig), p. 229 [Hereafter FCC].

67. FCC, p. 226.

68. *XII Corps: Spearhead of Patton's Army, Part 2*, by Lt. Col. George Dyer. (Hereafter XII Corps.)

69. "Flossenbürg Concentration Camp," Holocaust Education and Archive Research Team, http://www.holocaustresearchproject.org/othercamps/flossenburg.html. [Hereafter HRP.]

70. W97.

71. XII Corps.

72. Details and testimony from the Dachau Trials are taken from *United States vs. Friedrich Becker, et al., Case No. 000–50–46: Review and Recommendations of the Deputy Judge Advocate for War Crimes and Action by Approving Authority*, Deputy Judge Advocate's Office, 7708 War Crimes Group, European Command, APO 407, p. 12. A copy of this document may be found online at https://www.jewishvirtuallibrary.org/jsource/Holocaust/dachautrial/f13.pdf (hereafter USvFB).

73. Ibid.

74. CoCAR, p. 7, entry for "29 April 45."

75. Hoy, p. 26.

76. "Who Should Mourn?" by Robie Macauley. *The New York Times*, Letters to the Editor, August 8, 1976.

77. HRP.

78. USvFB.

79. Melchior, Ib. *Case by Case: A U.S. Army Counterintelligence Agent in World War II* (Presidio Press, 1993), p. 128. [Hereafter CBC.]

80. CBC, p. 129.

81. Letter to parents, 5.14.45, MARBL.

82. Letter to parents, 5.24.45, MARBL.

83. Letter by Capt. Oscar M. Grimes, 11.24.45, MARBL.

84. *Anthony Hecht: The Poet's View* (2001), a video, released on DVD, produced and directed by Mel Stuart.

85. Hoy, p. 26.

86. B, p. 12.

87. CEP, p. 78.

88. Letter to parents, 8.3.45, MARBL.

89. Ibid.

90. Letter to parents, 8.14.45, MARBL.

91. Ibid.

92. W97.

93. Letter to parents, 11.26.45, MARBL.

94. Letter to Kathryn Swift, 12.8.45.

95. "Japan," CEP, p. 77.

96. "Introduction," *Jiggery-Pokery: A Compendium of Double Dactyls,* edited by Anthony Hecht and John Hollander (New York: Atheneum, 1967), p. 16.

97. Letter to parents, 10.28.44, MARBL.

98. Hoy, p. 29.

99. From an undated talk given at The Folger Shakespeare Library in honor of Shakespeare's birthday, MARBL (hereafter Folger).

100. Review of "Selected Poems," by Diann Blakely, *Pleiades*, Vol. 32, No. 2 (Summer 2012).

101. "Rites and Ceremonies," CEP, p. 39.

102. Hoy, p. 24.

103. GL1, p. 26.

104. AEH, "At War with His Memories," a review of *Doing Battle* by Paul Fussell. In quoting his own review in his talk at the Museum of Jewish Heritage in 2004, he alters it slightly from the published version.

105. B, p. 7.

106. Interview with the author, June 2016.

107. Hoy, p. 35.

108. CEP, p. 211.

109. Hammer, pp. 97–8.

110. BOF, "Anatomies of Melancholy," by J. D. McClatchy, p. 192.

111. Hoy, p. 57.

112. "Introduction," by J. D. McClatchy, *Anthony Hecht: Selected Poems*, p. x.

113. Fan, p. 8.

114. *As You Like It,* Act 2, Scene 1.

115. CEP, p. 222.

116. CLP, p. 123.

Four: Mr. Ransom in Ohio, Mr. Tate in New York

1. Rhu, p. 22.
2. McC, p. 171.
3. Ibid.
4. McC, p. 172.
5. Author's interview with Nicholas Christopher, to whom AEH recounted this anecdote. The quotations from AEH are approximated from memory.
6. McC, p. 173.
7. AEH, "Poetry: John Crowe Ransom," *The Wilson Quarterly*, Vol. 18, No. 2 (Spring 1994), p. 93.
8. Hoy, p. 31.
9. Rhu, p. 22.
10. From a brief, unpublished history of Kenyon, by Professor Thomas Greenslade (hereafter Greenslade 1). A fuller account of Kenyon in the 1930s and '40s was published in 1977 by his father Thomas B. Greenslade titled *Kenyon College: Its Third Half Century* (hereafter Greenslade 2).
11. "In His Own Country," by Thomas Daniel Young, *The Southern Review* (Summer 1972).
12. *Robert Lowell: A Biography*, by Ian Hamilton (New York: Random House, 1982), p. 54.
13. McC, p. 174.
14. Fan, p. 8.
15. AEH, "Once Removed," *Kenyon Review*, Vol. IX, No. 2 (Spring 1947), p. 222. As was the case with a number of his earliest serial publications, AEH chose not to collect this poem. The first poem published in a magazine which AEH included in *Stones* was "Fugue for One Voice" in the *Kenyon Review* for Autumn 1948.
16. Letter to parents, 10.26.46, MARBL.
17. Richard Howard, interview with the author.
18. Blumenthal.
19. Greenslade 1.
20. Charles M. Coffin, ed., *The Major Poets: English and American* (New York: Harcourt, Brace and Company, 1954), p. 553.
21. One of AEH's most accomplished undergraduate poems, "Donne's Wind and Mine," employs complex Renaissance stanzas and an elaborate conceit of a ship at sea. It has the feel of a young poet's ars poetica: "But I, in need of a sail, / unfurl my lung, / And capture the breath of the sky, which rushes to rise / And spin in my rigging." MARBL.
22. Letter to parents, 10.26.46, MARBL.
23. JCR, p. 182.
24. JCR, pp. 180–1.
25. JCR, p. 183.
26. "John Crowe Ransom: 1888–1974," by Robert Lowell, in *Collected Prose*, edited

and introduced by Robert Giroux (New York: Farrar, Straus, and Giroux, 1987). [Hereafter Lowell.]

27. Hoy, p. 31.

28. Hoy, p. 30.

29. Letter to parents, 10.26.46, MARBL.

30. JCR, p. 181.

31. Letter to parents, 12.10.46, MARBL.

32. Hoy, p. 32. Pieces by Trilling and Bentley appear in the issue for Fall 1946. Hecht's poems appear two issues later. Nothing by Brecht appeared in the *Review* at this time, but the piece in question may have been "Personal Frustration: The Poetry of Bertolt Brecht," by Hannah Arendt, which appeared in the next volume.

33. AEH, "To a Soldier Killed in Germany," *The Kenyon Review,* Vol. IX, No. 2 (Spring 1947), p. 223.

34. From an undated interview conducted at the University of Rochester, Tape 19, transcript p. 12, University of Rochester Library (hereafter RochInter).

35. AEH, "A Friend Killed in the War," *Furioso*, Vol. III, No. 3 (Spring 1948).

36. From Ransom's poem "Somewhere Is Such a Kingdom."

37. CEP, p. 84.

38. CEP, p. 103.

39. JCR, pp. 187–8.

40. Rhu, p. 13.

41. McC, p. 180.

42. Ibid.

43. Hoy, p. 31.

44. Hoy, p. 32.

45. Lowell, p. 22.

46. "Third Avenue in Sunlight," CEP, p. 4.

47. Letter to parents, 10.26.46, MARBL.

48. McC, p. 176.

49. Hoy, p. 33.

50. Letter to parents, 8.23.47, MARBL.

51. Ibid.

52. Ibid.

53. Letter to parents, 9.10.47, MARBL.

54. Letter to parents, 9.19.47, MARBL.

55. Published posthumously in "Uncollected Hecht," edited by the author, *Poetry,* September 2011.

56. Hoy, pp. 36–7.

57. Telegram to parents, December 1947, MARBL.

58. "A Last Conversation with Robie Macauley," by Thomas E. Kennedy and Robie Macauley, *Agni*, No. 45 (1947), p. 182.

59. Sun.

60. *The Kenyon Review, 1939–1970: A Critical History*, by Marian Janssen (Louisiana State University Press, 1989), p. 168.

61. Sun. According to Jonathan Post, Empson commented on four of AEH's poems. He was particularly admiring of "Private Eye," which, uncollected, later ran in *The Kenyon Review*, Autumn 1948.

62. AEH, "A Few Green Leaves," *Sewanee Review*, Vol. 67, No. 4 (Autumn 1959), p. 568. [Hereafter Leaves.]

63. Hoy, p. 34.

64. Sun.

65. Leaves, p. 569.

66. "Christmas Is Coming," CEP, p. 89.

67. Hoy, p. 42. AEH overcame his reservations about the poem enough to include it in *A Summoning of Stones*, as well as among the poems he chose to preserve from that book in *The Hard Hours* and *Collected Earlier Poems*. Even so, the poem shared the flaws he found in his early work, when he looked back on *Stones* from the perspective of his mature poems, which began with the first poem in *HH*, "A Hill."

68. Leaves, pp. 569–70.

69. Hoy, p. 34.

70. Hoy, p. 33.

71. "The Private Eye: A Detective Story," *The Kenyon Review*, Vol. X, No. 4 (Autumn 1948), p. 627.

72. Hoy, p. 35. Hecht never warmed to leading workshops of student poetry, preferring to lecture on literature.

Five: Italian Journey

1. "Rome," CEP, p. 136.

2. Letter to parents, 6.25.49, MARBL.

3. Ibid.

4. "Seascape with Figures," from *A Summoning of Stones*, p. 41. [Hereafter Seascape.]

5. Letter to parents, 6.25.49. The second breakfast was ordered to scandalize their disapproving waiter. They were uncomfortably full when they disembarked, but they felt it was worth it.

6. Seascape, p. 41.

7. Ibid.

8. Ibid.

9. Hoy, p. 40.

10. *Bellow: A Biography*, by James Atlas (New York: Random House, 2000), p. 119. [Hereafter Atlas.]

11. *The Left Bank: Writers, Artists, and Politics from the Popular Front to the Cold War*, by Herbert R. Lottman (University of Chicago Press, 1982), p. 221. The first issue of *Les Lettres Francaises* included these words in its Manifesto of French Writers, signed by Georges Duhamel, Françoise Mauriac, and Paul Valéry.

12. Letter to parents, 7.13.49, MARBL.

13. Ibid.

14. Letter to parents, 6.28.49, MARBL.

15. Paul Henissart later became a *Newsweek* correspondent in North Africa and the author of *The Winter Spy* (1978) and other thrillers. His *Wolves in the City: The Death of French Algeria,* an account of the final, bloody year (1961–62) of Algeria's seven-year war for independence from France, is likely a source for Hecht's horrific account of an episode from that conflict at the end of "The Deodand," from *The Venetian Vespers* (1979). Reading his friend's horrific accounts of the war in Africa would have reminded Hecht of the unspeakable things they experienced at Flossenbürg, both personally and through survivor accounts.

16. Letter to parents, 8.18.49, MARBL.

17. Ibid. The café in question is quite possibly the opulent Caffè Florian, in the Piazza San Marco, where orchestral music can be heard until late in the evening.

18. Bellini's painting of St. Francis figures in "At the Frick," from *A Summoning of Stones,* and his *Transfiguration of Christ* appears in "See Naples and Die," from *The Transparent Man.*

19. This is the view from the canal-side bar at the Hotel Europa, Hecht's favorite vantage point for taking in the life of the city.

20. "The Venetian Vespers," from section II, CEP, pp. 229–30.

21. Rhu, p. 19.

22. Letter to parents, with the salutation "Kinderlein," 9.1.49, MARBL.

23. "The Art of Poetry No. 35," John Hollander interviewed by J. D. McClatchy, *The Paris Review* (Issue 97, Fall 1985). [Hereafter Hollander.]

24. AEH later penned this bit of light verse gently skewering Ginsberg and sent it off to Fred Morgan for his amusement:

    Said Albion Ginsberg to Gregory Crusoe,
    "We are the heirs of John-Jack Rousseau."
    Said Digory Corso to Alan Guitar,
    "Vice is a virtue if carried too far." [MARBL]

25. Interview with the author.

26. Hollander.

27. Interview with the author.

28. Hecht actively worked to prune back Auden's influence. He dropped a section from "Songs for the Air," which adopted an Audenesque music in the vein of the elegy for W. B. Yeats, when the poem was collected in *Stones* four years later. The dropped stanza, which appeared as the fourth and final section of the poem, appeared in *The Hudson Review,* Vol. II, No. 3 (Autumn 1949). It reads:

    Let us set in sounding phrase
    Words of honor and of praise
    Imperfections, which the tall
    Can walk under with no dread

That he's going to bruise his head
On its ceiling, which the weak
Can encompass if he speak
Bravely with it like a man,
Which the old and ugly can
Be embraced by and caressed,
By which naked things are dressed.
Let us set in sounding phrase
Words of honor and of praise
For the air that covers all.

The use of "praise" in the penultimate line suggests that Hecht is creating an outright pastiche of Auden's "In Memory of W. B. Yeats." In the end, he decided that this was not an effect (or close resemblance) that he wanted for his own poem. The version in *Stones* reverses the order of parts II and III and adds a new fourth section. He retains the same meter, though Auden's music is replaced by Marvell's in "Upon Appleton House." This revision does not seem to have been wholly satisfactory either. The poem was not among those that AEH chose to retain for the early poems appended to *The Hard Hours*.

29. Letter to John Hollander, 10.27.97, MARBL.

30. Letter to Norman German, 3.22.82, MARBL.

31. "Literature as Knowledge," by Allen Tate, from *On the Limits of Poetry* (Swallow Press and William Morrow, 1948), p. 48.

32. "Poetry as a Form of Knowledge," by AEH, "submitted in partial fulfillment of the requirements for the degree of Master of Arts, Faculty of Philosophy, Columbia University," pp. 68–9.

33. Letter from Al Millet in Amsterdam to AEH in Paris, late July 1950.

34. Among the popular Williams anthologies that included poems by AEH are *A Little Treasury of American Poetry* (1952) ("Japan," "Divination by Cat," "Hallowe'en," "The Place of Pain in the Universe," "Fugue for One Voice"), *The Pocket Book of Modern Verse* (Revised Edition, 1954) ("Samuel Sewall"), and *The New Pocket Anthology of American Verse from Colonial Days to the Present* (1955) ("Upon the Death of George Santayana," "Ostia Antica").

35. Interview with Mira Van Doren, by the author, February 2021.

36. Letter to parents, 8.22.50, MARBL.

37. Letter to Richard Wilbur, 11.15.50, MARBL.

38. Letter from Al Millet, late July 1950.

39. AEH's "On W. H. Auden's 'In Praise of Limestone,'" *Obbligati: Essays in Criticism* (New York: Atheneum, 1986), p. 32. [Hereafter O.]

40. Letter to parents from Monte Carlo, 10.24.50, MARBL.

41. Letter to Brad Leithauser, 4.19.80, MARBL.

42. Letter to Richard Wilbur, 11.15.50, MARBL.

43. "La Condition Botanique," CEP, p. 72. [Hereafter Condition.]

44. Condition, p. 74.

45. Condition, p. 75.

46. Letter to parents, late Feb., 1951, MARBL.

47. "Discovering Auden," by AEH in *The Harvard Advocate,* Vol. CVIII, Nos. 2–3, Special Issue (c. 1974) titled "W. H. Auden 1907–1973," p. 48. The issue also included contributions by William Empson, William Meredith, Randall Jarrell, Karl Shapiro, Dorothy Day, C. Day Lewis, Harry Levin, Richard Howard, Hannah Arendt, Elizabeth Bishop, Robert Fitzgerald, Tennessee Williams, Stephen Spender, Edward Mendelson, and others (hereafter DA).

48. Ibid.

49. Ibid.

50. "Ischia," by W. H. Auden, *Collected Poems* (Centennial Edition), edited by Edward Mendelson (Toronto: Modern Library, 2007), p. 541.

51. Ibid.

52. DA, pp. 48–9.

53. DA, p. 49.

54. Ibid.

55. Interview with Margaret Rosenthal.

56. DA, p. 49.

57. *Wystan and Chester: A Personal Memoir of W. H. Auden and Chester Kallman,* by Thekla Clark (New York: Columbia University Press, 1995), p. 4. [Hereafter Clark.]

58. Ibid.

59. Clark, p. 5.

60. Clark, p. 6.

61. Clark, p. 10.

62. Letter to Allen Tate, 10.16.51, MARBL.

63. Letter to parents, 7.16.51, MARBL.

64. Letter to parents, 10.4.51, MARBL.

65. DA, p. 49.

66. Letter to Allen Tate, 10.16.51, MARBL.

67. Hoy, p. 39.

68. Letter to parents, 10.4.51, MARBL.

69. Hoy, p. 43.

70. "La Condition Botanique," CEP, p. 74.

71. "A Deep Breath at Dawn," CEP, pp. 98–9, published, alongside poems by W. S. Merwin, James Wright, and others, in a section titled "A Group of Young Poets" in *The Kenyon Review* (Autumn 1951) under the title "Aubade," originally closed with these lines:

    Much turning of the earth, much turning away
    With hearts turned into bone by dreadfulness,
    And mouths incompetent, with little to say;
    Mars full of frenzy with his own success;
    Till any fool with eyes can see a wild

God, drooling and gurgling like a child.

Hecht's poem appeared in a particularly starry issue of the *Review,* which regularly featured marquee writers and critics. Also appearing in the fall issue were essays by Northrop Frye, Harry Levin, R. W. B. Lewis, and Austin Warren, along with a consideration of triptych paintings by Max Beckmann.

72. Hoy, p. 42.
73. Ibid.
74. Ibid.
75. Hoy, p. 44.
76. Letter to parents, 10.4.51, MARBL.
77. Hoy, p. 42.

Six: Roman Holidays

1. "A Roman Holiday," CEP, p. 101.
2. Letter to Allen Tate, 10.16.51, MARBL.
3. Ibid.
4. Hoy, p. 36.
5. Ibid.
6. *The New York Times,* 5.16.51.
7. Letter to parents, 10.4.51, MARBL.
8. Letter to Allen Tate, 10.16.51, MARBL.
9. Facsimile sent to John Guare, 3.21.01. This description was written in response to Guare's request for a brief memoir of life at the American Academy, MARBL. [Hereafter Guare.]
10. Ibid.
11. "A Roman Holiday," CEP, p. 100.
12. Hoy, p. 41.
13. *True Friendship: Geoffrey Hill, Anthony Hecht, and Robert Lowell under the Sign of Eliot and Pound,* by Christopher Ricks (Yale, 2010), p. 122. Hecht explores this method of affective landscape and of the paysage moralisé in his essay "The Pathetic Fallacy," in his first book of essays, *Obbligati* (1986). He would have known Auden's sestina "Paysage Moralisé" from *The Collected Poetry of W. H. Auden* (1945).
14. "Elegy," *Kenyon Review,* Vol. 14, No. 2 (Spring 1952), p. 324.
15. *A Summoning of Stones,* p. 24, not reprinted in HH or CEP.
16. We can assume that Hecht was writing about the "bounce of sex" from personal experience, though he had no sustained romantic relationships up to this point. It may well be that he retained the impression, formed in childhood from Fräulein and the *Journal-American,* that "sex was somehow wedded to disaster" (CEP, p. 159). Italy provided a counter impression of sex and love as "Pleasure without peer" (CEP, p. 92).
17. Hoy, p. 17.
18. Hoy, p. 18.

19. Hammer, p. 100. In his later life, Hecht kept a photo of Bellow in his study, alongside other friends and admired writers.

20. Atlas, p. 115.

21. Atlas, p. 205.

22. "Between the Love of Clizia and Mosca," *The New York Times*, February 23, 1986, p. 76.

23. Hammer, pp. 106–7.

24. AEH's memorial tribute to Brandeis, MARBL (hereafter Brandeis).

25. Ibid.

26. Letter to Philip Hoy, 4.2.99, MARBL.

27. Hoy, p. 46.

28. The original dedicatee of the poem, Sally Goldstein, was replaced by Arendt and Blücher shortly before the publication of *The Hard Hours*.

29. Blücher Archive, Bard College, https://www.bard.edu/bluecher/history.php.

30. "History of Bard," from the Bard website.

31. "Teaching a Different Shakespeare from the One I Love," by Stephen Greenblatt, *The New York Times Sunday Magazine*, Sept. 11, 2015, p. 60.

32. Letter to parents, 7.1.53, MARBL.

33. Ibid.

34. *Edwin Arlington Robinson: A Poet's Life*, by Scott Donaldson (New York: Columbia University Press, 2007), pp. 395–96.

35. *The Hudson Review*, Vol. 7, No. 2 (Summer 1954), pp. 302–308.

36. *The New Yorker*, June 5, 1954. [Hereafter Bogan.]

37. *The Kenyon Review*, Vol. 16, No. 3 (Summer 1954), pp. 473–81. [Hereafter Mizener.]

38. Mizener, p. 474 and p. 479.

39. Mizener, p. 480.

40. *Shenandoah*, Vol. 8, No. 1 (Autumn 1956), pp. 43–4.

41. "The Vow," CEP, p. 35.

42. Claire White, interview with the author.

43. *North of Jamaica*, by Louis Simpson (New York: Harper and Row, 1972), p. 161. [Hereafter Simpson.]

44. "Double Sonnet," CEP, p. 71.

45. Ibid.

46. "The Gift of Song," *The New Yorker*, January 16, 1954, p. 32.

47. Simpson, p. 163.

48. In fact, Pat married a Belgian aristocrat.

49. "Gurney's 'Hobby,'" from *Collected Critical Writings*, by Geoffrey Hill, Kenneth Haynes, ed. (Oxford: Oxford University Press, 2008), p. 425.

50. Letter to his family, addressed "Dear Tutti," 3.1.54, MARBL.

51. Interview with the author, June 2016.

52. *Communitas*, Vol. 1, No. 5 (May 6, 1954), p. 1.

53. *The Life of Saul Bellow: To Fame and Fortune, 1915–1964*, by Zachary Leader (New York: Knopf, 2015), p. 475. [Hereafter Leader.]

54. Leader, p. 457.

55. *Communitas*, Vol. 1, No. 7 (May 20, 1954), p. 4.

56. Letter to parents, 3.8.54, MARBL.

57. *Communitas*, Vol. 1, No. 5 (May 6, 1954), p. 1.

58. Letter to Henry Alen Moe, Guggenheim Foundation, 4.12.54, MARBL.

59. Letter to parents, 10.3.54, MARBL.

60. "An Offering for Patricia," published in "Uncollected Hecht," edited by the author, *Poetry*, September 2011.

61. Letter to parents, 10.3.54, MARBL.

62. *The New York Times Book Review*, April 4, 1954.

63. Richard Wilbur, interview with the author.

64. Hecht's impressions of Wilbur's process were reported to Robert Bagg in an interview, and recounted in "The Poet in Rome: Richard Wilbur in Post-war Italy," by Robert Bagg, *The Common*, October 1, 2012 (https://www.thecommononline.org/the-poet-in-rome-richard-wilbur-in-postwar-italy/).

65. Interview with the author, 6.4.15.

66. *Let Us Watch: Richard Wilbur—A Biographical Study*, by Robert Bagg and Mary Bagg (Amherst, MA: University of Massachusetts Press, 2017), p. 159. [Hereafter Bagg.]

67. Ibid.

68. Letter to parents, 1.30.55, MARBL.

69. Letter to parents, 11.55, MARBL.

70. Ibid.

71. Ibid.

72. Ibid.

73. Letter to parents, likely 11.30.55, MARBL.

74. "Abortion in American History," *The Atlantic Monthly*, May 1997.

75. Letter to parents, likely 11.30.55, MARBL.

76. Ibid.

77. Letter to parents, 12.2.54, MARBL.

78. Ibid.

79. Ibid.

80. Letter to parents, 1.14.55, MARBL.

81. CEP, pp. 35–6.

82. AEH reading at Sir George Williams University (SGWU, now Concordia University), Fall 1966.

83. *Poet's Choice*, edited by Paul Engle and Joseph Langland (Time Life Books, 1962), p. 202. (Hereafter Poet's Choice.)

84. AEH refers only to a poem of Lowell's from *Land of Unlikeness*, but Jonathan F. S. Post has identified it as "almost certainly" "The Boston Nativity," *A Thickness of Particulars* (Oxford: Oxford University Press, 2015), p. 38.

85. Poet's Choice, p. 203.

86. CEP, p. 16.

87. Letter to parents, 3.22.55, MARBL.

88. Although AEH was assisting, Auden read every entry himself.

89. *The Yale Younger Poets Anthology,* edited by George Bradley (New Haven, CT: Yale University Press, 1998), p. lxviii. [Hereafter Yale Younger.]

90. Ibid.

91. Letter from AEH to his father, 6.15.55, MARBL.

92. Ibid.

93. Ibid.

94. Letter to father, 8.19.55, MARBL.

95. Ibid.

96. Letter to parents, 11.9.55, MARBL.

97. Letter to parents, 11.20.55, MARBL.

Seven: "Marriages Come to Grief in Many Ways . . ."

1. "See Naples and Die," CLP, p. 38.

2. "The Origin of Centaurs," CEP, p. 33.

3. AEH later included this poem in *The Essential Herbert,* which he selected and introduced. That he chose Herbert above other possibilities attests to his deep affection for Herbert's poems.

4. *The Americanist,* by Daniel Aaron (Ann Arbor, MI: University of Michigan Press, 2007), p. 70.

5. Hoy, p. 47.

6. Letter to Philip Booth, 4.19.61, MARBL.

7. Hoy, p. 48.

8. "Jason," CEP, p. 9.

9. "The Vow," CEP, p. 36.

10. *The Hudson Review,* Vol. X, No. 1 (Spring 1957).

11. Hoy, p. 48.

12. Letter to William Arrowsmith, undated, late fall 1956, MARBL.

13. AEH later collected a number of these essays, talks, and notices in two prose collections, *Obbligati* (1986) and *Melodies Unheard* (2003).

14. Letter to William Arrowsmith, undated, late fall 1956, MARBL.

15. Letter to William Arrowsmith, 7.2.56, MARBL.

16. Letter to Daniel Aaron, 11.1.01, MARBL.

17. Daniel Aaron to Helen Hecht, 4.25.06.

18. The Baskin-Hecht collaborations for The Gehenna Press include *The Seven Deadly Sins* (1958), later included in *The Hard Hours; Predatory Birds* ["Birdwatchers of America," with lithographs by Aubrey Schwartz] (1958); *Struwwelpeter: A Poem by Anthony Hecht* (1958); *Æsopic: Twenty-Four Couplets by Anthony Hecht to Accompany the Thomas Bewick Wood Engravings for Select Fables* (1968), excerpts included in *The Hard Hours* under the title "Improvisations on Aesop"; *The*

Presumptions of Death (1995), later included in *Flight Among the Tombs*; *A Gehenna Florilegium* (1998), with flower poems later included in *The Darkness and the Light*; a projected book of ten biblical persona poems commissioned by Baskin and published after Baskin's death by The Double Elephant Press in 2001, with copper-plate etchings by Michael Kuch, included that same year in *The Darkness and the Light*. A collaboration with Aubrey Schwartz, *A Bestiary* (Kanthos Press, 1960/2), generated the suite of animal poems featured in *The Hard Hours*. Roughly a third of the original poems in that collection were the result of Hecht's collaboration with Baskin and, through Baskin, Schwartz.

19. Richard Michelson, interviewed by the author, 10.29.21, [Hereafter Mic.].

20. Ibid.

21. Ibid.

22. Ibid.

23. From 1974 to 1983, Baskin moved to Devon, England, near where Hughes was living. Baskin managed to acquire a press in England, and he and Hughes collaborated on Hughes's book, *A Primer of Birds* (1981), with woodcuts by Baskin, their first Gehenna Press project since Hughes left Northampton.

24. "Anthony Hecht," an interview by Daniel Anderson and Philip Stephens. *BOMB*, No. 62 (Winter 1998), p. 30. [Hereafter BOMB.]

25. "From the Life and Songs of the Crow," by Ted Hughes, based on Hughes's spoken account of Crow's creation on Faber/Penguin audiotape.

26. Mic.

27. Ibid.

28. Letter to Eleanor Cook, 1.9.97, MARBL.

29. Mic.

30. The Hecht archive at Emory.

31. Sun.

32. Ibid.

33. In a letter to Fred Morgan dated May 29, 1965, Hecht mentions that he recently interviewed Tate for *The Paris Review*: "It was very pleasant, as always, and he had some remarkably pungent things to say about your old pal and hero, Robt. Bly." [MARBL] The interview never ran in *The Paris Review*.

34. Baskin, a devotee of the poems of William Blake, produced an illustrated edition of "Auguries of Innocence" in 1959, sometime before this poem was written. Hecht's poem, written more than a decade after the scene depicted in the photograph that inspired it, appeared in *The Harvard Advocate* in 1973, while he was a visiting professor in Cambridge.

35. CEP, p. 139.

36. "Poets on Campus: 5 Talented Young Men Combine Poetry and the Classroom," by Sylvia Plath, *Mademoiselle* (August 1953), p. 291.

37. *The Unabridged Journals of Sylvia Plath*, edited by Karen V. Kukil (New York: Anchor, 2000), p. 384. [Hereafter Plath.]

38. Plath, p. 356.

39. Plath, p. 351.

40. Letter to Philip Hoy, 4.29.00, MARBL.

41. *The Complete Prints of Leonard Baskin: A Catalogue Raisonné, 1948–1983,* edited by Alan Fern and Judith O'Sullivan, with an introduction by Ted Hughes (Boston: Little, Brown & Co., 1984), p. 11. [Hereafter Prints.]

42. Ibid.

43. Prints, p. 19.

44. Ibid.

45. Evan Hecht, interview with the author.

46. Undated letter to Donald Hall, likely 1959, MARBL.

47. The Baskin pamphlet is titled "Predatory Birds." Hecht adopted the title "Bird-watchers of America" when the poem appeared in *Partisan Review* in Winter 1963.

48. CEP, p. 9.

49. Claire White, interview with the author. [Hereafter CW.]

50. Ibid.

51. Ibid.

52. Ibid.

53. Hoy, p. 48.

54. Simpson, p. 164.

55. Introducing the poem at a reading at Concordia University—Sir George Williams Campus in 1966, AEH explained that Louis Simpson was "a fine poet and very old friend of mine. I read a poem in one of his early books, called 'The Man Who Married Magdalene,' a fine and delicate poem, in which he imagines that this man who raged and stormed throughout his married life, upon the death of his wife finds it in his heart to forgive her and to acknowledge his abiding love for her. In fact, if I can remember the last stanza, it goes, 'But when he woke, and woke alone, he wept and would deny the loose behavior of the bone, and the immodest thigh.' I have chosen to make him far less forgiving in my version. He is a very angry man, and the whole poem takes place in a bar where he has been releasing his anger in a bibulous way for some time. His anger is not only personal, however, it's also theological. He is someone who believes in and accepts the ancient dispensation according to which Mary Magdalene had done something which could not, in fact, be so easily forgiven. And he regards the new dispensation as an antinomian heresy which leaves him bewildered and accounts for the rather promiscuous behavior he finds all around him in the bar."

56. Adam Hecht, interview with the author.

57. CEP, p. 59.

58. CEP, p. 60.

59. Hoy, p. 51.

60. Letter to Donald Hall, undated, MARBL.

61. *Robert Lowell: A Biography,* by Ian Hamilton (New York: Vintage, 1983), p. 280.

62. Letter to a C. B. [Brian] Cox [of the *Critical Quarterly*], 1.24.62, MARBL.

63. Helen Hecht, interview with the author.

64. Ibid.

Eight: Harder Hours

1. "Ubi sunt qui ante nos fuerunt?," *The Minor Poems of the Vernon MS.*, ed. F. J. Furnivall (Oxford: Early English Text Society, 1901), pp. 761–63. AEH takes this stanza of this 13th-century poem as epigraph for *The Hard Hours,* CEP, p. 1. The epigraph in its entirety translates as "Where is that laughing and that song, / that trailing and that proud going, / the hawks and the hounds? / All that joy is gone away, / that 'well' has come to 'wellaway,'/ to many hard hours."

2. CEP, p. 31.

3. "The Vow," CEP, p. 35.

4. Patricia Harris to AEH, 5.9.59, MARBL.

5. Letter to Anne Sexton, undated, MARBL. Jonathan F. S. Post, in *The Selected Letters of Anthony Hecht,* dates this letter as early May 1961.

6. Letter to Donald Hall, 3.5.61, MARBL. Hall and Pack took "The End of the Weekend," "'More Light! More Light!,'" "The Dover Bitch," "Third Avenue in Sunlight," and "Behold the Lilies of the Field," which represent the best of Hecht's new work when the anthology appeared in 1962. These poems replaced Hecht's poems from the 1957 edition: "The Vow," "La Condition Botanique," "Samuel Sewall," and "The Origin of Centaurs."

7. *The Flowers of Evil,* by Charles Baudelaire, selected and edited by Marthiel and Jackson Matthews (New Directions, revised edition 1962). AEH was among a group of poets added to the second edition of the book, which first appeared in 1955, and included translations by Richard Wilbur, Roy Campbell, Edna St. Vincent Millay, Karl Shapiro, Aldous Huxley, C. F. MacIntyre, and Allen Tate. Among AEH's cohort in the second edition are Robert Lowell, Robert Fitzgerald, Frederick Morgan, Stanley Kunitz, and Yvor Winters. Hecht's inclusion may be taken as a measure of his growing reputation after *Stones* and before *The Hard Hours.*

8. "To a Madonna: Ex-Voto in the Spanish Style," CEP, p. 19.

9. From Hughes's blurb for *The Hard Hours.*

10. Hecht wrote to one unidentified correspondent, addressed as Mr. Brown, that he felt "there is an intimate and subtle connection between poetry and drama," 1.6.02, MARBL.

11. AEH reading at the Poetry Center of the 92nd Street Y in New York City, 2.7.63, Poetry Center Archives [Hereafter 63Y].

12. Letter to J. D. McClatchy, 12.26.84, MARBL.

13. Richard Lincoln, interview with the author. [Hereafter Lincoln.]

14. Ibid.

15. CEP, pp. 7–8.

16. Letter to Shirley Hazzard, 2.25.00, MARBL.

17. CEP, p. 8.

18. "A Letter," CEP, p. 48.

19. Moss first published AEH on January 16, 1954, with the uncollected "The Gift of Song" (which appears in *Stones* as "Imitation," a title Moss disliked and asked to be replaced for the magazine). "Clair de Lune" followed on August 13, 1960. That fall, Moss wrote to request more poems, keen to include Hecht again in the magazine. At the end of the year, Hecht sent two of his most defining poems from *The Hard Hours*: "'More Light! More Light!'" and an untitled work that AEH referred to provisionally as "Poem" and which Hecht ultimately titled "A Hill." Moss and his readers, affectionately dubbed the Olympians, rejected "'More Light! . . .'" on the grounds that they "found the connection between the first three stanzas and the rest of the poem slightly ambiguous" [Letter from Howard Moss to AEH, 1.4.61, MARBL] (a juxtaposition that subsequent critics have praised for its resonance). Moss accepted "Poem," which he dubbed "A Vision" as a placeholder. It did not appear until February 21, 1964, two years after "A Letter." (The check for "A Hill" was sent well in advance of the publication, in January 1961, as Hecht was leaving on a trip to Mexico [with Natacha, most likely].)
20. Letter to Anne Sexton, 4.14.61, MARBL.
21. *Anne Sexton: A Self-Portrait in Letters,* Linda Gray Sexton and Lois Ames, eds. (Boston: Houghton Mifflin, 1977), p. 115.
22. Letter to Anne Sexton, 4.14.61, MARBL.
23. Cummings's reading took place in February 1961.
24. Helen Hecht's handwritten journal, begun in January 2006.
25. CW.
26. Letter to J. D. McClatchy, 12.26.84, from Rochester, MARBL. [Hereafter Mc-Letter.]
27. Letter to Anne Sexton, 10.28.61, MARBL.
28. Letter to Anne Sexton, 2.13.62, MARBL.
29. Patricia Harris to AEH, 2.25.61, MARBL.
30. Hoy, p. 49.
31. Mc-Letter.
32. "Circles," CLP, p. 167.
33. CLP, pp. 167–8.
34. CLP, p. 168.
35. CLP, p. 13.
36. CLP, p. 38.
37. Ibid.
38. Mc-Letter.
39. Hoy, p. 51.
40. Letter to Anne Sexton, 1.19.62, MARBL.
41. Hoy, pp. 50–1.
42. "Behold the Lilies of the Field," CEP, pp. 11–12.
43. "An Interview with Anthony Hecht," Philip L. Gerber and Robert J. Gemmett eds., *Mediterranean Review,* Vol. 1, No. 3 (Spring 1971), p. 7. [Hereafter Med-Rev.] This interview was the result of AEH's appearance in February 1970 on

the *Writers Forum* program at SUNY Brockport. In conversation with AEH are Gregory Fitz Gerald and William Heyen.

44. Hoy, p. 51.

45. Mc-Letter.

46. CEP, p. 31.

47. Ibid.

48. *The Literature of England: An Anthology and a History, Volume One—from the Beginnings to the Romantic Movement,* George B. Woods, Homer A. Watt, George K. Anderson, eds. (Chicago: Scott, Foresman and Company, 1936), p. 1967. The poem appears here in its four-stanza version, though it's possible that Hecht had seen it elsewhere in the version with ten stanzas.

49. Letter to Jason and Adam, MARBL.

50. *Sewanee Theological Review,* Vol. 34, No. 4 (1991), p. 74. Hecht would later populate much of his final collection, *The Darkness and the Light,* with poems based on Bible verses.

51. *Night Errands: How Poets Use Dreams,* Roderick Townley, ed. (Pittsburgh: University of Pittsburgh Press, 1999), pp. 52–3.

52. Ibid., p. 52.

53. Letter to AEH from Howard Moss, 9.20.62, *New Yorker* Records, Manuscripts and Archives Division, New York Public Library. [Hereafter NYPL.]

54. John Simon, from his introduction, 63Y.

55. Ibid.

56. *The Theory and Practice of Hell: The German Concentration Camps and the System Behind Them,* by Eugen Kogon, Heinz Norden, trans. (Berkeley Medallion, 1958), p. 97. The book appeared three years before AEH's poem was published in *The Nation* on 3.11.61.

57. CEP, p. 64.

58. Frederick Seidel, interview with the author.

59. "Recent Poetry," by Anthony Hecht, *The New York Review of Books,* June 1, 1963.

60. Ibid.

61. Hoy, p. 57.

62. "On Bewick's Blocks," by Philip Hofer. Hofer's brief note serves as an afterword to *Æsopic: Twenty-Four Couplets by Anthony Hecht to Accompany the Thomas Bewick Wood Engravings for Select Fables* (Northampton, MA: Gehenna Press, 1968).

63. The quotations in this passage from Chevy Chase are taken from an interview with the author.

64. Interview with the author.

65. Donald Fagan recalls Hecht in his memoir, *Eminent Hipsters* (2013). AEH gave Fagen a B- in "Shakespeare," a decent grade, given how tough Hecht could be with grading.

66. *The Listener,* Vol. 80, Issue 2067 Thursday, 11.47.68, p. 609.

67. CEP, p. 166. "Privates" was originally "tits," which Harry Ford deemed too common (Letter to Harry Ford, 8.26.78, MARBL). The desolate landscape of "smoke" becomes a key image in "Death the Whore," a monologue in the Baskin-illustrated "Presumptions of Death" sequence from *Flight Among the Tombs,* where it carries a resonance of the Holocaust (cf. the final stanza of "'More Light! More Light!'").

68. Bill Leonard, interview with the author.

69. Letter to Daniel Hoffman, 11.14.79, MARBL. AEH was grateful to Hoffman for his perceptive reading of "Rites and Ceremonies" in *The Harvard Guide to Contemporary American Poetry* (1979), pp. 581–86.

70. "T. S. Eliot," *Literary Imagination: The Review of the Association of Literary Scholars and Critics,* 5.1 (2003), p. 14. AEH read this essay at the "Writers and Beloved Writing" session for the eighth annual conference of the ALSC, Washington, DC, October 2002. [Hereafter On Eliot.]

71. Letter to Eleanor Cook, 10.12.02, MARBL.

72. On Eliot, p. 14.

73. Letter to Norman German, 9.16.82, MARBL.

74. "Abiding Questions: An Interview with Anthony Hecht," by Lawrence Rhu, *The Harvard Advocate,* Vol. CVII, Nos. 2 & 3 (Fall 1973), pp. 13–14.

75. Letter to Claire White, 12.12.66, MARBL.

76. CEP, p. 66. As AEH explained to Howard Moss in an undated letter (MARBL), the title is "a line from a Scottish lullaby ["O Can Ye Sew Cushions?," sung by a mother whose husband is away at sea] in which a crying child is asked if it can someday comfort a crying child."

77. CEP, p. 57.

78. CEP, p. 65.

79. Jonathan Post writes that "Hecht's lifelong involvement with Shakespeare not only aligns him with a past from which he sought both inspiration and differentiation; it also helps to distinguish him from some of his immediate contemporaries (*A Thickness of Particulars,* p. 175).

80. Hoy, p. 46. By the time of this ceremony, Hecht had left Bard for a professorship at the University of Rochester, where he would teach until the early 1980s. He was pleased to return to the city to help honor Blücher.

81. CEP, pp. 67–8.

82. CEP, p. 141.

83. *A Passover Haggadah: The New Union Haggadah,* edited by Herbert Bronstein, with drawings by Leonard Baskin (New York: Central Conference of American Rabbis, 1974), p. 17. [Hereafter Haggadah.]

84. CEP, p. 234.

Nine: Late Romance

1. *The Tempest,* V.i, lines 194–5.

2. In "Double Dactyl," *Esquire,* June 1966 [hereafter Esquire], AEH writes:

"[The form] is composed of two quatrains, of which the last line of the first rhymes with the last line of the second. All the lines except the rhyming ones, which are truncated, are composed of two dactylic feet. The first line of the poem should be a double dactylic nonsense line, like 'Higgledy-piggledy,' or 'Pocketa-pocketa' (this last of course, borrowed from *The Secret Life of Walter Mitty*). The second line must be a double dactylic name. And then, somewhere in the poem, though preferably in the second stanza, there must be at least one double dactyl line which is *one word long*. (Foreign languages may be employed.) But, and the beauty of the form consists chiefly in this, once such a double dactylic word has successfully been employed in this verse form, it may never be used again."

3. Ibid.

4. *Jiggery Pokery* received an enthusiastic response, though a letter to AEH from the critic Edmund Wilson (1.31.67) pointing out a number of typos in the book was irritating to Hecht as much for its tone as its content.

5. MedRev, pp. 4–5.

6. As further evidence of poetry's "small world" in the sixties and seventies, Loesser was, coincidentally, a childhood friend of Richard Howard.

7. One rift between Hecht and Hollander lasted for several years, after Hollander imperiously referred to Helen as "a moral idiot" [interview with the author]. Hollander's second wife, the sculptor Natalie Charkow, eventually wrote to Hecht to break the silence. Hollander felt that Hecht could be "exceedingly paranoid about what people thought of his work" and that a "screen or block of ice" would quickly descend if he felt a slight.

8. CEP, p. 39.

9. Ibid.

10. Haggadah, p. 48.

11. "Anthony Hecht, the Poet: Iambic Rhythm and Dignity," by Colin Walters, *The Washington Times*, 1982. [Hereafter WashPo.]

12. MedRev, p. 6.

13. MedRev, p. 5.

14. Ibid.

15. Letter to Ian Hamilton, 9.1.65. *The Review* issued a number of such pamphlets.

16. Letter to Harry Ford, 10.11.67, MARBL.

17. Review of *The Hard Hours* by Laurence Lieberman, *Yale Review*, Vol. LVII, no. 3 (Summer 1968).

18. "Formal Effects," by William Meredith, *The New York Times Book Review*, December 17, 1967, pp. 24–5.

19. From the book jacket of *The Hard Hours*, by Anthony Hecht (New York: Atheneum, 1967). AEH participated in Poetry International '67, organized by The Poetry Book Society and directed by Ted Hughes and Patrick Garland. Also on the bill were Pablo Neruda, Stephen Spender, Charles Olson, Patrick Kavanagh, Hugh MacDiarmid, Yehuda Amichai, Ingeborg Bachman, Robert

Graves, Yves Bonnefoy, Auden, Sexton, Empson, Berryman, and others. Hecht read ("The Dover Bitch," "Behold the Lilies . . . ," "The Room," "The Vow," "'More Light! . . . ,'" and "'It Out-Herods Herod . . .'") on a program with Bachman, Amichai, and Allen Ginsberg, before embarking on a reading excursion with Sexton around England.

20. Ibid.

21. Letter to Philip Booth, 5.2.68, MARBL.

22. Letter to Harry Ford, 4.17.68, MARBL.

23. "The Hard Hours," *Circling the Canon, Volume I: The Selected Book Reviews of Marjorie Perloff, 1969–1994*, David Jonathan Bayot, ed. (Albuquerque: University of New Mexico Press, 2019).

24. The Loines Award carried a purse of $2,500. AEH was nominated by Howard Nemerov and notified by Muriel Rukeyser and John Cheever, who chaired the grants committee.

25. Letter to Harry Ford, 7.11.68, MARBL.

26. Letter to George Ford, 10.20.68, University of Rochester Library.

27. Ibid.

28. Letter to L. E. Sissman, 10.2.69, MARBL.

29. Ibid.

30. Letter to Donald Finkle, 10.16.66, MARBL.

31. Letter to George Ford, 3.25.71, University of Rochester Library.

32. Letter to Philip Booth, 10.2.69, MARBL.

33. Letter to Elizabeth Bishop, 12.14.69, MARBL.

34. "Black Boy in the Dark," CEP, p. 110. The poem takes its title from a print by his friend Thomas Cornell, an artist whose images engage with social justice and to whom AEH's poem is dedicated. Baskin published a series of portraits from the French Revolution in *The Defense of Gracchus Babeuf Before the High Court of Vendôme* (Gehenna Press, 1964). Hecht owned a copy of Cornell's portrait of Frederick Douglass. The poem appeared in *Harper's* in July 1969. In *Masters* (JCR), AEH wrote of the scene at Yale that partly inspired the poem: the "soundless spectacle" of students, newly inducted to exclusive clubs, processing in academic gowns, was "closely observed by a small group of black teenagers, children who would never go to Yale, much less be invited to join such an elite. I was that evening no more than an outside observer, certainly more like the blacks than like the members or the initiates."

35. Letter to a Mr. Lyon, a colleague at U of R, 2.21.70, MARBL. Though Hecht and Lowell saw relatively little of each other, their struggles with mental illness formed a bond between them.

36. Letter to Harry Ford, 3.1.70, MARBL.

37. Letter to Philip Booth, 7.13.70, MARBL.

38. Letter to Alan Frost, 5.17.70, MARBL.

39. Another Atheneum title, W. S. Merwin's *Carrier of Ladders,* won the Pulitzer in 1971, with AEH on the jury.

40. CEP, p. 108. Hollander appears not to have been able to use the poem at *Harper's*; it appeared in *Encounter* (Vol. XXXVII, No. 1) in July 1971.

41. CEP, p. 116.

42. CEP, p. 37. AEH's translation of du Bellay ("Happy he who like Ulysses has made a successful voyage"), dedicated to Claire White, expresses a longing for home after years of absence.

43. The memories of Helen Hecht included in this chapter are taken from a series of interviews with the author.

44. From an undated account by Alan Frost. AEH befriended the Frosts, who were graduate students, during his first year in Rochester: "He would come over to our place several times a week, to share a meal and a bottle of wine, and know the comfort of a family. He would play with Melissa [the Frosts' daughter], who knew him as 'Uncle Tony'; and he and [Frost's wife] Lucy and I would discuss literature and politics, especially civil rights issues and the Vietnam war."

45. CEP, pp. 140–41. While "Peripeteia" did not appear in *The New Yorker* until February 11, 1974, AEH put the finishing touches on the poem in November of 1972.

46. CEP, p. 142.

47. Letter to Alan Frost, 3.24.71, MARBL.

48. HHJ, 80.

49. Letter to Donald Finkel, 12.3.79, MARBL.

50. CEP, p. 117. "Green: An Epistle" appeared in *The New Yorker* on May 14, 1971.

51. CEP, p. 120. One of Hecht's most extended and powerful uses of the pathetic fallacy can be found in the verse paragraph beginning "Whole eras, seemingly . . ." and concluding with "*rage?*" (CEP, pp. 119–20).

52. *The Tempest*, V.i.

53. Dr. Neil Weissman, interview with the author.

54. CEP, pp. 126–7.

55. Letter to Alan Frost, 3.24.71, MARBL.

56. Letter to Daniel Anderson, 1.24.98, MARBL.

57. CEP, p. 134.

58. Helen Hecht, interview with the author.

59. Letter to Harry Ford, 3.8.70, MARBL.

60. CLP, p. 135.

61. From a reading at the Folger Library in Washington, DC, October 22, 1987.

62. Letter to Philip Booth, 2.20.72, MARBL.

63. Letter to Dana Gioia, 12.12.95, MARBL.

64. Letter to Howard Nemerov, 4.20.72, MARBL.

65. CEP, p. 152. "The Odds" appeared in *The New Yorker* on November 8, 1976, with a typo (a freak instance, given the magazine's famed precision) in the first line—"leaves" for "loaves"—which, unfortunately, makes a nonsense of the poem's opening.

66. Evan Hecht, interview with the author.

67. Ibid.
68. Letter to James Merrill, 1.19.73, MARBL.
69. Letter to Robert Fitzgerald, 3.13.73, MARBL.
70. Letter to George Dimock, 5.2.75, MARBL.

Ten: Apprehensions

1. The title of AEH's most autobiographical poem. For a time he considered it as the title for the collection that he ultimately titled *Millions of Strange Shadows* (1977).
2. From "The Venetian Vespers," part VI, CEP, p. 247. AEH quotes Simone Weil, from *Waiting for God,* in a letter to the poet David Havird: "One of the principal truths of Christianity, a truth that goes almost unrecognized today, is that looking is what saves us," a quotation he also committed to his commonplace book. [Letter to Havird, 12.11.7, MARBL.] AEH also cites Ruskin, from the final volume *of Modern Painters*: "The greatest thing a human soul ever does in this world is to *see* something, and tell what it saw in a plain way. . . . To see clearly is poetry, prophecy, and religion—all in one."
3. CEP, p. 157.
4. Letter to Alan Frost, 9.4.70, MARBL.
5. Letter to Gerry Cambridge, 12.28.01, MARBL.
6. Letter to Nicholas Christopher, 2.3.84, MARBL.
7. Letter to Nicholas Christopher, undated [Shakespeare's birthday], likely from 1985.
8. Letter to Nicholas Christopher, 12.15.86, MARBL. It should be noted that these complaints about Rochester were leveled after AEH moved to Washington, DC. Clearly, his visceral aversion to the harsh climate lingered for years.
9. RochInter, Tape 20, transcript p. 14.
10. Ibid.
11. RochInter, Tape 18, transcript p. 8.
12. Letter to Brad Leithauser, 3.18.80, MARBL.
13. Hoy, p. 55.
14. Until his death in 1962, Plutzik frequently presented readings by prominent authors in the Welles-Brown Room in Rush Rhees Library near what is now The Plutzik Poetry Library and Archive at U of R.
15. Letter to Brad Leithauser, 3.18.80, MARBL.
16. John Irwin, interview with the author.
17. From an undated speech given as University Orator at the University of Rochester, MARBL.
18. Letter to John Irwin, 5.21.78, MARBL.
19. Evan Hecht, interview with the author.
20. Ibid.
21. CEP, p. 146. It is a cruel irony that Suttman fell out of touch and "saddest of all . . . split up from his wife" (Letter to Harry Ford, 2.7.77, MARBL).

22. CEP, p. 144. The title for "After the Rain" was suggested by Hecht's editor at *The New Yorker*, Howard Moss. The idea for the poem came to Hecht "on a stroll" with the Maryland poet Michael Egan. This "little pastoral," as he described it to Moss, encodes Hecht's war experience in words and phrases such as "barbed-wire fences," "ashes," "iron chain," "blacken," "trenched," "serpentine," and others.

23. Hoy, p. 107.

24. Letter to Harry Ford, 11.26.76, MARBL.

25. Adam Hecht, interview with the author.

26. Helen Hecht, interview with the author.

27. Letter to James Merrill, 4.17.74, Washington University Libraries.

28. Letter to Harry Ford, 3.11.75, MARBL.

29. Email to the author, 1.30.21.

30. CEP, pp. 156–7.

31. CEP, p. 157.

32. Ibid.

33. Letter to Harry Ford, 12.23.76, MARBL.

34. Mendelson.

35. Letter to David Bromwich, 2.12.82, MARBL.

36. Letter to Harry Ford, 3.25.77, MARBL.

37. Ibid.

38. Hecht's resentment and anger toward Donoghue did eventually dissipate, though not until quite late in his life, when his place in American letters was more assured. Even then, a bad review could cause Philoctetean psychic wounds. Unprompted, Donoghue later apologized, admitting he had been unfair in his review of *Shadows*.

39. CEP, p. 141.

40. RochInter, Tape 17, transcript p. 2.

41. RochInter, Tape 18, transcript p. 9.

42. A birthday tribute, commissioned by Helen Hecht, for AEH's 75th, MARBL.

43. Folger.

44. McC, p. 161.

45. *Meliora* ("ever better") is the University of Rochester's motto.

46. For more on this, see Jonathan F. S. Post's *A Thickness of Particulars: The Poetry of Anthony Hecht* (Oxford), which contains an excellent chapter on Shakespeare and Hecht.

47. BOMB, p. 32.

48. From an interview with David Mason posted to the Able Muse discussion board online on November 11, 2001, https://www.ablemuse.com/erato/showthread.php?t=5404.

49. "The Venetian Vespers," CEP, p. 234.

50. Letter to George Grella, 9.4.80, MARBL.

51. Letter to David Havird, 12.30.97, MARBL.

52. Letter to George Ford, 9.23.82, MARBL.

53. Postcard to Harry Ford, 7.8.77, MARBL.

54. *The Stones of Venice,* by John Ruskin (New York: John Wiley & Sons, 1878), Vol. I, Ch. I, Sec. XXXVIII, p. 27. Ruskin provides one of the epigraphs for "The Venetian Vespers," which emerged rapidly, in great chunks, after Hecht's return to the States.

55. Letter to Dimitri Hadzi, 3.31.79, MARBL.

56. Letter to George Ford, 7.8.77, MARBL.

57. Letter to Roger Hecht, 8.20.77, Roger Hecht Estate. As an added resonance, Helen Hecht recalled that "Death in Venice" was one of AEH's texts for freshman English at Smith; she had studied it with him in her first year there, 1957–8.

58. Letter to Brad Leithauser, 10.14.77, MARBL.

59. Hammer, p. 96.

60. Hoy, p. 79.

61. From AEH's memorial tribute to his brother, delivered on 4.28.90 at the Center for Ethical Culture in New York, MARBL. (Hereafter RogerMemorial.)

62. CEP, p. 229. Nims's consideration of the poem is included in *The Burdens of Formality* under the title " 'The Venetian Vespers': Drenched in Fine Particulars."

63. Mendelson.

64. Letter to Howard Moss, 12.13.77, MARBL.

65. Letter to Harry Ford, 3.25.77, MARBL.

66. BOMB, p. 31.

67. Letter to David Havird, 1.21.98, MARBL.

68. Hoy, p. 66.

69. Letter to David Havird, 1.21.98, MARBL.

70. Letter to Havird, 2.11.98, MARBL. Exodus 34:7 reads "Keeping mercy for thousands, forgiving iniquity and transgression and sin, and that will by no means clear the guilty; visiting the iniquity of the fathers upon the children, and upon the children's children, unto the third and to the fourth generation."

71. Hammer, p. 96.

72. Letter to Harry Ford 11.17.77, MARBL.

73. Letter to Ashley Brown, 12.24.77, MARBL.

74. Letter to Ashley Brown, 2.28.78, MARBL.

75. CEP, p. 213.

76. BOMB, p. 32.

77. Ibid.

78. Letter to Philip Hoy, 3.19.99, MARBL.

79. Adam Hecht, interview with the author.

80. RogerMemorial.

81. Ibid.

82. *Burnt Offerings,* by Roger Hecht (Lightning Tree, 1979), p. 20.

83. Letter to Harry Ford, 2.23.79, MARBL.

84. Letter to Harry Ford, 3.12.79, MARBL.

85. "Poets Who Have Learned Their Trade," by Christopher Ricks, *The New York Times Book Review*, 12.2.79.

86. RochInter, Tape 19, transcript p. 12.

87. Letter to Harry Ford, 2.10.80, MARBL.

88. Letter to Robert Fitzgerald, 2.21.80, MARBL.

89. Blumenthal. Blumenthal is quoting from the Hecht/Hoy interview. Hoy was told the anecdote by W. D. Snodgrass, who, Hoy believed, got it from Wright himself. Hecht retained no memory of the taxi ride or the reading with Wright, but he did admit to reciting on occasion passages from "Lycidas" in the voice of Fields (Hoy, p. 103).

90. Ibid.

91. AEH sent "Now Nights Abridge Their Hours" in a letter to Robert Fitzgerald on 3.11.80, MARBL. The italicized passage in the poem is from Robert Herrick's "To Live Merrily, and to Trust to Good Verses."

92. From "Poem without Anybody," CLP, p. 73.

Eleven: "Waiting for Things to Mend"

1. From "Peripeteia," CEP, p. 141.

2. Ibid.

3. From a journal by Helen Hecht, dated 4.8.11.

4. McC, p. 183.

5. Letter to Jacky Simms, 10.8.81, MARBL.

6. Letter to Nicholas Christopher, 9.14.83, MARBL.

7. Letter to George Ford, 10.27.86, MARBL.

8. Fan.

9. Letter to Philip Hoy, 10.26.00, MARBL.

10. McC, p. 163.

11. Helen Hecht, in her journal.

12. RochInter, Tape 19, transcript p. 12. Indeed, he had known about death from his earliest memories of suicides during the Depression and from combat in the Ruhr Valley in 1945, both of which he cited in this connection.

13. CEP, p. 195.

14. Letter to Harry Ford, 6.10.78, MARBL.

15. Letter to Brad Leithauser, 6.10.78, MARBL.

16. Letter to Brad Leithauser, 3.18.80, MARBL.

17. Letter to Brad Leithauser, 6.2.80, MARBL.

18. Hammer, p. 95. "The Transparent Man" appeared in *New England Review* in the Winter 1980 issue.

19. CLP, p. 81.

20. In one crucial revision to the first draft of "Yolek," the end-words *children* and *breakfast* (both taken directly from the source material) are replaced by *home* and *meal*. Why change these words? Hecht had something very particular in

mind, a kind of Herbertian typographical play that adds greatly to the meaning of the poem. As the critic Jeff Balch has pointed out, Hecht chose the end-words of his sestina for their final letters—y, o, l, e, k, and p, the "p" suggesting the Hebrew letter "pey," which, appearing on traditional Jewish gravestones, stands for poh, "here," as in "here lies." As Balch persuasively suggests, "With the name as a starting place, Hecht gave Yolek a resting place."

21. *On the Jews and Their Lies,* by Martin Luther, Martin H. Bertram, trans., p. 75 (https://www.prchiz.pl/storage/app/media/pliki/Luther_On_Jews.pdf).

22. CLP, p. 80.

23. AEH's written source for "The Book of Yolek" is the short essay by Hanna Mortkowicz-Olczakowa titled "Yanosz Korczak's Last Walk," from *Anthology of Holocaust Literature,* Jacob Glatstein et al., eds. The essay begins "The day was Wednesday, 5th August, 1942, in the morning." It later refers to "little Hanka with the lung trouble, Yolek who was ill" (p. 137). Other sources according to Hecht were the well-known photo of a boy being held at gunpoint in the Warsaw ghetto and AEH's own experiences at the liberation of Flossenbürg.

24. Hoy, p. 24.

25. Hoy, p. 26.

26. In *George Herbert: His Religion and Art* (Harvard, 1954), Joseph Summers notes Herbert's use of "hieroglyphics," which he defines as "a figure, device, or sign having some hidden meaning; a secret or enigmatical symbol; an emblem."

27. Fan, p. 8. Completed in 1981, "The Book of Yolek" was one of the first poems written for *Transparent Man.*

28. RochInter, Tape 19, transcript p. 12.

29. *On the Laws of the Poetic Art (The A. W. Mellon Lectures in the Fine Arts)* (Princeton, NJ: Princeton University Press, 1995), p. 137.

30. "Intimate Memory: Anthony Hecht on Poets and Poetry," *American Arts* (May 1983), p. 16. The interview, with an unnamed interlocutor, took place on March 10, 1983. [Hereafter AmerArts.]

31. Hecht, Anthony, et al. Anthony Hecht reading his poems in the Coolidge Auditorium, Oct. 4, 1982. Audio. Retrieved from the Library of Congress, <www.loc.gov/item/91740506/>.

32. In his introduction to "A Birthday Poem," for Helen, he added a long epigraph from José Ortega y Gasset's essay "The Dehumanization of Art" as a kind of mysterious "gloss" discovered only after the poem was published. The passage, from early in the essay, describes looking at a landscape through a window and explores the "human element" of the work of art as distinct from its aesthetic qualities.

33. AmerArts, pp. 16–7.

34. "Poetry Consultant's Office in an Aerie," by Clyde H. Farnsworth, Special to *The New York Times,* October 26, 1982. [Hereafter Farnsworth.]

35. WashPo.

36. Farnsworth.

37. O, p. 12.

38. O, p. 32.

39. "Books of the Times," by John Gross, *The New York Times* (Sept. 12, 1986), Section C, p. 25.

40. O, p. vii.

41. MU, p. 250.

42. O, p. 219.

43. Hoy, p. 106.

44. Ibid.

45. Ibid.

46. Helen Hecht, interview with the author. HH added "When [Tony's] parents died, Evan was, I think, five. It was then Dorothea's money, because Melvyn's family's money was pretty well dissipated. And Tony and Roger were the beneficiaries, but it was in a trust, very tightly controlled, and he got a very small amount. The trust ended with Tony's death and went to his three children."

47. Most of his parents' money had been put into a trust, to which he had very limited access.

48. Letter to Harry Ford, 6.26.86, MARBL.

49. Dia Center for the Arts, November 22, 1994.

50. "Joseph Brodsky: The Art of Poetry No. 28," interviewed by Sven Birkerts, *The Paris Review* (Issue 83, Spring 1982).

51. *Ecstatic Occasions, Expedient Forms: 65 Leading Poets Select and Comment on Their Poems,* David Lehman, ed. (Ann Arbor, MI: University of Michigan, 1996), p. 81.

52. Letter to Ashley Brown, 8.14.87, MARBL.

53. Hammer, p. 99. Hays Rockwell and his wife, Linda, are the dedicatees of Hecht's edition of *The Essential Herbert* (New York: Ecco, 1987).

54. Letter to Jacky Simms, 7.16.88, MARBL.

55. Ibid.

56. From an undated commonplace book. The notebook, likely acquired in Venice, depicts the buildings along the length of the Grand Canal.

57. Letter to Brad Leithauser, 5.14.89. MARBL.

58. *The Transparent Man* appeared eleven years after *Vespers,* and, though AEH suggests that it was a six-year gestation, a number of poems were composed earlier.

59. Evan started Vassar in the fall of 1990.

60. Letter to Roger Hecht, 9.9.89, Roger Hecht Estate.

61. Remarks by AEH at the memorial for Roger Hecht, The New York Society for Ethical Culture, April 28, 1990, 1 P.M.

62. Mendelson.

63. Letter to Nicholas Christopher, 3.24.90, MARBL.

64. Letter to Sandra Behrle, 5.19.90, MARBL.

65. Memorial tribute for Roger Hecht, MARBL.

66. *A William Maxwell Portrait: Memories and Appreciations,* Charles Baxter, Michael Collier, and Edward Hirsch, eds. (New York: Norton, 2004), p. 125.

67. Letter to William Maxwell, 11.4.88, MARBL. Hecht's word *haunted* resonates with the spectral voice in "Death the Whore," which was written a few years later. Hecht retained feelings of shame and regret regarding his affair with Stewart.

68. Letter to Brad Leithauser, 5.21.90, MARBL.

69. CEP, p. 189.

70. For a full account of the friendship between AEH and William MacDonald, see *A Bountiful Harvest: The Correspondence of Anthony Hecht and William L. Mac-Donald,* edited by Philip Hoy (Waywiser, 2018).

71. Fan, p. 8.

72. Letter to David Lehman, 11.3.89, MARBL.

73. Letter to Joseph Brodsky, 7.4.90, MARBL.

74. Hammer, p. 101.

75. From the website of the National Gallery, Washington, DC, https://www.nga.gov/research/casva/meetings/mellon-lectures-in-the-fine-arts.html.

76. Hoy, p. 107.

77. Letter to David Mason, 6.20.92, MARBL.

78. Letter to B. H. Fairchild, 11.17.92, MARBL.

79. Letter to Robert Beum, 3.11.96, MARBL.

Twelve: Presumptions

1. "Death Sauntering About," CLP, p. 89.

2. AEH wrote to Nicholas Christopher asking him to try to track down any books given by Roger to the Jefferson Market Library in the West Village, to no avail.

3. Letter to Francine du Plessix Gray, 9.6.00, MARBL.

4. Letter to Brad Leithauser, 5.21.90, MARBL.

5. Letter to David Mason, 10.20.90, MARBL.

6. Letter to Lakshmi Gopalkrishnan, 12.16.99, MARBL.

7. Hoy, p. 107.

8. Letter to David Mason, 10.20.90, MARBL.

9. Letter to Daniel Albright, 11.19.93, MARBL.

10. Letter to Daniel Anderson, 7.9.93, MARBL.

11. Hammer, p. 106. In a memorial tribute to Baskin at the American Academy of Arts and Letters, Hecht reiterated that "It was Leonard who initiated the collaborations we undertook." "Leonard Baskin: 1922–2000," read at the Academy Dinner Meeting on April 3, 2001. It is worth noting that Hecht was not consulting the images when composing his texts; once the subjects were agreed upon, Hecht worked on the poems independently.

12. Letter from Leonard Baskin, 1.10.1993, MARBL.

13. Letter to Daniel Albright, 1.4.93, MARBL.

14. BOMB, p. 30.

15. Hammer, p. 107. When Hecht first met Baskin at Smith in 1956, he was "producing a series of small sculptured figures with such titles as 'Dead Man' and 'Hanged Man.' He had at least as much reason as I to acquaint himself with the theme of mortality. His wife was slowly dying of multiple sclerosis. It was anguishing to witness, even on the part of an outsider, like myself. Of Baskin it must have required a stamina that was little short of heroic."

16. *The Presumptions of Death* was published by Baskin at The Gehenna Press in Northampton, MA, in 1995. The colophon reads: "Fifty copies . . . have been printed at The Gehenna Press . . . Arthur Hanson has printed the letterpress on Velke Losiny, a Czechoslovakian hand-made paper. The edition is arranged as follows: copies one to ten have a manuscript, a watercolor, a wood block & several hand-painted proofs; copies 11–50 comprise the regular edition. All the prints are signed by the artist. The colophon is signed by the artist & the poet."

17. Edmund White, interview with the author.

18. Letter to Joseph Brodsky, 9.30.93, MARBL.

19. Letter to Leonard Baskin, 10.7.93, MARBL.

20. CLP, p. 126.

21. Letter to Harry Ford, 12.11.93, MARBL.

22. MU, p. 176.

23. "An Eightieth-Birthday Ballade for Anthony Hecht," by Richard Wilbur, included in "Anthony Hecht at 80," a tribute at the Poetry Center of the 92nd Street Y, with readings by Nicholas Christopher, John Hollander, Richard Howard, Brad Leithauser, J. D. McClatchy, Elizabeth Spires, and Anthony Hecht, September 29, 2003.

24. From a journal entry by Mary Jo Salter dated March 11, 1995.

25. Baskin's wood engravings in the Gehenna Press edition of the poems were printed with color, which Harry Ford and Knopf were not able to reproduce in the trade edition. While the color of Baskin's originals adds warmth and pictorial interest, the black-and-white version have a starkness and a graphic severity appropriate to the elegiac tenor of the poems.

26. Claire White, interview with the author.

27. Mary Jo Salter in her diary for March 1995.

28. The *Poetry* feature included "Death Sauntering About," "Death the Mexican Revolutionary," "Death the Archbishop," "Death the Painter," "Death the Copperplate Printer," and "Death the Punchinello." Hecht toyed with the idea of writing a preliminary poem for the sequence, "what I think of as a sort of introduction to the text proper: the spiel of a carnival barker." The poem by that name, in fact, concludes the Presumptions when they were included in *Flight Among the Tombs*.

29. From the Hechts' guest book at 4256 Nebraska Avenue, NW, Washington, DC.

30. Letter to Daniel Anderson, 11.20.94, MARBL.

31. Undated letter to Daniel Anderson, Fall 1993, MARBL.

32. Letter to Dana Gioia, 1.8.97, MARBL.

33. Letter to Dana Gioia, 12.12.95, MARBL.

34. AEH's essay was later collected in *Melodies Unheard* under the title "The Sonnet: Ruminations on Form, Sex, and History."

35. "Introduction," *The Sonnets*, G. Blakemore Evans, ed., The New Cambridge Shakespeare (Cambridge: Cambridge University Press, 1996), p. 5. [Hereafter Cambridge.]

36. Cambridge, p. 28.

37. Cambridge, p. 7.

38. Cambridge, p. 26.

39. CLP, p. 55. Lysander's prose monologue recalls Caliban's prose disquisition in Auden's *The Sea and the Mirror*.

40. Later poems with Shakespearean elements include "In Memory of David Kalstone" (*As You Like It*), "Curriculum Vitae" (*Macbeth*), "The Transparent Man" (with an echo of Richard II's "with nothing shall be pleased until he is eased with being nothing"), "Death the Society Lady" (*Hamlet*), "Death the Punchinello" (*King Lear* and *Richard III*), "Death the Painter" (*King Lear*), "Whirligig of Time" (*Twelfth Night* and Sonnet 18), "For James Merrill: An Adieu" (*The Tempest*), "Poppy" (*Othello*), "Look Deep" (*The Tempest*), "Lapidary Inscription with Explanatory Note" (*Macbeth*), and numerous others.

41. Letter to Dana Gioia, 3.22.96, MARBL.

42. Ibid.

43. CLP, p. 142.

44. Letter to J. D. McClatchy, 2.30.96, MARBL.

45. CLP, p. 159.

46. At the suggestion of Brodsky's widow, Maria (née Sozzani), AEH agreed to read a poem by Auden at the memorial on March 8. They decided on "The Shield of Achilles," but then Maria thought "The More Loving One" would be a better choice. AEH obliged but privately felt that it was a "far slighter poem": "This may have been part of what has prompted me to embark on an elegy of my own." [Letter to J. D. McClatchy, 2.30.96, MARBL.]

47. The program aired on March 19, 1996.

48. Letter to Eleanor Cook, 1.9.97, MARBL.

49. Though writing poems was again his primary work, Hecht took on an editorial post at *The Wilson Quarterly*, introducing excerpts from poets he admired. The column ran until 1999 and paid $750 per issue.

50. "Living Ghosts," by John Bayley, *The New York Review of Books*, March 27, 1997.

51. "Old Guys," by William Logan, *The New Criterion*, Vol. 15, Issue 4 (December 1996).

52. Letter to Eleanor Cook, 8.1.96, MARBL.

53. Letter to Harry Ford, 2.15.97, MARBL.

54. Letter to Leonard Baskin, 5.4.97, MARBL.

55. Letter to Leonard Baskin, 5.26.97, MARBL.

56. Letter to Harry Ford, 7.28.82, MARBL. Hecht had mentioned an earlier health

issue in an exchange with Roger. When Roger wrote that he was suffering from an ulcer, Hecht in sympathy replied that he had had three over the years.

57. Letter to Philip Booth, 9.5.99, MARBL.
58. Letter to John Malcolm Brinnin, 11.13.97, MARBL.
59. "On Anthony Hecht," by John Hollander, *Raritan*, Vol. 17, Issue 1 (Summer 1997).
60. Letter to John Hollander, 11.1.97, MARBL.
61. Letter to George Core, 12.9.98, MARBL.
62. From "Evan Hecht in a Single Scull," undated typescript, MARBL. AEH never published this poem, feeling that it was "unsuccessful, as he was too close to the subject matter" [Helen Hecht, in an email]. The manuscript is struck through and contains a significant typo in the title, *skull* for *scull*.

Thirteen: Both Alike to Thee

1. Letter to B. H. Fairchild, 7.25.98, MARBL.
2. Ibid.
3. Letter to Robert Beum, 3.31.98, MARBL.
4. In an interview from the last year of his life, Hecht reports that he is no longer visited by the nightmares that had persisted for half a century.
5. Letter to Robert Beum, 5.29.98, MARBL.
6. Letter to Robert Beum, 10.27.98, MARBL.
7. Letter to Jacky Simms, 11.23.98, MARBL. Philip Hoy's Waywiser Press became AEH's English publisher after the discontinuation of the Oxford list, bringing out the UK editions of *The Darkness and the Light* and *Collected Later Poems*.
8. Letter to Philip Hoy, 12.22.98, MARBL.
9. Letter to Philip Hoy, 4.9.99, MARBL.
10. Ibid.
11. CLP, p. 224.
12. Letter to Jacky Simms, 12.23.99, MARBL.
13. Hecht had almost perfect recall of Bible verses. According to Helen Hecht, in an email, AEH "had a photographic memory. When he wrote critical essays, he would recall passages in books he had read long ago and be able to find them rather quickly among the books in his library."
14. Letter from Joseph Brodsky to AEH, 4.18.90, MARBL.
15. Letter to Joseph Brodsky, 5.18.82, MARBL.
16. Letter to Philip Hoy, 11.18.99, MARBL.
17. In composing "Mirror," AEH no doubt had in mind the poem of that title by James Merrill. Plath also has a poem called "Mirror," and McClatchy himself wrote a poem so called. (Other poets, including Rita Dove and Alexis Sears, have contributed more recently to the mini tradition of poems on this subject.)
    Though dropped from the manuscript, "Chromatic Fantasy" includes a stunning passage on raptors reminiscent of Baskin:
    The intimate vultures of Prometheus

> must be close at hand,
>
> cruising the updrafts,
>
> surfing the hot winds,
>
> hideous, bald,
>
> their bone beaks set
>
> to gouge right to the bone.

18. CLP, pp. 198–9.
19. CEP, p. 158.
20. From "Midrash" on myjewishlearning.com, edited by Rachel Scheinerman.
21. *Sewanee Theological Review*, Volume 37, Number 2 (1994).
22. Letter to Eleanor Cook, 8.11.00, MARBL.
23. Read at the American Academy of Arts and Letters meeting on April 3, 2001, MARBL.
24. After Baskin's death, one of his associates Michael Kuch printed Hecht's ten biblical poems, with twenty-five intaglios of his own. The book is dedicated to Baskin, and a portrait of Baskin as an angel with wings covering his eyes appears twice in this book.
25. Letter to Francine du Plessix Gray, 9.6.00, MARBL.
26. Letter to Daniel Anderson, 12.3.99, MARBL.
27. Letter to Agha Shahid Ali, 9.4.00, MARBL.
28. Letter to Eleanor Cook, 8.11.00, MARBL.
29. Letter to Brad Leithauser, 4.20.00, MARBL.
30. Letter to Philip Hoy, 4.29.00, MARBL.
31. "On Frost's 'The Wood-Pile'" was later included in *Melodies Unheard*.
32. The event took place on January 27, 2000. AEH read Sonnets 65 and 73, and passages from *Henry IV, Part 1*, I.iii; *Othello*, I.iii; and *Love's Labor's Lost*, V.ii.
33. Hecht ends his screed expressing his "pious hope" that the enterprise might meet "with complete defeat and great financial loss." This did not come to pass.
34. John Ruskin, from the introduction to *Deucalion*, Vol. 7 (Wiley, 1886), pp. 1–2. AEH quotes this passage in his essay on Seamus Heaney from *Melodies Unheard*, p. 214.
35. Quoted by AEH in "Seamus Heaney's Prose," from *Melodies Unheard*, p. 214.
36. Email to the author.
37. Letter to W. D. Snodgrass, 12.5.01, MARBL.
38. Ibid.
39. Letter to Frederick Morgan, 6.27.02, MARBL.
40. Sun.
41. "In Memoriam: Anthony Hecht," by B. H. Fairchild, *The Sewanee Review*, Vol. 113, No. 3 (Summer 2005), p. 466.
42. CLP, p. 226.
43. Letter to Daniel Anderson, 3.25.03, MARBL.
44. Ibid.

45. Letter to Dana Gioia, 6.10.03, MARBL.

46. Ibid.

47. This trip was rescheduled after earlier plans were canceled due to poor health. A long essay on Keats, written for that initial occasion (the Keats-Shelley Centenary Poetry Festival at the British School), was read in absentia and subsequently published in England in *The Keats-Shelley Review* and in the US in *The Yale Review* under the title "Keats's Appetite."

48. Letter to Eleanor Cook, 11.6.03, MARBL.

49. Letter to Tania Eriksen, 12.23.03, MARBL.

50. Letter to George Core, 6.5.04, MARBL.

51. Letter to Dimitri Hadzi, 4.12.04, MARBL.

52. "Keats's Appetite," *The Yale Review,* July 2004.

53. The poem appeared posthumously in the December 2, 2004, issue of *The New York Review of Books,* where Hecht had been a valued contributor of reviews and poems.

54. Fan. The description of morning recalls a passage from "The Grapes": "Mornings of course, it's we who get the light, / An especially tender light, hopeful and soft" (CEP, p. 186).

55. *The New York Review of Books*, October 21, 2004.

56. Philip Hoy, in an email.

57. Letter to George Core, 8.14.04, MARBL.

58. AEH, in an undated journal entry.

59. Paul Morrison, Adviser's Final Semester Summary, Fall 1942, Office of the Registrar, Bard College.

60. "Poet of Sorrow, and of Wit," by Benjamin Ivry, *The Wall Street Journal,* 10.26.04, p. D8.

61. BOF, p. 50.

INDEX